The British Press and Nazi Germany

The British Press and Nazi Germany

Reporting from the Reich, 1933–9

Kylie Galbraith

BLOOMSBURY ACADEMIC
LONDON • NEW YORK • OXFORD • NEW DELHI • SYDNEY

BLOOMSBURY ACADEMIC
Bloomsbury Publishing Plc
50 Bedford Square, London, WC1B 3DP, UK
1385 Broadway, New York, NY 10018, USA
29 Earlsfort Terrace, Dublin 2, Ireland

BLOOMSBURY, BLOOMSBURY ACADEMIC and the Diana logo are trademarks of
Bloomsbury Publishing Plc

First published in Great Britain 2021
This paperback edition published in 2022

Copyright © Kylie Galbraith, 2021

Kylie Galbraith has asserted her right under the Copyright, Designs and Patents Act, 1988, to be identified as Author of this work.

Cover image: Adolf Hitler at Reichsparteitag, 1934
(© Everett Collection Historical / Alamy Stock Photo)

All rights reserved. No part of this publication may be reproduced or transmitted in any form or by any means, electronic or mechanical, including photocopying, recording, or any information storage or retrieval system, without prior permission in writing from the publishers.

Bloomsbury Publishing Plc does not have any control over, or responsibility for, any third-party websites referred to or in this book. All internet addresses given in this book were correct at the time of going to press. The author and publisher regret any inconvenience caused if addresses have changed or sites have ceased to exist, but can accept no responsibility for any such changes.

Every effort has been made to trace copyright holders and to obtain their permissions for the use of copyright material. The publisher apologizes for any errors or omissions and would be grateful if notified of any corrections that should be incorporated in future reprints or editions of this book.

A catalogue record for this book is available from the British Library.

Library of Congress Cataloging-in-Publication Data
Names: Galbraith, Kylie, author.
Title: The British press and Nazi Germany: reporting from the Reich, 1933-39 /
Kylie Galbraith. Other titles: Reporting from the Reich, 1933-39
Description: London: New York: Bloomsbury Academic, 2020. |
Includes bibliographical references and index.
Identifiers: LCCN 2020033584 (print) | LCCN 2020033585 (ebook) |
ISBN 9781350102095 (hardback) | ISBN 9781350194427 (paperback) |
ISBN 9781350102101 (ebook) | ISBN 9781350102118 (epub)
Subjects: LCSH: National socialism–Press coverage–Great Britain. | Germany–Press coverage–Great Britain. | Hitler, Adolf, 1889-1945–Press coverage. | Germany–History–1933-1945. | Press–Great Britain–20th century. | Germany–Foreign public opinion, British. | Germany–Politics and government–1933-1945.
Classification: LCC DD256.5 .G233 2020 (print) | LCC DD256.5 (ebook) |
DDC 070.4/4994308620941–dc23
LC record available at https://lccn.loc.gov/2020033584
LC ebook record available at https://lccn.loc.gov/2020033585

ISBN: HB: 978-1-3501-0209-5
PB: 978-1-3501-9442-7
ePDF: 978-1-3501-0210-1
eBook: 978-1-3501-0211-8

Typeset by Deanta Global Publishing Services, Chennai, India

To find out more about our authors and books visit www.bloomsbury.com and sign up for our newsletters.

For Robin Prior and Robert Galbraith

Contents

Acknowledgements	viii
A note on sources	x
List of abbreviations	xi
Introduction	1
1 The British press	11
2 Hitler becomes chancellor	29
3 The destruction of democracy	49
4 The *Manchester Guardian* and the terror in Germany: A special case	75
5 A second revolution? The Röhm purge	97
6 'Cross and Swastika': The struggle for the churches in Germany	121
7 The Nazi persecution of the Jews	149
Conclusion	175
Appendix: British newspaper details	191
Notes	197
Bibliography	235
Index	259

Acknowledgements

The list of those to acknowledge for their support throughout this journey is long, but I will use this opportunity to thank some of the institutions and individuals who were key in completing this book. First, I would like to extend thanks to Bloomsbury Publishers for taking a chance on this book. I am grateful to the assistance and support of Rhodri Mogford, publisher in history, and Laura Reeves, editorial assistant, history. They have answered all my questions and offered support and kind words throughout this process. I would also like to acknowledge the University of Adelaide. The foundation for this book was my doctoral dissertation, which was completed in 2017. I have been fortunate to receive the continued support of the university, especially the Department of History, as I developed my thesis into the book that it is today.

Other institutions and archival repositories also deserve acknowledgement. These include the Barr Smith Library (BSL) at the University of Adelaide, the State Library of Victoria (Melbourne), the John Rylands Library (University of Manchester), the Bodleian Library (University of Oxford), the News International Archive and Record Office (London), UKPressOnline and Gale/Cengage Learning Database. Each of these institutions and repositories were veritable treasure troves of valuable archival sources that underpinned the research for this book.

In each of the libraries and archives mentioned there is a host of individuals that deserve recognition. These include Margaret Hosking (former research librarian at the BSL), Maria Albanese (BSL), Robin Secomb (BSL), Vikki Langton (BSL), Margaret Galbraith (BSL), Russell Wallace (State Library of Victoria), Nick Mays (News International Archive), Colin Harris (Bodleian Library, University of Oxford), John Hodgson (John Rylands Library, University of Manchester) and Craig Pett (Gale/Cengage). Their assistance, advice and help in finding source material and answering questions, some of which I am sure were exasperating, are greatly appreciated.

Throughout the entire process from doctoral thesis to book, the single most important influence has been Professor Robin Prior. We began this journey a long time ago, and it is no exaggeration to say that this book would not have been possible without him. I feel honoured to be able to call him a friend and confidante. Both Robin and Heather Prior have made me feel like part of the family. Robin has always been there for me and his support has been unwavering. These few lines do nothing to demonstrate what he means to me or how truly grateful I am for his support.

My own family has also been instrumental in helping me get this manuscript ready for publication. My family, particularly my mum Margaret Galbraith and my dad Ronald Galbraith, supported me, both materially and emotionally, as I worked to complete this book. Robert Galbraith, Ryan Galbraith, Erika Wiseman and John and Denise Elston also deserve mention. We do not choose our family but if we had to, I would still choose you all. I am so thankful for your words of advice and unwavering support, especially when I have been grumpy and irritable during this process. Scarlett Galbraith has provided countless cuddles and kisses. Many a hard day and night have been bearable by the love and cuddles from Roxi – my loveable but crazy pup. Bonnie and Cassie provided their support in the only way they know how, with head butts and cuddles.

Finally, I wish to thank and acknowledge my network of friends and colleagues who have supported me throughout this entire process. To Astrid Lane, Stephanie Thomson and Alison Wooding – I could not ask for better friends. Thank you for the many chats over coffee and shopping trips when we needed to avoid writing. I can rely on the three of you to push me to do my best. Acknowledgement must also be extended to both Professor Joanna Burke and Professor Jay Winter for their kind words, recommendations and encouragement which served as important inspiration during this manuscript process. There are, of course, many other colleagues and friends who inspired, assisted and helped me. The list is long and would likely take many pages, but a few deserve special mention. These include William Prescott, Daniel Ashdown, Dr Mark Neuendorf, Dr Bodie Ashton, Rachel Caines, Alex Jones, Dr Claire Walker, Dr Carol Fort, Professor Matthew Fitzpatrick, Associate Professor Andrekos Varnava and Professor Trevor Wilson.

A note on sources

Every care has been taken to ensure that as much information has been provided in the references to identify the source. When the article has been a Leader (or editorial) or Letter to the Editor, it has been signposted as such. Articles with taglines, such as 'From Our Own Correspondent, Berlin', 'From Our Special Correspondent' or 'From Our Diplomatic Correspondent' have been abbreviated (see 'Abbreviations'). These references do not include correspondent names as correspondents often went on leave or holiday and other journalists took over their duties under the same tagline. The exception to this is Frederick Augustus Voigt, special/diplomatic correspondent for the *Manchester Guardian*. Voigt's correspondence leaves no room for doubt as to which articles he wrote for the newspaper.

There are also articles without any author details such as short pieces in the *New Statesman and Nation* and *The Spectator*. Finally, articles that were attributed to a news agency, such as Reuters or Central News, have been cited as such.

Abbreviations

Berlin (etc.) Corr.   – 'From Our Own Correspondent in Berlin' (etc.)

Corr.   – 'Correspondent' (usually with author included)

Dipl./Spec. Corr.   – 'From/By Our Diplomatic/Special Correspondent'

Newspaper titles in references are displayed in full then abbreviated for the rest of the chapter. This also applies to archival institutions, whereby the full institution name will be included for the first time it is cited in the chapter. Subsequent references to the institution will be abbreviated.

Introduction

The poet W. H. Auden described the 1930s as a 'low, dishonest decade' in his poem 'September 1, 1939'.[1] In a sense it was; the 1930s witnessed the crisis of capitalism that became the Great Depression, the continued rise of fascism and dictatorships, and the rejection of liberal democratic values. It was also a decade in which a persistent fear, specifically of another war, pervaded international relations. This was compounded by the aggressive rhetoric of several states, in particular Italy, Germany and Japan. In the late 1930s this violent rhetoric turned into territorial aggression that violated international codes of conduct and eventually led to war. At the heart of this was Germany. The stability of Germany was of the utmost importance to her neighbours. The balance of power in Europe hinged on Germany. The advent of the brutal and violent Nazi dictatorship in 1933 was, therefore, viewed with concern.

For the British press, the 1930s were the 'golden age'.[2] The newspaper industry was at its peak. There were nearly 9 million wireless sets in British homes, and more and more people tuned in to news broadcasts, but the printed newspaper was still the most important and accessible form of news in Britain.[3] It was in the 1930s that the circulation wars reached their climax after the *Daily Express* took the title of largest daily circulation of 2,329,000. The combined circulation of national daily newspapers rose from 5.4 million in 1920 to 10.6 million in 1939; local daily and weekly newspapers did not see such growth.[4] The 1930s was also the era of the press barons. The interwar period saw a higher concentration of press ownership than ever before. The most powerful and influential of the press barons were Viscount Rothermere, and Lords Beaverbrook, Camrose and Kemsley.[5] The combined circulation of their newspapers (daily national, daily local and weeklies) was around 13 million.[6] Furthermore, the expansion of the national newspapers into regional areas meant that some proprietors had reach over huge audiences even when they owned relatively few newspapers.[7] Lord Beaverbrook, whose empire included the *Daily Express*, owned only four newspapers but the total circulation of these was 4.1 million.[8]

The British press, therefore, was in a prime position to observe and report the 'dark' decade. British journalist Malcolm Muggeridge described the 1930s as 'unusually eventful' and observed: 'There can seldom in ten years have been fewer days on which a chief sub-editor was embarrassed for lack of news.'[9] This was especially true for foreign news. The press had plenty to cover in the United States, India, Japan and China, to name a few, let alone on the European continent. Important news stories for British newspapers included US president Franklin Roosevelt's New Deal, Indian demands for greater independence from Britain, the Soviet Union's economic policies for rapid industrialization (that resulted in horrific famine), as well as the ongoing political turmoil in France, the assassination of Austrian chancellor Engelbert Dollfuss and the tragic death of Queen Astrid of Sweden in a motorcar accident. Some of the big stories for British popular newspapers included the disappearance and death of baby Charles Augustus Lindbergh Jr. and the resulting trial, the 'discovery' of the Loch Ness monster, the criminal banditry of Bonnie and Clyde and their dramatic deaths, the disappearance of Amelia Earhart and the explosion of the Zeppelin *Hindenburg*. The Italian invasion of Abyssinia, the Spanish civil war, the Japanese invasion of China and Germany's annexation of the Sudetenland and forced *Anschluss* with Austria were defining moments of the turbulent mid- to late 1930s.

In the 1930s Germany was one of the major news centres in Europe. Most British newspapers, at least at the national level, had teams of correspondents based in major cities throughout Europe. In Germany, correspondents were primarily based in Berlin where they had networks of sources and established connections who assisted in the gathering of news. Correspondents would also travel to where the news was, such as the *Manchester Guardian*'s Geneva correspondent Robert Dell who travelled to Leipzig in Germany to cover the Reichstag Fire trial in late 1933. Correspondents living and working in Germany were on hand to observe the advent of the Hitler dictatorship which sparked crisis after crisis in European relations. Hitler and the Nazi state treated the Treaty of Versailles with contempt and demonstrated a total lack of concern for European stability and peace. Inside Germany the Nazi Party, in control of the German state, overthrew Weimar democracy, crushed their enemies and implemented a ruthless dictatorship that completely rejected liberal democratic values.

The primary focus of this book is the domestic (or internal) situation in Germany rather than foreign policy, because central to the study is what the press understood about the *nature* of the dictatorship. In the 1930s the Nazi dictatorship challenged fundamental liberal values and institutions associated with democracy in a civilized country. The Nazis destroyed democracy and trampled civil liberties and freedoms, particularly religious freedom. This study focuses on how the press reported the emergence and development of policies and laws aimed at the establishment of the Nazi dictatorship and *Volksgemeinschaft*, or 'people's community'. This includes the process by which the Nazification of the German state was carried out, a process known as *Gleichschaltung* (coordination), as well as the brutal way in which the dictatorship treated enemies and outsiders.

The degree to which the British press covered and reported Nazi Germany is crucial, providing insight into what people in Britain could have known about the nature of the dictatorship on the eve of war in September 1939. To date, this has not been examined in any depth. Historians have explored British press responses to the foreign policy of Hitler's Germany in an attempt to understand the British government's policy of appeasement, but little effort has been devoted to how the press reported and understood the *nature* of the dictatorship. This leaves the historian with several questions. To what extent did the press report the destruction of democracy and the transition to ruthless dictatorship? Did the press grasp the significance of the establishment of the Nazi dictatorship? Did British newspapers report the brutal persecution of political and religious groups? Did they understand what was happening to the Jews of Germany? How much was known about the intimidation, barbaric thuggery and murder that was carried out in the name of the Nazi regime? And importantly, when the British government was appeasing the Nazi government, were they aware (or could they have been aware) of what type of state they were dealing with?

These questions are at the centre of this book, underpinning the central aims of examining the extent to which the British press reported and understood what was going on inside Nazi Germany prior to war and what the British public could have known about the regime by reading British newspapers in the 1930s. The wording here is deliberate; this book will examine what people *could* have known because it should not be assumed that everyone buying a newspaper read the foreign news section, nor is it assumed that people followed events in Germany. It is entirely possible that someone who purchased a daily newspaper might only read the sports section or the society news. And so, this book focuses on what people could have known and understood about the Nazi regime if they were reading (and following) press reports on Germany. It will examine the clues, signs and markers that could have informed the British public, and perhaps the British government, about the aims, goals and ambitions of Hitler's dictatorship.

Any study that tries to cover press reactions to particular events or time periods needs to set some parameters. This is no less true for this book. Not every newspaper could be covered because the research involved would have become unmanageable. Several considerations underpinned the choice in newspapers selected for this study. It was important to select newspapers that represented the political makeup of the press in the 1930s. Additionally, readership was an important consideration. Both quality and popular newspapers needed to be represented, just as the daily and weekly press needed consideration. Overall, in selecting the titles for this study, every effort was made to select titles that, together, would represent British press opinion in the 1930s. For this study, thirteen newspapers were selected: *The Times, Manchester Guardian, Daily Telegraph, Morning Post, The Daily Telegraph and Morning Post* (the result of the merger of the *Daily Telegraph* and *Morning Post* in 1937), *News Chronicle, Daily Express, Daily Mail, Daily Mirror, Observer, The Spectator, New Statesman and Nation* and the *Jewish Chronicle*. This list includes both daily and weekly newspapers and ranges across the political spectrum encompassing different degrees of political opinions and influence.[10] There are other newspapers that could have been added to this list, but these newspapers collectively offer fresh and relevant insights into the period and themes discussed in this book.[11] They range from class to popular newspapers, broadsheets to tabloids. Furthermore, their readership and circulation figures vary – the newspapers represent different sections of society, from the working class to the upper class and those in positions of power (such as the British ministers of parliament). Most of the daily newspapers, with the exception of the *Manchester Guardian*, were London based at the time.

The Times and the *Manchester Guardian* are at the forefront of the study, representing the conservative centre-right and the liberal-left respectively. In addition, on the centre-right were the *Morning Post, Daily Telegraph* (and from 1937 the *Daily Telegraph and Morning Post*) and the weekly newspaper *The Spectator*. On the liberal-left, the *Observer, News Chronicle* and the weekly *New Statesman and Nation* have been included. Three popular newspapers have been included – from the right, the *Daily Mail*, from the centre, the *Daily Express*, and from the left, the pictorial *Daily Mirror*. And finally, the weekly *Jewish Chronicle*, the most important Jewish newspaper in Britain, was selected. These newspapers incorporate different styles, readership, and ideological viewpoints. They provide an insightful and detailed cross-section of the British press in the 1930s.[12] This project is one of the most comprehensive studies of press responses to Nazi Germany.

The literature on responses to Nazism by the British press is not vast. But the field has not been entirely neglected. Franklin Reid Gannon wrote one of the first works on British press responses to Nazi Germany in 1971, titled *The British Press and Germany*.[13] His book focused on the responses of British newspapers to Nazi Germany between 1936 and 1939, in particular how the British government's policy of appeasement influenced the British press. Gannon's work deserves mention as it was one of the first that uncovered the efforts of British newspapers and their correspondents in reporting and covering the Nazi state's aggressive foreign policy. Two decades later, in 1991, *The Roots of Appeasement* by Benny Morris was released. Like Gannon, Morris examined British press reactions to Germany's foreign policy with a focus on appeasement. Morris, however, concentrated on British weekly newspapers. Both works only briefly touch upon events and themes discussed in this book leaving a noticeable gap in the field that this current study will fill.

More relevant to this study are several works that have examined press responses to the persecution of Jews in Nazi Germany. Deborah Lipstadt in *Beyond Belief*, Laurel Leff in *Buried by The Times*, Robert Moses Shapiro in *Why Didn't the Press Shout* and Andrew Sharf in *The British Press under Nazi Rule* all examine press responses to the escalating persecution and, later, murder of Jews in Nazi Germany (and Europe).[14] Underlying their analysis is the question, what more could have been done to save the Jews of Europe? According to Lipstadt, the inspiration for *Beyond Belief* came after a lively discussion with some students in which they expressed disbelief that the Allies, including people at home, could have known about the persecution and ultimate fate of Europe's Jews by reading American newspapers. On countless occasions people have remarked to this author that details about the true nature and violence of the regime could not have been known outside of Germany. If they had, surely the international community would have done something. As this book will demonstrate, few facts about Nazism were left unstated in British newspapers.

In their studies, Deborah Lipstadt and Laurel Leff examined the American press while Robert Moses Shapiro concentrated on American and international newspapers. This means that Andrew Sharf's *The British Press and Jews under Nazi Rule* is the closest to this current study as it examines British press reactions to the persecution of Jews under Nazism (which comprises Chapter 7 of this book). However, there are methodological issues with Sharf's work. It relies on clippings from newspapers that were collected by an Anglo-Jewish literary figure Joseph Podro, held in Yad Vashem. While this collection is valuable and the number of articles collected by Podro is impressive, relying purely on this collection limits the scope of Sharf's study. The articles are clipped which means that the context and placement of the article are lost to the researcher. In addition, and more importantly, Sharf is forced to rely on what just one person deemed important and necessary.

In the last few decades, historians have continued to explore printed and published sources in an attempt to understand responses to Nazism outside Germany before and during the Second World War. In 2003 Dan Stone's *Responses to Nazism in Britain, 1933-1939* was published, which examined literature on Nazism published prior to the war. Then, in 2012, Oliver Lubrich's *Travels in the Reich* was published. This edited collection features letters, diary entries and articles filled with observations about Nazism before and during the war. Building on this was the 2014 book *Britain, Germany and the Road to the Holocaust* by Russell Wallis. This book examined British attitudes to Nazi atrocities, providing insight into non-press responses to Nazism.[15] A year later, Colin McCullough and Nathan Wilson's edited collection of essays on press perceptions of *Kristallnacht* in *Violence, Memory and History* was published.[16] Contributions examined responses to *Kristallnacht* in Britain, France, Australia, Canada and France. It demonstrates the continued commitment of historians in assessing and understanding press responses to the horrors of Nazi Germany, particularly anti-Semitic violence. Michaela Honeicke Moore examined how America sought to interpret and understand Nazism in her work *Know Your Enemy*.[17] Of note for this work are her chapters on the efforts of key American correspondents living and working in Germany including Edgar A. Mowrer and William L. Shirer. More recently, Heidi J. S. Tworek's *News From Germany*, published in 2019, examined German efforts to establish a communication empire and the lengths that the Nazi dictatorship went in controlling and manipulating the news.[18] In recent years, Stephanie Seul has demonstrated an ongoing commitment to examining responses to Nazism in press and radio. Her work on the British Broadcasting Corporation (BBC) German-language broadcasts before and during the war is an important contribution to the field. She has also, importantly, written on responses to Hitler and anti-Semitism prior to the advent of the Nazi dictatorship. All of the mentioned works, published in the last few decades, demonstrate a commitment to investigating and understanding Nazism and Nazi Germany from new perspectives. Importantly they shed light on the ways in which Britain, and broadly the world, responded to the rise of dictatorships, the threat to democracy and the impending threat of war on the European continent.

In addition to the aforementioned titles are several books which touch on some of the themes in this book. Both the official *History of the Times* and David Ayerst's *Guardian: Biography of a Newspaper* briefly examine how the newspapers dealt with the Nazi dictatorship and appeasement during the 1930s.[19] Stephen Koss's *Rise and Fall of the Political Press in Britain: The Twentieth Century* is the most detailed study of the British press yet published.[20] He offers a balanced approach as to why the press reported what they did about Nazi Germany, arguing that editors were conscious of calming prevailing fears of war, but were also conscious of advertising revenues and circulation figures. However, Koss focuses more on how the press dealt with the threat of war in the late 1930s, rather than on internal matters. Sir Ian Kershaw in *Making Friends with Hitler* devotes an entire chapter to 'illusions and delusions' about Hitler in Britain, arguing that Hitler was a 'puzzle' to both the British press and the British government.[21] John Simpson's *Unreliable Sources*, published in 2010, examines how the twentieth century was reported but only provides a cursory examination of press coverage of Hitler, the emergence of the Nazi dictatorship and appeasement, and includes several sweeping generalizations of British press coverage and misinterpretation of events.[22] More recently *Reporting on Hitler* by Will Wainwright examined Rothay Reynolds and his time as foreign correspondent for the *Daily Mail* in Germany.[23] The books discussed here complement this study but do not impinge on it.

Studies that focus on the British press in the 1930s, and especially those that focus on Nazi Germany, have had an impact on how we understand foreign policy and appeasement in this period. Some of these could leave the reader with the impression, for example, that *The Times* was pro-German. In some studies, Geoffrey Dawson, as *The Times* editor, has been accused of misrepresenting the dictatorship by refusing to print articles that may have offended the German government. In a similar vein, the *Daily Mail* has been cast as a pro-Nazi paper for much of the pre-war period. However, in both cases, the situation was more complicated. Both newspapers, regardless of their ideological stance, covered and reported the development of the Nazi dictatorship and demonstrated a keen interest in what was happening in Nazi Germany. There were certainly differences in their reporting styles, but what this book demonstrates is that a reader could have followed developments in Germany in both newspapers. It is time to dispense with older stereotypes surrounding how newspapers like *The Times* and the *Daily Mail* covered Nazi Germany during the 1930s.

Newspapers have been recognized for their cultural importance as historical sources. Newspapers are not merely records of the past. They are valuable sources that, in addition to telling us how events unfolded, provide a wide range of responses and perspectives about any given event or time period as they were influenced by or tried to influence the public. In much of the recent literature dealing with Nazi Germany, newspapers are often only used as outlier sources – used to boost an argument or add some interesting perspective. Examples of this can be found in several recent books that explore Nazi Germany. These include Volker Ullrich's *Hitler*, which used articles from both the *Daily Mail* and *Daily Express*, and Tim Bouverie's *Appeasing Hitler*. This book puts newspapers at the forefront of the source material. The events and themes covered in this study were dictated by British press coverage of Germany from 1933 to 1939. The book is guided by what the press reported and covered in the pre-war period. The themes that emerged came from a close reading of each of the thirteen newspapers that comprise this project. The newspapers included were accessed in print, on microfilm and through digital databases.

The rise of digital databases has certainly made it easier for researchers to access newspapers of the past. Newspapers that were previously only accessible in hard-copy format or microfilm can now be readily accessed from the comfort of one's own office or home. Aside from the practical issues of accessing the newspaper, the rise of digital collections allows new methods of research, namely keyword searching. However, this presents methodological issues. As researcher Adrian Bingham pointed out in his article on the opportunities and challenges that digitization of newspaper archives presents to historians, keyword searches are a 'rather blunt instrument. The absence of a particular word does not necessarily mean that a subject is not discussed, it may merely indicate that an alternative terminology has been used.'[24] Furthermore, 'keyword searching treats the newspaper archive as a repository of discrete articles'.[25] He contended:

> There is a danger in this process of forgetting that newspapers were material objects that were bought, read and passed around, and that the location and presentation of individual articles is of central importance in understanding how these articles were received by readers and much significance was ascribed to them. It is also important to be aware of surrounding articles, pictures, headlines and advertisements, because this peripheral content also affects how the article in question is understood by the reader.[26]

In order to fully understand reporting trends of British newspapers in the 1930s, the research for this study was carried out by *reading* newspapers. What this meant was that each and every issue of each of the thirteen newspapers included in this study were examined for the period 1933 to 1939. While newspapers were accessed in different ways – microfilm, print or digitally – the method of research was the same. Every issue was read in order to understand the context and placement of relevant articles, as well as to determine what else was being reported and discussed each day. This was an enormous and laborious task, but it was necessary in order to appreciate the full range of press coverage and responses to the Nazi regime. The result is the most comprehensive study of press reactions to Nazism in this period to date.

In addition to the newspapers, material from several excellent archives across Britain was utilized.[27] This material includes diaries, letters, correspondence and memoranda from the two major newspapers at the centre of the book: *The Times* and the *Manchester Guardian*. Material collected from the archives of *The Times* and *Manchester Guardian* provided important insight into the interaction between correspondents and editors. These papers shed light on the role of the journalists, editors and proprietors within the newspaper structure and how they were involved in what would be printed. This is something that is often not evident just by reading newspapers themselves. Further, the personal papers of *The Times* editor Geoffrey Dawson, kept at the Bodleian Library, provided information about the duties of an editor as well as Dawson's connections with key government ministers. Monographs written by correspondents and newspapermen during the 1930s and 1940s have also been utilized to provide further insight into the experiences of foreign correspondents. Books published by correspondents on the European situation during the 1930s, such as Frederick Augustus Voigt's *Unto Caesar*, George Eric Rowe Gedye's *Fallen Bastions* and George Ward Price's *Extra Special Correspondent* were also used. These monographs were a chance for correspondents to shed editorial restrictions that had been placed on them while working in Germany and tell readers what they saw as the truth about the Nazi dictatorship.

The layout of this study is straightforward. It begins with a chapter devoted to the British press as an industry. This was deemed essential to give the reader insight into the press of the 1930s, particularly in terms of how the press functioned and operated. The gathering of news, the work of correspondents and the efforts of the editorial team will be examined in this chapter. It will draw particular attention to the variety of relationships under which editors and correspondents worked. For some correspondents, like F. A. Voigt, the working relationship he had with *Manchester Guardian* editor William Percival Crozier was one of deep respect and collaboration. For other correspondents, like Norman Ebbutt, the relationship could be fraught and tense, compounded by the stress Ebbutt experienced working in a dictatorship.

The rest of the study was determined by the themes and events that the British press focused on in their coverage of Nazi Germany between 1933 and 1939. The first part of the book focuses on the establishment of the Nazi dictatorship beginning with a chapter on the appointment of Hitler as chancellor. It will then move on to a chapter that charts the destruction of democracy and establishment of the Nazi dictatorship. An interlude will be provided with a chapter focusing on the campaign of terror perpetrated by the Nazis against their (real and imagined) opponents. While most newspapers underreported the terror, the *Manchester Guardian* proved itself committed to uncovering the excesses of the regime and, in doing so, came out as an outspoken critic of the new regime. The fifth chapter covers the Röhm purge or the Night of the Long Knives in mid-1934, an event that was reported widely by the British press. This chapter concludes with British press coverage of the death of President Hindenburg, an event that marked the final stage in the creation of the Nazi dictatorship, cementing Hitler's rule over Germany. The next two chapters examine the treatment of religious groups in Germany, specifically the suppression and attempted coordination of the Christian churches and the persecution of Jews.

Overall, the aim of this study is to examine and determine what people in Britain could have known about the Nazi dictatorship by reading British newspapers. But more than this, the book examines what the press understood about the nature of the Nazi dictatorship. In doing so it fills an important gap in the literature which has left the question of what was known and understood about the Nazi regime largely unanswered. And it is important because in 1939 Britain went to war with the Nazi state, after Germany invaded Poland.

* * *

1

The British press

In the early 1930s the newspaper press was the most popular means of conveying information to the vast majority of people in Britain. The ready availability of newspapers in Britain resulted in an extremely competitive market, as newspapers battled for the highest sales and circulation figures. The press covered every class and demographic – all audiences were catered for in different ways by different newspapers. In 1937 there were 1,577 newspapers and 3,119 magazines and periodicals being published in Great Britain alone.[1] In 1934 every 100 families bought 95 morning and 57½ evening newspapers each day, and 130 Sunday newspapers every week.[2]

The British press of the 1930s can be separated into distinct categories. There was the newspaper press, which is the primary interest of this study, as well as periodicals and magazines. Periodicals and magazines appeared weekly, fortnightly, monthly, quarterly and annually. In most cases the periodicals and magazines were specialized, focusing on one or two interest areas. The newspaper press mostly appeared daily or weekly. There were three main types of newspapers: 'quality', 'popular' and 'specialized'. The quality press had a readership of, primarily, the elite and educated of British society. This included the upper classes as well as politicians and prominent businessmen. Popular newspapers, as the title suggests, held popular appeal and were widely read by people of all classes across the country. 'Specialized' newspapers were aimed at particular groups of people or regions in Britain. For instance, those of Jewish faith were catered for by the *Jewish Chronicle*.[3] Newspapers could also be separated another way – by political affiliation. On the right or centre-right stood the conservative press such as *The Times* and the *Morning Post*. On the liberal left was the *Manchester Guardian* and to the left of that was the *Daily Herald*.

Newspapers could be further categorized as either broadsheet, like *The Times*, or tabloid, like the *Daily Express*, both in terms of size and content of the newspaper. As a general rule, broadsheets were distinguished by a traditional approach to newspaper layout with six or more columns and detailed, in-depth articles. Tabloids, on the other hand, were smaller in size and often contained large sensational headlines and photographs to attract readers. A quality newspaper usually had a broadsheet layout while the popular newspapers were usually tabloid. The broadsheet of the 1930s differed considerably from a broadsheet newspaper of today. Perhaps the most important difference was the front page which, in the 1930s, usually contained detailed advertisements in small print across seven columns. This would often continue for six pages. The newspaper would then have pages devoted to puzzles, book reviews, court news and so on. The news itself would not begin until around page ten. There would be a main page with a table of contents and news in short, as well as leaders and editorials, which were the main news articles offering opinion and analysis generally written by a team of leader-writers. Following this would be local or national news and foreign news, often several pages of each. Both the *Manchester Guardian* and *The Times* followed this layout.

The layout of the tabloid newspaper has changed little since the 1930s. Unlike a broadsheet, the front page of a tabloid newspaper contained the major news stories of the day with large pictures and headlines to attract readers' attention. The first three or four pages of the newspaper were dedicated to news stories, from local and national to foreign news. Depending on the newspaper, subsequent pages were a blend of letters to the editor, book reviews, gossip, women's health, fictional short stories, court news, opinions, leaders, financial and business and sporting news. For instance, the *Daily Mirror* often had three to four pages devoted to what they believed was women's news. This included gossip, romance stories and a page entitled 'A Woman's Point of View'.[4] Unlike a broadsheet, the tabloid newspaper did not follow a strict six- or seven-column page layout of the news. The layout often contained large headlines that dominated the page, with photographs, then accompanying text. While the layout of a broadsheet newspaper like *The Times* changed very little from day to day, the layout of a tabloid was dictated by current news stories. For instance, a major story with an eye-catching large headline would dominate front-page coverage one day, while the next day the front page might contain four or five shorter stories accompanied by small photographs. While *The Times* had a separate page devoted to foreign news, tabloid newspapers had local, national and foreign news sharing front-page coverage.

The news was collected and processed in a few different ways. For national or local news, each newspaper had a team of reporters or journalists who would travel to local towns or cities and collect the news. Reporters were also sent out by the newspaper's head office to cover a particular event or story for a feature article. News agencies helped to supplement what the reporters brought in. Local and national news was provided by Press Association, an agency which had been providing 'home' news service since its inception in 1868.

Foreign news, with which this study is concerned, was treated differently. Foreign news primarily came from abroad, but it could also be a foreign angle on a domestic issue, for instance, German reactions to the boycotting of German goods in Britain.[5] Most newspapers had a team of correspondents stationed in the major cities of Europe who would report breaking news or emerging trends back to Britain. In Berlin alone, in August 1937, there were thirteen chief and assistant correspondents working for British newspapers, as well as four for Reuters and two for other agencies.[6] One of the most important newspapers of the period, *The Times*, had 120 foreign correspondents working around the world, of whom around 40 were on the permanent staff or retaining salary, with the rest on a casual list of contributors.[7] Correspondents for *The Times* were kept anonymous, writing under the tagline 'From our own correspondent', while many of the popular newspapers liked to publish the names of their star reporters. Some of the weekly journals, such as *The Spectator*, also sometimes published the names of their reporters.

British newspapers also relied on foreign news services from agencies such as Reuters and Central News. Reuters had a long relationship with many British newspapers, notably the *Manchester Guardian*. The *Manchester Guardian* had been using Reuters for imperial and foreign news since the earliest days of the news agency in the nineteenth century.[8] In fact, from the 1930s to the 1950s, three *Manchester Guardian* figures served on the board of Reuters – J. R. and L. P. Scott, and William Haley.[9] For the *Manchester Guardian*, Reuters filled 'a gap in the paper's overseas coverage'.[10] Donald Read, who has written extensively on the news agency, explains that Reuters operated under four tenets – speed, accuracy, equal dealing and impartiality. Reuters aimed to be first to provide news (and mostly was) 'but not at the price of accuracy'. The news provided by Reuters was professed to be impartial, 'without bias in what it said, and objective in what it chose to report (or not to report)'.[11] The news collected by Reuters was made available to all clients and newspapers 'without exclusivity' and irrespective of political leaning.[12]

The news reports provided by Reuters served a valuable function for British newspapers and those working for them. Reuters could fill gaps that newspapers might have in coverage, either because the correspondent was pursuing other news stories or because the newspaper did not have a correspondent stationed in that location. It allowed newspapers to keep its readers updated on news that they might otherwise have missed. But it also gave correspondents the chance to pursue news stories that they identified as warranting further investigation. The *Manchester Guardian*'s Darsie Gillie was one such reporter. The news service provided by Reuters allowed Gillie to 'select the topics that interested him and leave the rest to Reuters and other news agencies'.[13] The services offered by news agencies, including Reuters, were invaluable to the *Manchester Guardian* after the removal of its Berlin correspondent Alexander Werth in 1933. For much of 1933 the *Manchester Guardian* relied upon news agencies for updates and news of developments in Germany, while Werth who was forced to relocate to Paris and special correspondent F. A. Voigt focused on particular topics like the persecution and terror of political opponents.

Once the news was collected by foreign correspondents the story would be sent, often by telephone or telegraph, to London. If the article was a feature, and not pressing news, it was sent by mail. When a report arrived, it would often be sent directly to the foreign editor's room. Foreign news was the responsibility of the foreign editor, who would enlist the help of his subeditors to check the story, as well as edit it to an appropriate length. The foreign newsroom would also send reports to all interested departments including leader-writers and, depending on the story, the editor.[14] Most newspapers only minimally edited original messages, preferring to keep the correspondent's voice or personality present. There were instances, however, where a foreign editor or editor altered an article to tone down the message of the article. There were also instances where an entire article would be cut to make way for another story breaking that day or because an editor did not want to take a particular line on a story or event.

There were many considerations about what was published and the way it was presented by the newspaper. On a broad level, the coverage of news could be affected, to varying degrees, by advertising contracts, circulation figures, readership concerns, the newspaper's proprietor and the editor. While it is difficult to gauge how much these considerations influenced what the newspaper actually published, it is important to keep them in mind when analysing how a newspaper approached a particular topic.[15] Advertising, for instance, was important revenue for newspapers and therefore could have considerable influence over the content and treatment of news. While an advertisers' concern could impact the editorial policy of a newspaper, a newspaper would not risk running with a major story just to please advertisers. If the newspaper ignored a breaking story just to satisfy advertisers, it risked losing sales and a subsequent drop in its circulation.

Attracting advertisers was also dependent on high circulation. This meant that while a newspaper wanted to satisfy its advertisers, it also had to serve its readers and maintain its high circulation.[16] This was the case for the *Daily Mirror*, a popular left-leaning pictorial newspaper that during the 1930s was in constant competition with the other high-circulation newspapers, including the centre-right *Daily Express*, and the more right-wing *Daily Mail*. Circulation had a significant impact on the way the many popular newspapers approached news. The popular press, especially, was in a constant circulation battle as each newspaper competed for the greatest daily sale. By 1938 the *Daily Express* had succeeded in gaining the title of 'World's Largest Daily Sale', with over 2 million sold per day, easily overtaking its main competitor the *Daily Mail*.

The most important consideration which impacted editorial policy was the control over their newspapers held by proprietors and editors. The influence of a proprietor over their newspaper had a lot to do with the proprietor's view of his role within the newspaper as well as his personality. In the 1930s the strongest newspaper proprietors were Harold Sydney Harmsworth (Lord Rothermere), who owned Associated Press including the *Daily Mail*, and William Maxwell Aitken (Lord Beaverbrook), who owned the London Express Newspaper Ltd. with the *Daily Express* at its forefront. Lord Rothermere took a keen interest in the *Daily Mail*'s approach to European news, especially the rise of Nazism. He helped to define the newspaper's policy in the 1930s, initially voicing his support and admiration for the Nazi regime with contributions to the *Daily Mail*. Perhaps the most notable instance of this was his infamous 'Youth Triumphant' article in July 1933 which celebrated the 'success' of the regimes first six months. But he also used the pages of the *Daily Mail* to campaign for air rearmament, a cause he felt passionately about and on which he wrote his book *Warnings and Predictions*, published in 1939.[17] Another of the big press barons, Lord Beaverbrook, also maintained tight control over his newspapers, particularly the *Daily Express*. With nearly 100 per cent shareholder interest in the *Daily Express* at one point, Beaverbrook was in a position to control every element of the newspaper.[18]

Not all newspapers were structured the same way. There were different degrees of proprietorship and of shareholder interest which tempered how much control a proprietor or chairman had over newspaper policy. This was the case for *The Times* which, while owned by two proprietors, Major the Hon. John J. Astor and John Walter, was governed by a trust established in 1924. The trust was dedicated to maintaining the tradition of political independence of the newspaper, as well as ensuring that the newspaper was not used for personal ambition or profit. In practice, however, the trust left the running of the newspaper to its editor,

Geoffrey Dawson. In fact, the only reason Dawson returned to *The Times* as editor in 1923 was on the condition that he receive no interference from the trust in making editorial decisions.[19]

Somewhat easier to discern in understanding newspaper policy was the role of the editor. Once again, everything depended on the editor's personality and his strength of character. This meant that one editor could be a 'mere cipher' while another 'the creative spirit of his paper's policy'.[20] All decisions, however, went through the editor. Each day the editorial team would sit down and decide the layout of the newspaper, the features and what stories were to be printed. In most cases, editors had their own ideas about what they wanted their paper to represent and the type of articles they wanted to print. This was probably best exemplified by the *Manchester Guardian*'s editor W. P. Crozier. While the *Manchester Guardian* was controlled by John R. Scott, Crozier was given full editorial control over the newspaper. Scott believed that a chairman's duty was to make the newspaper as profitable as possible, while all other decisions and considerations were for the editor.[21] For his part, Crozier felt it was his duty to inform the public about the true nature of Nazi Germany. To do this he assembled a strong team of correspondents and closely supervised the foreign news section throughout his time as editor. Furthermore, Crozier felt that since the German press had been muzzled it was important for him to provide continuous coverage of the German situation for the benefit of the *Manchester Guardian*'s German readership. As letters to the editor attest, many German readers appreciated the commitment the newspaper showed in covering developments in Germany in such detail.

The Times editor Geoffrey Dawson also expected no proprietorial interference and full editorial freedom. During the 1930s *The Times* was seen as the voice of the British government – a view taken seriously overseas, especially in Germany. This can be attributed to *The Times*' quality circulation as well as Dawson's closeness to the National Government, particularly Halifax and Chamberlain.[22] One only need glimpse at Dawson's diaries during this period for confirmation of the close contact Dawson had with some of the key political figures of the day.[23] In fact, at times, Dawson acted as more of a politician than a newspaper editor. But he took his role as editor seriously and took a keen interest in all aspects of the paper. He decided not to appoint a foreign editor because he was unable to find anyone suited to the job, although Robin Barrington-Ward assisted with many of the responsibilities.[24] In this way, he had direct control over foreign news and maintained close contact with the foreign correspondents, both while they were stationed in Europe and when they visited England.

Foreign correspondents working for British newspapers were, potentially, the most important link in the chain of supplying foreign news to the British public. Most newspapers had correspondents stationed in the capital cities of Europe. In Germany there was usually a correspondent stationed in both Berlin and Munich. The correspondent would spend most of his time in the city to which they were assigned but would also sometimes travel to prepare stories for a feature article or to cover a particular event, for instance, the Nazi Party's Nuremberg rallies. British newspapers of the 1930s benefitted enormously from having their own correspondents in Europe, especially in Germany. In most cases, foreign correspondents stationed in Germany had been there for a number of years before the Nazis came to power and were thus knowledgeable and experienced observers of the German scene. Foreign correspondent for *The Times*, Norman Ebbutt, had been stationed in Berlin since 1925, while F. A. Voigt had been the *Manchester Guardian*'s Berlin correspondent since 1920 before becoming special correspondent. This meant that Ebbutt and Voigt, among others, were witness to the struggling Weimar Republic and were in a position to appreciate what the Nazis coming to power in 1933 meant for democracy in Germany. Furthermore, these correspondents already had a network of sources and contacts from which they could draw on information about the evolving political situation.

There were, however, a number of factors which could detract from correspondent's pivotal role in supplying news from Germany. The first factor was possible conflict with or interference from the editors of the newspapers for which they worked. This could take the form of disputes over the approach to subject matter or the editing and printing of articles. This is clearly demonstrated in the case of Ebbutt. On a number of occasions throughout the 1930s, Ebbutt had his dispatches either edited or omitted from the pages of *The Times*. It was a source of frustration for him, as William L. Shirer recounted in his book *The Nightmare Years*. Shirer wrote how Ebbutt took great care to write accurately and in detail about the excesses of the Nazis, only for his newspaper not to publish 'much of what he reported'.[25] According to Shirer 'the unpleasant truths' that Ebbutt telephoned nightly to *The Times* were often left out.[26] Ebbutt turned to giving him these dispatches so that 'at least they would see the light of day'.[27]

As early as 1931 Ebbutt was complaining that his dispatches from Berlin were being cut and edited.[28] In April 1933 he wrote in a memo: 'I fear that, as usual, the articles will be found too long . . . Yet I feel incapable of doing anything more about than I have done, even if you give me up as a bad job.'[29] He defended the length of his articles, explaining that they had been written amid 'considerable difficulties', part of which was continued ill-health.[30] The stress of working under a dictatorship was already clear in 1933. *The Times* was covering more of the German situation than most newspapers but, for Ebbutt, it needed a greater commitment to longer and more detailed reports. In November 1934, Ebbutt complained to Ralph Deakin, who served on *The Times* Imperial and Foreign desk, that twelve of his recent articles had been cut, so much so 'as to leave the original distorted'.[31] He also complained of whole paragraphs being 'torn from their context giving a distorted effect to the whole message'.[32] Ebbutt also expressed concern that requests were being made for particular stories which, for him, set a 'dangerous precedent, as it tends to give disproportionate prominence to matters which do not deserve it'.[33]

Ebbutt was particularly concerned with the way in which his articles on the church situation in Germany were being edited or cut.[34] Ebbutt followed the Nazi persecution and repression of the Catholic and Evangelical churches closely. He had a network of contacts in German government and in official circles, including the Nazi Party, which gave him an advantage in that he was able to gain accurate, detailed and, importantly, current information about what was happening in Germany.[35] Ebbutt's articles were impeccably researched. He took a factual and detailed approach to his writing. For this reason, he had specific instructions for Printing House Square (PHS) about how his articles should appear in *The Times*. His annoyance at the way PHS dealt with his articles on the church situation can be seen in a letter to editor Dawson in December 1934. Ebbutt complained that his report had been altered and edited, putting other news above that of the church situation. He complained:

> The message has been knocked to pieces and put together with sensational headlines. The lead consisted of two of the last paragraphs of a carefully constructed dispatch torn from their context and placed above the Church story. They were not news and were only justifiable in the place originally assigned to them. As presented, they had little meaning and gave a distorted and sensational effect to the whole message.[36]

He worried that the managing of his articles would affect his credentials with some of his sources.[37] Ebbutt concluded that he could only think that whoever had changed the article wanted to add a sensational angle to its overall tone. He added that there had been a number of occasions where he would receive messages urging him to give a *bright touch* as he called it, to his reports from Germany. He explained: 'in the present circumstances it strikes me as rather impolite, to put it nicely, and requiring some discussion. Our problems, I should have thought, are difficult enough here for us to be spared schoolmasterly nagging.'[38] Dawson replied a few days later attempting to ease Ebbutt's concerns:

> I have however, had a word with the foreign sub-editors on the subject and emphasized the great difficulties under which you are working... I have made it clear that you must be allowed to be the best judge of what you can and cannot say, and of how your messages can be framed most discreetly. Do not allow yourself to be discouraged by an episode of this kind, which is now not likely to recur. You are doing first-rate work for the paper and everyone recognizes it.[39]

Despite reassurances, Ebbutt continued to encounter problems with editorial staff cutting and editing his reports, especially as Britain began to pursue a strategy of appeasement towards Germany's foreign aggression. However, by this time, with so much happening both inside the Nazi state and in terms of Germany's foreign relations, it was often necessary to cut articles. For Ebbutt this was no doubt frustrating, given the trouble and effort he had put in to obtain the information and write the reports. Problems of this kind, between Ebbutt and PHS, continued until his expulsion from Germany in 1937.

Conflict and disagreements between correspondents and editorial staff were not limited to *The Times*. George Eric Rowe Gedye, Vienna correspondent for the *Daily Telegraph*, was often at odds with newspaper staff who, at times, thought his articles too eager or indignant.[40] According to Gannon, Gedye was the 'prototype of the leftist British foreign correspondent between the wars', which inevitably conflicted with the conservative policy of his newspaper.[41] A keen observer of European politics, Gedye's abhorrence of the Nazi Party's ideology and practices was clear. He understood the brutal nature of Nazism early on, as an article entitled 'Impressions of Hitler's Germany', published in 1933 in *Contemporary Review* attested.[42] Gedye scathingly observed that the Nazis only embraced Germans in their 'Brotherly love', who

> have no Jewish blood in their veins, who reject all ideas of liberalism, democracy, socialism, trade unionism, the principles of Karl Marx, the political influence of the Catholic hierarchy, and parliamentarism, and submit themselves without reserve to worshipping the principle that salvation can come only through the divine and indisputable ordinances of men 'born to rule' by dictatorial methods.[43]

Discussing the Hitler dictatorship with a German writer, Gedye said the author told him that Nazism would last 'because it suits the Germans like a Savile Row suit an Englishman. Our people can be divided into three: One part wants to be kicked, another part to kick. These make up 90 per cent. The remaining 10 per cent looks on at the spectacle and weeps.'[44]

Gedye wrote passionately; his outrage over the Nazis' policies and actions was clear. His own ideological feelings prompted him to voice his revulsion at the Nazi movement. For this reason, his articles for the *Daily Telegraph* often had to be toned down.[45] In 1939, tensions between the *Daily Telegraph* and Gedye came to a head with the announcement of the upcoming publication of Gedye's book, *Fallen Bastions*. The book was advertised as the 'uncensored truth' about Austrian politics and the Anschluss in 1938 and was to be published by the Left Book Club.[46] *Daily Telegraph* editor Arthur E. Watson wrote to Gedye following the advertisement of the upcoming book, and asking him to come to London to discuss the fallout such a book would inevitably have. Gedye insisted on publishing the book. When no agreement could be reached, Gedye left the newspaper with six months' severance pay.[47]

Berlin correspondent for the *Manchester Guardian*, Alexander Werth, also had interference from his editor. In this case, however, editor W. P. Crozier and fellow correspondent F. A. Voigt felt that Werth's articles were not forceful enough.[48] In March 1933 Werth wrote an article about the terror of the Brown Shirts on the streets of Germany, particularly in Berlin, which included the unfortunate subheading, 'Rumours of a Terror'.[49] Voigt immediately contacted Crozier angrily asking, 'What is the good of having a man in Berlin if he cannot establish the truth?' He argued that he, for one, knew that there was a terror campaign being waged by the Nazis against their opponents.[50] Voigt expressed concern that the *Manchester Guardian* was not 'telling the truth of what is happening in Berlin'.[51]

After some discussion, Crozier withdrew Werth from Germany citing the danger of the situation in Berlin for someone of Jewish extraction – a point which Werth debated. Whether his removal was because of Voigt's criticism is unclear. Was he removed because Crozier felt he was not telling the truth? Or was he removed for fear of his safety? Before his transfer Werth wrote to Crozier trying to assure his editor of his safety: 'I really do not think that it's as bad as all that. I shall certainly not leave on my own initiative.'[52] He explained that the situation was 'calming down'.[53] Crozier, however, instructed Werth to leave Germany immediately for Paris. He wrote: 'You are not to think that you have not sent us all that you could, or should. I have been uneasy about your safety all the time, and should have been still more uneasy about your safety if you had sent us more complete accounts of what has been going on.'[54] He explained: 'We must be able to get a full supply of news, and we must be unhampered by the fear of serious consequences to our correspondent.'[55] Werth voiced his dissatisfaction to Crozier in another letter: 'Altogether I am feeling rather unhappy about your references to my personal safety. A journalist has to take certain risks – and I was fully prepared to take them; I feel that it was not my fault if you are now dissatisfied.'[56] The *Manchester Guardian* did not have a resident correspondent in Berlin until the end of 1933, when C. A. Lambert took up the post. For the rest of 1933 the *Manchester Guardian* relied primarily on Reuters for news from Germany, with regular special feature articles by Voigt.[57]

When C. A Lambert did take up the post in Berlin, he was under minimum risk instructions. Voigt continued his special reporting. As David Ayerst explained in his biography of the newspaper, even though the *Manchester Guardian* had limited financial resources and even though it was expensive to keep up a duplicate service, 'Crozier decided that there were some economies that must be made' so that the newspaper could continue to tell the truth about what was happening in Germany.[58] Throughout the 1930s the two services, 'Lambert's above-board and Voigt's underground', were kept, in the words of Ayerst, 'rigorously distinct'.[59] It was a commitment that was recognized by people in Germany. Voigt wrote to Crozier at the end of April 1933 that the *Manchester Guardian* is 'looked upon as the only paper in the world that can do justice to the German Republic'.[60]

Correspondents, in reporting from Germany, also had to be aware of the type of newspaper that they were writing for and tailor articles and reports accordingly. Popular newspapers, for instance, were more interested in sensational and dramatic news stories, often with a human-interest spin – something that their correspondents had to take into account. The *Daily Express*, for instance, was a newspaper that strove to, in the words of editor Arthur Christiansen, 'make the unreadable readable'.[61] Additionally, Lord Beaverbrook, proprietor of the *Daily Express*, was keen to avoid any future conflagration with Germany and pushed his newspaper to adhere to a policy of isolationism on questions of foreign relations. This editorial line became more pronounced as relations became strained between Britain and Germany, especially as Hitler demanded treaty revisions, rearmament and territorial expansion. In spite of this, the *Daily Express* had some distinguished correspondents including Sefton Delmer and Pembroke Stephens. Sefton Delmer was one of the first British correspondents to interview Hitler in 1931 and was the only journalist to have been invited to accompany Hitler, Göring and Goebbels on a tour of the wreckage of the Reichstag after it was set alight in February 1933. During the Second World War, Delmer worked as a black propagandist for the British government. Philip Pembroke Stephens, who replaced Delmer in Berlin at the end of 1933, took a particular interest in the persecution of the Jews. He was outspoken in his rejection of Nazi anti-Semitism. He was expelled from Germany in June 1934 for his reporting for the *Daily Express*.

In the early 1930s, most of Delmer's articles were scoops – the stories that other newspapers had not the chance nor the connections to get. These often took the form of interviews with high-ranking Nazis, exclusive articles or special coverage of an event. Delmer had established contacts within the Nazi Party, and other associated organizations including the police. He was friendly with Ernst Röhm, and knew Hitler after interviewing him in 1931. In April 1932 and February 1933, Delmer travelled with Hitler on his election tours of Germany. Delmer ingratiated himself with the Nazi movement in order to get the best stories for his newspaper. This did not necessarily mean he was sympathetic to Nazism as some of his detractors claimed, but he knew that these stories, each with a dramatic spin, would appeal to the readership of the *Daily Express*.[62]

The other major factor that affected the way a correspondent reported on the situation in Germany was the danger inherent in living and working in a dictatorship. The constant fear of arrest, violence or expulsion from Germany took a toll on the health of correspondents. In 1934, Ebbutt wrote to editor Dawson:

> Everything in Germany is torturous now. Straight stories are rare, and straight stories that can be taken at their face value are still rarer . . . in general you have to play the game as it is played in the country, or confine yourself to official statements and the frank purveying of wild rumours.[63]

Ebbutt's correspondence with PHS demonstrated the toll this had on his health. In early 1934 he took time away from Germany for health reasons. Dawson described Ebbutt's position in Berlin as a 'strained situation'.[64] In his uncompleted autobiography Ebbutt wrote: 'In January, 1936, I am ill, on the verge of a nervous breakdown, and the doctor orders me to go at once to the mountains in Czechoslovakia', where he could benefit from the 'fresh air'.[65] Over a year later, in August 1937, Ebbutt was expelled from Germany. A month after his return to Britain, he suffered a stroke. In 1944 he wrote: 'Before being expelled from Germany in August 1937, I had had warnings of my state of health, but not, until afterwards looking back, of the catastrophe which fell upon me.'[66] Ebbutt was paralysed down his right side and over the course of eight years had to learn to walk, write and speak again. He never wrote for *The Times* again.

Physical dangers were also present for foreign correspondents living and working in Nazi Germany. It is not an exaggeration to say that correspondents in Nazi Germany risked their lives to report the truth. The suppression, brutality and violence that were inflicted on Germans under the Nazi regime could also easily extend to foreign nationals, including correspondents. Throughout the 1930s, but especially in 1933, there were numerous cases of foreign nationals being molested in the streets for not raising their arm in the Hitler salute, or for looking *Jewish*. In early 1933 there were a number of cases of British and American nationals being beaten in the streets by Nazi *Sturmabteilung*, or Storm Troops (the SA).

The Nazi authorities continually attacked foreign journalists for spreading so-called lies and propaganda against the German nation in what today would be called 'fake news'. There were regular reports in British newspapers about arrests and expulsions of foreign correspondents. By staging regular press conferences with foreign journalists, the Nazis hoped to convince the correspondents to moderate their reports. For some, however, speeches by figures such as Hermann Göring and Joseph Goebbels had the opposite effect and were published in British newspapers and ridiculed. But, the threat of expulsion from Germany, either for a designated period or on a permanent basis, loomed over foreign correspondents. Prior to their expulsion, correspondents suffered intimidation and threats. In many cases they were arrested on bogus charges in an attempt to silence them. Often newspapers were suspended for several months for publishing an article the Nazis found undesirable. The *Manchester Guardian*, for instance, was suppressed for most of 1933 as a result of Voigt's reporting on the political terror campaign and the SA's brutal violence.

The expulsion of foreign correspondents began with some frequency after the Reichstag Fire. On 6 March 1933, three French correspondents were expelled for a period of two months for their reporting.[67] Visas could also be easily revoked by German authorities making it impossible for a correspondent to remain in Germany. There were also instances of correspondents fleeing Germany to escape police harassment and arrest. The *Manchester Guardian* published an official German statement on 9 March 1933 regarding the treatment of foreign journalists:

> In view of the mischievous reports on the political situation in Germany published in the foreign press, serious measures had been prepared against a number of foreign correspondents. Some of these questionable correspondents have escaped the police by leaving the country. As for the others, they have given assurances that they will avoid publishing reports of a mischievous tendency in

future, and refrain from using ambiguous statements. In view of these assurances, and in view of the more sensible attitude now taken by the correspondents in regard to the German situation, they have been spared expulsion, and have been granted a probation period of two months.[68]

This remarkable statement provides insight into the conditions facing correspondents who wished to tell the truth about events in Germany. Despite these statements, many British correspondents would continue to report events as accurately and in as much detail as they could. The regime responded with harassment, terrorization, arrest and expulsion.

One of the first instances of a British correspondent being arrested by Nazi authorities was that of Noel Panter, Munich correspondent for the *Daily Telegraph*. He was arrested in October 1933 by the 'political police' on charges of espionage.[69] The British consul-general at Munich was refused access to Panter, who had been imprisoned at the Ettstrasse prison. *The Times* reported that Panter had probably been arrested for his article about a SA military parade through Kelheim.[70] Several complaints were lodged with the German Foreign Office over Panter's imprisonment, including by the British ambassador Eric Phipps and Foreign Secretary Sir John Simon. He was finally released after nine days and ordered to leave Germany immediately. Once in Britain he wrote two feature articles about his imprisonment, drawing attention to the fact that most of those imprisoned, including political prisoners and Nazis, in the Ettstrasse prison were being held without charge, and for long periods of time.[71] German authorities tried to claim that he had not been expelled; however, on his attempt to work in Germany in June 1934 he was expelled again within a day.

The *Daily Express*' Pembroke Stephens was also expelled in 1934. He was arrested in May 1934 after he questioned some workers about the construction of a factory in the forest around Aken.[72] Stephens has suspicions that the installation could have been a secret armaments factory. He, along with his wife and her cousin, were held by the Secret Police. They were released soon after. Their arrest was big news and the *Daily Express* seized upon the fame of their Berlin correspondent and gave his articles special prominence. Rather than focus on the drama of the movement like Delmer had, Stephens focused on the effect Nazism had on Germans. He paid particular attention to the persecution and mistreatment of the Jews, criticizing the Nazi government. Unsurprisingly, due to the critical nature of his reports and the prominence of the articles following his arrest, Stephens was again arrested at the beginning of June 1934. This time he was expelled from Germany. According to an article written by

Reginald Steed in the *Daily Express*, the reason given by German authorities for Stephens's expulsion was the 'constant misrepresentation of the peaceful efforts of the German Government and frivolous and distorted reports in this connection which are an abuse of hospitality'.[73] Stephens, in a feature article on his expulsion, denied these claims. He declared:

> I affirmed my determination to tell the truth about Germany, even at the risk of imprisonment and expulsion. My friends chaffed me at the time, but events have proved my belief that it is impossible to tell the truth, the real truth about Germany, and remain an accredited correspondent in Berlin.[74]

Stephens wrote that there were only two alternatives open to him following his first arrest: 'either silence, humility, obeisance to officialdom, or the risk of continuing my work as if nothing had happened at all. I chose the second course and my expulsion was the almost inevitable result.'[75] Stephens continued to write critical articles about the Nazis from London but by this time the drama of his expulsion had worn off and the *Daily Express* began to tone down its focus on Germany.

Expulsion was not the only threat facing foreign correspondents working in Germany. Like the German populace, foreign correspondents also feared being arrested and were disappearing without a trace. *The Times* correspondent Norman Ebbutt recounted what he believed was a close call in early 1933. He witnessed police go into his flat one night when he was almost home. He turned and went back the way he came from to avoid them. He recalled in his unpublished biography that the incident had occurred 'just after the Reichstag fire when all sorts of people began to disappear in the night and had not been found locked up in the police stations in the morning'.[76] He described what had occurred:

> The porter said that the police did not enter at all the landlord's flat, which was a big flat on the ground floor but said they must enter Herr Ebbutt's flat above ... They may have looked over my things in the flat ... but if they had, they were thorough and left everything perfectly straight. There were no compromising documents or anything else in the least bit suspicious anyway ... The porter and his wife said that the police were after, so they thought, someone in the back court who did not materialise, but it was a very lame answer.[77]

The *Manchester Guardian*'s F. A. Voigt had an altogether more alarming encounter with Nazi authorities. As special correspondent for the *Manchester Guardian*, Voigt reported on mainly French and German news with focused coverage, distinct from the day-to-day coverage provided by the resident correspondents. His reports on the Nazi terror made the *Manchester Guardian* unpopular with the Nazi Party and the newspaper was routinely prohibited for sale in Germany. Voigt's reports meant that he was marked as an undesirable correspondent and any trips to Germany were clandestine affairs. He would sneak across the border and gather his information before returning to Paris, where he resided. He relied on a network of sources, particularly Max Wolf, a Swiss journalist-turned-informant for the *Manchester Guardian*, who would provide information about German affairs.

The encounter in question occurred in December 1933. In that month, Voigt received word that the Gestapo had begun operating in Paris. He wrote to editor Crozier that the situation had become grave. It would probably be best for him to leave Paris for a while as 'the Gestappa [*sic*] is determined to find out how my information is obtained'.[78] He proposed going to London to try to give the Gestapo the impression that he was permanently residing and reporting from London. However, before he could do this, the situation escalated. Voigt received word that a 'Nazi raid' on his apartment was imminent. The French authorities were concerned enough about information about the raid that they placed three detectives on personal detail with Voigt. One of them, wrote Voigt to Crozier, was 'armed with an automatic pistol of a size that I'm sure it must come under the category of heavy armaments' who 'sleeps in my room'.[79] Voigt explained to Crozier that the situation 'must be serious because it hardly ever happens that three men are detailed – usually it is only one or at the most two'.[80] The Nazi Government 'is determined to silence the M.G. at any cost'.[81] He believed they were not after him, but after 'my documents, and above all, my sources in Germany (which they would be able to deduce from my documents – had these been seized, there would have been hundreds of arrests as a result)'.[82]

Voigt did not take the situation as seriously as Crozier and London editor James Bone. They appealed for him to move back to London, or at the very least relocate to a hotel in Paris. Voigt, however, was notoriously stubborn and refused to move. By the end of December Voigt had received information that the situation was, in fact, more dire than he had earlier appreciated. Writing to Crozier, he explained:

> The Paris affair, so I now learn, was rather more serious that I at first thought. I had supposed that a burglary had been planned – possibly by French burglars engaged by the Germans. But apparently it was not to be a burglary but an assassination.[83]

Crozier's response was immediate. He instructed Voigt to move to a hotel immediately. Recognizing Voigt's stubborn nature, he also wrote to Voigt's wife, Eleanor, asking her to speak to her husband and convince him to move from his present home in Paris.[84] Voigt assured Crozier that the relevant authorities were aware of the situation. He explained that he did not think that it had been the German government that was behind the incident. Indeed, he believed that once they were aware of the situation, he was certain they would 'take steps to prevent anything of the kind from happening'.[85] Nevertheless, the French authorities took the matter seriously and according to correspondence between Voigt and Crozier, investigated the incident. While the situation had largely blown over by February 1934, the British Home Office, the Foreign Office and Scotland Yard were made aware of the situation. In light of the situation, Voigt's only concession was that he moved his most sensitive documents to London as a further protection for his sources. He also visited London more frequently to give the impression that he carried most of his work out in Britain.

On the face of it, foreign correspondents were the most important link in supplying news to the British public about the social and political situation in Nazi Germany. But there were a number of factors which could detract from this role. First and foremost was the interference of the newspapers for which they reported. From leader-writers to subeditors to the editor of the newspaper, interference could take many forms. It could take the form of requesting that a correspondent stick to a particular line, editing and distorting stories, or even completely ignoring and cutting whole articles. The requested approach to material could also impede the important role of a newspaper correspondent. As with Delmer, contacts and exclusive scoops were useless if the newspaper one wrote for was hesitant to get involved in European affairs. But perhaps the biggest factor that affected a correspondent's reporting was the dangers and risks inherent in reporting from a dictatorship. The Nazis used threats, intimidation and violence in an attempt to moderate and control what was written about the regime and what the outside world could have known about life inside Germany. The material they did manage to get out of Germany will be explored at length in this book.

* * *

2

Hitler becomes chancellor

On 30 January 1933, Adolf Hitler, leader of the National Socialist German Workers' Party, was appointed chancellor of Germany by President Paul von Hindenburg. Hitler and his Nazi Party were not unknown to the British press. Since the conclusion of the Great War the British press had followed and monitored the German political scene. However, after the failed Beer Hall putsch in 1923, the resulting imprisonment of Adolf Hitler and his associates, and the ban on the party most newspapers lost interest in the right-wing party. The resurgence of the party following gains in the German elections of September 1930 and July 1932 recaptured the attention of British newspapers. For the *Daily Express*, the rise of the Nazi Party in the early 1930s was deserving of their attention. Correspondent Sefton Delmer, a German expert, was not only the first British journalist to interview Hitler in 1931; he was also invited to accompany the Nazi leader on his election tour in 1932.

The Nazi Party's election successes in 1930 and 1932 had many British newspapers believing that a Nazi government or, at the very least, Nazi inclusion in German government was imminent. It was for this reason that British newspapers were not surprised when President Hindenburg appointed Hitler the new chancellor of Germany in January 1933. In announcing Hitler's appointment, the *Daily Telegraph* stated: 'The new turn given to the German political kaleidoscope on Saturday brought about, at last, the result that has so long seemed natural, if not inevitable.'[1] For the *Daily Telegraph*, 'logic' had prevailed with Hitler's appointment. Finally, explained the *Daily Telegraph*, Hitler had been given the ability of 'proving his powers of statesmanship'.[2] Other newspapers made similar statements. In a leading article, *The Times* commented: 'That Herr Hitler who leads the strongest party in the Reichstag and obtained almost a third of more than 35,000,000 votes in the last election, should be given the chance of proving that he is something more than an orator and an agitator was always desirable.'[3]

For some British newspapers, the inclusion of Hitler and the Nazi Party in German government was not only imminent; it was necessary. As *The Spectator* summed up: 'It has been evident for some time that the experience of a Hitler administration was something that Germany had to face, if only to get it over.'[4] There was no other alternative, explained the newspaper; President Hindenburg realized that 'the Hitler experiment must be tried sooner or later'.[5] In a similar manner, the *News Chronicle* explained that it had become clear that 'until Herr Hitler had been given a fair trial every other possible German Government was hopelessly handicapped'. The newspaper stated: 'Whatever such a Government might do, there was always this strange figure behind its back outbidding it every time with windy promises of doing far better if given the chance. Now the chance has been given.'[6]

While the British press had believed that a Hitler administration was imminent and inevitable, what they did struggle to understand was the precise nature of the Nazi leader's appointment. Few details were provided by the president or members of the German government about the reasons for Hitler's appointment. For this reason, in the days and weeks that followed, reports were often plagued by doubt, suspicion, rumour and misunderstanding as the press grappled with the rapidly changing political situation in Germany. Misconceptions about the nature of the new government began with the dismissal of Chancellor Kurt von Schleicher and the subsequent appointment of Hitler in his place. Drawing on Schleicher's military background and ties to the army (he was a general during the war and was appointed minister of defence during Papen's chancellorship), the *Daily Express* published a sensational account of what it believed had occurred under the headline 'Hitler Smashes Military Plot'. With front-page coverage, the newspaper reported:

> A startling disclosure of a military plot to seize power in Germany threw light last night on the sudden move which made Adolf Hitler, ex-labourer, the Chancellor of Germany. . . . The ex-Chancellor, General von-Schleicher, had persuaded a number of officers and generals to establish a dictatorship while the country was still without a Government.[7]

With dramatic flourish the newspaper declared: 'Hitler, the popular hero, with his old enemy, von Papen, the autocratic Junker, joined hands to defeat the soldier's plot.'[8] Needless to say, the *Daily Express* had the story wrong. There was no impending military plot. But in the early days of his succession rumour abounded.

For many British newspapers, it seemed the only way that Hitler's inclusion in government would be tolerated was with certain conditions and curtailments placed on the party and its leader. This gave rise to the popular idea that Hitler was a prisoner or pawn of the new cabinet. This view was subscribed to not only by the British press but also by leading German politicians at the time, namely former chancellor Franz von Papen and Nationalist leader Alfred Hugenberg. Both politicians believed their positions in the new government would serve to check Hitler and the Nazi Party. The precise nature of the new cabinet was the subject of much discussion in British newspapers. For some newspapers, the fact that the cabinet included the strong figure of Papen as well as a significant number of Nationalists proved that Hitler would be held prisoner by more dominant political forces. The *Daily Telegraph* drew attention to the position of Papen reporting that he 'promises to be the controller of the new Hitler Cabinet. He has been given powers never before held by a Vice-Chancellor.'[9] To this end, reported the *Daily Telegraph*, 'Almost all the important departments of the Reich have been withdrawn from Herr Hitler's influence.'[10] Hitler was 'Chancellor in little but name, and is virtually a prisoner of his own Ministry'.[11] The *News Chronicle* described Papen and the other non-Nazi ministers in the new cabinet as 'watch-dogs' of President Hindenburg.[12] The *Daily Express* painted the most vivid picture of what it saw was Hitler's position in the new cabinet:

> [H]e has entered the Chancellor's palace only to find himself a shackled prisoner of von Papen and Dr. Hugenberg, his Nationalist colleagues, not to mention the grand old watchdog in the President's palace next door, Field-Marshal von Hindenburg. . . . [Hitler] has recognised his prison as a prison.[13]

But not all newspapers subscribed to this view. Some British newspapers urged caution in viewing Hitler as a prisoner of stronger conservative forces. Both the *Daily Mirror* and the *Manchester Guardian* recognized that while the makeup of the cabinet was designed to keep 'check on Hitler', his fellow Nazis held important posts; Wilhelm Frick was named minister of the interior and Hermann Göring was appointed minister without portfolio and acting commissioner for the Prussian Ministry of the Interior.[14] The *Manchester Guardian* observed with some accuracy:

> The Hitler Government is a coalition of Nazis and Hugenberg Nationalists, although the latter are more numerous in the Cabinet three of the most 'strategic' posts are held by Nazis, and it is by no means certain that the Nazis will be the 'prisoners' in this new Government.[15]

For the *Manchester Guardian*, Göring's appointment as acting Prussian minister of the interior and Frick as Reich minister of the interior was 'highly significant'.[16] The newspaper explained to readers that 'With these two posts in their hands the Nazis hope to "cleanse" both the Civil Service and the police of Republican influences, and to turn them into obedient instruments of party policy'.[17] The *Manchester Guardian* was one of the few newspapers to pick up on the significance of the makeup of the new cabinet.

Most newspapers struggled to understand Hitler's acceptance of the chancellorship under the conditions set by President Hindenburg. For some it seemed that Hitler had given up his aims of total power. As the *Daily Mirror* reported: 'Hitler has achieved the ambition of his life . . . but not without giving up a great deal of his "all or nothing policy".[18] Did this mean that Hitler had given up his ambitions of overturning German democracy and creating a National Socialist state? For the *New Statesman and Nation*, this seemed to be the case. The newspaper explained to readers that what Hitler had achieved was

> [H]ardly the glittering prize he clamoured for . . . though he is Chancellor of the German Reich, he is not the head of a Nazi Government, but of a mixed body of Die-hards . . . it is not likely that they are going to be ciphers, or to give Hitler a free hand to make a new Germany on 'National Socialist' lines. We shall not expect to see the Jews exterminated, or the power of big finance overthrown.[19]

The *Daily Telegraph* conveyed a similar sentiment: 'Herr Hitler in office is very far from being the national and international peril that he has so often vowed himself to become if given the chance.'[20] For the *Morning Post*, Hitler's acceptance of the chancellorship was 'proof that he has given up the ambition to rule Germany alone at the head of his party'.[21] He had not gained the majority of the electorate which had always been his 'declared aim'.[22] 'Heads will scarcely "roll in the dust", as he promised in the autumn', reported the *Morning Post*.[23]

Some British newspapers expressed cautious optimism, hoping that Hitler would become more moderate now that he was in power. The *Jewish Chronicle* was one such newspaper. Mirroring the response of many Jews in Germany, the newspaper commented: 'the most solid hope that still remains is that the Nazi chiefs may acquire, in office, that sense of responsibility which they could not feel when wooing the passions of the rabble.'[24] 'Will Adolf Hitler, the statesman, be as successful as Adolf Hitler, the agitator?' the *News Chronicle* asked.[25] Other newspapers were not so optimistic. Even if Hitler was a prisoner in the current cabinet, he had expressed his contempt for democracy on a number of occasions. Therefore, as *The Spectator* observed: 'This is less Hitler's hour of triumph than his hour of trial. At last he has the chance of proving himself, and in the process he will in all likelihood make or break his party, and quite possibly the Weimar Constitution, too.'[26] *The Times* echoed a similar line. For the newspaper, German parliamentary democracy depended 'upon the unknown quality of Herr Hitler's constructive powers, and of his ability for the first time to exercise power with responsibility'.[27]

In general, it can be said that the British press failed, with the notable exception of the *Manchester Guardian*, to perceive the deadly intent of the Nazi Party to remain in power at all costs, and overate the power of the rather feckless conservative elites to rein them in. They were well aware of the tactics used by the Nazis in previous years to further their purpose but the beatings inflicted by the Storm Troops on their political opponents and the general intolerance of the Nazis of any divergent view were somehow discounted by many of the press in their early appraisals of Hitler. The willingness of the press to give the Nazis the benefit of the doubt, to 'normalize' them, meant that the British public were off to a shaky start in their ability to establish the inwardness of the new regime.

* * *

At the beginning of February 1933, the *Manchester Guardian* described Berlin as 'fairly quiet' – the feeling in the city was one of 'expectation'.[28] The Nazis 'are expecting to see wonders' while others were 'waiting with mixed feelings of distrust and curiosity'.[29] It was in this climate that the Reichstag was dissolved, and an election scheduled for 5 March 1933. The election campaign marked an important turning point in press understanding and reporting of Hitler's fledgling coalition. Misunderstanding and uncertainty about the nature of Hitler's chancellorship gave way to suspicion and unease as repression became the hallmark of the pre-election period. Throughout February the British press reported how the Nazis' election campaign was dominated by brutality, violence and the suppression of civil liberties, demonstrating contempt for the democratic election process. At the call of the elections, the Nazis began to wage a ruthless campaign against rival political parties.

One of the first steps taken by Hitler that alerted the British press to his true nature was one that was personal for many correspondents. It was the freedom of the press itself. The newspaper press in Germany was an important tool used by political parties during election campaigns and, for that reason, it was one of the first democratic institutions targeted by the Nazis. The Nazis' war on opposition newspapers was made possible by a decree, originally prepared under the Papen administration, that came into force on 4 February 1933.[30] The 'Decree for the Protection of the German People' was used by the Nazis to ban opposition newspapers and meetings, thereby severely limiting the ability of rival political parties to stage an effective election campaign. To the British press, this decree was a powerful weapon which, in the hands of the Nazis, could effectively wipe out any, and indeed all, newspapers in Germany. The *Manchester Guardian* stated that the decree was worded in such a way that 'almost any article may come under it'.[31] The *Morning Post* explained that the 'effect of the decree largely depends on its interpretation by the Ministry of the Interior and the Government Press Bureau' which were in the 'hands of Nazis'. Therefore, it was likely that 'many of the opposition newspapers whose journalistic ethics, if not impeccable, are incomparably superior to those of Herr Hitler's Party Press, should be disquieted by the penalties which await them if they are considered to have violated the new Decree'.[32] As the German newspaper *Berliner Tageblatt*, quoted by the *Manchester Guardian*, put it, the new decree 'will make it possible for the Government to exterminate completely any paper'.[33]

The effect of the decree was swift. On 6 February 1933 *The Times* reported that *Vorwärts*, the principal organ of the Socialist Party, had been suspended for three days, along with eight Socialist newspapers in Silesia and eighteen Communist newspapers throughout Germany, based on a 'charge of infraction of the sedition clause of the penal code'.[34] The reason for suspension, according to *Vorwärts* and quoted by *The Times*, was that the newspapers had published the Socialist election manifesto which urged voters not to resort to violence but instead use the 'weapon' of the ballot paper. To the *Manchester Guardian*, the suppression of *Vorwärts* 'gives one a sufficiently clear idea of the methods with which the Nazis propose to conduct the election campaign'.[35] The *Daily Express*' Sefton Delmer described the effects of the prohibitions: 'The newspaper stall at the corner of our street . . . has rather a different appearance to that which it had three weeks ago. There are far fewer newspapers on sale than there were.'[36]

British press reports on the prohibition of German newspapers ranged from a few lines in popular newspapers like the *Daily Express* to in-depth analysis in quality newspapers such as *The Times*, the *Manchester Guardian* and the *Daily Telegraph*. The suppression of the German press was of interest to newspapers of all political leanings – this was not a matter of politics but a matter of the freedom of the newspaper press itself. *The Times*, the *Daily Telegraph*, *Morning Post* and the *Manchester Guardian* published frequent, if not daily, reports as newspaper after newspaper was prohibited in Germany for periods ranging from a few days to a few weeks, even several months. For instance, on 16 February the *Daily Telegraph* reported how suppressions continued even though the opposition press, threatened by heavy financial losses through suspension, has already become exceedingly tame . . . Violent language is now confined to the Government press, which day after day hurls unbridled insults at its political opponents.[37]

The *Daily Telegraph* then went on to list prohibited newspapers and included follow-up reports on new suppressions on 18, 20 and 24 February. Despite some press prohibitions being quashed by the courts in Germany, the *Daily Telegraph* explained: 'the voice of public opinion has been almost completely stifled in this country. A minority of the nation is given absolute freedom to say what it likes about the majority, which has been completely cowed by the ruinous Press prohibitions.'[38] During the month of February, the suppression and prohibition of the German press remained a primary focus of British press reports on the election campaign.

While Communists and Socialists had their newspapers suppressed, their election posters and placards banned and their election demonstrations prohibited, the Nazis used the same methods that were denied to their opposition to wage a vigorous campaign. Election posters, wireless, speeches and demonstrations, and Nazi-controlled newspapers such as the *Völkischer Beobachter* were used to their full potential by the Nazis. Their efforts to win votes were reported extensively by the British press. This became the primary avenue by which the British press came to understand Nazi aims and goals. The British press closely followed and documented these propaganda pieces in the Nazi newspapers, as well as the election speeches given by Hitler and fellow Nazis, in order to gain an understanding of what the new Hitler government intended for Germany.

By the middle of February, it had become clear to many correspondents that Hitler intended to secure complete power, regardless of the outcome of the election process. British newspapers published official speeches and broadcasts by Hitler and his fellow Nazis which demonstrated a contempt for the election process, and for democracy in general. *The Times* drew attention to a speech given by Hitler which clearly demonstrated contempt for the democratic process. In the speech he declared: '"If the German people should desert us that will not restrain us. We will take the course that is necessary to save Germany from ruin."'[39] Importantly, this passage was omitted from official reports – a fact picked up by *The Times*. The correspondent noted that even though it had been censored it had been heard by millions who listened to the broadcast. *The Spectator* also referred to the passage, explaining to readers: 'It is now evident that every conceivable expedient is to be invoked to secure the return of the present Government in Germany at the elections on March 5th'.⁴⁰

The Times Berlin correspondent Norman Ebbutt took an astute interest in the changing relationship between the National Socialists, the state and the electorate. His articles provided readers with the chance to understand the true intentions of Hitler and his Nazi Party towards German democracy. On 16 February, Ebbutt informed readers:

> It can now be stated on the best authority that the Nazi partners in the present Nazi-Nationalist alliance are avowedly working to establish the 'Nationalistic State' by which their followers certainly understand the Hitlerist State – irrespective of opposition, and expect to realise their ambition in the immediate future.⁴¹

Ebbutt recognized that the Nazis' suppression of their political opponents, through means of controlling the press and propaganda, was the precursor to Hitler's attempt to subvert, and thereby destroy, the democratic electoral process of the Weimar Republic. In another article, Ebbutt explained to readers that 'The elections might be important if their results were allowed to count; but no attempt is now made to disguise the intention of the Hitler-Papen Government, and especially the Nazi part of it, to "find other means" of remaining in power if it does not obtain a majority'.⁴²

Other newspapers could not compete with the level of detail and the frequency of reports that were in *The Times*, but they did make similar points. The *Manchester Guardian* drew readers' attention to a speech by Walter Funk of the Nazi Party and chief of the government press department: 'I want you to all grasp the brutal fact that the accession of Hitler to power did not mark a mere change in Government but a change of regime in Germany'.⁴³ This was powerful proof of Nazi intentions, reported the *Manchester Guardian*:

> Herr Funk said that Parliamentary Government was 'finished'. The Nazi position could not have been defined more clearly, more precisely, and – to use Herr Funk's own adjective – more brutally . . . If the Nazis have their own way Germany will be Fascist within a few months, perhaps within a few weeks.⁴⁴

It was clear to the press that the German elections were no great hurdle to the Nazis' quest for power; they were now a mere formality. As the *Daily Telegraph* explained: 'Herr Hitler, Chancellor of Germany, to-night committed himself to the definite statement that, failing a majority at the elections on March 5, he intends to govern with a minority'.⁴⁵ In his speech, 'Hitler added significantly:

"I did not make the present constitution."[46] This was also reported in the *Observer*.[47] Harking back to initial reactions to Hitler's Chancellorship, the *Manchester Guardian* remarked: 'Nobody is speaking any more of Hitler and Göring being the prisoners of Von Papen and Hugenberg. The Hugenberg people are beginning to show signs of nervousness.'[48]

While the press picked up on the fact the Nazis were actively working to undermine the democratic process, there was less certainty about the future, specifically what would happen after the election. This was partly to do with the difficulty in obtaining accurate information about the evolving situation in Germany. Towards the end of February 1933, the German press was largely muzzled and, as the *Manchester Guardian* put it, all decisions were made 'behind closed doors'.[49] The *Manchester Guardian* summed up the difficulty in obtaining information: 'The general public knows next to nothing of what is going on behind the scenes. The papers to-day are either ignorant or reticent, and even some of the best informed people have to supplement a great deal of the official information with more or less reliable verbal reports and rumours.'[50] For the most part, correspondents had to piece together what was happening from official reports and speeches, supplemented by information from informants and conversations on the streets of Berlin and around Germany. There were exceptions to this – *The Times* Norman Ebbutt had access and connections in German political circles, while Sefton Delmer of the *Daily Express* had established close contact with the Nazi Party and other organizations, including the police. Their reporting styles, and the way they utilized these connections, had marked differences. While Ebbutt wrote soberly and factually, Delmer favoured a more sensational and dramatic style – one that he knew appealed to readers of the *Daily Express*.

By getting close to the Nazis, the *Daily Express*' Sefton Delmer supplied dramatic news stories that appealed to readers who wanted an insight into the personality of the new chancellor of Germany. Having access to Hitler and the Nazi Party meant that Delmer was able to provide the *Daily Express* with 'scoops' – the stories that other newspapers had not the chance to report or did not have the connections to get. The *Daily Express* sought to give its readers an exclusive and personal insight into the Nazi election campaign and main figures of the party. Undoubtedly the figure at the forefront of Delmer's scoops was the new German chancellor. One of Delmer's exclusive scoops was secured with an invitation to accompany Hitler on his election tour of Germany. Flying in Hitler's plane, Delmer provided readers with not only descriptions of Hitler's speeches but also of the leader himself. He described Hitler as a 'middle-aged man in a fawn coat, with a kindly reddish face beneath a mop of carefully brushed brown hair'.[51] He even included a description of the lunch the leader ate – 'a cheese sandwich' – eaten while 'turning over the leaves of an illustrated magazine, lingering interestedly over the picture of a beautiful woman'.[52] But, most vividly, Delmer described Hitler as he disembarked the plane to greet those waiting: 'His blue eyes . . . were now staring fiercely straight ahead of him, hypnotising all that came within their range of vision. Hitler's mouth was grim and aggressive. This at last was the real Hitler – the Messiah of Militant Nationalism.'[53]

* * *

With the election campaign almost at a close, a dramatic event captured the attention of the British press. It was the fire in the Reichstag which broke out on the night of 27 February 1933. The *Daily Express* led the way with its coverage of the fire. Sefton Delmer was able to exploit his connections with the party, getting invited to accompany Hitler, Göring, Goebbels and Vice Chancellor von Papen on a tour of the still-smouldering Reichstag. Delmer described arriving at the scene of the fire soon after it was lit 'watching the flames licking their way up the great dome into the tower'.[54] The reactions of the leading Nazis to the arson were described in detail in the resulting article entitled 'Nothing Shall Stop Us Now', published on 28 February 1933. Of Hitler's anger at the scene, Delmer wrote: 'Never have I seen Hitler with such a grim and determined expression. His eyes, always a little protuberant, were almost bulging out of his head.'[55] Acknowledging the arrest of one man and the alleged presence of a number of communist deputies Goering declared, according to Delmer, 'This is undoubtedly the work of Communists.'[56] Delmer recorded how Hitler watched firefighters battle the fire with 'a savage fury blazing in his pale blue eyes', and, when he met with Von Papen, Hitler declared: 'This is a god-given signal! If this fire, as I believe, turns out to be the work of Communists, then there is nothing that shall stop us crushing out this murder pest with an iron fist.'[57] With Delmer present, Hitler seized on the opportunity to expound the dangers of communism. With dramatic flourish, Hitler announced to the foreign journalist:

> God grant, that this is the work of the Communists. You are witnessing the beginning of a great new epoch in German history. This fire is the beginning . . . You see this flaming building . . . If this Communist spirit got hold of Europe for but two months it would be all aflame like this building.[58]

Delmer's exclusive access gave readers an insight into the fire which no other newspaper was able to provide. No other British correspondent was permitted access to the burning building or witnessed the immediate reactions of Hitler, Göring, Goebbels and Papen as they surveyed the damage. The Berlin correspondent for the *Daily Mail* described his attempts to gain access: 'Just after 10p.m. I tried to get to the burning building. A policeman warned me to go back, and the production of a police-card was to no avail. "Not even members of the Reichstag are allowed to approach," he said.'[59] But correspondents were able to provide readers with their own accounts of the fire and the devastation it wreaked on the historic building. For instance, *The Times* correspondent recalled:

> Your correspondent, who by chance was passing the Reichstag shortly after 9 o'clock, saw the central dome surmounting the rectangular Parliament building, with its four corner towers, blazing furiously – a beacon which must have been visible for miles . . . fire engines from all parts of Berlin came tearing through the Tiergarten, and hundreds of police in lorries and on horseback arrived and cleared the streets.[60]

For visual effect, many newspapers, including the *Daily Mail*, *Daily Express*, *Daily Mirror* and the *News Chronicle*, also printed large photographs of the fire to accompany articles.

British press coverage of the fire was dominated by sensational accounts. Revelations that the arsonist, Marinus van der Lubbe, had ties to the Communist Party led some newspapers to make wild speculations about the intent behind the fire.[61] The fact that van der Lubbe was not a member of the German Communist Party did not stop the Nazis from linking the party to the fire. British newspapers reported how the communist headquarters at Karl Liebknecht house in Berlin were raided shortly after the fire. Raids were accompanied by wide-scale arrests of members of the Communist Party. Some of the wildest reports of communist plots came from the German authorities which were quoted at length in British newspapers. They revealed the raid had uncovered 'proof' that the party had been planning revolts to undermine the present government and throw Germany into chaos. The raid had, wrote the *Morning Post*, allegedly unearthed 'plans for revolution and civil war'.[62] Accepting the Nazis claims the *Daily Mail* observed the uncovered documents demonstrated,

> [R]evolution and civil war throughout Germany were planned to begin on Saturday, the eve of the general election. They state that the Communists intended to assassinate a number of prominent men and had plans for poisoning large quantities of food and for killing people wholesale. The Communists further intended to disguise themselves in Nazi and police uniforms and shoot down their political enemies in the streets.[63]

Needless to say, there was little evidence of the alleged plots, but the Nazis exploited the fire and the political background of the arsonist.

Nazi authorities used the fire as a pretext to push through an emergency decree. The introduction of the decree was widely reported in British newspapers. The Decree of the Reich President for the Protection of People and State, or the Reichstag Fire Decree as it became known, was introduced through by the Nazis and signed by President Hindenburg. This was despite the fact that it seriously undermined his presidency by ceding powers to the cabinet, led by Hitler. The decree, drawing on plans and discussions that dated back to the 1920s, ushered in emergency measures that severely restricted the rights and civil liberties of the German people, imposed draconian measures including the death penalty for violation of the decree and permitted the Reich government to intervene in the federated states to restore order and security.[64] British newspapers widely reported the introduction of the decree. While many newspapers reported the measures against the German states, they spent more time focusing on the suspension of key articles of the Weimar constitution that governed freedom and civil liberties. The *Manchester Guardian* explained to readers that the following freedoms and rights had been suspended: 'personal liberty, the right of free expression of opinion, the freedom of the press, security against house searching, the right of holding meetings and forming associations, the privacy of letters, telegrams, and telephone calls'.[65] The *Daily Mail* quoted repealed articles of the decree which included Article 114, 'guaranteeing freedom of person' and 'Article 118, which states: Every German has the right to express his opinion by work, writing, printing, or picture.'[66]

The British press also drew readers' attention to the introduction of draconian measures for breaches of the decree. In effect this meant that the government could use repressive measures against opposition groups which could include detaining people in 'protective custody' for indefinite periods of time without judicial interference.[67] Additionally, the decree introduced the death penalty for a range of broadly defined crimes including, quoted *The Times*,

> [A]ttempting the life of the President, or members of the Reich Government, or Reich Commissioners, or of conspiring with others in such an attempt, or of incitement to such an attempt . . . cases of grave disturbances of the peace, of deprivation of liberty with a view of using the victim as a hostage, of high treason, of incendiarism, of causing floods or explosions, and of poisoning to the common danger.[68]

Under the decree, the government could pursue the death penalty in charging arsonist van der Lubbe for the arson in the Reichstag. The *Manchester Guardian*, *News Chronicle*, *Daily Mail* and the *Morning Post* also drew readers' attention to the application of the death penalty for breaches of the decree. The *News Chronicle* alerted readers to this point of the decree with the headline 'Hitler's Death Decree'.[69]

In his report on the Reichstag Fire Decree, the *News Chronicle*'s John Segrue referred to the German government as a 'dictatorship'.[70] Segrue had good reason for using this term – he and other correspondents had witnessed the Nazis contempt for democratic processes. The latest expression of this contempt had taken the form of the Reichstag Fire Decree. Official government statements did little to diminish this. According to Segrue, a government spokesperson commenting on the decree announced to foreign journalists: 'This Government is going to stay in office. The only alternative to it is Communism. Parliamentary and democratic government is done with for ever in Germany.'[71] For Berlin correspondent John Segrue, this statement left little doubt as to what the decree, in the hands of the Nazis, would mean for democracy in Germany. He reported: 'The decree, stated to have been framed for "warding off Communist acts of terror that may endanger the security of the State", sets up in effect a dictatorship far exceeding in strictness any form of government that has hitherto existed in Germany.'[72]

Other newspapers were just as astute in recognizing what the decree meant for Germany. The *Morning Post* reported to readers: 'The Reichstag fire has overnight hastened and intensified the movement towards Fascist dictatorship in a degree that would have seemed incredible yesterday.'[73] The *Manchester Guardian* argued the emergency measures placed Germany 'under an absolute dictatorship', while the *Daily Mail* wrote that the decree had ushered in the 'end of democracy'.[74] For the immediate future, reported *The Times*, the decree meant that the 'Left Opposition has thus been completely silenced'.[75]

The Nazis made wild accusations to justify the introduction of the decree. British newspapers reported these justifications. The *Daily Telegraph* referred to official government declarations that the decree had been

> necessary to thwart a wholesale communist plot. This, it is asserted, aimed at leading up to civil war by acts of incendiarism, bomb outrages, poisoning of wells, and other horrors. Terrorism was to be begun all over Germany.[76]

Given the severity of the decree and the wide-scale arrest of political opponents, it did not take long before British newspapers began to raise questions about the fire. Most British papers generally accepted that Marinus van der Lubbe was behind the arson, but they were suspicious of Nazi claims that the fire had been the German Communist Party's signal for civil war and revolution. The *Morning Post* was one of the first newspapers to speak out about the allegations levelled against the Communist Party. Under the subheading 'Democracy Finished', the *Morning Post*'s correspondent declared: 'The charges amount almost to accusations of political insanity, so certain was the act of arson to play into the Government's hands'.[77] A day later, on 2 March, the *News Chronicle* weighed in:

> While the campaign of dictatorship against the so-called 'Red terror' grows more violent, doubts as to its wisdom – as to its honesty even – continue to spread here . . . I have still to meet an intelligent German, not blinded by party passion, who believes that the Communist Party countenanced Monday night's attempt to burn down the Reichstag, or that they have been hatching a revolutionary plot, of which hair-raising particulars are being printed hourly in the Nazi and Nationalist newspapers.[78]

The *Manchester Guardian* made similar statements declaring that there were 'millions of people in Germany to-day who simply cannot and will not believe the extraordinary stories circulated about the "Red" revolution which has only just been averted'.[79] The details provided about the alleged plot were 'too fantastic' and 'incredible' for most to believe. [80]

The *New Statesman and Nation* went further not only dismissing the charges against the Communist Party but also challenged the idea that van der Lubbe was the arsonist. The *New Statesman and Nation* took the opportunity to survey the situation on the eve of the 5 March election:

> Germany has gone this week from purgatory to hell. The burning of the Reichstag building was the signal for an outburst of savage decrees, of wholesale arrests and of blood-curdling threats against all adversaries of the regime. The Nazi leaders, of course, seized upon this arson as 'a heaven-sent opportunity'. A great many people believe that it was not Providence, but the Nazis themselves, who arranged it, for it is incredible that this foreign incendiary could have been left free to do all he did in the building without the custodians, and others behind them, knowing anything about it. The pretence that it was a plot of the German Communist Party, which had everything to gain by keeping quiet with its enemies in power, is too thin to take in any sane man ; but unhappily insanity is widespread in Germany to-day, and the lie will help the Government in fermenting the fear of the populace and the fury of their own gunmen against the Reds.[81]

The *New Statesman and Nation*'s in-depth commentary on the methods employed by the Nazis to secure power in Germany was a defining feature of the British weekly press at this time. Weekly newspapers often sought to contextualize the week's events in lengthy articles that combined a blend of commentary and analysis. For the *New Statesman and Nation* this took the form of vocal condemnation of the Nazi government. These articles were intended to expose the Nazis' brutal practices and ruthless drive for power. One of the earliest articles published in the newspaper of this type appeared on 11 February 1933, barely a fortnight after Hitler was appointed chancellor of Germany. It referred to the popular notion that Hitler 'had been tricked by die-hards', commenting, 'already doubts are arising lest they have bitten off more than they can swallow'.[82] The *New Statesman and Nation* then juxtaposed the Nazis' own election campaign with the repressive measures employed against their opponents. During the campaign, 'there has been a skilfully organised Nazi stampede of the nation, by a dexterous combination of honeyed words from Hitler with the seduction of pageantry'.[83] This had taken place against 'a background of terrorism': 'frank murders of Socialists and Communists go unpunished; the now official Nazi press has a superb technique by which these crimes are presented as the splendid actions of provoked heroes.'[84] In addition, the newspaper reported, 'The Chancellor's slogan of two Four Year Plans was an unblushing demand for irresponsible power'.[85]

Just days from the March elections another weekly newspaper, *The Spectator*, provided its own analysis of the situation in Germany. Correspondent Harrison Brown described the surprise among the German population at the 'rapidity with which Fascism in its ugliest form has burst upon Germany'.[86] He wrote: 'Every day sees the perpetration of acts weeks earlier would have been scouted as impossible . . . The press is in chains, liberty has disappeared, telephones are constantly tapped, letters may be intercepted, and nobody known to be interested in politics can consider himself safe.'[87] It was difficult, Brown wrote, to 'convey the state of tension prevailing in Berlin to-day, and still more the rapidity with which the realization of insecurity has burst upon the ordinary citizen'.[88] Brown painted a bleak picture of the outcome of the election and the future of German parliamentary democracy. He described how Germany had become 'one of the world's black spots', observing: 'Force is in control and . . . force will inevitably have its hour of triumph.'[89] While he notes that a 'democratic Germany will no doubt re-emerge', he explained to readers that 'there is a chapter of force to live through first'.[90] Indeed, he added, 'force wielded by incompetents can be a tragic business'.[91] The elections, he noted, 'will of course be a farce'.[92] Weekly newspaper the *Observer* made similar statements with its correspondent stating: 'What has happened in Germany can only be called a volcanic eruption in politics . . . with the resolve of the Nazis to keep in power in any case, to-day's voting is a farce. The situation could hardly look darker.'[93]

While the British weekly press could not compete with the daily press in up-to-date coverage of events as they occurred in Germany, they were able to explore the increasingly repressive atmosphere in more depth. As a whole, however, the British press had covered the election campaign in detail. British newspapers recognized early on that the election campaign had been unique – one-sided from the start, and increasingly characterized by terror. On the eve of elections, British newspapers explained to readers that the elections scheduled for 5 March would count for little; the Nazi Party would disregard the results of the election if they did not obtain their desired majority. Summing up the whole sorry situation *The Times* explained to readers: 'There cannot, of course, be the slightest doubt that the present Government intend to remain in office whatever the result of the election; and to that extent the consultation of the people is a farce.'[94] The *Daily Telegraph* noted:

> The German Nation will be asked on Sunday whether it wants to be deprived of its political rights. The answer will have no effect on major events. Both the partners in the Cabinet have put it beyond any doubt that, if democracy is unwilling to cut its own throat, they are determined to perform the operation for it. But, as is usual before executions, the condemned man is being allowed to express his last wish.[95]

The *Daily Mail* tried to be more diplomatic, although it did cite the inevitability of the death of democracy in Germany: 'The Government parties, the National Socialists, led by Herr Adolf Hitler, the Chancellor, and the Nationalists hope that the nation will give them an overwhelming majority, and thus enable them to abolish parliamentary rule in Germany altogether.'[96]

Despite this bleak outlook, there was some hope that voters would be able to freely express their choice in the election. The *Manchester Guardian*, in a leader article on 4 March, reported:

> The German voter, in spite of the repression of the last few days, can still exercise the faculty of choice. Neither intimidation nor the suppression of his newspapers and meetings can stop the Socialist or Communist or Catholic from voting for his party lists. If this were not a fact the electoral efforts of the Nazi party would be empty of all meaning.[97]

But the newspaper's lead correspondent, Alexander Werth, who lived and worked in Berlin, was not convinced. He believed the fear and repression that pervaded Germany might impact voter turnout. He explained: 'No one can tell how this vague fear of the Storm Troops, which undoubtedly exists, will influence the elections. It is said that in small towns in particular many people will abstain from voting.'[98] President Hindenburg had assured those concerned that 'he would do everything within his powers to assure freedom of the voter and prevent any excesses in the election campaign'.[99] But, on this, Werth reported: 'This statement is a little surprising when one considers that the Socialists, for instance, are not even allowed to display election posters.'[100] *The Times* Berlin correspondent Norman Ebbutt came to similar conclusions, reporting:

> While adequate measures may be taken to protect the polling stations, and while the counting of votes may be scrupulous, the present aspect of Germany suggests that many people will be frightened to go to the poll at all . . . The reasons for the fears which possesses these people must be found between the lines of such brief announcements as that which told yesterday of the discovery of 'a workman' murdered in his dwelling; in the flight and self-concealment of prominent Socialists and Communists; and in the innumerable arrests.[101]

The German elections dominated foreign news coverage on 5 March 1933. Despite fears for the freedom of the elections, polling day, observed *The Times*, 'passed off yesterday, at any rate until the closing of the polls, with comparative tranquillity'.[102] As the votes were counted, it was clear that the election had been a success for the Nazis. This was of little surprise to British newspapers. *The Times* reported: 'The result, it need hardly be said, was a complete victory for the Chancellor and his Nationalist-Socialist followers.'[103] *The Spectator* remarked: 'The result of the German elections . . . was what might have been expected after a campaign in which the opposition parties had been virtually silenced by terrorism of varying degree.'[104] Popular newspapers, like the *Daily Express*, *Daily Mail*, *Daily Mirror* and the *News Chronicle*, gave front-page coverage to the elections. Dramatic headlines such as 'Hitler's Great Triumph at the Polls' (*Daily Mail*), 'Sweeping Victory for Hitler' (*Daily Express*) and 'Germany Votes for Nazi Rule' (*Daily Mirror*) were accompanied by large photographs, especially of President Hindenburg and Hitler at the polling stations.[105] The dramatic headlines announcing the election results were not restricted to the popular press with a number of quality newspapers using similar language – 'Triumph for the Nazis' (*The Times*) and 'Hitler Sweeps Germany' (*Morning Post*).[106]

In their coverage of the election, British newspapers provided readers with a breakdown of votes polled. *The Times*, for instance, included a table that accounted for all 39,162,419 votes cast.[107] Included in the table were the Nazi vote – 17,264,298 (288 seats), the Nationalists – 3,130,715 (52 seats), Socialists – 7,032,612 (118 seats), Communists – 4,845,003 (81 seats) and even the Württemberg Wine-Growers Party – 83,563 (1 seat).[108] *The Times* also printed a follow-up article that compared the results to the November 1932 elections. From this it was clear that the Nazi Party had increased their votes from previous election in which they had polled 11,737,391 votes and gained 196 seats. In the March 1933 election, they had secured 92 more seats than the 1932 election. *The Times* also compared the losses suffered by the Nazis' opponents, particularly the Communists and Socialists. The Communist Party had secured 4,845,379 votes, or 81 seats, down from 5,980,540, or 100 seats; while the Social Democrats had only lost 1 seat, from 121 to 120 seats.[109] This approach was taken by a number of other daily newspapers, including the *Morning Post*, *Daily Express*, *Daily Telegraph*, *News Chronicle*, *Daily Mail* (who contrasted the results against both the July 1932 and November 1932 elections) and the *Manchester Guardian* which compared results of the last four elections.

What was clear from the results was that although the Nazis had increased the number of seats in the Reichstag, they had not secured the majority they had desired. Despite an intense propaganda drive and the brutal suppression of the opposition, the Nazis only had a majority in partnership with the Nationalists. In an early report the *Daily Mail* explained: 'It would seem already clear that the Nationalist Socialists will not have the sole majority which they had hoped for, that is to say, they will not have a majority *without* the Nationalists.'[110] Summing up the election result the *New Statesman and Nation* commented: 'Herr Hitler has won a victory at the polls, but it was not the resounding triumph that he wanted, and he is still faced . . . with a solid and formidable opposition and with exceedingly difficult friends at his side.'[111] To John Segrue of the *News Chronicle*, the election result demonstrated that there was still strong opposition to the Nazis:

> Not only did the Chancellor fail to get a majority over all other Parties for his own Party, but to-day's voting clearly shows that organised Labour in Germany now, as in the past, resolutely refuses him its support and remains loyal to those 'Marxist' Parties which it is his ambition to crush.[112]

While the Nazis had gained ninety-two seats in the Reichstag, the major opposition parties had still managed to hold onto most of their seats. Unsurprisingly given the campaign of persecution and repression, the Communist Party had lost the most seats, but they still retained eighty-one seats in the Reichstag. The German Socialist Party, according to *The Times*, retained 120 seats in the Reichstag (losing only 1 seat), while the Centre Party actually gained 3 seats, giving them a total of 73.[113] The elections demonstrated that, for the most part, the German people voted for the same political parties they had voted for in previous elections. That is to say, those that supported conservative and left-wing political parties were still willing to show their support despite the campaign of violence and repression against these parties that had plagued the lead-up to the election.

The fact that many political parties had retained their voters while the Nazi vote increased significantly was attributed by a number of British correspondents to 'new voters'. Correspondents in Berlin noted in their reports that polling on election day had been 'exceptionally heavy'.[114] The *News Chronicle* reported in some towns that 90 per cent of the electorate had turned out to vote – a 'considerable' increase from the November 1932 elections.[115] The *Daily Mail* explained: 'The German people flocked in their millions to elect a new Reichstag to-day, and the size of the poll has easily broken the record established last November, when 35,247,192, or 77 per cent. of the electorate recorded their votes. More than 39,000,000 have been counted.'[116] For the *Daily Telegraph* it was clear where the 'extra' votes had come from: 'Evidently the Nazis have succeeded in mobilising the greater part of the normal abstainers. This has undoubtedly been the main source of their enormous gains.'[117] Breaking down the votes the *Manchester Guardian* commented:

> With the exception of the Communists... none of the other great parties have lost more than a tiny fraction of their votes ... and out of 5,000,000 votes won by the Nazis 4,000,000 have come to them from former non-voters. It is there hitherto neutral and politically inexperienced people who have made this election such a success for the Nazis. These people and not the Socialists or Centre voters have been impressed by the Communist scare, by the loud assertions that Germany was on the eve of an indescribably horrible Bolshevik revolution.[118]

For the *Manchester Guardian* then, the Nazi propaganda drive had been 'tremendously efficient', for 'their poll has increased much less at the expense of the other parties than through their ability to persuade the non-voters, especially women and other people who had never taken any interest in politics – to go to the polls this time'.[119]

What the elections meant, in the words of the *Manchester Guardian*, was that Germany now faced 'a long period of Hitlerism'.[120] While *The Spectator* reported that 'it remains now to see how he will use the power he has grasped', the most likely scenario was that Hitler would seek to consolidate his position.[121] *The Spectator* surmised:

> The Government, so long as its two component parts hold together, can command a majority in the Reichstag, and there should be no difficultly in carrying a Bill conferring extensive powers on the Cabinet, after which the Reichstag itself will no doubt disappear from view indefinitely.[122]

And, while the newspaper observed a two-thirds majority was required to change the constitution, 'even that should not be unattainable, for the Nazis have quite effective means of discouraging such Communists as are not under lock and key, and a good many Socialists as well, from attending the Reichstag'.[123] The *Manchester Guardian* also predicted the continued arrest of Communist deputies which would enable them to 'keep an absolute majority in the new Reichstag even without the help of their allies the Nationalists'.[124] This would mean, to enact any changes to the constitution 'there must be a two-thirds majority, which cannot be forthcoming without the assistance of the two Catholic parties'.[125] In the days following the elections speculation was rife about what Hitler and his party would do now that they had secured power. Like *The Spectator* and *Manchester Guardian*, other British newspapers including *The Times*, *Daily Mail*, *Morning Post* and *Daily Telegraph* offered their own speculative assessments. For *The Times* what was clear was that 'Herr Hitler and his Nazi movement have won all along the line and established their virtual control over the country'.[126]

By this point, in early March 1933, the British press was in prime position to report what followed as the Nazi Party established control over the German state and ushered in the end of democracy. The British press had already witnessed and reported the lengths to which the Nazi Party would go to secure power. With the announcement of Hitler's appointment in January 1933, the British press had been willing to give the newly installed Nazi government the benefit of some doubt. However, the passing of the 'Decree for the Protection of the German People' and the ruthless election campaign that brutally targeted their political opponents helped to remove the scales from the eyes of the press. By this stage, the press was under no illusion as to the intentions of the Nazis to remain in power whatever the result. The manner in which Hitler exploited the Reichstag Fire only confirmed for the British press that Hitler and the Nazis were intent on destroying democracy in Germany. As the campaign developed, their reporting was, in general, accurate and frank. Correspondents, with the insights gained from their experiences during the election campaign, were in good stead to observe and report the next phase in the Nazis' quest for total power.

* * *

3

The destruction of democracy

Following the March 1933 election, the British press was confronted in Germany by a Nazi regime that was now likely to be permanent. That democracy would be destroyed seemed beyond question. The precise course that destruction would take was less clear. British newspapers had little time to speculate or reflect before the Nazis began their promised assault on democracy. The first stage of this assault was against those sources of power that still remained in Germany – the federated states. One day after the elections the *Daily Mail* reported the fall of the first state, Hamburg. With the headline 'Nazis Seize Hamburg: Dramatic Election Day Coup' the newspaper's Berlin correspondent described how Nazi Storm Troops had 'seized control of Hamburg, which is the stronghold of Communists and Socialists, while the Senate was in session, and hoisted their Swastika flag over the City Hall'.[1] This had taken place, reported the correspondent, as the 'National Socialists and their allies, the Nationalists, were sweeping the polls yesterday'.[2] For the *Daily Mail* the forcible takeover of Hamburg demonstrated that the Nazi government in Berlin 'intends to smash the opposition of all States having governments which are out of harmony with National Socialism'.[3] This action was also reported by the *Daily Telegraph*, the *Manchester Guardian*, the *Morning Post* and *The Times*.

It became strikingly clear to British correspondents in the following days that the seizure of Hamburg was only the beginning in a Nazi campaign to take control of state governments. On 7 March Hermann Göring, at the time Prussian minister of the interior, was quoted in *The Times* as stating:

> [T]he enormous ascendency of the National Front, especially in the South German States, no longer gives the South German Governments the right to continue to govern in the name of the people, as the people have placed themselves behind Adolf Hitler there, too.[4]

The aggressive actions of Nazi Storm Troops throughout Germany confirmed for many British correspondents the reality of Göring's threats. During the election campaign, Nazi Storm Troops had been effectively employed to suppress the opposition. Now, as the strong arm of the party, they were helping to carry out the brutal assault on democracy. The *News Chronicle* captured this in a report on 8 March 1933 describing how 'Nazi Storm Troops and Steel Helmets continued their "war" upon cities where the local authorities display their reluctance to accept the political situation created by the Chancellor's triumph'.[5]

From this 'war' emerged a process along which the takeover of the states was conducted. Public buildings, including town halls, and official residences were seized by bands of enthusiastic yet menacing Storm Troops. This was accompanied, in a symbolic gesture of the increasingly revolutionary nature of the new government, by the hoisting of the Nazi swastika flag. Local governments were pressured to resign and cede control to their National Socialist counterparts. In addition, the party headquarters and press offices of the local political parties, especially the Communists and Socialists, were targeted and raided. This was often accompanied by a wave of arrests of members of the local Communist, Socialist and even the Catholic Centre Parties. And, in a move that would have sinister consequences, a National Socialist would be put in charge of the state police. According to Nazi officials the seizure of the states was carried out in an effort to restore law and order – a claim that was often repudiated in press reports.

The British press was particularly interested in the resistance of the southern states to Nazi attempts at consolidation. The question of the political future of the southern federal states was featured in several articles during the election campaign in February 1933, as the press reported tension between the government in Berlin and the state governments. Several correspondents even questioned whether the southern states, particularly Bavaria, would attempt to cede from the rest of the Reich if the Nazis won the election. British newspapers commented that while the realignment of northern Germany along National Socialist lines had been met 'without too much resistance', the southern states would not be as accommodating.[6] Yet, as British newspapers reported, even the southern states did not last long in resisting the Nazi onslaught. On 8 March 1933, British newspapers reported resistance from the state governments, including in Württemberg. The following day, on 9 March, the *Daily Mail* recorded that the police in four more states (Saxony, Württemberg, Baden and Schaumburg-Lippe) had been brought, 'under the control of the Reich'.[7] On the same day, the *News Chronicle* reported that 'up and down Germany, scores of buildings were "seized" by Storm Troops and Steel Helmets in a mood of patriotic fervour, which shows no signs of abating. In Berlin raids upon the Reichsbank, the ex-Kaiser's palace, the Stock Exchange and University ended with the hoisting of the Hitlerite flag on the buildings.'[8]

The most important state in the struggle, by far, was Bavaria. As all the other German states fell under Nazi control, Bavaria was seen as the state that represented the most resistance to the Nazis. Of the southern states, Bavaria was the largest and the most politically significant. Bavaria was the last state to be absorbed by the Nazis and the British press keenly reported on events as they transpired. On 9 March, the *Daily Telegraph* had announced from Munich the arrival of 'Several high officials of the Nazi movement' who were to report 'how best the Government of Bavaria can be reconstituted in order to fit in with the balance of power in the Reichstag'.[9] The article suggested that a compromise between Berlin and the state government was on offer, but if the local authorities firmly resisted the regime there was likely to be trouble.[10] The view that Hitler would 'compromise' on control of the state was to prove wide off the mark, as the *Daily Telegraph* had to acknowledge on 10 March when the newspaper reported 'Hitlerites seize control in Bavaria'.[11] The *Daily Telegraph* went on to provide readers with a concise, yet detailed, account of events in Bavaria, highlighting the overwhelming strength of the Nazis and the relative ease in which they seized control. A special representative for the newspaper described the atmosphere in Bavaria: 'Munich awoke this morning to rumours of an impending Nazi "Putsch". By midday these rumours had been partly confirmed, and an expectant public knew that it stood on the threshold of a dramatic afternoon.'[12] By the evening, the Nazis were 'the masters of Munich'.[13] The correspondent described what had happened:

> The newly appointed Reich Commissioner for Bavaria, Gen. von Epp, who had arrived from Berlin by air, informed Dr. Held, the Premier, that he had been empowered by the Reich Minister of the Interior to assume the supreme control of affairs. Dr. Held was forced to comply with the request, but has addressed another telegram of protest to Herr Hitler. Nazi Storm Troops to-night occupied the Bavarian Parliament and several other State buildings.[14]

The Nazis celebrate with 'a tremendous Nazi victory demonstration was held on the Odeonsplatz'.[15] On 11 March, the *Daily Telegraph* proclaimed: 'The Hitler Government now has complete control of Bavaria and the other big German states.'[16] Already the effects of Nazi control were being felt in Bavaria: 'hundreds of arrests have been made. Many papers have been suppressed and officials dismissed.'[17] For readers unaware of the significance of Nazi advances against the states, the correspondent explained:

> With the capture of Munich the Nazis' conquest of the German states is complete. They now control the situation in all the capitals of the Federal States. The only remaining opposition comes from their partner in the Cabinet of the Reich (the German Nationalists), and it does not seem to be very strong.[18]

The *Daily Telegraph* provided readers with a clear picture of the process through which the Nazis had secured their hold over the federal states in Germany. For Bavaria this involved the arrival of Nazi officials in Munich, threatening demands and ultimatums made against the local government, and finally the seizure of the power structures of the state. The *Daily Telegraph*'s correspondent highlighted the overwhelming strength of the Nazis and their efforts to wipe out all potential opposition.

The *Daily Telegraph* was not alone in reporting the seizure of Bavaria. Popular newspapers and quality newspapers alike included lengthy reports about the Nazi takeover of Munich, often making the story a feature of their foreign news section. As a major news centre, many British newspapers had correspondents stationed in Munich who were on hand to observe the takeover.

The *News Chronicle* gave front-page coverage to the news with the headline 'Nazi troops besiege Bavarian Cabinet; Munich Frenzy', and the *Daily Express* declared, 'Hitlerites Capture Bavaria; Hostile Cabinet cowed by Storm Troops', which was also featured on the front page.[19] For the *Morning Post* the takeover was of the 'greatest importance':

> never before would it have been possible for Berlin to intervene in this way in Bavaria. It makes clear the absurdity of the speculations still entertained in some quarters abroad upon the possibility of detaching Bavaria from the Reich.[20]

Indeed, several newspapers had referenced rumours that the Bavarian state might try to cede from the Reich following the Nazis assumption of power. This was, however, a misguided notion and one quickly dismissed by correspondents who had witnessed the ruthlessness of the Nazis in securing hold over the German states.

Since the 5 March elections correspondents had been in a race to keep up with events and the takeover of Bavaria, the last of the states to fall under Nazi control, was an opportunity for correspondents to review, analyse and reflect. As Berlin correspondent for *The Times* remarked, 'the sequence of events has been almost bewildering in its rapidity'.[21] For the *Manchester Guardian*, the rapid seizure of the states 'confirmed probably beyond dispute that what is going on in Germany to-day is a first-class revolution'.[22] Setting aside the methods so far employed by the Nazis and focusing purely on the results, the revolution 'has been successful beyond all expectations'. In the last week, reported the *Manchester Guardian*, the 'succession of coups in all the Federal States, including Bavaria, during the past week has placed the police of the entire German Reich under their control'. Indeed, reported the newspaper, the Nazis 'have scored one success after another'. Examining the current spate of Nazi action, the *Manchester Guardian* observed:

> A list of the present Federal Administrations shows that wherever there is not a purely Nazi Government there is a police commissioner, and in every case this police commissioner is a Nazi. In the states now under commissarial control there are to be either new elections or drastic changes in the Government, with the inevitable result that in every case Nazis will have before long not only the virtual but also the formal control of public affairs.[23]

Throughout this, 'their Nationalist colleagues have merely looked on with surprise and bewilderment'. *The Times* also picked up on the Nazis control over the police but noted that the Nazis still needed control over the German army, the *Reichswehr*, 'to make Germany a completely Hitlerist State'.[24]

For British newspapers, the swiftness of the takeover was, in the words of the *Observer*, 'astonishing'.[25] *The Times* explained that 'Germany herself probably does not fully realize yet what has happened to her'.[26] The *Observer*'s correspondent in Munich noted the changed atmosphere in the city. He described what he had witnessed:

> As I write uniformed Nazis often pass the window of this cafe. The police patrols have been doubled, and they are now often accompanied by an SA or SS man. Some of the big multiple shops have been closed, or have closed voluntarily. Yesterday Nazis moved on anybody curious enough to stand at their closed doors. Probably much the same scenes are going on all over Bavaria.[27]

To the British press the takeover of the states, by all appearances, had occurred with little real resistance. This was surprising for the *Manchester Guardian* and its lead Berlin correspondent questioned whether this could prove to be the undoing of the Nazis. The question of hidden resistance loomed over the Nazis victories, declared the correspondent. In a report published on 11 March 1933, the correspondent commented:

> The Nazis know, of course, that their revolution has succeeded 'too easily', and that there are potential tremendous forces in the country which are hostile to them. Otherwise it would be impossible to explain why they should need to persecute Communists, Socialists, and even Roman Catholics. They realise that a revolution like this cannot succeed unless all hostile elements are suppressed, and they know that the mere installation of Nazi police commissioners in the

Federal States and the hoisting of Nazi flags on all Government buildings do not in themselves mark the completion of a Fascist revolution.[28]

However, other newspapers such as the *Daily Telegraph* focused on the futility of attempts to reverse Nazi aggression in Germany observing that the opponents were 'completely cowed'.[29] The state, reported the *Daily Telegraph*, was now in a 'state of terrorism'. This was the reality in the 'new Germany'.[30] Explaining the situation for readers, the *Daily Telegraph*'s correspondent observed:

> The Brown Shirts have cowed the whole of Germany into submission, in spite of the fact that their ranks are by no means in the majority of the population. The whole German people – even Bavaria has toed the line – are now dancing to the tune set by the Hitler organisation. It seems to the foreign observer that their opponents, be they Socialist, Communist, or Catholic, are so terrified of reprisals that all hope of effective protest has gone. There is no freedom of speech or print in this modern Germany.[31]

The next step in the takeover of the states was on the local level. The local elections held on 12 March 1933 saw the Nazis secure their hold over town councils, the country diet and the provincial diet across the German states. On 14 March the *Daily Telegraph* reported that the mayors of Berlin, Cologne, Frankfurt, Mannheim and many other towns had been driven out.[32] Of Nazi (and Nationalist) victories in the local elections the *Manchester Guardian* wrote: 'Thus the Nazi revolution is winning all along the line.'[33] For *The Times* the takeover of the states and government on the local level meant that the '"seizure of power" by Herr Hitler's Government is almost complete':

> During the past week the Nazi steam-roller has passed over every one of the seventeen Federal States of the Reich and has left a Brown uniformity behind it. Bavaria, Baden, Württemberg, and Saxony are virtually governed by Nazi Dictators, styled Reich Commissioners and invested as such with almost unlimited powers. Such of the smaller States as were not already in friends hands have been, so to speak, forcibly converted into Hitlerite citadels.[34]

Just like the *Manchester Guardian* days earlier, *The Times* described what was happening in Germany as revolutionary. *The Times* correspondent explained to readers:

> So complete has been their victory that the rest of the world hardly yet realizes that what has happened throughout the length and breadth of Germany is no mere change of Government, no sudden swing of the political pendulum from Left to Right, but a real Revolution. No other term indeed can fairly be applied

to the change from a more or less constitutional democracy to what is to all intents a two-party Dictatorship in which one party has almost a monopoly of dictation.[35]

Once again, *The Times* stood out for its coverage of events in Germany, providing both analysis and detail. But, importantly, other newspapers also covered the seizure of the states drawing readers' attention to the increasingly 'revolutionary' character of the new Nazi-Nationalist government. The *Daily Telegraph*, for instance, was one of the few newspapers that documented the process by which the seizure of the state of Bavaria by the Nazis was accomplished. The *Manchester Guardian* also keenly reported events and provided lengthy appraisals of the progression of the Nazi 'revolution' for its readers. A number of popular newspapers also covered the takeover of the German states, with the *Daily Mail* at the forefront of popular press coverage with reports appearing almost daily. The *Daily Express* did include a couple of articles, particularly regarding the seizure of Bavaria. The *Daily Mirror* was much more sporadic in its reporting and, apart from reports on the German elections, was largely silent on the progression of the Nazi 'revolution'. It is startling that the conservative right-leaning *Daily Mail* provided more coverage on the Nazi takeover of Germany than the left-leaning *Daily Mirror*.

For the most part, the British press covered the Nazi takeover of the German states. The press as a whole recognized that the seizure of the states was an important step in the Nazi 'revolution'. In reporting the seizure of the states, the press focused on three key areas. The first was concerned with the actual seizure of local governments and councils, specifically the forced resignations and removal of non-Nazi mayors and other government officials and the appointment of Nazi commissioners. Second, the press drew attention to the takeover of the police in most states, recognizing that this was an important step in preventing any resistance from those coming under increasing persecution, particularly members of the Communist and Socialist parties. And finally, reports drew attention to the hoisting of the Nazi swastika flag on public buildings and official residences throughout Germany. British newspapers recognized that the seizure of the states was an important (first) step in what was increasingly becoming the 'Nazi revolution'.

* * *

Following the coordination of the federal states of Germany, focus turned back to Berlin and the impending meeting of the newly appointed Reichstag. Scheduled to open with a ceremony on 21 March 1933, reports in the intervening period focused on the continued suppression of the Communist and Socialist Parties and, in particular, the campaign of violence directed against individuals in what was soon to become labelled by correspondents as the 'Brown Terror'. It had become increasingly clear before and after the March elections that the Nazis were intent on driving Communists and Socialists out of politics. Raids on Communist and Socialist headquarters and offices, as well as trade union offices, were accompanied by an announcement by Interior Minister Wilhelm Frick, reported in the *Manchester Guardian* and several other newspapers, that there would be 'no Communists in the Reichstag when it meets on March 21'.[36] Frick was reported as declaring that 'not only Communists but also the Socialists must be exterminated'.[37] The *Manchester Guardian* clarified: 'Presumably he did not mean "exterminated" in the literal sense – though for the simple Storm Troopers such phrases have at times been misleading – but that the Nazi Government is determined to crush Socialism and Communism in Germany is certain.'[38] What was clear from the reports was that Communists and Socialists in Germany were destined for newly established concentration camps, where they would receive 'retraining' to become 'useful citizens'.[39]

The absence of the Communists from the Reichstag meant that the Nazis, with support from the Nationalists and Centre Party, would be able to pass an Enabling Bill which would allow for constitutional amendments, reported *The Times* in mid-March.[40] A few days later *The Times* reported attempts by the Nazi newspaper *Völkischer Beobachter* to undermine the Socialist Party. The article explained that if the Socialist deputies were prevented from participating in the Reichstag, the government (Nazi and Nationalist) would have the majority required to pass the Enabling Bill and 'Centre support could be dispensed with'.[41] It was clear that the Nazi-Nationalist government were intent on further constitutional changes and were prepared to silence any opposition by any means possible, from discrediting the political left (and individual members of the Communists and Socialists) to throwing elected Reichstag deputies into a concentration camp.

What did the British press understand about the proposed 'Enabling Bill'? The press widely reported the publication of the draft text of the bill prior to the opening of the Reichstag. In doing so, British newspapers conveyed to readers what the promulgation of an Enabling Act would mean for the already beleaguered Weimar democracy. As the popular *Daily Express* reported, the '"Bill for the Relief of the Distress of the German People and the German Reich", which will be laid before the Reichstag to-morrow, is nothing less than a blank cheque authorising Hitler to rule Germany with dictatorial powers for four years'.[42] Another popular newspaper, the *Daily Mail*, explained to readers that the 'law, if accepted, will give the Government very wide powers to carry on without the Reichstag for a period which, it is expected, will run into years'.[43] For the *Morning Post* the bill was important as it 'bestows upon the present Cabinet dictatorial powers regarded at least as wide as those of any Government in the world, possibly wider'.[44] To assist readers in understanding the significance of the bill, the correspondent went on to provide a thorough and detailed summary of the nature of the bill. An extended excerpt deserves inclusion as it gives an insight into what a reader could have understood about the bill under discussion by the Reichstag:

> The Reichstag will be asked to empower the Government to legislate on any subject, to decree the Budget, to alter the Constitution (except that it may not declare the Reichstag or Reichsrat abolished), and to ratify treaties.
> The Chancellor is to promulgate the laws instead of the President.
> Legislative rights of the Reichsrat and of the President fall into abeyance.
> The Bill is to remain in force until April 1, 1937, unless the present Government resigns before that date. In the meanwhile the Cabinet can make any change in the Constitution, suspend the independence of the judges, administer the finances without making public the state of the Budget, and therefore the expenditure of the Army and Navy. It can, in fact, do anything except declare that the functions of the Parliament has ceased to exist.
> From the moment this law is passed no German has a right of appeal of any kind against a Government measure.
> The President himself loses all his functions except that of head of the army, and even this function can be taken from him by a Government resolution. The Reichswehr, the last control upon the autocratic powers of Herr Hitler could thus be completely at his disposal, and the President would thereby become an ornamental figurehead.[45]

Concluding its commentary on the bill, the *Morning Post* reported that 'The Government will not hesitate to take the necessary steps to secure that the Bill becomes law'.[46]

Unlike the *Morning Post*, the *Manchester Guardian* did not include extended commentary on the proposed bill, nor did it include excerpts from the released draft. However, even with limited coverage, the *Manchester Guardian* was clear about what the bill meant for German democracy. With the headline 'Absolute Power for Hitler; Dictatorship Plans', the *Manchester Guardian* stated that the bill would give the Hitler government 'powers more complete than those enjoyed even by Stalin or Mussolini'.⁴⁷ It is not entirely surprising that the *Manchester Guardian*'s coverage of the bill was limited. Editor W. P. Crozier had just decided to withdraw correspondent Alexander Werth from Berlin over fears for his safety. The newspaper had also started to focus more on the increasing terror campaign that was being waged by the Nazis against the political left. Indeed, the report about the Enabling Bill featured below an article on the opening of the first concentration camp at Dachau.

On 21 March 1933 the newly appointed Reichstag was ushered in with an elaborate ceremony in the town of Potsdam. The ceremony itself was held in the garrison church, because the Reichstag in Berlin had sustained significant damage in the fire on 28 February 1933. The location was significant, explained British newspapers. *The Times* informed readers that it was 'once the Imperial centre of Court splendours and military display' as well as, noted the *Manchester Guardian*, the location 'where Frederick the Great is buried'.⁴⁸ The historic nature of Potsdam played heavily in the day's celebrations, as the *Manchester Guardian* acknowledged: 'The atmosphere was charged with a peculiar mixture of revivalism and imperial memories'.⁴⁹ British newspapers described in vivid detail the day's festivities where the Nazi flag flew alongside the German Imperial flag. *The Times* reported: 'The day, nominally no more than the occasion of the opening of a Reichstag which enjoys no credit at all in Nationalist Germany, was deliberately celebrated as that of the rebirth of the German Reich.'⁵⁰

In contrast to the celebrations for the opening ceremony, the 'business meeting' of the Reichstag held in the evening of 21 March 1933 took on a different tone, with the *News Chronicle*'s correspondent commenting that the scene at the Kroll Opera House was a 'sombre' one.⁵¹ The stage-managed pageantry was gone, but Nazi flag still featured heavily. Noticeably absent were the eighty-one newly elected Communist deputies, most of whom had been arrested. For the other two main opposition parties, the Catholic Centre Party and the Socialist Party, observed the *News Chronicle*,

> there hung a gloom resulting partly from the recent campaign against political liberty in Germany and partly from a feeling that at the end of the two-day session the Reichstag, by according the necessary two-thirds majority to the measure conferring full powers upon the Government, will decree its own doom.⁵²

Any attempt to thwart the passing of the Act would, according to a Nazi press statement quoted in *The Times*, 'mean a challenge that the Government would at once take up'.⁵³ The *Manchester Guardian* also referred to this statement noting: 'Non-acceptance by the Reichstag of the Enabling Bill . . . would be considered tantamount to a declaration of war, and its consequences would be visited not only upon the parties themselves but also upon their supporters.'[54] In view of this the *Manchester Guardian* observed: 'It is expected that the two Catholic parties – the Centre and the Bavarian People's party – will, despite certain misgivings, help the Government to obtain the requisite two-thirds majority for the bill in order to avert a dangerous aggravation of the situation.'[55]

It was not surprising then that the Enabling Bill passed. The *News Chronicle* reported the news with front-page coverage with correspondent John Segrue informing readers that the bill had secured for the Hitler government 'dictatorial powers'.[56] Of the passing of the Act the *Manchester Guardian* stated: 'In view of the threats made by the Nazis on Wednesday to the non-Government parties, the passing of the bill is not surprising.'[57] All parties except for the Socialists voted for the bill, reported newspapers such as *The Times*, *Manchester Guardian* and the *Daily Mail*, which easily gave the government the two-thirds majority required to pass the bill. Reporting the passing of the Act, the *Daily Mail* informed readers that the final tally of the vote amounted to 441 votes to 94.[58] As the only party to outwardly oppose the bill, the Socialists were targeted by the government with arrests reported before and following the vote. A number of newspapers noted the arrest of Carl Severing, 'one of the most famous German Socialists', who was, according to *The Times*, arrested on his way to the meeting of the Reichstag, allowed to cast his vote against the bill and then rearrested.[59]

For the British press the Enabling Act was an important step in Hitler's quest for total and uncontested power throughout Germany; however, it was unclear at this stage exactly what lay ahead for Germany. With the passing of the Act Hitler had been established, in the words of the *Daily Express*, 'as open dictator of the Fatherland'.[60] The press understood the intent of the Enabling Act. It could remove the Reichstag as a legislative body and give Hitler sweeping new powers. Hitler still had a way to go before securing total power over Germany, but the Enabling Act was an important step in this process. The Enabling Act, as the *Morning Post* had reported, would help sweep away some of the most important tenets of the constitution. Importantly, the law undermined the position of the president, transferring more power to Hitler, including, for instance, the ability to promulgate new laws. Many newspapers simply summed this up by reporting that the Nazis had essentially been given a blank cheque to do what they wanted in Germany.

The next step in the Nazis' destruction of democracy took the form of a concerted attack on trade unionism. The *News Chronicle* was one of the first newspapers to recognize this. On 25 March 1933, as part of its coverage of the passing of the Enabling Act, the *News Chronicle* reported: 'The first use Chancellor Hitler proposes to make of the dictatorial powers conferred upon him yesterday by the Reichstag will be to abolish German trade unions as they are at present organised.'[61] Indeed, the headline for correspondent John Segrue's article was 'German Trade Unions to Go'. It was obvious the unions were to be the next target, Segrue pointed out; one only needed to look at 'The Chancellor's writings and speeches . . . . He is known to hold the view that trade unions have become an obstacle to industrial development'.[62] Indeed, surely 'the trade unions are well aware of their impending doom'.[63] Even before the Nazis came to power, explained Segrue, 'Herr [Theodor] Leipart, the secretary of the Trade Union Federation, was at pains to show that the movement was "Marxist" no longer'.[64] However, this would likely not matter. What would happen, reported Segrue, was that trade unions 'in the British sense would cease to exist in Germany'.[65] In its place 'one huge trade union, having at its head a Government Commissioner, will replace the dozens of unions now in existence'.[66] Leipart was reported as having submitted a memorandum to Hitler 'accepting the principles of the State supervision of the unions', and at the same time taking steps to distance the union movement from the Socialist Party.[67] According to Segrue, union leaders who were both leaders of the movement and Socialist members of parliament would soon have to choose 'between politics and their trade unions work'.[68] Segrue, somewhat naively, stated that trade union leaders could possibly remain in the state union so long as they distanced themselves from Socialist connections, something that the existing unions had already initiated.

While rumours of the impending doom of the trade unions circulated, press reports turned their focus to the first National Socialist May Day which was to be marked by celebrations on an 'unprecedented scale'.[69] As *The Times* reported, '"German Socialism" is to be honoured. The Nazis mean to outdo all Socialist May Days.'[70] The *Manchester Guardian* was more scathing of Nazi plans to stage a National Socialist May Day that combined both the trade union Labour Day celebrations with traditional May Day spring festivities. The spring festival that had, in the past, been May Day was a 'distinctly bourgeois activity' with 'maypoles and flowers and sprigs of birch and broom'. The May Day envisioned by Hitler was one that attempted 'gallantly if unconvincingly to combine the two festivals' where 'not only the Socialists but National Socialists can join'.[71] However, commented the *Manchester Guardian*,

> The deception will not succeed; there is something pitifully ludicrous in the spectacle of Hitler, Göring, and Goebbels leading the German workers in

a merry romp around the maypole. There would hardly be enough common interests to make the party go: the Socialism in the Nazi programme is a mere name for their intention of restoring the depressed German middle class to its privileged position. Even in wolf's clothing, Hitler and Göring remain petty bourgeois sheep.[72]

Socialism in Germany was in a perilous position, the *Manchester Guardian* concluded: 'In Germany the Social Democrats and the Communists must be phoenixes if they are to rise from the ashes of the Reichstag fire.'[73]

Few British newspapers reported the festivities of Labour Day, but the swift and brutal suppression of German trade unions was the subject of considerable coverage. The seizure on 2 May 1933 was, in the words of the *Daily Mirror*, the result of a 'sudden swoop', in which Hitler 'strengthened his wide power by a dramatic coup – the seizure of all free trade unions'.[74] The *Daily Mirror* described the action as a 'surprise blow at socialism'.[75] However, for the more astute observer, the suppression of the trade unions was not unexpected. The *New Statesman and Nation* was one such newspaper, commenting:

> The knockout blow administered to the German Trade Unions on Tuesday comes as no surprise. It was known that it was only a question of time, and hopes that the submission of the Labour leaders might save their organisations were clearly doomed to disappoint.[76]

For those living in Germany, however, the seizures came as a surprise. *The Times* commented that the 'the secret of the impending seizure of the trade unions had been well kept' in Germany and the seizures were 'carried out with ruthless efficiency'.[77] *The Times* also reported the mass arrests that accompanied the seizures of trade union buildings and offices:

> [T]he president of the Trade Union Federation, Herr Leipart, and 11 other leaders of the Trade Union Federation (among them a former Minister for Economics Herr Wissell, and a prominent trade union leader, Herr Grassmann); the presidents of 28 trade unions affiliated to the Federation; two senior officials of the Workers' Bank; and three editors of trade union journals. Herren Leipart and Grassmann, according to the officials statements, were, after arrest, 'taken to hospital on account of illness'.[78]

They had in fact been arrested and beaten, which resulted in hospitalization, as a report in the *Manchester Guardian* made clear.[79] Most reports in British newspapers cited that fifty trade union officials and representatives had been arrested on 2 May 1933 and placed under 'protective arrest'. The *Manchester Guardian* further noted that those arrested would, according to official government statements quoted in the newspaper, 'be released shortly if not found guilty of any offences'.[80]

For the *Daily Telegraph* the action against the free trade unions was 'the real meaning of German May Day celebrations'.[81] It had been, reported the newspaper, 'the hardest blow so far by the Nazis at the Socialists. Its reaction among the working class cannot at the moment be ascertained'.[82] The centrality of Hitler in the decision to smash trade unionism was noted by the *Daily Telegraph*:

> The seizure is very characteristic of the judicial anomalies at present existing in Germany. According to the Government Press, it was not carried out by any authority known to the law, but by 'the National-Socialist Committee of Action, commissioned by Adolf Hitler'.[83]

The Times also drew attention to the role of the Nazis in the takeover of the unions:

> The seizure of the trade unions, which have played so important a part in the last 50 years of German history – and whose capacity for resistance to a Fascist regime was overestimated by nearly everybody – was carried out by the Nazis as a party. The Government's part in it is the passive one of non-intervention, but there can be no question that the party as acted as the instrument of policy.[84]

Nazi justifications for the seizure of the trade unions featured heavily in British press reports. The *Daily Mail* covered a proclamation made by Robert Ley, who would head the German Labour Front that was to emerge from the seizure and amalgamation of the trade unions. In it he declared the reason for the seizure was that the 'trade unions remained under Socialist influence' and so the action against them had been 'done for their good'.[85] Every trade union member needed to understand that '"Adolf Hitler is thy friend. Adolf Hitler fights for thy freedom. Adolf Hitler gives thee bread"'.[86] Furthermore, all members 'must be delivered from the devilish teaching of Marxism'.[87] Robert Ley's statement about the seizures was also quoted in *The Times*, specifically where Ley referred to the free unions as 'those Red criminals who for generations misused you, good-humoured, honest and upright German workman, in order to dispossess and disinherit you and the whole nation'.[88] Herein was the reason for the crushing of the unions; a justification that was summed up by the *Daily Mirror* quite simply as a move to 'to suppress Marxism'.[89] The *Morning Post* pointed out, with some justification, that German trade unions had long since ceased to be Marxist in any real meaning of the term. In their view, the real motivation for the move against the unions was the overall Nazi policy 'of controlling all important organisations in the country'.[90] This was reiterated by *The Times* who informed readers that although the trade union leadership was willing to see their status sink to that of a provider of banking and other social insurance, 'This was not enough for the Nazis, and the Socialist trade unions have gone the way of all other potential opposers of their onward march'.[91] With these statements, *The Times* offered insight into the reason for the seizure of the trade unions – they were a bulwark in the Nazis' quest for total power across the German state. The correspondent added: 'Herr Hitler said yesterday that the next aim of the Government was to increase and consolidate its power until the whole nation lay within its dominion'.[92] With this article a reader of *The Times* could be in no doubt that the seizure of the trade unions was another step in the Nazis' attempts to eliminate opposition and secure their hold over the German state.

The weeklies reflected on what this might mean for German society. *The Spectator* held out a ray of hope, noting that sometimes, 'Opposition driven underground can be ultimately more dangerous than opposition in the open. But so far effective opposition hardly exists even underground in Germany. Its day no doubt will come, but no man can say when or in what conditions.'[93] The *Observer*, however, saw no hope and no prospect for optimism: 'All present possibility of opposition has been annihilated. Without a struggle, almost without a cry, freedom as the English-speaking races conceive it has perished in the Reich.'[94] Perhaps it was the *New Statesman and Nation* that summed up the situation best. It provided a detailed summary of the state of play in Nazi Germany after the destruction of the trade unions. It deserves to be quoted at length:

> [T]hey [trade unions] are – for the time being, and probably for a long time to come – as effectively broken as the political parties of the Social Democrats and the Communists. The Nazis are now very nearly complete masters of the situation. Any resistance that might have come from the proletariat they nipped in the bud. Their bourgeois allies, the Nationalists and Junkers, who thought that Hitler, with his Brownshirts and his popular histrionics, was to be their catspaw, have been hopelessly duped. The Stahlhelm has been overcome with scarcely a struggle and merged in the Nazi forces. President von Hindenburg is no more than a rubber stamp of the Government. And the Government is a coalition only in name; its non-Nazi members are ciphers, and may disappear at any moment. What is to be the next stage in this triumphant revolution? So far we have had nothing but destruction – the elimination of 'Marxism', the hounding down of the Jews, the filching of the States' autonomy and the suppression of private rights. The technique has been at once simple and clever, combining

terrorism with a pretence of constitutional forms, elaborate play-acting and appeals to mass emotion.[95]

* * *

The British press did not have to wait long for the next stage in the National Socialist revolution. Only days after the seizure of the trade unions and the arrest of union officials and members, the Nazi government began the process of suppressing and dissolving all other political parties in Germany. Despite the trade union leadership distancing themselves from the Socialist Party prior to their takeover, in the eyes of the Nazi Party the unions and the Socialist Party were the same – symbols of the labour movement. And so, merely days after reporting the seizure of the trade unions, *The Times* reported the confiscation of Socialist Party funds and property, in what was described by the Berlin correspondent as 'the final blow' to the party.[96] As the correspondent explained:

> With many of its leaders abroad, its Press suppressed, the Socialist trade unions already taken over, and its 7,000,000 voters in confusion, the Socialist Party was already dying: and this is the *coup de grâce*. It is difficult to see German Socialism rising again: if and when the turn of the tide comes some new and more resolute force would have to be waiting to take it.[97]

This latest attack on the Socialists took place on 10 May and was reported in the British press on 11 May. *The Times* reported that funds contributed by Socialist Party members had been seized. In addition, their publishing concerns, which included many news printing offices, had been shut down, and the grounds and buildings, once owned by the party, had been taken into state ownership.[98] The reason given for the action, reported *The Times*, was that '"numerous cases of malfeasance" (by Socialists) had been discovered since the seizure of the Socialist trade unions and the taking over of the Socialist Workers' Bank'.[99] *The Times* was not taken in by these Nazi justification. They dismissed the allegation of Marxist corruption brought forth by the Nazis as a sham, suggesting that they were as plausible as 'the frequent reports of people being shot "while trying to escape"'.[100] The *Morning Post* also reported the seizure of the Socialist Party's assets under the headline, 'Hitler the Ruthless', and, like *The Times*, saw the future of the party in Germany as a hopeless case:

> The Socialist Party still exists in theory – the Reichsbanner has dissolved itself in despair – but it is completely incapable of action. It has now no Press and no property; even the property of those leaders who were members of the Braun

Cabinet has been seized. Many leaders are in exile, others are in prison, and the remainder are incapable of any sort of political activity.[101]

While the *Daily Mirror* only included a short article on the seizure of Socialist funds, the dramatic language employed could leave readers in little doubt what the move meant: 'With one bold sweep, Hitler the "Iron" Dictator of Germany, yesterday crushed organised Socialism in the country.'[102] But, it took the *Manchester Guardian* to express disbelief in the enormity of the Socialist Party's demise:

> The complete collapse of the Socialist party, which commanded over 7,000,000 votes in the election last March compared with the 17,000,000 cast for the Nazis, is certainly one of the most remarkable events in recent years. Before the rise of Hitler the Socialist party occupied first place in numerical strength, and after the last election was still the second largest, with 125 seats compared with the Nazis' 287.[103]

While it would be over a month before the Socialist Party was officially dissolved and banned, it was clear to the British press that this latest attack on the already floundering party was, as so many newspapers reported, the 'death-blow'. Like the Communist Party in Germany, the Socialist Party had endured press suppressions, violence and raids on both their residences and offices, most of which was reported by British newspapers. With the Communist Party all but suppressed and most of its deputies and supporters in prison or in concentration camps, the Socialist Party was the last pillar of organized socialism in Germany. This did not stop the Socialist Party from trying to save some vestige of the party and party leader Otto Wels, and other Socialist officials left for Prague where they established the party headquarters in exile.[104] The *Manchester Guardian* was one of the few newspapers that reported the move to Prague, with an article on 7 June 1933.[105] It was used by the Nazi government as a pretext for the total ban of the party, issued on 21 June 1933. *The Times* reported:

> Recent events, he [Frick] stated in explanation of the order, had provided incontrovertible proof of treasonable Socialist undertakings against Germany and the legitimate German Government. Leading members of the party, such as Herren Wels, Breitscheid, Stampfer, and Vogel, had been settling in Prague for weeks past in order to conduct the treasonable campaign against national Germany.[106]

What this proscription meant was summed up by *The Times*: 'All Socialists who still belong to elective bodies like the Reichstag, State Diets, or municipal councils are immediately to be deprived under the order of their seats and salaries. Meetings of the party or dependent organizations are not allowed, nor may Socialists newspapers or other publications appear.'[107] Given the existing persecution of Socialist deputies, the seizure of assets, property and the suppression of the Socialist press, *The Times* called the ban 'a superfluous order'.[108] This was merely the nail in the coffin of the already maligned Socialist Party: 'This measure will, of course, hit the remaining Socialist Deputies and other leaders, but it can hardly do much more than has already been done to smash the party organization.'[109] Other newspapers like the *Manchester Guardian*, the *Observer*, *Daily Mail*, *Daily Express* and *Morning Post* printed similar articles about the proscription of the party; an action that had effectively wiped out 'active political opposition' in Germany, to quote the *Daily Express*.[110] As with *The Times*, the reason given for the action was treasonable offences committed by the Socialist Party against the German state.

With the destruction of the largest labour movement in Europe the other German political parties were soon dissolved. Between June and July 1933, the British press recorded the demise of all other political parties in Germany. Of these, the most widely reported was the struggle of the Nazis' coalition partner, the Nationalist Party led by Alfred Hugenberg. It had become clear, especially following the March elections and the passing of the Enabling Act, that the Nazi-Nationalist alliance was an unequal one. The British press was not only interested in the increasing marginalization of the Nationalist Party in politics but also keenly reported the outrages by Nazi Brown Shirts against the *Stahlhelm* (or Steel Helmets), the paramilitary league aligned with the Nationalist Party.[111] For instance, the violent suppression of the Stahlhelm in Brunswick by the local SA at the end of March 1933 was reported by several newspapers. The incident at Brunswick involved raids on Stahlhelm offices and property, the arrest of all leaders and a general ban or dissolution of the local organization on suspicion, according to *The Times*, 'of opening its ranks to "Marxists," and even of "preparing counter-revolutionary acts"'.[112] The ban was soon overturned by the intervention of Franz Seldte, who, as Hitler seemingly forgot, was minister of labour in his government, as well as leader of the Stahlhelm.

Nevertheless, the whole incident was a particularly illuminating example of the deteriorating relations between the two parties, as *The Spectator* reported:

> It has been obvious from the first that a split must come sooner or later between Herr Hitler and Herr Hugenberg, each with his band of retainers. At Brunswick the Stahlhelm, charged with the heinous crime of admitting Marxists to its ranks (everyone who is not a Hitlerite is a Marxist now), was disarmed by the local

Nazis on the instructions of the Brunswick Minister for the Interior, himself of course a Nazi, and it is not yet clear how far the efforts of the Reich Ministers to patch the affair up have been successful.[113]

For the *Daily Telegraph* it also emphasized existing divisions within the coalition: 'The old saying holds good that the régime which is divided against itself cannot stand. This Brunswick incident emphasises the division.'[114] Further, *The Times* observed: 'the incident shows clearly how unsafe it is to regard German affairs as settled for a period of years'.[115]

The conflict between the Stahlhelm and the Nazis came to a swift conclusion at the end of April 1933 and was reported by several quality newspapers, including *The Times* and *Manchester Guardian*. In mid-April 1933, *The Times* reported that violent outbursts between the 'uniformed organizations' of the Nazi and Nationalist arms of the government, the SA and the Stahlhelm respectively, 'have engaged the serious attention of the government, and this blemish – amongst the only remaining one – on the countenance of a Germany which has now been thoroughly "Hitlerized" seems likely soon to be removed'.[116] Indeed by the end of April 1933, *Manchester Guardian* announced: 'Herr Franz Seldte, head of the Stahlhelm . . . has joined the Nazi party, carrying the Stahlhelm with him.'[117] The merger of the Stahlhelm into the SA signified to *The Times* that: 'it would seem only to be a matter of time before the Nationalist Party itself, in spite of the efforts of Herr Hugenberg, is submerged by the Nazi tide'.[118]

In early May, *The Times* reported the further alienation of the Nationalists, documenting the appointment by Hitler of 'Statthalter' (State Governors) for several states across Germany, including Württemberg, Baden, Saxony and Brunswick, where none of the newly appointed governors were Nationalists. Of this latest move by the Nazis, *The Times* declared: 'The progressive elimination of Nationalist influence by the party which the Nationalists helped into power has now reached a point at which the disappearance of the Nationalist leader, Herr Hugenberg, from the Government seems almost inevitable.'[119]

In June 1933 the final blow came, and Nationalist leader Alfred Hugenberg was forced to resign as Reich minister of economics and minister of food and agriculture. His party was soon dissolved. As *The Times* had been reporting throughout the spring of 1933, the Nationalist Party and the *Stahlhelm* had been subject to intimidation and repression by its National Socialist coalition partners. With the *Stahlhelm* placed under Hitler's leadership in April and increasing numbers of the Nationalist Party defecting to the Nazi Party, Hugenberg was in an isolated position. He became even more vulnerable following the suppression of the Nationalist Fighting League, or the 'Green Shirts' (the rather feeble

Nationalist equivalent of the SA), in June 1933. As the *Daily Mail* declared of Hugenberg's position following the forcible suppression of the Nationalist Green Shirts: 'He is powerless.'[120] The *Morning Post* observed: 'The Government's action makes Dr. Hugenberg's resolute clinging to office even more undignified in the eyes of the general public, and is probably another effort on the part of his Nazi enemies to force him to resign.'[121]

Then on 28 June 1933, the British press reported that Alfred Hugenberg had tendered his resignation to President Hindenburg. The *Daily Mail* provided some context for readers just in case they had not been following the situation. The newspaper explained to readers that Hugenberg took the step of resigning because 'the Nationalist party, whose leader he is, would be dissolved, as most of the other parties have been'.[122] The *News Chronicle* also reported: 'After a fierce conflict behind the scenes with Chancellor Hitler, Dr. Hugenberg, Minister of Economic Affairs and Leader of the Nationalist Party, sent his resignation to President von Hindenburg this evening.'[123] After threats of forcible dissolution, the Nationalists 'decided to capitulate to the Nazis [and] . . . announced that they had decided to dissolve the party'.[124] The following day, on 29 June, the *News Chronicle* explained to readers:

> Even among the millions of Germans who hate Hitlerism, little sympathy is shown to-day for Dr. Hugenberg, the politician who intrigued to put the Nazis in power in the hope, so swiftly shattered, that he and other Nationalists would dictate the policy.[125]

Of Hugenberg's resignation *The Times* stated: 'It will certainly be regarded as a miracle if the resignation is not accepted.'[126] The *Morning Post* too acknowledged that the acceptance of Hugenberg's resignation by President Hindenburg was a 'foregone conclusion', and for that reason focused more on the future of the Centre Party which was reported as awaiting 'execution'.[127] The newspaper explained: 'Only the Centre Party remains to be dealt with, and the delay is presumably due to a desire not to offend the Vatican.'[128]

Statements made by leading Nazis following the resignation of Hugenberg confirmed that it was only a matter of time before the Nationalist Socialists were the sole party in Germany. The *Manchester Guardian* quoted a statement by Hermann Esser, a Nazi Bavarian minister, in which he demanded the dissolution of political parties in Germany: '"They are no earthly use any more", he declared. "They have to disappear in the interests of the inner political consolidation which is essential for the final aim of our movement – namely Germany's freedom, work and bread".'[129] Just a day later, Goebbels was quoted as declaring to a meeting of the 'old guard': 'Except for the Nazi party, there must be no other party or organisation.'[130]

The acceptance of the resignation of Alfred Hugenberg by President Hindenburg marked the end of the Nationalist Party. On 29 June the *Morning Post* reported: 'The terms on which the Nationalist party has dissolved itself are more advantageous than might have been expected.'[131] These terms, according to the *Daily Telegraph*, stated that:

> [T]he former German Nationals are to be admitted into the Nazi party on a footing of complete equality, and are to be protected against all prejudicial treatment. German Nationals who have been arrested on political grounds are to be liberated immediately, and no further action taken against them.[132]

With this *The Times* informed readers: 'Thus a balance is struck in the two Ministries between the "old guard" of the Nazi party and the Nationalist or Conservative forces now bound to it by a "treaty of friendship" and destined to eventual absorption.'[133] One of the best articles that reported the downfall of Hugenberg and the Nationalist Party appeared in the *New Statesman and Nation* on 1 July 1933 which, laden with irony, reported:

> The Nazis have been having another busy week. Herr Hugenberg, the Nationalist leader, has been forced at last to resign, and his Party has 'dissolved itself'. This action is charmingly described in an official announcement as a proof of the goodwill of the Nationalists to the Government. There have been more wholesale arrests of Socialists, Communists and Trade Unionists, attacks on the Catholic and Protestant churches, and a determined drive against the Bavarian People's Party. Herr von Papen has gone to Rome to discuss the Catholics' position in Germany and, it is said, to negotiate a Concordat with the Vatican. He should have his work cut out![134]

The only other major political party in existence was now the Catholic Centre Party. That this situation would not continue was made clear by Goebbels. The *Manchester Guardian* quoted Goebbels: 'There is no longer room for the Centre Party . . . we should render a service to the Catholic Church in causing the Centre Party to disappear.'[135] The Bavarian People's Party, another Catholic party, was soon dealt with. In the March 1933 elections, the Bavarian People's Party had been marginalized, losing a number of seats. The party's offices were raided, and its leaders arrested. This was carried out, reported the *News Chronicle*, 'with the object of stamping out what the Nazis describe as "political Catholicism".'[136] *The Times* explained the action was, to quote Adolf Wagner, Bavarian minister of the interior, part of the revolution which 'will continue its course until every force which does not unite with it is eliminated'.[137] The following day *The Times* acknowledged: 'The Centre Party alone now stands in the way of the outward achievement of the "totalitarian" State, and the Nazis are plainly threatening to dissolve it by force if it does not dissolve itself.'[138]

Negotiations between the Vatican and the Nazi government were carried out in June and July 1933.[139] However, the result of these negotiations was not as widely reported as one might expect. Most newspapers only published a short paragraph on the conclusion of the Concordat discussions. In fact, the *Manchester Guardian*, *The Times* and the *Daily Mail* were the only newspapers to discuss the outcome of the negotiations between the German government and the Vatican in any detail. On 1 July 1933, the *Daily Mail* reported: 'No doubt now remains that the last independent political party left – the Centre party, representing the Catholics of Germany – will disappear like all the others.'[140] On the same day, the *Manchester Guardian* acknowledged: 'A completely Nazified Germany is now only a matter of hours.'[141]

The actual dissolution of the Centre Party was reported more widely as it signified the end of political parties in Germany. As the *Manchester Guardian* reported: 'With the announcement by the former Chancellor, Dr. Brüning, that the German Centre party has dissolved itself, the last vestige of Parliamentary opposition to the Nazis has been eliminated.'[142] According to the article, a last manifesto on the part of the Centre Party declared: 'The German Centre party is no more. Its retirement from the scene of political history occurs, like its birth, under the stars of a new age.'[143] *The Times* also quoted the Centre Party's 'farewell message':

> In the sincere endeavour to collaborate in the reconstruction of the State and the national community the former supporters of the Centre should not and will not allow themselves even to-day to be outdone by anybody. 'Let the hour of farewell be an hour of respectful remembrance of our great leaders and of sincere gratitude to all who have stood loyally by the old flag. If we now dismantle the framework which has served its time, it is with the firm will to continue serving the nation as a whole, true to our proud tradition, which has always put the State and Fatherland before party.[144]

With the dissolution of the Centre Party, the Nazi Party became the sole political party in Germany. As the Centre Party issued its final farewell to the German public, British newspapers reported Nazi proclamations that the 'revolution was over'.[145] While the statement was primarily intended to publicly curtail the continued efforts of the SA to secure control over Germany and reassure the

German public that the revolutionary violence was due to come to an end, it also demonstrated, to quote the *Daily Express*, the National Socialist Party 'has become the state'.[146] *The Times* agreed:

> With the disappearance of all other parties, the attainment of full and unchallenged power throughout the land and the consequent completion of the 'totalitarian' Nazi State, Herr Hitler and his advisors have evidently decided to apply the brake firmly to the party machine.... The National-Socialist Party has thus become sole bearer of the State. All power in this State lies in the hands of the Government, which is led by the Chancellor alone, and in which all decisive posts are occupied by trustworthy National-Socialists.[147]

On 16 July 1933, the *Observer* reported the passing of several laws, including a decree which made it compulsory for state officials to greet each other with the Hitler salute and, significantly, a law that banned the formation of new political parties. The newspaper commented:

> Now that the last of the old parties has disappeared from the political stage, it is stated, and the impatience of the Nazis for the realisation of the total State has expressed itself, the Government came forward with all these new measures guaranteeing the permanency of the Nazi regime and making it impossible for anyone else to seize political power from the triumphant Nazis.[148]

With these latest developments in mind, the *New Statesman and Nation* asked in August 1933:

> Is there still a Germany to-day apart from Hitler? It appears to be unthinkable. The news which comes from Germany daily speaks of a sudden transformation of an entire nation – of the end of all parties, of the disappearance of all non-Socialist organisations and leaders, of the cessation of all non-Fascist though. There is nothing outside Hitler.[149]

Special correspondent for the *Manchester Guardian*, F. A. Voigt, found the demise of parliamentary democracy in Germany particularly troubling. He expressed disbelief at the destruction of the political left:

> Everywhere there is surprise that the German Left did not 'go down fighting'. Those formidable labour organisations that were unsurpassed in the world, this great Socialist movement, this Communist party, the most powerful that existed outside Russia, this Catholic Centre with its skilful leaders who, since the Revolution, were never without a share of Governmental power – why, it is asked, did they all collapse like some old worm-eaten building in a storm? No struggle, no resistance, no protest, not even a defiant gesture – nothing! Why?[150]

Perhaps the answer lay in the fact that democracy was imposed on Germany with ideas of 'English Liberalism and Wilsonian idealism'; it was not a 'struggle for freedom' as it had been in England and France, a battle where democracy had grown 'teeth and claws'.[151] From the beginning political parties in Germany had been working against this imposed democracy. He stated: 'a freedom introduced from abroad is never so precious as the freedom that comes from within and, having been won by hard sacrifice, is the more fiercely defended'.[152] The desire to overthrow parliamentary democracy blinded political parties to the reality of Hitler's aims and aspirations. As Voigt explained in an article on 28 June: 'Conservatives who play with Fascist ideas play with instruments for the destruction of themselves and all they stand for.'[153] Voigt expanded on this idea in his third instalment of commentary on the Hitler dictatorship:

> Why did not Parliament suppress the Counter-Revolution, which was hostile, above all, to Parliament itself? The Reichstag never had a collective consciousness, never had a sense of its own dignity. The Nazis, the Communists, many of the Nationalists, and even some of the 'People's party' entered the Reichstag so as to work against it . . . The German Parliament itself prepared the way for non-Parliamentary government. Nazis and Communists both wanted dictatorships (though of different kinds), and were equally zealous in their efforts to weaken and discredit Parliamentary institutions.[154]

Furthermore, wrote Voigt, the very system that Hitler worked to overthrow enabled each and every measure that undermined the German democratic system:

> [A] revolution or a counter-revolution is easy when it is subsidised and sheltered by the regime it works to overthrow. . . . Organised labour fought at a tremendous disadvantage – it could not win the immediate fight, all it could hope for was to stave off defeat until 'better times' came along.[155]

* * *

British newspapers, with correspondents in Germany, captured with some accuracy the Nazis' destruction of democracy in each of its stages. Beginning immediately after the March elections, correspondents reported the attack on the freedom of the German states. The forcible coordination of the states culminated in the seizure of Bavaria, an event reported by many British newspapers. The takeover of the states was recognized by the press as an important step in the Nazis pursuit of total control over the Germany. Equally importantly, they recognized the intent of the Enabling Act. For the British press, this constitutional amendment laid the foundation for the Nazi dictatorship. Newspapers, like the *Morning Post*, quoted the Act at length in order to give readers a clear picture of exactly what the amendments meant for German parliamentary democracy. It was clear from these reports that Hitler had drastically increased his power and, at the same time, limited that of President Hindenburg. Newspapers now discussed the Nazi coordination of the state as part of a 'revolution'.

A crucial part of this process was the destruction of the political Left. At the beginning of May, British newspapers reported the assault on organized labour. The trade unions were swiftly destroyed in one fell swoop. Not only were the offices taken over and funds seized, but trade union leaders were ruthlessly pursued and arrested. It was not just the liberal and left-leaning newspapers that reported this series of actions against trade unions. *The Times*, *Daily Telegraph*, as well as popular newspapers like the *Daily Express* and *Daily Mail*, reported the seizure of the trade unions in May 1933. This can perhaps be put down to the fact that the seizure of the unions was understood to be part of the assault on democracy. It was an integral part of the organized Left and, for that reason, was a bulwark in the Nazis' pursuit of complete control.

For the press, the next assault on democratic values came with the forcible dissolution of political parties. British newspapers keenly reported the proscription of the Socialist Party, which had followed months of arrests and violence against their members. They paid special attention to the resignation of Nationalist leader Alfred Hugenberg and reported the capitulation of the Nationalist Party. But it was the dissolution of the Centre Party (and Bavarian People's Party), secured through the Concordat with the Vatican, that caught the attention of many British newspapers. This was because, with the disappearance of the Centre Party from German politics, the Nazi Party had become the sole political party in Germany. For the British press, democracy had been destroyed in Germany. In just six months the Nazis had been able to dismantle Weimar parliamentary democracy, destroy the political left and establish control over Germany. And British newspapers had reported the entire process.

Here it should be noted that not only did the press report these steps in the destruction of democracy, but the press *understood* what was happening and conveyed that to readers. It did not take long for British newspapers to recognize that what was happening in Germany was no ordinary change of government and documented that for readers. As a result, even a cursory reading of a British newspapers could have given readers a good idea of the destruction of democracy in Germany.

As the votes were being counted after the March elections, the SA was storming government buildings and seizing control. British newspapers wasted no time in reporting this, and in reporting and following the rest of the actions taken by the Nazis to violently and forcibly dismantle democracy. The seizure of the states, the Enabling Act, the suppression of the trade union movement and the dissolution of the political parties in Germany were reported as fundamental steps in the destruction of democracy. By the end of this process it was clear to the British press, and could have been clear to readers, that Hitler and his Nazi Party were firmly in command of the government in Germany.

All sections of the British press reported the destruction of democracy, whether it was because the events were dramatic and would appeal to readers, or because correspondents and their editors felt a moral urgency to speak out. The frequency of articles on the destruction of democracy certainly varied between newspapers but, overwhelmingly, the British press reported the major events. The degree of reporting in the first six months of 1933 demonstrated that the British press was vitally interested in the death of democracy in Germany. It was a different case when it came to covering the campaign of political terror in Germany; there were clear divisions in reporting between newspapers. The terror was a subject on which British newspapers differed and disagreed. These resulting reports, and the divisions they created, will be explored in the next chapter.

* * *

4

The *Manchester Guardian* and the terror in Germany

A special case

British correspondents witnessed and reported the violence that accompanied the Nazi Party's election campaign in February 1933. Most also reported the wide-scale arrests of Communists and Socialists after the Reichstag Fire and the opening of the first concentration camp near the town of Dachau in March 1933. But far fewer reported the brutal terror campaign that followed and then accelerated after the Nazis' election win. The terror in Germany was a campaign of political repression, led by the Nazis, particularly the *Sturmabteilung* or Storm Troops (SA), against the political left. Communists and Socialists were the primary targets. They were arrested en masse and taken to Brown Houses (warehouses, houses and office buildings used by the SA for the purpose of imprisonment and torture), prisons and, from late March 1933, concentration camps where they were beaten, tortured and, in some cases, murdered. Many were held in 'protective custody' (without charge) in makeshift prisons and concentration camps for months. Some correspondents did try to report what was happening in Germany, particularly the early stages of the terror. In one case this reporting received a backlash from readers. Other correspondents tried to report the terror but were silenced by the newspapers they wrote for. There were also a number of newspapers that did not report the terror in 1933 at all, and some that even denied its existence. This left a gap in reporting, one that would be filled by the *Manchester Guardian*. It would be these reports that defined the newspaper as the most outspoken critic of the Nazi regime.

In early 1933, *The Spectator* attempted to bring news of the early days of the terror in Germany to the attention of their readers. Correspondent Harrison Brown wrote an article in early March 1933 which described an atmosphere of fear that pervaded Germany, particularly in Prussia, brought on by the violence and repression of the SA and auxiliary police. Brown explained to readers: 'It is difficult to convey the state of tension prevailing in Germany to-day, and still more the rapidity with which the realization of insecurity has burst upon the ordinary citizen.'[1] He wrote that Germany was now 'under martial law and the tyranny of gunmen, and the most unpolitical of citizens look forward with something like panic to a future of apparent chaos.'[2] Brown recounted how the 'insane orgy of unchecked violence proceeds': 'Nazi outrages had been committed for impunity for several weeks. . . . For the capital alone the casualty list last week was a regular feature. Three or four people each night were either shot down in cold blood or killed in political scraps.'[3] While the article contained some rumour and conjecture, including questioning whether Göring was going to kidnap President Hindenburg and re-establish the monarchy, and did not actually refer to a 'terror campaign', it did convey to readers the sense of desperation and fear that had spread throughout Germany.

But not all readers were appreciative of Brown's investigative report. His story was met with a flurry of letters to the journal suggesting that much of the detail given by Brown was exaggerated or invented. *The Spectator* made the decision to print many of these letters in the next few issues. One reader, Ernst Deissmann of Lexham Gardens, complained: 'Your editorial notes on the German situation and Mr. Harrison Brown's article "Terror in Germany" in last week's issue of *The Spectator* can hardly claim – to put it mildly – to have maintained the high standard of reliability and impartiality which one has come to expect from your quarter.'[4] His letter criticized *The Spectator* not only for its reporting on the increasing terror but also for its reports on the Reichstag Fire Decree, the suppression of the German press and political parties, exclaiming that 'what has taken place during the last few weeks falls nothing short of a national revolution' and that 'one is bound to admit that normal standards for political and parliamentary life are for the time being not appropriate measures of judgement'.[5] Deissman was annoyed not just at *The Spectator*'s reporting but also other 'sections' of the press:

> Instead of seeing things in their proper proportion, sections of the English Press have, during the last few weeks, given the widest publicity to a series of deplorable clashes and acts of violence in which altogether not more than a few hundred Nazis and Communists were involved. . . . Ten or fifteen cases of violence against particularly unpopular opponents have been described and dealt with at the greatest length. Of the thousands of meetings and demonstrations which have taken place undisturbed all over Germany, hardly a word has been mentioned.[6]

Another reader, I. Posner, wrote to *The Spectator* that in light of Brown's recent article 'one cannot help thinking that for you Communism would be better in Germany than the Hitler system'.[7] At this, the editor responded: 'Almost anything – except Communism – would be better than an administration owing its position to such methods as upholders of the Hitler system have pursued in the recent election.'[8] The editor of *The Spectator* also responded to another letter, printed on 24 March 1933, in which the writer A. Munthe complained: 'As a student of history I must protest against the letters you have been publishing on this subject. The very phrase strikes anyone living in this peaceful, orderly, kindly country as utterly ludicrous.'[9] The letter then proceeded to give a lengthy historical overview of Germany, which Munthe claimed the correspondent, Harrison Brown, knew nothing of. *The Spectator*'s editor made it clear where his newspaper stood:

> No facts in recent history are established more incontestably – to a large extent on the evidence of witnesses essentially friendly to Germany – than the numerous cases of murder, assault, and various forms of intimidation for which the Nationalist Socialist Party in Germany has been responsible in the last two months. Out of the mouths of its spokesmen, Captain Göring and Dr. Goebbels, the party stands convicted. The organised economic boycott of the Jews is the climax. *The Spectator* has consistently shown itself a friend of Germany, but it is a friend of freedom first. Resort to violence is not condoned by styling it revolution.[10]

The Spectator continued to receive and print letters in response to Brown's report and articles throughout March and April 1933. Some of these letters were from people living in Britain but they also included some from people who had either recently travelled to Germany or resided in Germany. In early April 1933, *The Spectator* printed several articles by Sir Evelyn Wrench, former editor and major shareholder of the newspaper. Wrench urged 'an impartial attitude towards Germany and show that we are really desirous of understanding the German aspirations'.[11] Wrench was referring to the persecution of the Jews in Germany but, regardless, it was a disappointing turnaround for the newspaper.[12] *The Spectator* did not report the escalation of the terror, nor did they return to reporting the violence of the regime in 1933. In late October 1933, a Harrison Brown from 'Royal Automobile Club' wrote to *The Times* explaining that the world needed to 'judge Nazi Germany by her deeds, not the rhetoric of her leaders'.[13] Hitler's 'professed desire for peace' was at odds with the violence which had 'become an integral part of a system which retains 80,000 people in confinement without charge'.[14] He wrote: 'Those who are personally acquainted with conditions there are unable to accept the statement that a few minor excesses occurred in the early days, but that they have now ceased.'[15] He concluded: 'the Terror continues.'[16] Was this the same Harrison Brown who wrote the article on the terror for *The Spectator* in early 1933? It is unknown but the knowledge of the violence in Germany in the letter makes it seem likely.

The Times itself was restrained in reporting the terror in Germany. The newspaper did publish reports by Berlin correspondent Norman Ebbutt about the creation of concentration camps and provided readers with updates on those arrested and imprisoned, but there was little attempt to combine the details of Ebbutt's reports as evidence of a terror campaign. There was limited editorializing. Details about the concentration camps and arrests were often included as part of a larger article that dealt with other developments in the German situation. The newspaper did not refer to a campaign of terror.

On several occasions in 1933 *The Times* did publish testimony about the conditions in the concentration camps. One, by a 'correspondent lately in Germany', described his 'repulsion' at witnessing such 'inhuman treatment'.[17] Another report was by a young man who had been imprisoned in the Oranienburg concentration camp.[18] But, on another occasion, *The Times* refused to print an investigative report by one of its correspondents, Stanley Simpson, that chronicled the cruel and harsh treatment of prisoners in Dachau concentration camp. Berlin correspondent for *The Times* Norman Ebbutt wanted the paper to do more in uncovering and reporting the terror campaign. For that reason he supported the publication of the investigative report. Ebbutt was frustrated that his articles continued to be cut and edited by *The Times*. As early as February 1933, the *Manchester Guardian*'s Berlin correspondent Alexander Werth wrote to editor W. P. Crozier informing him that 'Ebbutt . . . showed me the article he wrote on Monday, and it was pretty violent; – yet, at the London end, they cut out everything that was in the least likely to offend Hitler'.[19]

Stanley Simpson, who had been living and working in Munich at the time, sent *The Times* the article in late 1933. It was the result of months of 'examination' by Simpson, and exposed the 'conditions at Dachau'; the information for which came from 'various sources, ex-prisoners, Nazi SS guards, the widows and relatives of the victims'.[20] It would have been the most outspoken report on the terror and concentration camps that the newspaper had published. It went beyond reports on the camps previously published, providing more detail and greater scope, especially about the horrors inflicted upon prisoners. For Simpson, it was a story that must be exposed because 'If the facts about Dachau can be made known to the whole world it is possible that several lives may be saved and countless torments prevented'.[21]

At this point, it was approved by Ralph Deakin, on the Imperial and Foreign News desk. However, deputy editor Robin Barrington-Ward was concerned about the accuracy of the report and requested that Ebbutt be contacted to confirm the details. Barrington-Ward questioned whether Simpson was getting carried away with 'atrocity stories'.[22] Correspondence between Deakin and Barrington-Ward testified that if the story could be authenticated and 'If Simpson is thoroughly trustworthy, and Ebbutt can find no serious flaw, the article will certainly have to be given, probably in company with a discriminating leader'.[23] Ebbutt, for his part, was supportive of the article being published, writing to Deakin: 'we should publish it and take the opportunity of challenging Hitler and Goebbels in a leading article'.[24] Ebbutt went so far as to write an introduction that would accompany the article when it was printed:

> [W]e have felt bound to publish this, despite the official German assurances that little or nothing of the kind has occurred or is occurring in the concentration camps, not because we wish to keep nagging about a particular aspect of German internal policy . . . but because it comes from sources we cannot dismiss lightly and it becomes more and more clear that until this matter is cleared up relations between British public opinion and the N-S regime will be seriously hampered.[25]

Since the article only dealt with the conditions in the first half of 1933, Simpson continued to collect testimony and facts about continued brutality in the camp that had taken place from August onward. During this time, the article went through several galley proofs, demonstrating Deakin's willingness to publish the report. However, in February 1934, Deakin was instructed to write to Simpson that the article would not be printed. As Barrington-Ward explained: 'the editor [Dawson] is now inclined to feel that what has appeared lately in The New Statesman and Nation really disposes of this article'.[26]

What had probably happened was that Dawson had decided not to print the report because, as Lee Kersten pointed out in her article on the matter, the editor 'thought it better not to annoy the German government at that time'.[27] The *New Statesman and Nation* had published an article on treatment of prisoners in a concentration camp but it focused on an entirely different concentration camp and, therefore, did not render Simpson's article outdated or void in any way. Whatever the reasons for the decision, *The Times* had decided not to print an important report on the terror campaign and the conditions endured by thousands in concentration camps. This was in spite of the endorsement of

Berlin correspondent Ebbutt. *The Times* would report on many aspects of the terror but would not report some of the grislier details about the concentration camps nor would it at any point refer to a campaign of terror.

Several other British newspapers did print articles that, at the very least, mentioned the violence in Germany. Of these, the *New Statesman and Nation* best conveyed to readers the nature of the violence. Several articles in 1933 referred to violent arrest and imprisonment of Communists and Socialists. In January 1934 the *New Statesman and Nation* published a report on conditions in Sonnenburg concentration camp which had 'found its way out' of the camp. It was the same report that Dawson had cited as the reason for not publishing Simpson's Dachau article. The report was printed under the headline 'The Terror Continues'.[28] The editor of the newspaper explained that the terror 'continues unabated, though with increased secrecy'.[29] The *Jewish Chronicle*, the *Observer* and the *News Chronicle* also printed several articles about violence in Germany, particularly in the concentration camps. In June 1933, the *News Chronicle* gave front-page coverage to an article by special correspondent and Liberal MP Robert Bernays which described his experience touring a 'big' concentration camp at Breslau.[30] The article was restrained. Bernays stated to readers: 'it is not for me to make any comment on the political morality of Concentration Camps'.[31] His 'memory' of the camps was of 'prisoners watering the flowers behind the barbed wire. They had been planted in the shape of a swastika'.[32] That a liberal left-leaning newspaper could seemingly be so naive was disappointing. Another feature article that appeared in the *News Chronicle* also missed an important chance to expose the brutality of the regime. Lady Oxford (Margot Asquith) obtained an interview for the *News Chronicle* with Alfred Rosenberg, the head of the NSDAP Office of Foreign Affairs.[33] She raised the issue of the concentration camps but was seemingly distracted by Rosenberg protesting against the idea that Hitler and the Nazi Party wanted war.[34] It was a missed opportunity for the newspaper, especially as the *News Chronicle* later reported that particular issue of the newspaper had sold out in Berlin in seconds.[35]

Other British newspapers went so far as to downplay the terror. The *Morning Post*, like the *News Chronicle*, was seemingly convinced by the forced unity displayed at concentration camps during propaganda tours for foreign visitors and journalists. A special correspondent for the *Morning Post* described prisoners as 'cheerful' on a visit to Dachau: 'Many prisoners were sitting on wooden seats near their sleeping quarters or lying in the sun on the grass banks of the swimming pool, some of them sucking on empty pipes.'[36] Prisoners 'looked well' and there was 'no shortage of food'.[37] The *Daily Express* did report the arrest of Communists and Socialists but described it as the inevitable outcome of the Communists war on Nazism. But, in 1933, the newspaper focused more on the persecution of the Jews with feature reports by correspondent Pembroke Stephens. There were also several newspapers that did not even try to tell the story of the terror. Both the popular *Daily Mirror* and conservative *Daily Telegraph* did not report it at all.

The *Daily Mail* was perhaps one of the most extreme examples of a newspaper that tried to ignore and downplay the terror. After reporting the initial arrest of Communists and Socialists after the Reichstag Fire in late February 1933, the *Daily Mail* remained silent on the activities of the SA. In July 1933, they broke their silence but in a rather bizarre fashion. In that month the newspaper published an article by proprietor Viscount Rothermere, entitled 'Youth Triumphant', which praised the new regime and denounced those who had criticized it. His hatred of the left, and of communism, came through in the article:

> The most spiteful detractors of the Nazis are to be found in precisely the same sections of the British public and Press as are the most vehement in their praises of the Soviet regime in Russia. These ranters, who can see nothing in the Bolshevist slave-labour camps but an admirable example of civic organisation, shut their eyes to the practical achievements of the Nazi movement and shudder at the sight of the enthusiasm it has aroused in every walk of life in Germany.[38]

Unsurprisingly, Rothermere ignored the existence of the concentration camps set up by the Nazis, where forced labour was already being utilized. In addition, he denied the existence of a campaign of violence:

> They have started a clamorous campaign of denunciation against what they call 'Nazi atrocities', which, as anyone who visits Germany quickly discovers for himself, consist merely of a few isolated acts of violence such as are inevitable among a nation half as big again as ours, but which have been generalised, multiplied, and exaggerated to give the impression that Nazi rule is a bloodthirsty tyranny.[39]

He called critics of Nazi methods 'the old women of both sexes' and referred readers to the example of Italy where the 'incidental extravagances of the early days of Fascism are forgotten. In the same way the minor misdeeds of individual Nazis will be submerged by the immense benefits that the new regime is already bestowing upon Germany.'[40]

The *Daily Mail*, by categorically denying the existence of a campaign of violence, was an extreme example of a British newspaper's response to the terror in Germany. Most British newspapers failed to report, in any depth, the terror campaign perpetrated by the SA, SS and Gestapo against political opponents in

1933 and 1934. Some newspapers simply did not report the horrors perpetrated by the regime and others omitted any reference to a 'campaign of terror', while some sought to downplay the brutality of the regime. Others tried, and failed, to get the story of the terror into the pages of their newspaper. What this all meant was that there was a serious gap in the reporting of the establishment and practice of the dictatorship in Germany. There was a noticeable vacuum. Fortunately for British readers, the *Manchester Guardian* stepped in to fill the void.

* * *

The *Manchester Guardian* stood out for its reporting on the terror in Germany in 1933, with unrivalled coverage of the phases of the political terror, and articles that gave readers a vivid, detailed and often graphic insight into the horrors committed by the Nazi regime. However, in early 1933, the newspaper's editor W. P. Crozier balanced the desire to tell the truth about Germany, specifically the brutalities of the regime, with the need to have a correspondent in Berlin. At the beginning of February, following Hitler's appointment as chancellor, Berlin correspondent Alexander Werth asked editor W. P. Crozier whether he should go 'full steam ahead' and 'be certain of being kicked out' of Germany or whether he should be 'objectively "moderate"' and, in doing so, reduce the likelihood of being expelled.[41] Crozier replied: 'I should prefer that you did not get yourself expelled, if it can be avoided . . . On the whole stick to the facts and avoid strong judgements.'[42] For special correspondent F. A. Voigt this was not acceptable. Voigt took issue with the *Manchester Guardian*'s reporting on Germany, particularly Berlin correspondent Alexander Werth's dispatches. He was particularly annoyed at an article by Werth which stated, 'there are rumours about a sort of Nazi Cheka' and blamed the 'nervous tension' in Berlin for stories of 'abductions, tortures, and secret executions', and which included the unfortunate subheading, 'Rumours of a Terror' – an addition by a subeditor and not Werth's doing.[43]

Voigt also informed Crozier that correspondents working for other newspapers felt the *Manchester Guardian* should do more in reporting the terror. The *Morning Post*'s Berlin correspondent, Darsie Gillie, had been threatened by the German government. His newspaper backed off printing critical reports. Gillie had contacted Voigt, 'begging me to do what I can to get something at least that tells the real story into the Guardian – the Morning Post will not speak up as he would wish it to'.[44] As far as Voigt was concerned 'on the German news the Guardian is being beaten hollow by the Times and the Telegraph (not to speak of the French papers) whereas it should be the other way about'.[45] Voigt implored Crozier to permit him to go to Germany to collect information for a series of articles on the terror:

> [W]hat is happening in Germany is so awful that I cannot possible remain deaf to it. . . . The Brown terror is not just one of the many dust-ups that have been going on in Europe in the last few years – it is a frightfully dangerous inrush of barbarism into the civilised world.[46]

Initially Crozier was hostile to Voigt's criticisms, but he also wanted to tell the full story of the violence in Germany. He was also concerned about the safety of correspondents if the *Manchester Guardian* were to expose the increasing brutality of the regime. He wrote to Geneva correspondent Robert Dell of his concerns about Voigt's request to travel to Germany to investigate the violence:

> I should regard him as being in greater danger than Werth. That would not worry Voigt, I daresay, because as you say he is a man of great courage . . . I am extremely anxious to get and to give everything possible about the Terror, and I detest the idea that the 'Times' or any other paper should be thought to be doing more about it than we are. On the other hand I do not desire to get Voigt murdered which, if he went, I should be afraid of every day.[47]

Shortly after, Crozier withdrew Werth as Berlin correspondent and sent Voigt to Germany to collect information from sources and informants for a series of articles on the terror.[48] It was the first in a series of visits that Voigt made in 1933. The articles that resulted from this trip established the *Manchester Guardian* as an outspoken critic of the Nazi regime.

Voigt's articles commenced publication in the *Manchester Guardian* in March 1933. They were based on evidence and testimonies from confidential sources (some of whom had been targets of Nazi aggression) which he had collected on his recent trip to Germany. Voigt's aim with these early reports was to reveal the extent of the terror and debunk rumours that the violence was merely the excesses of overzealous Storm Troops. Furthermore, Voigt wanted readers to understand that the terror was continuing after the initial arrests after the Reichstag Fire, and indeed after the elections. As he wrote in his first report on the terror, printed on 25 March 1933:

> Now that the Brown Terror has ebbed, every effort is being made to show that, except for a few deplorable excesses, there never was a terror. It is necessary to state in categorical fashion not only that there was a Terror but that the facts, so far from being exaggerated, have been understated (although many false rumours have gotten into print). The Terror was also entirely unprovoked. Had

there been resistance to the counter-revolution or any conspiracy against it there might have been some excuse for rigorous action, but there was no resistance. In spite of this, scores of perfectly inoffensive people, many of whom had never taken part in active politics, have been killed and hundreds have been injured (many of them in a horrible fashion).[49]

There were difficulties in determining the full truth, wrote Voigt, but it was important to understand:

[T]he Terror did not consist of sporadic excesses, that it was not a series of disorders, that it was not mob rule, but that it was systematic and an integral part of the counter-revolutionary offensive. This is not in the least disproved by the fact that there were individual excesses which the Government did not condone.[50]

And just as important, Voigt established:

For the Terror as a whole the regime is responsible. Although it has ebbed it has not ceased. There are continual raids by Brown Shirts; there were at least two in the 'Norden' quarter of Berlin on Tuesday. Arrests are being made the whole time. Prisoners are continually being shot 'while trying to escape', and dead bodies are continually being found. The number of persons now imprisoned or interned goes into many thousands.[51]

Voigt expanded on the responsibility of the Nazi government for the terror campaign in another article, in which he examined the nature of the emerging regime. He argued that it was not possible to put the terror down to 'natural excesses':

[A]s for the belief that the violence of the last few weeks has been of the kind natural in a period of excitement, it is necessary to state categorically that this belief is wholly erroneous. To hold it is wholly to misconceive the character of the Hitlerite counter-revolution. The German Government, and more particularly, Captain Göring, who, no less than Hitler himself, is the dictator of Germany, by admitting a few and denying the many excesses (while designating the few as perfectly natural, indeed excusable ...) ... attempt not only to conceal by far the greater and by far the more terrible part of the truth, but also to make themselves and their so-called 'revolution' appear unique and resplendent by reason of the kindness and the magnanimity of its leaders and the prodigious decency and self-discipline of their followers.[52]

The intent behind the action of the Nazis, particularly the SA, towards those considered enemies of the regime was clear:

The Opposition (collectively and individually) must not merely be defeated according to normal constitutional procedure, it must be broken up, demoralised, and intimidated by physical force – this, and this alone, is the real intention of the Dictatorship towards that Opposition.[53]

Like *The Spectator* the *Manchester Guardian* came under attack by readers, who criticized the paper for its hardline stance on the violent methods of the Nazi regime. In fact, some of these letters, complaining about the reporting of the *Manchester Guardian*, were in response to Werth's articles, and came in before Voigt's appeared. The *Manchester Guardian*, like *The Spectator*, decided to print many of them

> because they show the state of mind, and in particular the ignorance of recent events, prevailing in Germany. As however, the newspapers of the Left are either suppressed or terrorised and the newspapers of the Right either would not or could not print accounts of the outrages which began on March 3, nothing else is to be expected. To accusations against our own columns it is necessary to reply. The full story of the Terror has not yet been told.[54]

Readers criticized the reporting of Berlin correspondent, with one reader, Joan Gray, alleging Werth's articles were '50 per cent fantasy'.[55] Gray stated: 'I can hardly think a newspaper as renowned and important as the "Manchester Guardian" would lower itself to propaganda of such cheap and unworthy style.'[56] Other letters were printed in the same issue, written primarily by readers who lived in Germany.

The *Manchester Guardian* received more letters of criticism following the publication of Voigt's articles on the terror in late March. The primary criticisms levelled against the newspaper, especially from those living in Germany, were that his reports had either been falsified or at the very least exaggerated. Some readers admitted that while violence had occurred, it was only a natural given that what was happening in Germany was a revolution, not a mere change of government. For these readers some excesses and violence were expected; one just had to look at Russia to see that revolutions were violent affairs and by comparison the revolution in Germany was rather peaceful. As one reader wrote on 1 April 1933: 'seldom has a revolution been so free from violence and so quickly over'.[57] Another letter, authored by a group of Germans, declared:

> As in every revolution, news and reports from Germany are bound to be contradictory. We feel, however, that the British public is receiving up to this day a distorted view of the great events in Germany, since most English observers

lay all the stress upon certain incidents on the surface and overlook the deeper significance of the present struggle of the German national to lay the foundation for the future.[58]

For other readers the arrest and intimidation of political opponents, especially the Communists, were necessary as they posed a grave threat to order and security in the Reich. For instance a letter printed on 24 March 1933 by an 'Englishwoman' in Germany read:

> [W]ith regard to German politics, you are wrongly informed. Your reports of the Nazi Terror are ridiculously distorted. Decent people here only speak of the Communist Terror. All my friends are pleased that the Communist Terrorists are being put down.[59]

For these readers it was important that the Communists be suppressed; any Jews or Socialists caught up in the arrests and violence must have been 'Communist sympathizers' or so the argument went.

Not all letters were critical; the *Manchester Guardian* also received letters from readers applauding the efforts of the correspondents (and the newspaper) in trying to get the full story out to readers about the political (and religious) persecution in Germany. On 28 March 1933, for instance, one reader wrote: 'It is pretty obvious that we in this country, thanks to the well-organised news service of such journals as yours, know more of the German, or rather the Hitler-Nazi, Terror than the peaceful citizens of Germany itself.'[60] Historian A. L. Rowse wrote to the paper:

> Your readers are grateful to you for publishing that batch of letters putting the Nazi point of view in your issue of March 24. It enables us to judge the extent to which people's common sense, let alone their political judgment, can be swamped by nationalist hysteria.[61]

What these letters revealed was that reports about the terror in Germany divided readers. For many readers of the *Manchester Guardian* the reports on the terror were so fantastic that they could not be true. Most of the letters, printed in March and April 1933, were written by men and women who either lived in Germany, or had recently visited the country. Prominence was given to these letters because, for Crozier and the *Manchester Guardian*, the letters confirmed the degree to which people in Germany (and even in Britain) were ignorant of their new government's actions, particularly the brutal persecution of the political left. Crozier used these letters as proof that free speech had been suppressed in Germany. A letter printed on 30 March 1933 is a particularly good example:

If I were in England reading the British reports I might get the impression that it is a most dangerous thing to live in Germany to-day. Yet here I am living my ordinary quiet life and, up to now at least, wholly unmolested. And this though I am one of the much-abused believers in internationalism and though I have, in the past, written in pacifist German papers with the greatest decision against anti-Semitism.[62]

He explained that British subjects and, for the most part, Jews should feel safe in Germany, but acknowledged: 'Communists must avoid Germany, as against Communists the condition here is that of war.'[63]

Voigt's articles on the terror were the envy of some correspondents from other newspapers. According to Voigt, Norman Ebbutt and Douglas Reed of *The Times* were upset that their own newspaper refused to give prominence to the violence in Germany.[64] As Voigt wrote to Crozier on 30 March 1933: 'I must add – and this was impressed upon me in Berlin – that the M.G. is looked up to as the only paper in the world that can do justice to the German Republic.'[65] This was reiterated by French prime minister at the time Édouard Daladier who, according to Voigt, 'thinks the Guardian is the best paper of all. Its editorial policy is magnificent (his own expression), while that of the Times makes him sick.'[66]

The *Manchester Guardian*'s scathing reports did not escape the attention of the German authorities. The Nazi Party, already trying to suppress reports about Germany from appearing in foreign newspapers, prohibited the sale and distribution of the *Manchester Guardian* in Germany. The newspaper was informed of the decision by a telegram from the Wilhelm Frick, minister of the interior, which instructed that the newspaper would be prohibited 'until further notice'.[67] The *Manchester Guardian* responded publicly by stating in the newspaper:

> This paper is not the first to be prohibited in Germany, nor will it be the last. Dictatorships abhor freedom and fear truth. The tyranny which attacks its own citizens, however distinguished, however humble, because of their opinions or their race, is unlikely to spare the foreigner who practices outspokenly the freedom on the suppression of which its own existence hangs. . . . But other things besides newspapers are forbidden activity in Germany to-day: pacifist leaders, liberal writers and thinkers, Jews who are the ornament of their professions, Jews who are only honest workmen. A newspaper is, therefore, in good company. And, forbidden or not, it cannot be stopped from exhibiting what it believes to be the facts.[68]

As Alexander Werth had previously stated, the *Manchester Guardian* was the 'best-hated foreign paper' in Germany.[69]

The decision to ban the newspaper did, however, complicate matters, especially the question of Werth returning to Berlin as resident correspondent. It was clearly something that troubled Werth who, while wanting to return to Germany and recognizing the importance of having someone in Berlin to report on German affairs, was worried about living there given the reaction to Voigt's articles. Even before the *Manchester Guardian* was prohibited Werth wrote to Crozier: 'Voigt is urging me to go back to Berlin at once. That is all very well: but I do not quite see why he should have all the fun of stirring up the hornets' nest, and then ask <u>me</u> to take the consequences.'[70] Voigt did not advocate for Werth's return for long. In April 1933, he wrote to Crozier to request that Werth remain in Paris for his own safety. He thought that the atmosphere in Germany was too poisonous for a correspondent of Jewish extraction and, as a result, Werth would find it difficult to work effectively.[71] Crozier agreed.[72] In early May 1933, he wrote to Voigt suggesting that it was not worth sending a correspondent to Berlin. For the moment, the paper would have to rely on Voigt and his articles.[73]

The *Manchester Guardian* did not have a correspondent in Germany for many months. In September 1933, Geneva correspondent Robert Dell was sent to cover the Reichstag Fire trial. His time in Germany was short. After a few weeks he was withdrawn from Germany after a German friend was arrested and closely questioned about the activities of the *Manchester Guardian*, specifically the identity of the newspaper's special correspondent. According to Voigt, Dell's friend was asked by the Gestapo interrogators: 'Who . . . is the swine-hound who is slinging mud at Germany in the M.G.?'[74] Dell left Germany for France at the beginning of November 1933. He wrote to Crozier of his relief at leaving Germany, describing it as a 'horrible country . . . . It is worse than anybody could imagine who has not stayed in it for some time. The apologies for the Nazis of some silly sentimental fools in England and elsewhere make the men here, who know what it really is, furious.'[75]

After Dell withdrew, the *Manchester Guardian* did not have a correspondent in Germany until December 1933, when C. A. Lambert took over as Berlin correspondent. This did not mean, however, that the *Manchester Guardian* ceased to report on the German situation. Voigt continued to gather material by clandestine visits into Germany to collect information from his network of sources. His articles painted a horrific picture of life in Germany, especially for those unlucky enough to be considered opponents of the new regime. The *Manchester Guardian* was able to print these articles without fear of retribution – the newspaper was already prohibited in Germany, complaints by the

German government had already been made to the British government (and were ignored) and no correspondent for the newspaper resided in Germany, which meant there were no fears for their safety which might have impacted the editorial policy. This meant that the newspaper could focus on printing the truth about the terror.

* * *

Voigt's initial reports for the *Manchester Guardian* on the terror established the scope and intent of the campaign of violence. He made it clear that complicity and responsibility for the terror lay with the Nazi regime. They were guilty of waging a terror campaign to annihilate their opposition, the political left. In April and May 1933, Voigt's articles built on these earlier reports by providing details and examples, often graphic, on the nature of the terror. These articles were, in part, a response to readers who had claimed that the 'terror' was something invented by reporters and correspondents. The articles exposed the actions of the SA and the SS and documented cases of abuse, torture and murder. They were the direct result of Voigt's continued investigations into the violence in Germany perpetrated by the Nazis, particularly the SA.

On 8 April 1933 the first of this type of report was printed in the *Manchester Guardian*. It was entitled 'Examples of Nazi Terror', and was written from Frankfurt. In it Voigt documented several cases where people had been intimidated and beaten in their own homes:

> In the small hours of this morning a workman's home was raised by Black Shirts ... drawers and cupboards were ransacked and windows, pictures, and crockery smashed ... two girls were threatened with revolvers. One of them was struck in the face by a Black Shirt – her face is still swollen. Your correspondent has inspected the raided premises. He has also spoken with the victims and witnesses of several recent beatings.[76]

It was not just suspected Communists and political opponents that suffered the violent wrath of the SA:

> At Worms also a number of Jews were arrested, shut up in a pigsty and beaten on the buttocks, so that the flesh was bruised and lacerated. They were then made to hit one another.

As a precaution against claims that the press was inventing these stories of violence, Voigt stated to readers: 'The names of three of the victims are known to your correspondent.'[77]

The torture and subsequent death of other Jews were also documented. For Voigt it was imperative that the horrific particulars of the terror were documented as well as his own role as onlooker, witness and reporter, especially with the *Manchester Guardian* under continued attack from sections of its readership. And, in case a reader was to further question the reliability and accuracy of the reporting, the *Manchester Guardian* printed several photographs as evidence in the 8 April issue. It included a photograph of the ransacked house mentioned in Voigt's article and several photographs of inmates in the concentration camp at Oranienburg.

These cases were not exceptional – similar incidents were occurring all over Germany, reported Voigt in another article printed in April 1933:

> [D]igging only an inch below the surface, which to the casual observer may seem tranquil enough, will in city after city, village after village, discover such an abundance of barbarism committed by the Brown Shirts that modern analogies fail.[78]

The brutality, Voigt reported, was difficult to comprehend because the crimes 'by their very magnitude and persistence tend to stifle the protests or even the interest of the outside world simply because the normal civilised mind can no longer accommodate the ever-growing accumulation of horrors'.[79] This, he wrote, was the 'Brown Terror in Germany'.[80] In Cassel, for instance, beatings by the SA 'have left the victims bruised, bleeding, and lacerated human wrecks, with minds dazed or blank'.[81] They were carried out 'systematically and according to a general plan – general, that is to say, for all Germany – in the "Brown Houses" that are nothing less than torture chambers'.[82] Voigt established that these beatings 'were not carried out in the heat of a political struggle but in cold blood, and on victims who were helpless and who were found guilty of no offence whatsoever'.[83]

So far, Voigt reported: 'Against the Brown Shirts there is no defence, for the torture they inflict there is no redress.'[84] The German government 'knows exactly what is going on. It had received abundant evidence in the form of sworn statements, medical certificates, photographs, reports from witnesses, but it does not take the slightest notice'.[85] Voigt had also been able to collect this type of evidence from his sources in Germany. This included victim testimonials of experiences in the 'Brown Houses of Berlin'.[86] Voigt explained that for many of these testimonials the 'details are unprintable'.[87] This changed in early June when the *Manchester Guardian* printed the testimony of a Bulgarian doctor who had been arrested by the SA and taken to one of the many torture houses. His story vividly captured the brutal treatment of prisoners in the Brown Houses at the hands of the SA. He recounted his first beating:

> The Brown Shirts then began to beat me with their rubber truncheons, leather whips, and 'Stahlruten' (rods of flexible steel). They seemed to be in a mad, bestial rage. They jumped on chairs and tables and struck downwards at me without mercy. Most of the blows fell upon my head. The blood streamed down my face. Then someone hit me with an iron bar, there was a whistling noise in my left ear, and I collapsed and lost consciousness.[88]

When he was arrested, he was already ill with influenza and so his condition deteriorated quickly following the beatings. He was initially refused treatment but, following another beating, he was finally taken to hospital. When he was discharged, he was informed the arrest had been a mistake.[89]

For the *Manchester Guardian*, these witness testimonies were evidence of the brutality of the Nazi regime, as well as evidence of the campaign of terror. They were intended, in part, to dispel readers' doubt about the veracity of reports printed in the *Manchester Guardian* in March and April 1933. By the end of June 1933, the *Manchester Guardian* was able to add more detail to the story of the terror in Germany, as information and testimony about the concentration camps began to emerge. The opening of the first concentration camp at Dachau had been reported by British newspapers in March 1933, but it took longer to find out what was happening inside the camps and by the time that details were emerging most British newspapers had moved on to other news. For the *Manchester Guardian*, however, the use of the concentration camps marked an important shift in the terror. Even then, Voigt observed: 'No more than occasional glimpses of what goes on in the German concentration camps are possible, so elaborate are the precautions taken to secure secrecy.'[90] But, he explained, even these glimpses 'leave no doubt at all as to the inhuman treatment of the interned prisoners'.[91] It was also difficult to estimate how many were imprisoned as 'estimates vary from 13,000 to 50,000 or 60,000'.[92] What Voigt did establish was that the victims were those who 'were first ill-treated in one of the "Brown Houses", which are really torture chambers . . . before being sent to a camp'.[93] In these camps 'the treatment combines hard labour, rigorous military discipline, ferocious corporal punishments, and the arbitrary ill-treatment of individuals'.[94] Importantly Voigt established: 'Few, if any, of the prisoners have been tried – many of them do not know why they are interned.'[95]

By July 1933, the terror had entered a second stage. According to Voigt, this stage was defined by a final push to 'destroy all potential resistance or rivalry'.[96]

The concentration camp occupied an important place in this new stage. In early July 1933 Hitler had called a halt to the violence and excesses by the SA. The revolution, Hitler declared, was over. Other sources of possible resistance were now targeted. As Voigt reported: 'There is probably not a single German pacifist known as such who is not in prison, in exile, or in a Concentration Camp.'[97] This new phase of the terror was

> [D]riving hundreds of trade union officials from their homes. Even those Socialists who accepted the regime are being beaten. It threatens the Conservatives – all they ever stood for is in danger of total destruction. Priests of the Catholic Church are being arrested. The Protestants who, like the Conservatives, supported the Nazis are not being spared, and many of the Evangelical clergy must prepare to suffer for their religion.[98]

Those targeted were innocent; their treatment at the hands of the Nazi guards was brutal and inhumane. Voigt reported:

> Hundreds of men whose integrity is beyond any doubt are being arrested all over the country and are being sent to endure lives of suffering in the Concentration Camps. In the Camp at Bornicke (between Nauen and Kremmen), for example, there are eighty prisoners. . . . Some of the prisoners work in the Camp, others are 'loaned' out to employers in the neighbourhood – that is to say, they are used for 'slave labour'. The prisoners are continually goaded on to greater efforts by blows from whips of rhinoceros hide.[99]

These reports added a new layer to the story of the terror in Germany. They were further testimony of the violent methods of the dictatorship. Voigt's reports established that the terror was not just part of the revolution but, increasingly, a crucial part of the dictatorship.

* * *

With the revolution reported as concluded, the central role that terror played in the Nazi system of governance was made clear in reports in the *Manchester Guardian* in late 1933. By this point, the *Manchester Guardian* noted, the 'Brown Terror' had largely subsided. The system of terror that replaced it was far more horrific, as the *Manchester Guardian* established in articles printed in October 1933. In two articles the *Manchester Guardian* charted the shift in SA-led violence to Gestapo and SS terror and persecution. The story was first reported by 'a correspondent', possibly Robert Dell who was in Germany at the time reporting on the Reichstag Fire. The correspondent observed that the 'beatings by Nazi

Storm Troopers have greatly diminished and may cease altogether in their old form. They are evidently discouraged by the authorities, because such action on the part of the S.A. infringes on the functions of the S.S. .'[100] The 'Brown Houses', the 'notorious as Nazi torture chambers in the early days of the Hitlerite Terror have been partly replaced by the prisons or detention barracks of the "Gestapo" (the Secret State Police) . . . . The chief terrorist force in Germany now is the "Gestapo".'[101] The article had been based primarily on the testimony of a victim and described the horrific treatment he had endured at the hands of the SS, who had beaten and tortured him over several days.

Voigt also recognized this important shift in state-sponsored violence and terror in Germany in his own article days later. He reported that the function of the SA had shifted – the violence of the early days of the regime had given way to a more organized system of terror: 'The cruelties practised in the prisons of the "Gestapo" are worse than those that went on in the Hedemannstrasse and the other well-known Brown Houses, for they are more secret, more systematic, and more prolonged.'[102]

The violence of the unruly SA had been replaced by a more systematic and organized terror carried out by the Gestapo and SS. Voigt referred to this terror as a 'legal terror' in a letter to Crozier in November 1933.[103] This legal terror was being conducted with the greatest secrecy. This had implications for how the British press would observe and report on life in Germany. The *Manchester Guardian* still had an important role to play in uncovering and reporting on the systematic terrorization of the German population. Voigt wrote to Crozier:

> They will try to conceal it and I think they'll succeed with the Times, the Telegraph and the Morning Post, for there will be superficial order (unless there is resistance and a fight in Germany – this is still not altogether impossible). People will say, order has been restored, there is firm Government and so on. But the M.G. can, I think, do a great service by exposing the character of the regime.[104]

In light of this, it was important that the *Manchester Guardian* continue to give prominence to articles about the terror and violence in Germany. In December 1933, as concerns for his safety in Paris grew, he wrote the following to Crozier:

> I have had a good deal of information about the Terror and from people who have supplied me at great risk to themselves. There is no mention in the German press of the hundreds of arrests that have been made in the last few weeks and, of course, nothing is said about the ill-treatment of the prisoners. Many – indeed most – even well-informed Germans know nothing about these things. . . . I have

had appeal after appeal, with the information that has come to me (by various routes) that it be published with all speed . . . I don't want to be a nuisance and I quite understand that you are hard pressed for space, but perhaps it would be possible to show a slight bias in favour of speedy publication of messages . . . . When I get such reports – and they come to me at great risk – a number of people wait, day in day out, with keen anticipation for them to appear. Many of the facts I get are unprintable or they are so fantastic (although true) that I suppress them, for plausibility comes second only to truthfulness. . . . All other papers of any standing have stopped publishing the facts about the Terror (although the Terror is worse than ever) and this, it seems to me, makes it all the more desirable that the M.G. should not stop.[105]

Crozier, as editor, was on board with Voigt's requests and the *Manchester Guardian* continued to report print reports on the violence and terror in Germany in late 1933 and into 1934. Every care was made to distinguish the new Berlin correspondent C. A. Lambert's reports from Voigt's reports. Lambert, who took up the post as Berlin correspondent in November 1933, reported under 'Our Own Berlin Correspondent', while articles by Voigt were given the clear tagline, 'From Our Special Correspondent'. Voigt's reports had established the *Manchester Guardian* as an outspoken critic of the Nazi regime. While other newspapers had remained silent, or merely omitted details of the terror from their reports, the *Manchester Guardian* had continued to report and uncover details of the brutalities committed in the regime. And importantly, Voigt had established that the terror was not merely a by-product of the 'revolution' taking place in Germany but played an important part in the conduct of the Nazi state.

The *Manchester Guardian* was definitely the exception to the rule when it came to reporting the terror in Germany. As correspondent Voigt repeatedly informed readers, the violence in Germany was part of a campaign of terror – it was not a series of sporadic excesses by unruly Storm Troops. It was part of a system of terror for which the Nazi regime was responsible. Some other newspapers had tried to report the terror, while others ignored or denied it. But when other British newspapers went silent, the *Manchester Guardian* filled the vacuum.

The *Manchester Guardian* was the only newspaper that provided sustained coverage of the brutal nature of the Nazi regime throughout 1933 and into 1934 and beyond. Voigt's analysis of the role of the terror in the consolidation of the Nazi dictatorship set the *Manchester Guardian* apart from other British newspapers. For Crozier, as editor, it was extremely important to keep news of the brutal persecution of political opponents and religious groups in the news as a constant reminder of the reality of life in Germany under the Nazis. This decision not only saw the *Manchester Guardian* prohibited for sale in Germany but also put correspondents, such as Voigt and Dell, in danger. But for these correspondents the risk was worth it because in risking their safety, Voigt and Dell, as well as the newspaper's other correspondents, exposed the brutal nature of the Nazi regime. As Franklin Reid Gannon wrote of their efforts: 'The *Manchester Guardian*'s leaders and articles on all aspects of the Terror in Germany, and Voigt's reports as "Our Diplomatic Correspondent" and especially as "Our Special Correspondent", stand out as humanitarian and journalistic monuments to the men who wrote them and the paper which printed them.'[106]

* * *

5

A second revolution?
The Röhm purge

On 1 January 1934 *The Times*, in an article entitled 'A "happy and free" Germany', reported that the Nazi government had welcomed the new year 'with hearty optimism'.[1] Since coming to power in 1933 the Nazi government had secured its hold over the political apparatus of the state and, outwardly at least, crushed all opposition. *The Times* recorded that 'the theme of the day' for the government was the 'moral revival of Germany' and the 'unity of the people'.[2] In official statements and press declarations in Germany 'not a dissentient voice breaks into the jubilant chorus; there is barely a mention of the problems of the future'.[3] Yet, underneath this façade of unity, British correspondents, closely monitoring the situation in Germany, identified tension and disquiet. Of particular note for British correspondents was the tension that seemed to exist between the Nazi government and its paramilitary army, the *Sturmabteilung* or Stormtroops (SA). However, few would guess that this tension would culminate in a murderous purge of the SA that took place between 30 June and 2 July 1934.

While the press reported tension and discontent within the Nazi German government and its associated apparatus, they were in the dark about the mounting pressure on Hitler to 'solve' the problem of the SA. By the middle of 1934 this underlying tension had escalated and in late June Hitler made the drastic decision to violently purge the SA of its troublesome elements, in particular its long-serving head Ernst Röhm. For the British press, and indeed the German public, the purge came as a surprise. The behind-the-scenes discussions, meetings and plots that led to the June purge remained a secret from both the British press and the German public. Even today, with the noticeable absence of documents relating to 'Operation Hummingbird' (or accounts not tainted by association to the Nazi Party), historians face difficulties piecing together the lead-up to the murderous purge of the SA.

Is it any surprise then that the British press struggled to understand the putsch? What they did do in the days that followed was report the purge in detail. Most newspapers gave it front-page coverage (popular newspapers) or made it a feature in the foreign news section (daily quality newspapers). The story of Hitler turning on his own paramilitary army was a sensational story. While 1934 started off quietly for foreign correspondents reporting on Germany, by mid-1934 the focus of foreign news in British newspapers had turned squarely back on German affairs. For the British press, the passing of President Hindenburg in August 1934 and the oath of loyalty by the *Reichswehr* (German army) to Hitler as newly appointed Führer was the final step in the establishment of the National Socialist dictatorship.

* * *

In the weeks following the purge the press struggled to piece together what had happened and, importantly, why Hitler had decided to take such drastic action against the movement's own paramilitary organization. There had been few signs to indicate that such violent and murderous action would be perpetrated by the government. Articles on the SA did continue to appear in early to mid-1934 but they were sporadic. The *Manchester Guardian*, for instance, continued to update readers about the violence perpetrated by the regime. In early 1934 it reported that while the SA were more closely monitored than they had been in the 'wild' days of 1933 they and the Gestapo continued to commit barbaric acts of torture against so-called political opponents.[4] Just the previous month, in December 1933, the *Manchester Guardian* reported that the SA had grown to more than 2 million men.[5] In the article, the *Manchester Guardian* quoted Ernst Röhm who declared that the SA were not soldiers but 'the bearers of the will and the philosophy of the Nazi revolution'.[6] Röhm was clearly trying to allay concerns over the rapid growth of the SA and growing concerns that the organization would supersede the *Reichswehr* and become Germany's new armed forces.

For the most part British newspapers focusing on the German domestic scene observed and reported on the evolving religious struggle, especially attempts to create a 'German church', the continued suppression of political opponents and the persecution of Germany's Jewish population. These reports were interspersed with articles about concentration camps, the economy, decreasing unemployment and the occasional special feature or interview in the case of the popular newspapers. For instance, on 17 February 1934 the *Daily Mail* featured an interview with Hitler by special correspondent George Ward Price in which the chancellor expounded his views on foreign affairs, German nationalism and winning over his opponents.[7]

In early 1934 British correspondents began to pick up on tension within the government, the party and the SA in 1934. H. Powys Greenwood, writing for *The Spectator*, marked the one-year anniversary of Hitler's appointment as chancellor, reporting: 'revolution is in the air . . . The mental strain is intense, the atmosphere charged with electricity'.[8] He clarified that while there was a feeling of 'revolution' this did not 'mean that there is the slightest chance of the present *régime* being overthrown'.[9] But, the government was faced with discontent in Conservative circles and this was something that the chancellor would have to deal with.[10] Similarly, the *Observer* noted that while Hitler was 'firmly in the saddle', there was 'a long way to go before the whole nation accepts its [the Nazi government's] major theses'.[11]

For the *New Statesman and Nation*, the atmosphere in Germany could be compared to the later days of William II where 'an atmosphere of nervous threats and personal intrigue' existed.[12] The 'mystery' of Hitlerism 'becomes increasingly obscure' and it was difficult to determine whether the 'experiment' would be successful. As the *News Statesman and Nation* reported, tension existed both in government and within the movement as the so-called Right and Left of the party battled for dominance. Röhm often 'indulged in ambiguous but ominous threats', advocating the continuation of the revolution at home. The 'flamboyant militarism' of the SA was alarming to Germany's neighbours, especially France, and the idea that the SA would likely make up a significant portion of a new *Reichswehr* only added to these concerns. In a recent speech, Röhm had announced that if Germany were to be 'attacked from outside', the Storm Troops would 'fanatically defend her soil', as would all other Germans.[13] Claims from some in the regime that the SA was 'a company of peaceful young persons' were clearly contradicted by these statements.[14] Again focusing on the problems within the regime in mid-June 1934, the *New Statesman and Nation* reported that the SA was a 'heavy burden' on the state as 'disbanded warriors without jobs to keep them busy are apt . . . to be a danger to the body politic'.[15] In all, 'Hitler has plenty of anxieties to keep him busy at home'.[16]

For British newspapers, the problems within the regime were made further evident in a speech given by Vice Chancellor Franz von Papen at Marburg University on 17 June 1934. In the speech, Papen called for an end to the months of political turmoil and, according to the *Manchester Guardian*, warned against a coming 'second revolution . . . staged by "Nazi fanatics"'.[17] It was, reported the *Manchester Guardian*, the most sustained and formidable criticism of the ugly sides of National Socialism to which the Propaganda Minister and his like can have listened since they came to power. No wonder they are angry. But if Von Papen spoke effectively, he spoke with triple weight because he spoke for many others, not least for the President.[18]

The speech was swiftly banned by Propaganda Minister Joseph Goebbels but not before it had been printed in some German newspapers and distributed both in Germany and abroad. *The Times* observed that 'every effort is being made to preserve a strict silence, although the commotion beneath the surface, by all accounts, is of the liveliest kind'.[19] In a broadcast Deputy Führer of the Nazi Party and Reich Minister without Portfolio Rudolf Hess warned 'monarchists and other reactionaries against entertaining false hopes' as well as those 'National Socialists who might be contemplating a "Second Revolution" without the Fuhrer's orders'.[20] *The Times* explained that Hess's declaration was a good reflection of Hitler's policy 'to steer as straight a course as possible and resist the currents flowing too strongly to left or right'.[21]

For the British press, Papen's speech brought the problems in the dictatorship and the mounting pressure on Hitler to deliver on promises made in the days of revolutionary fervour to the forefront of public discussion. Both the *News Chronicle* and *Manchester Guardian* observed increasing discontent. The *News Chronicle* reported that the 'storm of criticism grows in violence', while the *Manchester Guardian* stated that 'discontent with them is widespread – in Berlin it has become almost general'.[22] Special correspondent for the *Manchester Guardian*, F. A. Voigt, observed that problems were intensified by corruption which 'reaches high and low, particularly amongst the organisations created by the Nazis themselves, the "S.A." and the Secret State Police'.[23] The *Reichswehr*, reported Voigt, had made it clear to Hitler that they would not be absorbed by the SA. Additionally, 'the scheme by which officers of the "S.A" were to become regular army officers was not acceptable to the regular army chiefs'.[24] Voigt summed up the situation within the regime asking: 'Can there be a move "towards the Right" so as to produce a reformed regime with Hitler remaining as Chancellor, with part, at least, of the "S.A." disbanded, with some of the Nazi leaders discarded . . . with the support of the Reichswehr and of certain leading conservatives?'[25] The SA were due to go on leave for a month and, Voigt observed, 'It will be interesting to see how many of them will come back'.[26]

For the *News Chronicle* the time for action was upon the government. Diplomatic correspondent Vernon Bartlett warned that if Hitler did not act and get rid of problem elements there was an increasing likelihood of a coup *against* the Nazi dictatorship. In a feature article, Bartlett wrote:

> Herr von Papen is not a clever or courageous man. It is certain that he would not have made such a speech unless his friend and protector, President von Hindenburg, had told him to do so. And behind Hindenburg are the officers of the Reichswehr, the industrialists, the landowners, the upper middle-class, and most of those people whom the rank and file of the Nazi Movement are determined to dispossess. The crisis has reached this point. Unless the more bitter and extreme elements in the National Socialist Party are cleared out of office within the next few months there will quite probably be an attempted *coup d'état* by the Reichswehr.[27]

For *The Times* Papen's speech was likely 'intended to inspire a moment which might help Herr Hitler to check exaggerations in his movement and carry out a purge of certain fanatical elements, which has been admitted to be overdue even among moderate National Socialists'.[28] One can assume what the newspaper was imagining was more the dismissal of officials and party members rather than their brutal murder.

It had become clear to a number of British correspondents that the time had come for something to happen. Whether it would be action by the National Socialists or an attempted coup by conservative forces or the *Reichswehr* was still unclear at this stage. What correspondents did not know was that preparations for the brutal purge of the SA were already being made behind-the-scenes and kept secret from everyone not essential to the plan. The press, like most Germans, were left to guess what might lie in store for Germany and for the Nazi dictatorship. And, so, when news of the bloody purge broke it took British correspondents (and indeed most Germans) by surprise.

* * *

The violent purge of the SA (Operation Hummingbird) commenced on Saturday 30 June 1934 and continued until Monday 2 July 1934. Because the action was carried out on the weekend, news of the purge was not reported in British newspapers until Monday 2 July 1934. Three popular daily pictorial newspapers featured the story on the front page of Monday's issue – the *Daily Express*, *News Chronicle* and *Daily Mirror*. The *News Chronicle*'s front-page article had the headline 'Hitler's Week-end of Ruthless Slaughter: Army Now in Control', with the subheadings, 'Storm Troop chief and seventeen leaders executed; von Papen prisoner at home; President gravely ill; Brown Army to disappear; "All Quiet" in Berlin'.[29] The article also featured a photograph of Hitler performing the Nazi salute to marching *Reichswehr* troops.[30] Most of the *News Chronicle*'s front page was devoted to news of the purge with only a few other side articles about home news, including an article about England's third test team, a train hold-up in London and a story of a disgraced mayor who had been found guilty of seduction in a court of law. The main article on the purge was printed in a larger font with bold type and reported the final moments of 'Captain Roehm' before he was executed. It included mention that he was offered the chance of suicide prior to his execution. The *News Chronicle* explained the purge had taken place to counter an 'attempted revolution' which was a 'plot between discontented Storm Troop leaders and General von Schleicher, to overthrow the Hitler regime'.[31] John Segrue, the *News Chronicle* Berlin correspondent, reporting from Berlin explained that Germany was finally 'quiet to-night':

> Chancellor Hitler being, ostensibly, the master of the country. His position, however, is fundamentally changed as a result of happenings to-day and yesterday. The Brown Army which was the main prop of the Nazi regime, has in fact disappeared and will not be recreated as before.[32]

Of all British newspapers, *The Times* stood out for its reporting of the purge. The newspaper provided readers one of the most thorough accounts of how events played out in Munich which included the arrest and subsequent murder of SA leader Ernst Röhm. The newspaper devoted most of its foreign news section on 2 July 1934, to coverage of the purge. Pages fifteen and sixteen of this issue featured news of the purge, with four out of seven columns on page sixteen devoted to the news from Germany. The main article, entitled 'Herr Hitler's Coup; A Midnight Descent on Munich', opened with:

> Herr Hitler and his chief lieutenants stuck suddenly on Saturday at Brown-Shirt leaders and non-Nazi 'reactionaries' who were alleged to have been conspiring to bring about a 'second revolution'. Many prominent and highly placed men were shot or 'committed suicide'.[33]

The Times also established that 'A second reason given for the authorities' drastic action is the degrading private conduct of some of the Storm Troop leaders' – a reference to the homosexuality of Röhm and his deputy commander Edmund Heines.[34] This introductory piece led into an article by the newspaper's Berlin correspondent, titled 'Story of the Crisis', which was remarkable in its detail and depth. The correspondent chronicled justifications for the purge, detailed how events unfolded, remarked on the responses by the German public, covered General Göring's press conference in Berlin, listed names of the other victims and commented on the 'inevitability' of such action. Under the subheading 'An Alleged Plot', the correspondent first detailed how Röhm was alleged to have been planning a 'second revolution' 'without the Führer's knowledge and with the support, or friendly interest, of a foreign Power'.[35] General von Schleicher and others were said to have been 'linked up in some way or other with the revolutionaries in the conspiracy'.[36] Röhm had been 'arrested, deprived of all offices, and publicly disgraced'.[37] It was announced that Röhm had been given 'the opportunity to draw the logical conclusions of his treasonable conduct. He did not take the opportunity, and has been shot', reported *The Times*.[38]

The level of detail provided in *The Times* article of how events had unfolded, obtained from an official but anonymous source, was unrivalled.[39] According to this account, the Führer had hardly slept for some days but nevertheless he had flown in the middle of the night from Berlin to Munich with Dr Goebbels and others. His attitude during the flight was 'one of tremendous resolution'.[40] Once Hitler had arrived in Munich, he learned that overnight local Storm Troops had begun mobilizing after being told that the Führer and the army was against them. This action had been quelled by Bavarian minister of the interior Wagner, and its leaders had been suspended. They were later arrested in Hitler's presence. Hitler 'faced them alone, and himself tore off their shoulder straps'.[41] Hitler and his associates then

> [D]rove at 5:30a.m. to Bad Wiessee, where Röhm was at his country house. Chief Group leader Heines was also there.... The Führer entered, and in person arrested Chief of Staff Röhm, who yielded 'silently and without resistance' in his bedroom. In Heine's room immediately opposite 'a shameful picture' met the Führer. 'Heines was in bed with a youth; the repulsive scene which accompanied their arrest cannot be described. It pitilessly reveals the conditions reigning in the circles around the former Chief of Staff'.[42]

But, *The Times* correspondent established, the homosexuality of the Storm Troop leader and his deputy commander was not a secret, especially to Hitler. The correspondent explained that 'The unfortunate tendencies prevailing in those quarters have been known since long before the revolution'.[43] This was not a case of Hitler discovering that Röhm and others were homosexual and retaliating, instead 'it would appear from an official statement' that Herr Hitler, who had long spared the offenders in consideration of their service to his movement, suddenly lost patience with them when the plot was discovered'.[44]

Similar versions of this account of events in Munich on 30 June 1934 appear in the contemporary literature today, including, but not limited to, Norbert Frei's *National Socialist Rule in Germany*, Richard J. Evans's *The Third Reich* in *Power* and Volker Ullrich's *Hitler*.⁴⁵ It is therefore remarkable that the correspondent for *The Times* was able to obtain such a detailed account so soon after the purge. The details of what happened in Berlin and other places were often less precise. Other newspaper accounts relied on details from Göring's statements to the press and, in the days and weeks that followed, other official announcements and eyewitness testimony. None could rival *The Times* eyewitness account for detail.

The Times also conveyed to readers the early reactions of the German populace following the purge. The newspaper's Berlin correspondent described 'extraordinary scenes' at newspaper stands as the public scrambled to find out what had happened:

> A newspaper seller arriving with these sheets was instantly submerged by a clamant crowd. Eventually he fought his way out hugging the tattered remnants of his wares, ran off with the crowd hotfoot after him, and took refuge in a doorway. Then special editions followed in rapid succession, each with new and more extraordinary tidings.⁴⁶

The reaction of the public was 'remarkable', wrote the correspondent: 'There was nowhere consternation.' Overall, 'the public as a whole is evidently impressed by the graphic description of the Führer's personal reckoning with traitors, and at any rate glad that something has been done'.⁴⁷ There had been a feeling of disillusionment and even disgust at the SA, with complaints about the 'extravagant uniforms', the 'showy' 'luxurious' cars and the lavish entertainments in which the SA leadership indulged.⁴⁸

Viewing the purge by focusing on purely 'practical results', Hitler had 'set in train the big "purge" which has long been considered overdue in moderate circles'.⁴⁹ *The Times* explained that the purge was proof of Hitler's 'determination, and the tendency of his principal advisors, to steer a middle course'.⁵⁰ According to *The Times* Berlin correspondent it had been well known that 'moderate National-Socialists, as well as Herr von Papen and "reactionaries", had long had in mind a list of "radical" revolutionaries, either fanatics, exploiters of office, or a mixture of both, whose disappearance from high posts was desirable in the interests both of better conditions at home and Germany's reputation abroad'.⁵¹ It was noted that both Röhm and Edmund Heines were on that list. Of Schleicher, however, it was observed that 'intrigues were going on round' him but it was hard to conceive that he had wanted the chancellor removed from his post. The lengthy article in *The Times* provided readers with a thorough overview of events as they had transpired over the previous weekend. While much of the information was comprised of initial findings and testimony, the article was detailed and, somewhat surprisingly, correct on a number of points. *The Times* seemed to accept official justifications that Röhm had been planning a 'second revolution' but, at the same time, recognized that Hitler had been planning some action against the '"radical" revolutionaries'.[52] Despite the brutality of the purge and the fact that some of the victims were clearly innocent, including Elisabeth von Schleicher, *The Times* accepted the government line that the Nazi perpetrators were moderates steering a 'middle course' and cleaning up 'conspiratorial "reactionaries"'.[53]

Other newspapers also made much of Hitler the moderate. In the *Daily Mail* this view was given its most strident form. Reporting the purge, the *Daily Mail* proclaimed Hitler the saviour of his country:

> Hitler's love of Germany has triumphed over private friendships and fidelity to comrades who had stood shoulder to shoulder with him in the fight for Germany's future. He has acted with the knowledge that the best men in Germany desire to see the country purged of those whose influence was evil and whose plots were a perpetual danger.[54]

The *Daily Mail* went further than *The Times* in covering the reaction of the German public reporting that there was 'rejoicing in Germany as if the nation had awakened from a nightmare. A fresh wind is blowing through the land'.[55] The newspaper's special correspondent George Ward Price immersed himself in the story, describing to readers his efforts to uncover what had happened over the weekend. With the dramatic flourish that underpinned the newspaper's reporting style Price reported:

> News which has just come into my possession throws an entirely new light on Saturday's tragic events. I have received the following details of the great plot which was discovered and which led Herr Hitler to take measures of so violent a nature.

George Ward Price then went on to describe the plot in detail:

> What Hitler had discovered was that the leaders of the Storm Troops with Captain Roehm at the head were conspiring with the leaders of the Army to overthrow his government, to drive him from power, and to take the direction of Germany into their own hands. A list of Ministers of the proposed Government fell into the hands of Hitler's secret service. It included the names of General von Schleicher, General von Frisch, Commander of the Army, Captain Roehm, and Gregor Strasser, ex-National Socialist.

Price also dramatically described how it was not just key political figures in Germany involved in the plot; indeed 'Hitler learned further that the benevolent support of a foreign Power had been guaranteed for this Government, whose fixed intention would be the restoration of the monarchy.'[56]

The *Daily Express* also accepted the official government line that the SA had been planning a coup. In its front-page coverage of the purge the *Daily Express* declared: 'With these executions, and the death of nearly thirty Storm Troop commanders who were despatched on Saturday, the Brownshirt mutiny against Hitler is regarded as having been completely crushed.'[57] In documenting the purge the *Daily Express* optimistically stated: 'The failure of the coup and its energetic suppression have filled all with new hope for immediate peace.'[58]

The weekly newspapers did not add anything new, providing readers with an overview of events with little inference or opinion. Relying on official statements, including one released by the National Socialist Party in Munich (and made available through the official German news agency), one of several articles printed in the *Observer* on 1 July reported that the 'ruthless' action could be seen as a 'cleaning-up process'.[59] Like some of the popular daily newspapers, the newspaper emphasized the sordid nature of some of the most notorious leaders. Nevertheless, the *Observer* did conclude that the purge demonstrated that Hitler was willing 'to proceed strenuously and ruthlessly against any opposition of any kind whatever, and from whichever direction it comes'.[60]

Perhaps most surprising was the initial reporting of another liberal-left newspaper, the *Manchester Guardian*, which was uncharacteristically cautious in its initial coverage of the purge. As with many British newspapers, the *Manchester Guardian* devoted most of its foreign news section on 2 July 1934 to news of the violence in Germany. The newspaper included several articles on the purge which described how events had transpired but also included short biographies on some of the victims, including Schleicher, Röhm and Heines, as well as a leader article and a special feature article. It was the special feature article by 'a close observer of German affairs' that urged some caution in accepting the government line regarding the purge but, at the same time, examined scenarios in which the victims would form an unlikely alliance. On the one hand, the 'observer' urged caution in accepting official government justifications for the purge:

> It would be unwise to take the statements made by Hitler, Göring, and the German news agencies at their face value. Until there is more evidence to the contrary it is permissible to suspect that the 'plot' which Hitler is alleged to have crushed never existed.[61]

But the *Manchester Guardian*'s writer was careful not to take this line of thinking too far, and examined the possible reasons that Röhm and the SA might join forces with conservatives like Schleicher:

> It was inevitable that the Storm Troops should be inarticulately angry with the course events were taking. The many genuine idealists among them saw their hopes of 'German Socialism' receding every day. The ruffians, who have brought disgrace upon the name of Germany, saw that their licence to do evil when and as they pleased was being limited and might be cancelled. Both types were naturally nervous at the prospect of a month on leave without the certainty that they would find their uniforms again in August.[62]

At this point, the writer was also careful of dismissing the involvement of Schleicher in such a plot, explaining that 'It may at first appear incredible that the Junker General von Schleicher should have been concerned in such a scheme with such associates. But shrewd intriguers sometimes lose their judgement, and better men than Schleicher have been taken in by less impressive plotters.'[63] As Schleicher was sidelined from politics and 'his friends cold-shouldered him', he may have 'turned towards the Nazi 'Radicals'. This line of thinking posited that if Schleicher could not come back to office through the *Reichswehr*, he might come back to office through the Storm Troops.[64] The caution of British newspapers, including the *Manchester Guardian*, is not altogether surprising. Merely one day after the violent purge all British newspapers had to go on were official government statements and announcements made to the press.

However, at least one liberal-left newspaper, the *News Chronicle*, was prepared to cast doubt on claims that the Nazis Storm Troops had teamed up with Schleicher. Indeed, lead correspondent John Segrue believed such allegations were ridiculous and official attempts at 'enlightenment' on details of the 'mutiny' had so far been 'unsatisfactory'.[65] With front-page coverage, his report read:

> The plotters seem to have acted in a singularly nonchalant fashion, ill-suited to their temperaments, and hardly making for the success of their projects. . . . It is suggested both that the Storm Troop leaders wanted a 'second revolution' – that is, one to enforce their pure Nazi doctrine – and that their allies were General von Schleicher and the reactionaries, including Herr von Papen, who, however, has not been mentioned by name: men to whom Nazism is hateful, and who influenced the restoration of normal conditions in Germany. To explain away this contradiction, it is suggested that the Storm Troop leaders were using the 'reactionaries', or that the 'reactionaries' were using the Storm Troop leaders in a project of mutual destructive purposes.[66]

Segrue also found the claim that Papen and Schleicher had worked together unbelievable, especially as the former had ousted the latter, working to replace him with Hitler in January 1933. Furthermore, Segrue found the idea that Schleicher, 'a man of high personal character, and a patriot', had worked with a foreign power (alleged to have been France) 'difficult to believe'.[67] In all, Segrue was highly suspect of official statements regarding the weekend's events.

* * *

As the facts about the purge became more widely available, the attitude of the press began to harden. Indeed, just a day after initial reports the *Daily Telegraph* stated in a leader on 3 July:

> The method of June 30 was to make sure of silence either by shooting out of hand or by immediate execution after summary court-martial. If the Chancellor is at all susceptible to foreign opinion he can hardly fail to observe that the world which had no sympathy with traitors has still a very strong regard for the forms of law.[68]

Correspondents focused, in particular, on the rising death toll which by 5 July 1934 was approximately sixty, according to the *Manchester Guardian*.[69] The newspaper's Berlin correspondent wrote of the difficulty in determining precise figure of fatalities: 'How many of the hundreds of prisoners known to have been taken will meet their death through so-called suicide or through the firing parties of the black-uniformed S.S. . . . following summary party justice, can only be guessed at.'[70] The so-called justice of Nazi actions was also commented upon. *The Spectator* mocked this so-called Nazi justice, reporting:

> The hurriedly-summoned courts-martial and the firing-squads have completed the purge; and the leaders, priding themselves on their splendid energy in butchering their ex-colleagues, receive their meed of deeply-felt thanks and sincere appreciation from the remote and enfeebled head of the State. 'Law and order', then, for the present at least, seem to be re-established. But whose law, and whose order?[71]

For the *News Chronicle* the purge was symptomatic of the way that the Nazi regime worked. Simply put, it was the

> dictatorship at work. The bloody methods pursued in Berlin and in Munich last week-end are not exceptional. They are merely one more illustration of the price which has to be paid for its alleged 'efficiency' and the results, inevitable in one

form or another, which follow when tyrants encroach on liberty, and then, as always, fall out among themselves.[72]

By 3 July, so just one day on from first reports of the purge in British newspapers, *The Times* had dropped any talk of 'moderates'. On that day it printed a leader comparing the methods of the German dictatorship to the 'bloody intrigues of [Shakespeare's] *Richard III*'.[73] This, observed *The Times*, was 'the stage of political development to which Germany has reverted'.[74] The leading article was entitled 'Medieval Methods' and, to some extent at least, compensated for *The Times* silence on the terror. *The Times* summarized the actions of the regime declaring that 'So far as methods of government and respect for human life are concerned, Germany has ceased for the time being to be a modern European country'.[75] Quite simply, Germany had 'reverted to medieval conditions'.[76] Despite establishing this, the newspaper offered little sympathy for the murdered Nazi Storm Troop leaders stating: 'No pity need be wasted on the dead Nazi leaders, who on every reckoning have richly deserved their fate. So long as they were in authority at the head of the Brown Army they were a menace to peace and to all orderly progress'.[77] But, *The Times* did vehemently denounce the bloody and ruthless measures taken by the regime in dealing with the SA and called into question the Germany's standing as a civilized European country in the wake of the violence:

> What is ominously symptomatic of the present state of Germany is the savagery, the disregard for all the forms of law which are the indispensable safeguards of justice and which are sacrosanct in every modern civilized State. What is of still deeper significance is the indifference – even the complacency – with which this resort of to the political methods of the Middle Ages is apparently regarded.
>
> In other countries, and especially in Great Britain, the reports were received at first with incredulity by all who did not realize how completely the common standards have ceased to apply in Germany. It seemed inconceivable that the head, even the despotic head, of a modern Government should order the arrest and the summary execution of numbers of his principal lieutenants. It is even harder to believe since among the victims chosen for the massacre were men who had been his closest associated and had been rewarded with high office and entrusted with great powers. This might be credible in Russia, or in the Turkey of Abdul Hamid's time, or in some medieval monarchy. It could not occur in a great European country in the twentieth century.[78]

After a shaky start, where British newspapers had only official statements to base their reports on, the press quickly found its voice. The difference in reports published on 2 July to those published a day later on 3 July, and in the days that followed, was stark. The press wholeheartedly denounced the violent methods employed by Hitler, Göring and others in dealing with the alleged coup in Germany. The methods employed were barbaric, medieval and were at odds with the way that Western European countries operated. For *The Times*, *Manchester Guardian*, *News Chronicle*, *The Spectator* and *New Statesman and Nation*, the true nature of the dictatorship had once again reared its ugly head. As the *New Statesman and Nation* wrote on 7 July 1934: 'Whatever views may be held in Germany of Hitler's latest exploit, it has found no approval abroad. It is generally felt that to murder your comrades in arms is a different thing from murdering your enemies, even when unarmed.'[79]

Criticism of the purge in British newspapers did not escape the attention of German authorities. On 5 July 1934 *The Times* reported that, in official circles, there was 'deep disappointment' at the 'foreign condemnation of the methods of last week-end'. As *The* Times reported: 'Yesterday's leading article in *The Times* and other British comments have now been given publicity here as examples of foreign inability or unwillingness to understand German internal affairs.'[80] Propaganda and Press chief Joseph Goebbels vigorously attacked the foreign press. In reporting these outbursts, the *Daily Telegraph* informed readers of the confiscation and prohibition of several British newspapers including their own. But, reported the *Daily Telegraph*, British newspapers were not the only foreign newspapers targeted. Goebbels attacked the press of the world. He alleged their reports were a 'campaign of lies' and likened them to the 'fairy tale propaganda against Germany during the War'.[81] The *Daily Telegraph* quoted Goebbels's attack on the press:

> I believe that I speak in the name of the whole German people if I protest with disgust and indignation, and declare with all frankness, that the German Government will not tolerate in this country foreign journalists who thus set nations against each other and conjure up an atmosphere which makes honourable and unprejudiced relationships between peoples impossible. . . . This has nothing to do with freedom of opinion. What is here sowing its wild oats is the worst form of revolver journalism, which can do honour to no people.[82]

The *Morning Post* also quoted Goebbels's statements, drawing particular attention to his condemnation of the work of foreign correspondents:

> One would have thought . . . that the international Press, with its well-paid special correspondents in Berlin, would have reported the matter objectively. But except for a few serious newspapers, the great part of the foreign Press had published hysterical and malicious lies.[83]

The *News Chronicle* was dismissive of Goebbels's comments, responding:

> From a responsible Minister, so grave a charge would demand serious investigation. From the lips of a gentle-man who apparently thinks that the indiscriminate shooting without trial of scores of persons held to have been engaged in a 'revolt' which, in fact, never took place, is a quite normal and praiseworthy incident in the life of a patriotic Government, it is unworthy of attention.[84]

But the *New Statesman and Nation* put blame for any errors or miscommunication at the door of the Nazi government:

> No doubt he [Goebbels] could point to errors in some of the reports as to the fate of this or that victim in Hitler's bloody coup. But for this he and his colleagues have only themselves to blame; they do their best to hamper journalists in getting at the truth in Germany. The real cause of Goebbel's fury, however, is obviously the hostile judgment which the foreign press has passed, with practical unanimity, on the gangster exploit of June 30th.[85]

In addition, the *Daily Telegraph* reported that both the London *Daily Express* and the *Observer* had been banned in Germany for eight weeks for their reporting on the purge.[86] The *Daily Express* reported on 11 July that all copies of its newspaper that had arrived in the previous few days had been 'confiscated and destroyed by order of the Government'.[87] Other newspapers had been criticized by Goebbels including the *Daily Telegraph*, *Morning Post*, *Manchester Guardian*, *Daily Mail* and the *Daily Herald*. The *Morning Post* explained that its own newspaper had been criticized for one passage regarding a comment about President Hindenburg's wishes.[88] The article explained that the *Daily Telegraph* and *Daily Express* 'were evidently the most serious offenders'.[89] In future, explained the *Morning Post*, for those foreign newspapers still allowed to circulate 'newsagents will be allowed to keep foreign newspapers in stock, but not to display them as they do at present'.[90]

On 13 July 1934, at the Kroll Opera House, Hitler addressed the Reichstag about the violent purge. It was hoped that the speech would provide some answers about the motivation for the purge. *The Times* reported that the German nation was still waiting for an explanation for the violence as 'the country has still been vouchsafed no other information about the revolutionary-reactionary-international plot than that contained in the official announcements of June 30'.[91] In the event, the speech was a disappointment. The *Manchester Guardian* reported that the speech 'adds nothing of significance to what was already known'.[92] It was merely a description of events and a justification for the action. It seemed that the *News Chronicle*'s prediction about the speech had been correct: 'The object of this manoeuvre is apparently to settle Herr Hitler a little more firmly on his pedestal as the popular idol, his position having been a little shaken by recent unfortunate events.'[93]

Despite revealing nothing new, Hitler's speech to the Reichstag was reported widely and in detail by British newspapers. British correspondents not only described the atmosphere in the Reichstag but also quoted Hitler's address at length. The *Daily Express*, for instance, reported how the mostly National Socialist uniformed deputies greeted a 'brown-uniformed' Hitler with 'thunderous "Heils"'.[94] For the *Daily Express*, Hitler's performance during the speech revealed the duality of his character. Reported by a '*Daily Express* Representative who listened in'

> During the greater part of the speech Hitler's voice was wild, screaming, hysterical . . . the voice of a man on the verge of breakdown. Not since the early days of his career has he spoken more fanatically. The roars of applause that greeted him from the serried rows of Storm Troopers can only be likened to the hoarse roar of a Roman mob at the arena. . . . Then suddenly the hysterical note died, and the calm, assured tones of the statesman took its place. It was impossible to know which was the real Hitler.[95]

The speech was a long one, continuing for one hour and forty minutes, according to the *Manchester Guardian*. It revealed all the intricacies of the plot planned by Röhm and Schleicher to overthrow Hitler's government. Rather than focusing on Hitler's performance, the *Manchester Guardian* printed excerpts of the speech itself. With the 'evidence' before him, Hitler stated:

> I could only make one decision. If the disaster was to be prevented I must act like lightning. Only ruthless and bloody intervention could prevent the revolution from spreading. There was no question then, that it was better that a hundred mutineers and conspirators should be destroyed than that ten thousand innocent S.A. men on the one side and ten thousand innocent men on the other side should be led to death. . . . It was perfectly clear to me that only one man could and must go and act against Röhm, who had broken his loyalty to me and I had to call him to task for this.[96]

Hitler defended his actions. He, according to the *Manchester Guardian*, declared:

> If anyone raise the charge against me that we did not use the ordinary courts for the sentencing, I can only say that in this hour I was responsible for the fate of the German nation and that I myself was the supreme court of the German people for this twenty-four hours.[97]

Notably, Hitler also made the following clear: 'I gave the order to shoot those who were mainly guilty of this treason, and I furthermore gave the order to burn out the tumours of our inner poisoning.'[98] For British newspapers this statement was significant. The translation of Hitler's declaration differed in some newspapers, but the point remained the same – Hitler did not shy away from the fact that it had been his decision to shoot and summarily execute those who were part of the alleged plot. Importantly though, while accepting responsibility, Hitler justified his actions and, in doing so, amplified the danger that the so-called plot or 'second revolution' had posed to law and order in Germany. And while Hitler's address did not reveal the names of all the victims (as some had hoped), it did reveal the death toll from the purge – seventy-seven – which included, according to the *Morning Post*:

> Nineteen high Storm Troop leaders, 31 ordinary Storm Troopers and members, and three black uniformed leaders were shot as participants in the plot.
> Thirteen Storm Troop leaders and civilians were shot 'in resisting arrest', and Three 'committed suicide'.
> Five members of the party not Storm Troopers were shot for complicity.
> Finally, three S.S. men who were guilty of 'disgraceful mishandling of prisoners' were also shot.[99]

Overall, Hitler's address to the Reichstag was seen by the British press as somewhat of a propaganda failure. The *Daily Telegraph* reported, although on what evidence is not clear, that the German public were 'not convinced' by Hitler's justifications for the purge. On 16 July 1934 the newspaper commented:

> Germany has had time to think. The spell the Chancellor cast over his listeners has worn off; the glamour has faded from the story of vice conquered and virtue triumphant; intelligence has returned to the masses. The result is that to-day thinking Germans are unanimous in believing the speech was 'empty'. Where has all the rhetoric led? Where is the evidence for the plot? These are the questions asked.[100]

Hitler failed to present any documents as evidence despite the fact that 'countless documents' had been found and read by Hitler. So far, reported the *Daily Telegraph*, no documents had been 'submitted to competent court for proper examination'.[101] *The Spectator* called the speech 'empty', with an article printed on 20 July, stating:

> The speech he delivered was unconvincing. The story he told was uncorroborated and could as well have been fabrication as fact. The promised list of victims of the terror has never been forthcoming. Apart from a few notorious cases mentioned by Herr Hitler himself no one knows who was killed or why.[102]

While foreign newspapers could express dissatisfaction with official explanations of the purge, *The Spectator* reminded readers that 'Public opinion in Germany today has no means of making itself articulate'.[103] But, explained the newspaper, 'the scepticism and disillusionment reported by British and other newspaper correspondents in Germany are in all the circumstances more likely to develop than diminish'.[104] *The Spectator* echoed the earlier report by H. Powys Greenwood, published in February 1934, in which he noted discordance within the government, with the observation:

> [T]he fact has to be faced that two of the legends on which the Hitler *régime* is based, the legend of a united party extending till it becomes a united State, and the legend of an administration capable of making good its promises, have been finally and comprehensively shattered. Unity has not been restored to the Nazi Party because a hundred or two representatives of the immediately discordant elements are shot in cold blood, shot while resisting or shot while trying to escape.[105]

The Spectator noted that 'Intimidation no doubt has its temporary effect, but Herr Hitler himself must be more intensely conscious than any man in Germany at the possibility of fresh challenges to his authority at any moment and in any quarter'.[106] With this comment, *The Spectator* seemed to suggest that opposition to the regime was possible. In reality, if the German people were unhappy or unconvinced by Hitler's explanations for the purge, they had precious few ways of expressing their opinions. And one of the lessons to be drawn from the purge was that *any* dissent, real or imagined, would be ruthlessly crushed by the regime. It was expecting rather a lot of the German people that they would openly express their opinions in a dictatorship which had not hesitated to shoot senior members of its own leadership. Hitler's fulminations perhaps looked as unconvincing in Berlin as they did in London, but at least in the latter city it was safe to say so.

Conversely, an article by Italian historian and journalist Professor Guglielmo Ferrero that appeared in *The Spectator* in the same issue was more critical and established the fruitlessness of any attempts at open dissent in Germany.[107] Ferrero used the purge as an example of the illegality of the Nazi regime and all Fascist regimes:

> Will the events that have been taking place in Germany at last open the eyes of the free countries? Will they make them realise that the Nazi and Fascist governments differ from representative governments in this above all, that they are illegitimate governments which have set out to discover a new principle

of authority outside the principles of Monarchy and Democracy, and, having failed to find it, rest on no principle of law whatever? The heads of the Nazi government, like the Fascists, are endeavouring to convince the word by public speeches that they have established a marvellous *régime*, dazzling in its novelty. But all this fine talk does little to conceal from discerning eyes the incurable weakness of the two *régimes* – the absence of any legal title, clear, precise, and recognised by the people.[108]

The lesson that should be drawn from the Röhm purge, in this view, was that life under Hitlerism could be nasty, brutish and short, and other states should wake up to the reality of this. *The Times* felt that the recent action did open the eyes of many to the dictatorship. Hitler's announcement that he was the 'supreme court' in Germany had shattered many of the illusions about National Socialism. Importantly, *The Times* reported, it also shattered illusions about the dictatorship in Germany:

> [T]he chapter of the 'clean-up' in the history of National Socialist Germany may be said to have been closed as far as it ever can be closed. Its final significance cannot yet be judged, for it has destroyed something that is unlikely ever to be completely reconstructed: the illusion of indestructible patriotic unity, of the eternal loyalty to each other which the National Socialist leaders so often proclaimed. . . . None can tell what this new and shaken frame of mind will ultimately lead.[109]

* * *

News of President Hindenburg's failing health set aside any remaining questions about the purge. After a long bout of illness, the aged President Hindenburg died on 2 August 1934. His death was an important turning point in the Nazis' pursuit of total and unrivalled power. For the British press, it was the final step in the establishment of the Nazi dictatorship. Prior to his death many British newspapers had offered theories about what might occur in the event of the president's death. A few correspondents had theorized that Hitler would combine the Offices of Chancellor and President, concentrating all power into his own hands. For instance, *The Times* accurately summarized:

> The idea has often been discussed that the application of the National-Socialist *Führerprinzip* (principle of leadership) to the State should be completed by the creation of the post of *Reichsführer*, which would thus unite these two offices. It would not be surprising, in the event of the President's death, if a Bill were passed making this change, and if this were quickly submitted to a national plebiscite.[110]

This was not the only theory offered. Other alternatives were raised, and discussed, by British correspondents but it was understood that whatever step taken would not lessen the gains already made by the Nazi government. For instance, some newspapers suggested that an honorary president might be appointed. The *Daily Telegraph* suggested that while it might be decided that there might not be another president, it was also possible that 'Some generally respected man will be made President as mere figurehead'.[111] An article provided by Reuter in the *Manchester Guardian* put forth the Duke of Brunswick, the son-in-law of the ex-Kaiser, General Field Marshal August von Mackensen (stated to be a former rival of Hindenburg's and popular hero in Germany for his war record), or President von Hindenburg's son, Colonel Oskar von Hindenburg (a landed estate owner in East Prussia), as possible candidates for the title of 'honorary' president.[112]

As the president's end approached many newspapers printed articles celebrating his life, written by prominent British statesmen and writers. Conservative MP and head of the Admiralty during the First World War, Winston Churchill, wrote a feature article for the *Daily Mail* while former British prime minister during the war, David Lloyd George, wrote a special article for the *Daily Express* entitled 'My Old Enemy' that appeared on 2 August 1934.[113] On the same day that David Lloyd George's article appeared in the *Daily Express*, President Paul von Hindenburg died in Germany. News of his death appeared in British newspapers the following day, on 3 August 1934. But, in reporting the president's death most British newspapers focused more on the advent of Hitler to the position of, in the words of the *Daily Mail*, 'the world's most powerful ruler'.[114] With Hindenburg's death, Hitler had combined the positions of chancellor and president thereby contradicting the terms of the Enabling Act of March 1933 which had guaranteed the rights of the president. The *News Chronicle* summed up the news with the headline: 'Hitler out-Kaiser's the Kaiser.'[115] Berlin correspondent for the newspaper stated that with the new title Hitler

> becomes Head of the Army and of the Navy and the whole bureaucracy, State and Municipal, of the land; he will have the nomination of all German Ambassadors and Ministers; foreign diplomatists will be accredited to him; and the final decision between peace and war so far as Germany is concerned will rest in his hands.... The technical legality of last night's decree is nowhere challenged. By exercising the 'full powers' conferred on the Government by the Nazi Reichstag in January 1933, Herr Hitler could disregard constitutional niceties.[116]

In all, Hitler's new powers were 'far exceeding those exercised by Signor Mussolini or Stalin, powers even beyond the ambition of any Eastern potentate'.[117] The *Manchester Guardian* similarly reported that Hitler had become 'the most powerful dictator in Europe, if not the whole world'.[118] He had become more powerful than the Kaiser ever was because 'he is dictator over a unified, non-Federal Germany and is untrammelled by a Legislature which qualified the former Imperial ruler's sovereignty'.[119] Importantly, it meant that Weimar democracy had been dealt its final blow – the constitution had been 'swept aside'.[120]

What final powers Hitler would hold would be left to a plebiscite, but the *Daily Telegraph* stated that there was 'No room was ever left for doubt concerning the result'.[121] As a leader in late August observed: 'The atmosphere of Germany is not healthy for opposition to the governing power. The concentration camps and the events of June 30 are sufficient warning to those who would openly express dissent.'[122] The propaganda of the previous weeks had 'not been directed against opponents, of whom none dare to reveal themselves. Its intent has been to secure from the German people a vote so overwhelmingly in favour of Herr Hitler as to impress indelibly the foreign mind.'[123] Even though there was clear discontent and disillusionment among the German population, Hitler's success in the plebiscite was certain.

* * *

Whatever the purge had meant to accomplish for Hitler in his relations with the government and the army, it was a disaster for the regime in the eyes of the British press. Instead of the press congratulating Hitler and the government for dealing with the rowdy and violent SA, they denounced the state-sanctioned execution and murder. Initially, the press' reaction had not been so clearly defined. In the eyes of the press, bereft of information about what had actually happened, the Röhm purge was first portrayed as a victory for the moderates against the wilder elements in the party. As events became clearer, however, the true nature of the purge (if not always its intent) was subjected to unrelenting criticism. The action had taken place outside of the legal framework of the state and, for that, the regime was condemned. It confirmed to many correspondents and their newspapers what they already knew, or at least suspected – that the Nazi 'government' was a brutal dictatorship. The violent purge sparked widespread outspoken criticism of a kind not seen even during the months of political terror in 1933. For this was not just illegal violence; it was violence perpetrated by the Nazi government against its fellow members and colleagues. It was no longer violence by some rowdy SA members against members of a rival party, like the Communist Party, but was state-sanctioned, government action. Legality and due process had been overturned for the weekend of 30 June to 2 July 1934, and the head of the state had assisted in the murder, or execution, of fellow ministers and officials. And for this the Nazi government was condemned by the British press. It was a rare occasion in which most British newspapers, with the exception of a few popular dailies, criticized and denounced the Nazi regime. This reaction clearly surprised the Nazi government who attacked the press for their coverage and, particularly, their condemnation of the action.

As for the plebiscite, it did not demonstrate to the foreign powers, or the British press, the complete unity of Germany under National Socialism. The plebiscite was not a complete success for Hitler's government, especially given the propaganda that surrounded it. Surprisingly for the Hitler regime, and the British press, there was some opposition which saw approximately 6 million who either voted no or abstained from voting. Commenting on these votes the *New Statesman and Nation* observed:

> In the circumstances, when every vote of abstention required physical courage as well as independence of mind, the vote of four million against Hitler, and the two million abstentions and 800,000 spoilt ballot papers are of real significance.[124]

The initial excitement and enthusiasm for the regime was wearing off. H. Powys Greenwood of *The Spectator* remarked that 'Opposition and discontent in the Third Reich is increasing, as every observer of Germany has noted, and as was indeed to be expected'.[125] But, noted Greenwood, '84 per cent of the qualified electorate, consisting, in proportions difficult to estimate, of the enthusiastic, the luke-warm, the resigned, and the intimidated, are prepared to accept the Führer's rule'.[126] At present, 'Herr Hitler's position may for the present be regarded as absolutely unassailable'.[127] At the Nazi Party rally in early September 1934 Hitler was, reported the *Morning Post*, 'hailed like a King'.[128]

Despite declarations from Hitler that the revolution was over – and that Germany was now a completely National Socialist state – opposition and tension still existed in Germany, not least among the Christian churches in Germany. Throughout its reporting on the Röhm purge and the death of President Hindenburg, the British press continued to cover the struggle of the churches in Germany against attempts by the Nazis to bring them into line. Even as the focus turned to foreign affairs, specifically German rearmament and its aggressive territorial demands, British newspapers still demonstrated an interest in the internal affairs of the country. The British press continued to give space to domestic affairs. This included reporting the increasingly brutal persecution of the German Jewish population as well as the undermining of the Christian churches in Germany, to which we now turn.

* * *

6

'Cross and Swastika'

The struggle for the churches in Germany

In September 1934, a month after the plebiscite that confirmed Adolf Hitler as Führer of Germany, *The Spectator* printed a lengthy piece on the struggle of the churches in the Nazi state entitled 'The Cross and the Swastika'. Attempting to explain the conflict, particularly where the Protestant or Evangelical churches were concerned, the newspaper acknowledged that 'It is not easy to understand the German church dispute in all its bearings'.[1] The struggle of the Protestant churches against the state could not be merely explained as hostility to National Socialism or even 'to the unification of the Protestant churches of the various German provinces, or to the fusion of the Lutheran and Reformed churches, or (in most cases) to episcopal government with a Reich Bishop at the head'.[2] What they resisted, if one were to try to sum it up, was 'the patent attempt to make the Church serve the purposes of the State' and to subject it to arbitrary decrees.[3] The attacks on the opposition continued and, reported *The Spectator*, 'will be maintained'.[4] But, the newspaper noted, so far the opposition 'has withstood the attack successfully for eighteen months now. Only men ready to suffer their convictions could have achieved that, and it is only if they are prepared to suffer still that the cause they care for can survive.'[5] *The Spectator* concluded by stating that

> The Christian Churches of all lands, perhaps of this land most of all, owe them no small debt, for so long as they stand firm contact can be kept with a true Protestant Christianity in Germany at a time when it is hard to recognize the officialised Protestant religion in that country as Christianity at all.[6]

And, importantly, 'a battle fought anywhere for freedom is fought for freedom everywhere'.[7] With this article, *The Spectator* conveyed to readers the importance of the church conflict in Germany. This was not simply a group (or groups) in opposition to Nazism; the conflict concerned the freedom of the Christian churches and their position in the state without interference, especially in terms of church doctrine and teachings. What *The Spectator* article demonstrated was that while the church situation was a difficult one to report, it deserved attention and coverage. *The Spectator* was not the only British newspaper to feel this way.

In the 1930s, the suppression and attempted coordination of the Christian churches in Germany captured the attention of the British press. From 1933 till the onset of the Second World War British newspapers, to varying degrees, followed the struggle of (and for) the churches in Germany. For quality newspapers like *The Times*, *Manchester Guardian* and weekly newspapers like *The Spectator* and the *New Statesman and Nation*, the attempted coordination and suppression of religion in Germany was a matter of extreme importance. News about the church struggle was often featured alongside articles about the increasing persecution of Germany's (and later Austria's) Jews, as well as reports charting Germany's rearmament and increasing territorial demands. For the press, interest in the church conflict in Germany was centred on two themes – the struggle for religious freedom and autonomy and the existence of opposition within a dictatorship. British newspapers reported the struggles of the both the Catholic Church and the Protestant churches in their attempt to retain autonomy, independence and spiritual freedom.

* * *

Prior to 1933, the Nazi Party enjoyed more election success in areas with predominant Protestant populations. For many Protestants the nationalist, right-wing policies of Adolf Hitler and his party were appealing. Pastor Martin Niemöller, who would later become a leading figure in the church opposition movement, advocated for a spiritual renewal of Germany and even voted for Hitler in the 1933 elections. Catholic interests, on the other hand, were represented by the formidable political party the Centre Party, led by former chancellor Heinrich Brüning, and the Bavarian People's Party. A number of Catholic bishops and prominent Catholics had denounced Nazism prior to 1933. Fritz Gerlack, publisher of the Catholic weekly newspaper *Der gerade weg* (*Straight and Narrow*) attacked Nazism in an article printed in July 1932 entitled 'National Socialism is a Plague'. He was one of two Catholic victims on the Night of the Long Knives in 1934.[8]

Catholicism was one of the early targets of the Nazis following the appointment of Adolf Hitler as chancellor in January 1933. It first came under attack in the Nazi Party's war against parliamentary democracy in early 1933. An integral part of this was the suppression, isolation and persecution of political groups, particularly the parties of the left. But, importantly, this also involved the undermining and removal of the influence of the Catholic Church from politics – specifically the Centre Party and the Bavarian People's Party. Early reports by British correspondents detailed attempts by the Centre Party to accommodate and work with the Nazi Party 'in building up the Fatherland'.[9] But the Nazis, intent on becoming the sole political party in Germany, shunned these conciliatory efforts. Instead, Hitler sought to destroy the Centre Party by other means. He opened negotiations with the Vatican in Rome to secure the removal of political Catholicism from Germany. The negotiations led by Vice Chancellor Franz von Papen on behalf of Hitler resulted in the *Reichskonkordat*, or Concordat, between the Holy See and the German Reich which was signed on 20 July 1933. It guaranteed the independence of the Catholic Church, especially the freedom of Catholic youth organizations and schools. In turn, the Catholic Church was to remain outside of politics; Catholic clergy were not allowed to participate in political activity, and the remaining Catholic political parties, the Centre Party and the Bavarian People's Party, ceased to exist.

The signing of the Concordat was reported by *The Times*, *Manchester Guardian*, *Daily Mail*, *Morning Post* and the *Daily Express*. The *Daily Mail* summed up the Concordat, informing readers that it 'defines the respective spheres of Church and State in Germany'.[10] The *Manchester Guardian* reported that this was to be achieved by 'the complete withdrawal of Catholic priests and Catholic organisations, particularly the Centre Party, from politics'.[11] Quoted by the *Daily Mail*, Hitler announced that the Concordat:

> [G]ave sufficient guarantee that the members of the Roman Catholic Association [the Centre Party and Bavarian People's Party] will henceforth place themselves unhesitatingly at the service of the National-Socialist State . . . I am happy in the conviction that a period has now ended in which, unhappily only too often, religious and political interests were in apparently insoluble opposition. The concordat will in this direction serve the cause of peace, which all desire.[12]

With the signing of the Concordat, the Catholic Church was sidelined and removed from politics. What this meant was that the Nazi Party had become the sole political party in Germany. Days later, British newspapers reported the promulgation of a new law forbidding the revival or creation of political parties.

The signing of the Concordat came after months of violence against Catholic priests, politicians and members of Catholic organizations. This had been reported by several newspapers, including the *Manchester Guardian*. Special correspondent for the *Manchester Guardian* F. A. Voigt expressed surprise at the swiftness of negotiations and the silence of the Vatican to attacks on its clergy, which included arrests and meetings that were broken up 'often with great brutality'.[13] He wrote: 'That the Holy See should have contemplated such outrages almost without a murmur . . . is perhaps surprising – all the more so since Hitlerite conceptions are fundamentally hostile to those of Roman Catholicism.'[14] *The Times* had also reported the violence against the clergy and associated organizations. One notable incident occurred in Munich in June 1933. A congress of the Roman Catholic Journeymen's Societies meeting in Munich was violently broken up by SA.[15] Priests were reported to have been brutally removed from the Congress and taken out into the street where they were beaten in full view of passers-by. Reported justification for the attack centred on allegations that the members had worn 'yellowish' shirts and had sung the Horst Wessel song with 'incorrect words' and had made comments about liberating Germany from Hitler.[16] The congress was subsequently called off by its members.

The Concordat did not necessarily mean an end to disagreements and conflict between the National Socialist state and the Catholic Church. As Voigt commented in July 1933: 'whether the new concordat is anything more than a pause in a gigantic struggle between two conceptions that can with difficulty – if at all – live side by side in the same state is unpredictable at the moment'.[17] For Voigt:

> Hitler's 'Totalitarian State' is incompatible with Roman Catholicism or indeed Christianity. The whole future of religion as such has been darkened by the Hitlerite challenge in Germany – and perhaps not in Germany alone – and deep misgivings are felt by German Catholic and Evangelical clergy alike.[18]

'But', he wrote, 'for the time being Catholic Germany has been silenced and Hitler has gained a big success, a success which for all the brutality of the methods employed shows that the German dictatorship is by no means incapable of skilled diplomacy'.[19] Voigt acknowledged that the Vatican did gain one advantage with the Concordat:

> Whereas in Italy Catholicism is the religion of the overwhelming majority of the people and, therefore, as a matter of course a State religion, in Germany, it is the religion of a minority. By the new concordat it acquires a status of a State religion side by side with the Evangelical Church.[20]

As British newspapers would report, attacks on the clergy and other Catholic figures did not end, but some concessions were initially made. For instance, several British newspapers reported the freeing of priests who had been imprisoned in concentration camps. The *Morning Post* reported that Hitler had ordered the 'release of all priests and leaders of such organisations arrested in connection with their dissolution, and has forbidden such measures to be taken in the future'.[21] Additionally, the *Morning Post* noted that Hitler had reversed the Prussian order for the dissolution of several Catholic organizations.

Nevertheless, instances of violence and arrest continued and were reported by British newspapers. In November 1933, the *Morning Post* printed excerpts from a speech by a German Bishop[22] who alleged that

> 140 Catholic Priests are under preventive arrest, and in the Palatinate Catholic priests are paraded through the streets bare-foot and with posters bearing libellous inscriptions hanging over their shoulders in sandwich-board fashion.[23]

And, in December 1933, the *Manchester Guardian* reported the arrest of several Catholic priests by the Bavarian secret police. Their arrest was for 'spreading atrocity stories about the conditions in the Dachau concentration camp'.[24] The charge that priests were becoming involved in politics by denouncing the actions of the National Socialist government was a common excuse for the arrest and imprisonment of priests and members of the church.

In 1934, despite the Concordat, tension only increased between the Catholic Church and the Nazi government. The *Manchester Guardian* reported: 'an unacknowledged state of war exists in many parts of Germany between the servants of the State and the Roman Catholics'.[25] The Reich Concordat was a 'comprehensive document', but 'as all history has shown, it is not easy to define the limits of the temporal and spiritual spheres . . . the German "totalitarian" State has shown itself exacting of the Church's interpretations'.[26] In practice this meant:

> Catholic associations may exist for social and religious purposes, yet their full freedom has, in fact, been constantly restricted by police command in many parts of Germany. The right of priests to preach is undisputed, yet sermons criticising anti-Semitism and the frantic vapouring's of 'German Christians' have led to violent attacks in the official Nazi press upon their preachers.[27]

The *Manchester Guardian* explained that the government line on church affairs was hard to define because 'It is not hard to find innumerable contradictions in official definitions of the Government's attitude towards the Church'.[28] So while Papen tried to reassure Catholics, 'less prominent colleagues in executive positions translate policy into practice'.[29]

Relations were further strained in April 1934, when the pope publicly denounced the treatment of Catholic youth organizations in Germany during his Easter message. Referring to the conditions of the Concordat, *The Times* explained that the Vatican had received 'a promise of protection and recognition by the "Nazi" State of non-political associations and organizations of Catholics'.[30] However, a delay in their recognition as well as declarations from Baldur von Shirach, leader of the Hitler Youth, that his organization was going to 'absorb the Catholics this year' had caused concern.[31] The *Observer* commented:

> Every observer of German internal affairs knows quite well that the Nazi-Catholic conflict is not merely a political duel; it is a life-and-death struggle for the souls of German Catholic youth. However much Rome may hate Moscow materialism from which National Socialism claims to have saved it, it does not intend to hand over the education of millions of German Catholic youth to mystically-minded, brown-shirted, pagan pantheists.[32]

The freedom of the Catholic press was also at stake, reported *The Times*, following a judgement by the Duisburg District Court[33] in which a ruling essentially declared 'the so-called Catholic Press is superfluous'.[34] *The Times* explained: 'Their right, which is admitted by the Concordat, publicly to teach and explain the doctrines of their Church would be materially restricted were the Roman Catholic Press to disappear from the Reich.'[35]

Throughout the 1930s, British newspapers reported ongoing tension between the Nazis and Catholic Church over issues such as youth organizations, education, freedom of the press, and racial and social policies. These protests and the ensuing negotiations between the Vatican and the Reich government were often reported by the British newspapers. In 1934, for instance, the *Daily Express* noted the success of a request made by the Vatican that Catholic doctors and nurses in Germany be excluded from taking part in the new sterilization programme launched by the Nazi government.[36] Also, in 1934, the *Observer* reported that following the Pope's denunciation of the treatment of Catholic organizations in Germany, Hitler had sent an emissary to Rome to negotiate and attempt to 'end the conflict'.[37]

The conflict, however, did not end there. By 1937 most British newspapers observed that the situation had become 'specially acute'.[38] *The Spectator* noted tensions between the Vatican and the Nazis were so high that the Pope would probably denounce the Concordat.[39] In early 1937, an encyclical by the Pope was circulated to churches in Germany and read from pulpits. It reviewed the history of the Concordat and charted breaches of the agreement. The pope declared that he had signed the Concordat '"despite grave misgivings" because he believed it to be in the best interests of the Church and of the German people'.[40] There had been continual breaches, declared the pope according to the *Daily Mail*, but 'that is not the fault of the Church'.[41] He alleged the Nazi government

> has been guilty of mis-application of the Concordat, of evasion of its provisions, of undermining its context, and finally, of more or less open violations of its stipulations and of the unwritten law governing its extent.[42]

Despite the pope's statement and frequent incursions on the terms of the Concordat by Nazis (local officials, governments and, at times, the Reich government), the agreement between the Nazi regime and the Vatican remained in place prior to and during the war. The press continued to record and report the tension that existed in the uneasy relationship between the Catholic Church and the German government in the 1930s. Excesses, disagreements and negotiations were reported by British newspapers including *The Times*, *Manchester Guardian*, *Morning Post*, *Daily Mail* and *The Spectator*, but for most British newspapers the main religious struggle was the one taking places in the Protestant churches.

* * *

The Protestant Church struggle was different to that of the Catholic Church. While the conflict between the Catholic Church and the Nazi government had centred on questions of political and cultural influence, the struggle of the Protestant churches was focused on issues of faith, religious doctrine and membership. At its very heart, it was a struggle for the freedom of faith. This was something that most British newspapers understood from the beginning of the church conflict when it broke out in the spring of 1933.

In committing to covering the Protestant Church struggle, or *Kirchenkampf*, the British press had a difficult task ahead. The coordination or attempted *Gleichschaltung* of the Protestant churches was complex, messy and often chaotic. This could be said not only of the church struggle itself but also the various groups at the centre of the conflict. This included the Faith Movement of German Christians, a nationalist, anti-Semitic group that aligned themselves with Nazism but also other groups such as the German Faith Movement, a group that desired a more 'German church' based on pagan and Nazi ideals rather than Christian ones. Furthermore, the pastors and other church figures in opposition to forcible coordination by the German Christians and the Nazi state were by no means a unified group. One of the key opposition groups that featured in British news reports was the Pastor's Emergency League (*Pfarrernotbund*) led by former U-Boat commander, Iron Cross recipient and theologian Martin Niemöller, a pastor whose parish was in Dahlem, a leafy affluent district in Greater Berlin. The Pastor's Emergency League was created in 1933 after Niemöller sent out letters inviting members of the Young Reformer's League (an earlier group made up of church members who were in opposition to the German Christians), of which he was a member. The Pastor's Emergency League then grew into the Confessing Church in May 1934 as a result of the Barmen Declaration which denounced any attempt at state control over the church. In all, the church conflict was dominated and characterized by competing factions of members with strong personalities who held differing and opposing views which caused frequent squabbles.

Despite the difficulty in understanding the church struggle, newspapers like *The Times*, *Manchester Guardian* and the *Morning Post* provided sustained coverage, especially from 1934. Of these, *The Times* excelled in providing the most detailed and sustained coverage. A regular reader of *The Times*, wanting to follow what was happening in Germany, would have been able to follow every development in the church conflict. This did mean it would have been difficult for readers who had not been following the conflict to simply pick up the newspaper and expect to be provided with a summary of events. Berlin correspondent Norman Ebbutt wrote his articles for readers who read *The Times* each day and who were invested in following developments in Nazi Germany. The *Manchester Guardian* and *Morning Post* also closely reported the conflict but provided readers with more background, summarizing aspects of the conflict in their articles. The *Manchester Guardian* was aided in this with reports by its special correspondent (and later diplomatic correspondent) F. A. Voigt. His special features provided detailed analysis, focusing on key areas of life under Nazism. Other newspapers, much more sporadic in their coverage, had to provide more background and context as they drew readers' attention to a recent development, such as the arrest of Pastor Niemöller in 1937. Their coverage was less comprehensive but still gave readers insight into Nazi efforts to coordinate the Christian churches in Germany. As a whole, however, the British press conveyed to readers the struggle of the Protestant churches against attempts to coordinate them under Nazism.

The Times was one of the first British newspapers to draw attention to early moves to create a unified Reich Church. In April 1933, *The Times* published an article by a 'German Churchman' who declared that the 'reconstruction of the Evangelical Church' was underway.[43] The twenty-eight disparate churches in Germany were to be 'removed' and consolidated into 'two great Church federations

... with a common central organization'.⁴⁴ Basically, as *The Times* summarized in May 1933, 'The Nazi principle of "leadership" is in large measure to supersede that of democracy'.⁴⁵ What this article referenced was early efforts by the Faith Movement of German Christians (known as the German Christians) which had begun its campaign to redefine and restructure the Protestant Churches of Germany. This was by no means an easy task as *The Times* had established. The Protestant churches in Germany comprised of twenty-eight disparate churches made up of predominantly Lutheran and Reformed (or Calvinist) churches, loosely held together in a confederacy. The German Christians, with the backing of Hitler and the Nazi government, sought to create a single, unified German Protestant Reich Church along National Socialist lines with an emphasis on strong nationalist, ethnic and racial ideals. At its head would be a Reich Bishop who would lead the way in creating the new church.

Moves to create a unified church were not initially met with much church protest. But conflict did arise over the question of who would be appointed the Reich Bishop to preside over the Reich Church. The German Christians wanted Dr Ludwig Müller for the role, an army chaplain from Königsburg and patron of the German Christian movement. Müller also had the backing of Hitler who, on 25 April 1933, had appointed him his 'personal representative in the negotiations for the formation of the new "Reich Church"'.⁴⁶ This was opposed by some pastors who organized themselves as the Young Reformers Movement. This movement, of which Pastor Martin Niemöller was a member of, was similar to the German Christians in its nationalistic fervour and support of Hitler and his Nazi government.⁴⁷ But what separated both groups were questions surrounding the role of the state and the church; the Young Reformers wanted to maintain the separation of church and state and ensure the independence and freedom of the church from interference by the state. The German Christians waged a rigorous campaign for their candidate but when votes were cast for the Reich Bishop, Friedrich von Bodelschwingh, a Lutheran pastor from the Westphalian city of Bielefeld, was elected instead of Müller.⁴⁸ *The Times* reported that the German Christians were not prepared to accept the election result. They were

> determined to make a stubborn fight for their candidate, and are using the ingenious methods of agitation so successfully applied by the Nazis in the political sphere to extend their influence among the rank and file of churchgoers.⁴⁹

One of the 'ingenious methods' included the appointment of Dr August Jäger, a lawyer and former church councilman, as Nazi state commissioner for the

Evangelical churches in Prussia, to assist in carrying out the seizure of the churches for the German Christians. As Klaus Scholder summarized: 'Jäger never left any doubt that the only goal of his activities in church politics was the radical, political co-ordination of the church, and that he would make use of every means to this end.'[50] Jäger placed the entire Prussian Church under police jurisdiction. As a result, many pastors were suspended, fired or arrested.[51] He removed many church administrators and replaced them with German Christians.[52] The Nazi Party and the German Christians mounted a vigorous campaign against Bodelschwingh. Finally, amid increasing pressure, Bodelschwingh resigned. According to *The Times*, he declared in his resignation that the appointment of a Nazi commissioner (Jäger) 'rendered it impossible for him to fulfil the mission entrusted to him.'[53]

Church elections were then scheduled for 23 July 1933 to elect new members for a national synod who would then be responsible for electing a new Reich Bishop. In the meantime, Müller was (illegally) announced as the new Reich Bishop. Jäger continued his efforts to bring the Prussian churches into line, sparking protests from churches in Prussia, Hanover and Hesse. These protests were made because the appointment of a commissioner was seen as 'an encroachment on the constitutionally guaranteed independence of the Prussian Evangelical Churches'.[54] In addition, reported *The Times*, 'utterances of some of the "German Christian" extremists have given rise to a fear lest it be hard to keep the substance of the Christian faith intact.'[55] At the end of June 1933, Müller proclaimed himself, without any authority, head of the Evangelical Church Federation and president of the Church Council. These appointments, reported *The Times*, made him 'virtual dictator of the Prussian Churches'.[56] Ushering in this new period, pastors were instructed to read a message to their congregations which *The Times* summarized: '[T]he Church is being "delivered" by the State from its condition of disorder, and that the Church must be thankful for all the trouble the State, occupied as it is with such enormous tasks, is yet taking in reorganizing it.'[57] In future, pastors were ordered to refrain from any 'criticism of the State or even of measures contemplated by its commissioners' – '"Church political activity", either from the pulpit or in the parishes will, the pastors are told, render them liable to prosecution', which could include 'disciplinary action and even dismissal'.[58]

Unsurprisingly, these moves were met with vigorous protest. This prompted President Hindenburg to intervene. At the beginning of July 1933, he wrote a public letter to Hitler expressing, according to *The Times*, his 'deepest concern' over the church situation.[59] President Hindenburg's intervention in the conflict sparked the interest of other British newspapers which had previously given little space to the struggle. The *News Chronicle* gave the story front-page coverage and the dramatic headline, 'Hindenburg's Clash with Hitler: Call to Save Churches'.[60] The article read: 'In dramatic fashion tonight President von Hindenburg intervened to protect the German Evangelical churches from the attacks that have been made upon them by the Nazis.'[61] The newspaper quoted extensively from Hindenburg's public letter and summarized the reasons for discontent within the churches. This intervention seemed timely given the upcoming elections for the national church synod, and it was hoped that the conflict would be resolved, especially after it was revealed that Hitler had requested Interior Minister Wilhelm Frick to monitor the situation. This was important, explained the *News Chronicle*, because even though the position of the regime was 'unassailable' 'it gets daily more evident that difficulties beset his effort to acquire the goodwill of the millions of Germans who persistently voted against him' in the March 1933 elections.[62]

As the church synod election loomed, British newspapers reported intimidatory tactics used by the German Christians against their opponents.[63] The *Morning Post* reported that while the freedom of the elections was 'guaranteed by the Chancellor' 'so strong a suggestion has already been created by the Press that the church opposition is also a political opposition, that this belief will undoubtedly dominate the polling'.[64] The pastors who opposed the Nazification of their churches were at a severe disadvantage as most of the candidates for elections were German Christians. Few in the opposition camp were represented and the *Morning Post* reported: 'the prospects of the church opposition winning on Sunday are very slight'.[65] *The Times*, like the *Morning Post*, reported that complaints of intimidation had been lodged by opposition pastors and that it would be 'inevitable that the pressure of the vast Nazi organization should have worked in favour of the "German Christians"'.[66] Three days later British newspapers recorded widespread victories for the German Christians. *The Times* summed up the church election result with the headline 'Extremist majority in Church elections'.[67]

At the end of July 1933, with the success of the church elections behind them, the German Christians proclaimed Müller as official Reich Bishop, or Primate of the unified German Evangelical Church. As *The Times* reported, this meant:

> The German Christians have had their way – legalized by elections in which the mighty face of 'the movement' and Herr Hitler's personal support were behind them, and in which the opposition laboured under difficulties which can only be appreciated at close quarters – and there can now be little doubt that German

Christian influence will be paramount in clerical appointments and in the life of the Church.[68]

For the moment, the German Christians were triumphant but, as the British press would go on to report, the opposition pastors refused to succumb to the extremist 'Nazi' church group.

* * *

The opposition movement continued to grow in late 1933. Resistance was especially acute following suggestions from German Christians that the Reich Church introduce an Aryan paragraph, based on the one introduced in Law for the Restoration of the Professional Civil Service on 7 April 1933.[69] The introduction of an Aryan paragraph to the church constitution would see the implementation of Nazi racial ideals in the church, which would include the dismissal and exclusion of all clergy and church officials that were considered non-Aryan.[70] It would, for instance, exclude pastors and clergy who had been born Jews but had been baptized and converted to Protestantism. This was a blatant and direct attack on the church. Suggestions about the adoption of an Aryan paragraph were discussed in August and September 1933 at the same time that Müller was enforcing an authoritarian structure on the Prussian Church. In November 1933, the *Manchester Guardian* and *The Times* reported efforts by some German Christians to push through a stricter Aryan clause for the 'purification of German Christianity'.[71] On 15 November 1933, *The Times* reported a 'demonstration' by German Christians, which was attended by 20,000 German Christians including the group's leader Bishop Hossenfelder. During the rally, 'radical demands were made'.[72] *The Times* correspondent stated that one of the demands was the

> ruthless application of the 'Aryan Paragraph' . . . excluding from the ministry all pastors with Jewish blood even far back, the segregation of all members of the Church of Jewish or other foreign racial descent and their inclusion in special religious communities (the so-called 'Ghetto church' idea), the elimination of the crucifix, the whole of the Old Testament, and 'superstitious' portions of the New Testament.[73]

The speaker of these inflammatory remarks was Dr Reinhold Krause, the head of the German Christians in Berlin.[74] Even Müller was alarmed by the rhetoric of the speech. *The Times* reported the Reich Bishop had 'issued a declaration sharply denouncing Dr. Krause's speech'.[75]

Discussions about the introduction of an Aryan paragraph sparked vigorous protests from opposition pastors who had, in early September 1933, organized into the Pastors' Emergency League, led by Martin Niemöller. Their protests were not so much about the anti-Semitic rhetoric of the German Christians' proposal but about church independence, specifically the 'curtailment of confessional freedom'.[76] They saw the Aryan paragraph as a serious attempt at interference by the state in church affairs.[77] The *Manchester Guardian* reported that members of the Pastors' Emergency League, which was founded in September 1933, read a message of protest from their pulpits in over 3000 churches. The newspaper commented: 'the pastors who have spoken up deserve all credit for their courage'.[78]

Protests from the opposition pastors, namely the Pastors' Emergency League (which later grew into the Confessing Church), were covered in more detail by British newspapers in 1934. Just days into the new year, on 4 January 1934, Müller introduced the 'Ordinance concerning the Restoration of Orderly Conditions in the German Evangelical Church'.[79] The decree, according to *The Times*, contained an order 'forbidding all public discussion of Church policies or the use of Church premises for statements in regard to Church policies'.[80] The decree was also reported by the *Manchester Guardian* and the *Morning Post*. In response, the Pastors Emergency League drafted a declaration denouncing this interference in church affairs which was to be read aloud from pulpits. According to the *Morning Post*, the opposition pastors felt it was their 'unshakeable belief . . . that the Church must return to the faith of the Bible. A firm stand must be made against the intrusion of heathen elements into the doctrines of the German Evangelical Church.' The opposition to interference in church affairs was, reported the *Morning Post*, 'the most dogged and perplexing that the Nazis have encountered since coming to power'.[81] And, stated the newspaper, it showed no signs of abating, instead it 'is steadily increasing in strength'.[82]

This escalation in the church situation captured the interest of the popular liberal newspaper, the *News Chronicle*. In the days following the announcement of Müller's decree the *News Chronicle* covered the situation in detail, at times with front-page coverage. Of the decree, the newspaper explained to readers that pastors must refrain from 'misusing' church services for 'church-political' purposes or risk suspension and loss of salary.[83] The reading of the declaration of protest drafted by Martin Niemöller and others, which was read from pulpits during Sunday service, made the front page of the *News Chronicle* on 8 January 1934. It featured the dramatic headline: 'Pastors Defy German Primate, Gravest Church Crisis Since Reformation, Historic Declaration from 6,000 Pulpits.'[84]

It was probably an exaggeration to say that it had been read aloud from 6,000 pulpits but, nonetheless, the *News Chronicle* captured the importance of the declaration. Importantly, the *News Chronicle* stated, 'each [pastor who publicly read the declaration] affirmed "before God and his congregation" that threats of suspension or material loss would not induce him to maintain silence in regard to questions affecting the Bible and the Church'.[85] By reading the protest declarations to their congregations, pastors 'expose[d] themselves to suspension and even to deposition from office, with consequent economic ruin'.[86] They were, however, 'ready to face persecution'.[87] This placed Reich Bishop Müller in rather an awkward position, as the *News Chronicle* made clear:

> Bishop Mueller, the Nazi Primate, is in an embarrassing dilemma. To maintain his authority he ought to suspend or remove from office the 5,000 to 6,000 pastors who defied him on Sunday from their pulpits. Yet, so drastic an action is hardly practicable, although he is contemplating it.[88]

Opposition had now 'reached the remotest parts of the land'.[89] In the meantime, the German Christians, reported the *News Chronicle*, were 'clamouring for the use of repressive measures against their opponents. It is not so certain that the Chancellor, who is known to view the conflict with distaste, will accede to Bishop Mueller's demand'.[90] Müller appealed to Hitler to use the police and, if necessary, the SA to 'crush the resistance of close on 6,000 pastors [Pastors' Emergency League] who are defying his attempt to make German Protestantism a part of the Nazi State'.[91] It was fast becoming, reported the *News Chronicle* at the end of January 1934, a 'stormy European situation'.[92]

Hitler, however, was according to *The Times* 'anxious to bring about peace' in the church before 30 January 1934, so that there would be 'no flaw in the celebrations of national unity'.[93] The recent conflict looked to jeopardize that. The conflict had escalated to such a degree that Hitler took the unusual and unexpected step of intervening. *The Times* had reported that Hitler had earlier met with President Hindenburg who had requested he do all 'he could to bring about peace in the Church'.[94] Following this meeting with Hindenburg, Hitler hosted a conference which was intended as a mediation between the German Christians and the leaders of the opposition including Bishops Theophil Wurm (Württemberg), August Marahrens (Hanover) and Hans Meiser (Bavaria), as well as Pastor Martin Niemöller. However, the meeting did not go as the opposition had hoped. Within moments of the meeting convening Hermann Göring, minister of the interior for Prussia, launched a vigorous attack on Niemöller accusing him of disloyalty to the state.[95] The subject of the attack was a transcript of a phone conversation, which had been recorded by the secret police, between Niemöller and his colleague, which was read aloud to all those in attendance at the meeting.[96] For *The Times* Berlin correspondent, this process was known only too well by foreign correspondents whose own phone calls were subjected to the 'listening-in gang' and 'recorded by that invisible third'.[97] The attack by Göring deeply unsettled the opposition but, as *The Times* reported, they 'seem to have survived the shock and remain unified'.[98] However, it had 'left the situation more doubtful than ever'.[99] The correspondent explained that '[w]hatever indiscretions individual members may have committed, the Church conflict remains'.[100]

Just days after the meeting, *The Times* reported that Müller, seeking to solidify his position in the church, issued an emergency decree 'investing in himself all powers of the Prussian Church Synod . . . . He thus becomes sole arbiter of the Prussian Church'.[101] Almost immediately Niemöller was retired from his pastorship and taken in for questioning by the secret police. On this occasion he was released. According to the *Manchester Guardian*, Neimöller remained defiant and, despite his suspension, continued to conduct services at his church in Dahlem. Niemöller was determined to challenge the constitutional validity of the suspension before the Supreme Court at Leipzig. Niemöller's congregation, it was reported, 'maintain the view that in the Prussian Church a pastor is primarily responsible to his congregation'.[102] The *Manchester Guardian* added: 'Whether the opposition can continue in the face of the powerful forces ranged against it remains to be seen, but it is clear that it is still alive.'[103]

In August 1934 the National Synod, made up of mostly German Christians, met and passed through legislation designed to further the goal of creating a National Church. What this essentially meant was the southern churches, which up until this point had refused to be 'coordinated', would be forced to join the Reich Church under Müller's control. The first decree passed legalized all of Müller and Jäger's recent measures; the second prepared the way for the takeover of the churches in Württemberg and Bavaria. The *Manchester Guardian* summed up the new measures: 'Henceforth legislative power is vested in the new Reich Church, to the exclusion of the regional churches. . . . The three remaining "rebel" Churches – Hanover, Bavaria, and Württemberg – lose their autonomy.'[104] Furthermore, plans were made for all pastors to 'swear obedience to the Führer of the German nation and state, Adolf Hitler . . . and devote themselves to the German nation with every sacrifice and effort befitting a German Evangelist'.[105]

As British newspapers would report, this latest move sparked more protests from opposition theologians and pastors. They issued a statement denouncing the National Synod proceedings as, according to the *Manchester Guardian*, 'illegal and arbitrary'.[106] They also denounced the oath. The statement was read from the pulpits of churches associated with the opposition (Confessing Church) movement. The *Manchester Guardian* quoted part of the declaration:

> This so-called national synod, its proceedings, and its resolutions are invalid, according to spiritual law and temporal law. Those who obey them break the constitution and the law of the Church, and they are exhorted not to make themselves accessory to such breaches.[107]

The *Manchester Guardian*'s Berlin correspondent called the statement 'a courageous declaration couched in strong and unequivocal language', the reading of which could see the pastors facing prison.[108] Indeed, he added, 'a number' of pastors had already been imprisoned for reading the declaration.[109] This protest was 'the first time for many months that the Opposition – to whom virtually all avenues of expression have been closed by the State, and police backing given to the Primate, Bishop Müller, and his Church government – have ventured upon a public pronouncement'.[110]

Amid protests over the legality of forced retirements and suspensions, Müller and Jäger mounted an aggressive campaign against the southern churches to bring them into line under the new national synod. But, as *The Times* reported in September 1934,

> [T]he incorporation of the resisting regional Churches is not proceeding smoothly. Both the Bavarian and the Württemberg Churches have formally refused to recognize their incorporation under the law of Reich Bishop Müller's Administration making them subject to its legislation, and Bishop Wurm, of Württemberg, has declared the appointment of an Administrative Commissioner [Jäger] invalid.[111]

Bishop Theophil Wurm, head of the church in Württemberg, was then suspended which sparked further protests. *The Times* reported, following the announcement of Wurm's suspension, 'disturbances broke out . . . meetings of protest were held, at which the greatest indignation was expressed by churchgoers at the attempt to saddle Dr. Wurm with implication in a financial scandal'.[112] Wurm, it was reported, had refused to accept 'his suspension, the legality of which he challenges, and continues to regard himself as head of the Regional Church'.[113]

There were also 'striking demonstrations' in Munich, reported the *New Statesman and Nation*, where Bishop Hans Meiser 'had preached a vigorous sermon of protest' at moves by the German Christians on his church.[114] He also denounced what was taking place in Württemberg.[115] Following the sermon, 'the huge congregation marched through the streets singing Luther's hymn, "'Ein' feste Burg ist unser Gott" [A Mighty Fortress is our God], to demonstrate in front of the episcopal palace, until they were eventually dispersed by police and S.A. men'.[116] The *New Statesman and Nation* explained: 'It is probable that Dr. Müller will beat the resisters, temporarily at least. But his victory will be costly, for he is widening and deepening opposition to the regime'.[117] This last comment in the *New Statesman and Nation* was most likely in reference to a speech by Müller in Hanover on 19 September in which he declared that he and the German Christians wanted 'a German Church free from Rome'.[118] In the speech, reported by several British papers including *The Times*, Müller announced his desire for 'one State, one Nation, one Church'.[119] Sections of the speech were censored when published but the message was clear. The last line about a 'Rome-Free' single church shocked many in Germany and abroad, as it was taken (and seemingly intended) to mean the amalgamation of both the Catholic and Protestant churches into one Reich Church.

The speech was also reported by some British newspapers that had previously given little space to the conflict. The *Daily Mail*, for instance, reported that Catholics were to 'join with Protestants in his National Church; if they do not, Dr. Mueller will "cope with them"'.[120] For the *News Chronicle*, which had been following the church situation, 'Dr. Mueller's thunderings appear a strange mixture of the odious and the merely ridiculous'.[121] But, acknowledged the newspaper, they should be taken seriously. The plans reported the newspaper, 'would be incredible if it did not follow so neatly the lines on which the other Nazi leaders have acted in other fields'.[122] Catholics in Germany were disturbed and the Vatican sought assurances from the German government that the Concordat was still in place. In turn, Foreign Minister Constantin von Neurath warned Müller about making any further inflammatory speeches. Despite this, Müller and Jäger continued to pursue the forcible incorporation of the southern churches.

In October 1934 the conflict further escalated when Bishop Würm, of Württemberg, was arrested for his continued refusal to acquiesce to the Jäger's intimidatory tactics to bring the church into line. Less than a week later, Bishop Meiser of Bavaria was removed from office. The *Daily Mail* dramatically reported:

> The fires of revolt which have been smouldering in the Protestant churches of Southern Germany since Reichbishop Müller and his National Synod began their attempt to reorganise the Bavarian State Church burst into full flame to-day.[123]

The reason given for Bishop Meiser's removal, reported *The Times*, was his 'persistent refusal to carry out the legitimate decrees of the Reich Church administration'.[124] Furthermore, 'the chiefs of the State Regional Synod and other prominent pastors and members of the Synod were also dismissed yesterday by Dr. Jäger'.[125] The article noted: 'Dr Meiser is now understood to be under "house arrest." His movements are strictly supervised by a detective and he himself is confined to his residence.'[126] Meanwhile, in response to Meiser's removal and as a show of support, church services were full across Bavaria and crowds gathered outside Mesier's residence.[127] In response to Jäger's aggressive tactics, the Bavarian Protestant Church announced its split from Müller's church administration. The declaration issued by the Bavarian Church described Jäger's methods as 'tantamount to an act of war'.[128] 'Dark forces are at work', the declaration stated: 'The Evangelical faith is threatened and the door has been opened to every kind of heresy.'[129] The Bavarian Church also encouraged other churches to protest the 'church administration which is unconstitutional and a violation of the faith', explaining that in doing so, 'We realise that the burden we lay on their shoulders is a heavy one'.[130]

British newspapers also reported that the Confessing Church, based largely in Prussia, had announced that it too was 'breaking off all relations with the official "Reich" Church'.[131] The *Manchester Guardian* reported that events in the south had demonstrated 'that all hope that the 'German Christians' will ever change their policy must be abandoned'.[132] This left the Confessing Synod with no other option except 'formal separation and a declaration that Reich Bishop Müller and his adherents, through denying the fundamental principles of the Gospel, "can no longer be regarded as a Christian Church"'.[133] This essentially meant that it would form a new church, and a new church constitution, the *Manchester Guardian* reported.[134]

Seemingly, even the German Christians were becoming alarmed at Jäger's (and Müller's) methods. The *News Chronicle* summed up the situation with a headline on 16 October 1934, 'German Pastors Winning; Nazis Seeking a Way Out'.[135] The article stated that efforts to crush the Bavarian Church were proving a 'fiasco'.[136] On 19 October 1934 *The Times* reported that Dr Christian Kinder, leader of the German Christians, had visited Jäger to demand his resignation over the Bavarian crisis.[137] *The Times* explained:

> The impression is gained that the Party-State is at last beginning to realise that the unification of the German Evangelical Church desired by Herr Hitler, and, indeed, no less by the Confessional community of the so-called Opposition, cannot be satisfactorily achieved through a Church regime and a Church Party

which are overtaken every few months by a grab crisis and are in a state of constant dissension.[138]

Here, *The Times* still assumed that Hitler wished to see the Protestant churches united into a National Church. In reality, Hitler was busy distancing himself from the church conflict. The *Daily Telegraph* reported that Hitler was to meet with Jäger, the result of which would probably be Jäger's dismissal. Even Müller was now trying to distance himself from Jäger, reported the *Daily Telegraph*, explaining that latter had lost the support of his Primate. Müller was also at risk of losing the support of Hitler – he had few options left to try to unite the church and 'win over the protestant community to his side'.[139] Jäger was finally dismissed at the end of October. The *News Chronicle* announced the news with the dramatic headline: 'Hitler Removes Church Goering; Dr. Jaeger Forced to Resign'.[140] In reporting Jäger's dismissal, *The Times* also reported the indefinite postponement of a ceremony in which Müller was to make an oath of loyalty to Hitler.[141]

The dismissal of August Jäger as Nazi commissioner for the Evangelical churches coincided with the release of the southern churches' leading figures, Bishop Meiser and Bishop Würm. *The Times* reported that both 'have been unconditionally released from "house arrest" or other restrictions on their liberty'.[142] *The Times* commented: 'The release is a tactical sign of the new turn in the Protestant Church conflict'.[143] For the southern churches the peak of the church crisis was over. On 31 October 1934, the *News Chronicle* reported the situation 'transformed'; Jäger had been dismissed and Hitler had met with the opposition, specifically Bishop Würm, Bishop Meiser and Bishop Mahahrens (of Hanover) and assured them that orders had been circulated to the police, SA and secret police 'forbidding them to take any further part in Church matters'.[144] The *News Chronicle* explained that if there was no deviation from this order, 'it would appear that the German Evangelical Church has regained its freedom'.[145] The *News Chronicle* reported that this had 'caused the utmost relief among the leaders of the so-called opposition, for they are convinced that once the church is allowed to shape her own destiny the abuses which have existed during recent months will disappear, and there will be a return to the Christian spirit'.[146] But, the newspaper noted, this sense of optimism was felt more by the southern churches than the Confessing Church and the 'rebel' Pastors' Emergency League.[147]

Reich Bishop Müller was left, reported the *Manchester Guardian*, trying to 'preserve the crumbling edifice of his Church government'.[148] The *Observer* reported: 'Deprived of his strong right arm, Dr. Jäger, Reichbishop Müller now finds himself captain of a ship in which most of the crew refuse to sail under his orders.'[149] The *Morning Post* described how Müller's 'authority is being flouted by something like half the Protestant Church', indeed 'the Reichbishop has now suffered the humiliation of having his newspaper banned by the Propaganda Ministry'.[150] As far as Propaganda Minister Joseph Goebbels was concerned, the church conflict 'has been settled in Germany'.[151] As part of his announcement to this effect, Goebbels criticized both the German and foreign press for their reporting of the conflict in the southern churches. The *Manchester Guardian*, reported that Goebbels had declared the German people 'were never interested in what is called the quarrel of the Churches . . . only a malevolent foreigner can be interested in the domestic quarrels of the German people over these matters'.[152] The *Morning Post* printed a different extract from Goebbels statement: 'The Churches must disappear once and for all from our assembly halls. Let them settle their differences in their churches before God.'[153] In December 1934 *The Times* reported that Interior Minister Frick had declared: 'The German nation was sick and tired of the Church conflict and took no interest whatever in the quarrels of the pastors.'[154]

* * *

In fact, the conflict was far from over. Once again, it was *The Times* which led the way with reports on new developments in the conflict. In September 1935, the newspaper reported that the conflict in the churches had taken another turn when former Prussian minister of justice Hanns Kerrl was appointed by Hitler as Reich Minister for Ecclesiastical (Church) Affairs. Müller had been sidelined and Kerrl had been brought in to restore order following the chaos created by the German Christians. As Goebbels's statements made clear, the regime was sick of the conflict. Several decrees swiftly followed, including the 'Law for the Safety of the German Evangelical Church' which, despite its title, made Kerrl, according to *The Times*, 'virtually Church dictator'.[155] *The Times* reported that the new law was seen by the opposition to give the 'Herr Kerrl more rights over the Protestant Church than the Pope has over the Roman Catholic communion'.[156] More decrees followed, reported *The Observer*, that were 'aimed at crushing completely all opposition forces in the Protestant Church struggle'.[157] To that end, Kerrl had so far approached his task with 'real Nazi fervour'.[158] But, *The Observer* commented, the problem 'has proved harder to solve than he imagined'.[159] Already Kerrl had to

> appeal to the Chancellor, who gave him, apparently, permission to use the ultimate Nazi method of dealing with opposition, political and spiritual – dictatorship and force. Thus, after thirty months of conflict, the Nazi State has

nothing more to offer its opponents than threats of prison and concentration camp.[160]

Naturally, the opposition churches opposed new measures to pacify them and bring them into line. Most of their original grievances about interference in church affairs remained. This time the Catholic clergy joined in opposition efforts. In January 1936 the *News Chronicle* reported: 'Breaking a long silence, Protestant pastors and Roman Catholic priests today denounced Nazi religious persecution in vigorous language'.[161] For Protestant pastors, the appointment of Kerrl was seen as an attempt 'to turn the Evangelical Church into a branch of the Nazi Party'.[162] A declaration to this effect was read, in defiance, from 'hundreds of Prussian Protestant pulpits'.[163] In January 1936, Niemöller followed this up with a pamphlet denouncing the actions of Kerrl's Ministry. It was swiftly confiscated by the secret police and, according to *The Times*, the offices and houses of members of the Confessing Church had been searched for copies.[164] The *Manchester Guardian* managed to get a copy and printed an extract:

> The paralysis of the Evangelical Church in Germany must be resisted before it is too late. The freedom of the Church to obey God's Word must be maintained. If this cannot be done without a fight the fault is not with the Confessional Church. . . . We must obey God rather than men.[165]

F. A. Voigt described the pamphlet as 'the boldest attack that has yet been made on the new ecclesiastical policy of the German Dictatorship'.[166] In July 1936, Niemöller again issued another protest on behalf of the Confessing Church. This time the protest was sent directly to Hitler. The *Daily Express*, which obtained a copy, reported that it was specifically concerned with the continued existence of concentration camps, unrestrained action of the secret police and even 'what is held to be the deification of Hitler'.[167] It was not just about opposition to efforts to control or suppress the church but was beginning to move dangerously close to criticism of the regime even if that was not what Niemöller intended.

The regime's response to this latest protest was a new round of arrests. Those arrested were often faced with long periods of imprisonment and harsh treatment. British newspapers reported the arrest of well-known figures and prominent churchmen throughout 1937. After years of struggle against efforts to coordinate and dominate the Protestant churches in Germany, Pastor Niemöller was arrested in July 1937 for, to quote *The Times*, '"slanderous sermons", which for some time past have caused "public unrest"'.[168] He had, according to the *News Chronicle*, been vigorously denouncing the arrest of his colleagues from the pulpit in his church in Dahlem.[169] The *Manchester Guardian* reported that given that most of Niemöller's colleagues had already been arrested, and the pastor himself had been interrogated twice in the previous fortnight, 'it was merely a matter of time before the most widely known figure in the Confessional Church should suffer the same fate'.[170]

The *Morning Post*, *Daily Telegraph*, *News Chronicle* and, of course, *The Times* and *Manchester Guardian* reported Martin Niemöller's arrest. Most, including the *News Chronicle*, quoted the official communique issued by the Nazi government following his arrest. The official announcement also denounced the foreign press, which was not surprising given the sustained coverage of the church situation by several British newspapers. The announcement stated:

> Niemoeller for a long time has made inciting speeches in Church services and lectures, and has made disparaging remarks about leading personalities of the State and movement, and has spread untrue assertions about the Government measures in order to disquiet the population. . . . His statements were a permanent part of the contents of the foreign press hostile to Germany.[171]

With his arrest, reported the *News Chronicle*, 'the whole conflict between the German State and the Christian churches – the Roman Catholic as well as the Protestant – reaches a new stage of severity'.[172] It was an important development in the conflict and came at a time in which two further church decrees were passed, designed to 'spell the end of Church independence'.[173]

The *Manchester Guardian* was highly critical of the actions of the Nazi state in arresting Niemöller and condemned the regime for its ongoing persecution of the churches. The newspaper described the conditions under which Niemöller had lived in the months leading up to his arrest, providing insight into the intimidatory methods employed by the dictatorship:

> The arrest was decided upon many months ago, and Dr. Niemöller has been closely shadowed by agents of the Gestapo. Indeed, his movements were so circumscribed that he has long been in a state resembling arrest – his passport was taken away from him so that he could not leave Germany . . . and he was constantly summoned to the Alexanderplatz, which is the Scotland Yard of Berlin. His telephone calls were overheard, his letters were opened, his associates were questioned. But nothing could have been discovered to justify legal proceedings against him. Not that this would deter the police and the judiciary of the Third Realm in the ordinary way; those who have been sentenced or sent to concentration camps without a sentence, even when there has been no basis for a charge, are numerous in Germany. But Dr. Niemöller is well known both in his own country and throughout the world.[174]

The Times provided detailed reports about the wave of arrests that accompanied Niemöller's. In mid-July 1937, the newspaper reported that while some pastors had been released, thirty-four were in custody, including 'a woman secretary of the Dahlem Parish Council'.[175] Niemöller was released from Moabit prison but was immediately rearrested by the secret police 'and taken to police headquarters in Alexanderplatz'.[176] In August, *The Times* reported that more arrests had been made following a Protestant demonstration in Dahlem (the Berlin suburb where Niemöller's church was located). The arrests number 150, reported *The Times*, 'of whom 48, mostly pastors, have been detained'.[177] As the correspondent reported on 3 August 1937: 'The cat-and-mouse game, as played by the authorities with variations, individually and collectively, with the Confessional Movement in the German Evangelical Church, continues steadily.'[178]

The Times' coverage of the church conflict had been closely monitored by the German authorities. In an attempt to silence *The Times*, the newspaper's Berlin correspondent Norman Ebbutt was expelled from Germany in August 1937. The Nazi authorities tried to claim that 'Norman Ebbutt has for years past conducted his Correspondence in a manner exclusively hostile to Germany, and has abused the hospitality extended to him.'[179] Goebbels's mouthpiece, the newspaper *Angriff*, alleged:

> There are a whole lot of foreign correspondents, among them Anglo-Saxons, whose work does not stop at the transmission of distorted reports, but whose far more extensive activity consists in a constant interference in the internal affairs of Germany.... This work has nothing to do with journalism, but this close entanglement of foreign correspondents with State-opposing groups is neither more nor less than counter-revolutionary activity. Many of them, if they knew what we know about them, would probably leave voluntarily, by the next train, this country whose indulgence and hospitality they abuse in such an unseemly way.[180]

Ebbutt vigorously defended his work as Berlin correspondent attacking statements made against him in the German press, and by German authorities. He believed it was his reports on the church struggle that had got him expelled. He called the allegations against him 'nonsense' and argued that the Nazis had come up with these lies 'because convincing objects to correspondents on journalistic grounds cannot be found'.[181]

Ebbutt's expulsion was covered widely by international newspapers. It garnered international attention and was condemned by the international press. French newspaper *Journal des Débats* (quoted in *The Times*) praised Ebbutt's reporting, agreeing with him that it was his reports on the church conflict which had seen him expelled:

> He is particularly disliked because of the admirable way in which he has kept himself informed of the wave of religious persecution now surging in Germany. Thanks to his telegrams, which we often quote, the chief events in the war against Christianity have now become known. It is hoped in Berlin that, once his voice has been silenced, opinion abroad will be kept ignorant of all that they want to hide. The regard and admiration which all his colleagues have for this great journalist can only be increased by the treatment to which he is now subjected.[182]

For the *Manchester Guardian* Ebbutt's expulsion was an alarming warning to other foreign correspondents living and working in Germany. Working conditions were hard enough, and now 'naked reprisals have been introduced'.[183] The *Manchester Guardian*'s Berlin correspondent explained to readers:

> the outlook generally for the treatment of foreign correspondents is highly unfavourable. Whether further retaliation against British correspondents will be made is not yet known. . . . the impression is gained that the attitude of the authorities will be even more severe in the future than hitherto, and that reasons even slighter, judged at least by British standards, may be found for further expulsion of foreign journalists.[184]

Norman Ebbutt would not write for *The Times* again. Following his return to Britain he suffered a major stroke and spent years recovering. However, despite not having Ebbutt's expertise, the newspaper continued to print articles about the church conflict as did the *Observer*, *Manchester Guardian* and *News Chronicle*.

* * *

The trial of Pastor Martin Niemöller was reported as the climax of the Evangelical Church conflict by the British press. The British press keenly reported the trial, especially the verdict. The court acquitted Niemöller of the crime of treason against the state but found him guilty, in the words of the *New Statesman and Nation*, of 'making pulpit pronouncement "disturbing to public order"'.[185] He was sentenced to seven months and a small fine. Since he had been confined to prison for longer than the prison term handed down to him, his sentence was deemed time served. This meant that the pastor was to leave the court as a free man. British newspapers applauded the verdict. The *Manchester Guardian* reported: 'There can be no question that the judgment is in the interest of justice.'[186] The case demonstrated 'police rule in Germany is not absolute'.[187] However, the victory for the pastor was short-lived. He was swiftly rearrested outside the courthouse by the Gestapo on Hitler's personal order. The *New Statesman and Nation* was outraged at this decision: 'What justice, even in a *gleichgeschaltet* [Nazi coordinated] German court, had to concede to Pastor Niemöller, the Thuggery of Nazism has taken away.'[188] The newspaper reported:

> Unluckily for him, the court decided that his preliminary detention awaiting trial should be deducted from the sentence and ordered his immediate release. The sequel was his seizure by the Gestapo and his despatch, without further judicial procedure, to the horrors of a concentration camp.[189]

The *News Chronicle*'s assessment of Niemöller's re-arrest was similarly scathing:

> The leniency of the sentence, in contrast with the boasted severity of Nazi justice, was so striking that the first instinct of public opinion outside Germany was to congratulate both Dr. Niemoeller on a moral victory and also the German authorities on what looked like their ability to exercise moderation. Mercy is so infrequent in a dictator State that one could almost overlook the fact that, by democratic standards, Dr. Niemoeller had committed no offence for which even a formal conviction was appropriate. The Nazis are, however, determined to correct at the earliest possible moment the impression that they are capable of a gracious act.... Released from jail, he is to be sent to a concentration camp. So German "trials" are not so different after all from the judicial farces of Moscow. Justice in Germany, as in Russia, is apparently no more than a camp follower of the dominant party.[190]

Niemöller was taken to Sachsenhausen concentration camp.[191] He remained a political prisoner until the end of the war. The *Manchester Guardian* reminded readers that the imprisonment of the regime's opponents in concentration camps was an old tactic used by the Nazis, similar to measures introduced and used during the terror in 1933 and 1934. The *Manchester Guardian* explained: 'No charges need to be made against him and he cannot claim trial. Political prisoners in the concentration camps are usually detained by this extra-legal machinery.'[192] Voigt commented that the imprisonment of Niemöller was a return to the 'old tactics' of the Gestapo whereby a well-known figure in opposition to the regime was imprisoned, as a political prisoner, for a lengthy time 'until he has been forgotten by the outside world just as Thälmann [the Communist leader] has been forgotten'.[193] The *New Statesman and Nation* commented:

> There, in the tortures of indefinite 'preventive custody', a brave man who fought for his country and whose only offence against 'patriotism' is that he demanded public toleration of religious belief, will rot lest God should steal a shred of

veneration from the Führer. Heil, Hitler! The engulfment of a once civilised nation in the code of Caligula would seem to have approached completion.[194]

Martin Niemöller's imprisonment marked the end of united and coherent opposition. This was not to say that opposition was crushed, but the Confessional Church without Niemöller was a movement that had lost its confidence. Prior to the trial the *Daily Telegraph and Morning Post* had commented: 'The continued imprisonment of Pastor Niemoeller has had the desired effect of placing a handicap on the resistance of the Confessional Church to State interference.'[195] A 1938 Gestapo report noted that the Confessional Church was feeling a 'weariness' in their struggle and had lost their sense of purpose.[196] But in all this Niemöller was not forgotten. In July 1938 the *Manchester Guardian* marked a year since Niemöller had first been arrested with an article about the pastor. The *Manchester Guardian* reported that the German authorities have been 'surprised at the concern shown in Germany, but the number of deputations which have asked for his release, and by the kind of men who have formed these deputations'.[197] Despite attempts by the regime to silence the Confessing Church, 'the German people, and especially those faithful to the Confessional Church, can be trusted not to forget Pastor Niemöller'.[198]

The British press continued to report the church conflict in late 1938 and early 1939, albeit more sporadically. At this crucial stage in the relationship between Britain and Germany and at a time when the peace and stability of Europe was at stake, British newspapers like the *News Chronicle*, *The Times* and *Manchester Guardian* still reported developments in the struggle over the churches. Many British newspapers were now focusing more on the persecution of the Jews under Nazi control as the situation became more barbaric and brutal, especially following the *Anschluss* with Austria in 1938, but occasional articles about resistant pastors or state measures against the churches still appeared.

* * *

In the 1930s the British press was committed to reporting tension and conflict between the Nazi government and the churches in Germany. Reports began to appear shortly after Hitler's appointment as Chancellor as the Nazi Party began making moves against other political parties, including the Centre Party. The clash with the Catholic Church was over relatively quickly, with the signing of the Concordat in July 1933. There were infringements of the Concordat and complaints by the Vatican about the treatment of Catholics in Germany, which was reported by many British newspapers, but by 1934 the focus of reports on the churches in Germany centred on the struggle taking place in the Protestant churches.

Most newspapers, at one point or another, printed something about the Evangelical Church conflict. Some of these articles were sensational pieces that examined Nazi conceptions of Christianity. Others were informative but sporadic. But newspapers like *The Times, Manchester Guardian, Morning Post, Daily Telegraph* and *The Spectator* committed themselves to following and reporting the church struggle in detail. The *Manchester Guardian, News Chronicle* and *New Statesman and Nation* wholeheartedly denounced the actions of the German Christians, the Gestapo and the state. They were scathing in their assessment of the conflict. For these newspapers the treatment of the churches in Germany was an example of the brutal methods of the dictatorship. *The Times* was more detail orientated, with less editorializing. Ebbutt was wary of sensationalizing the news from Germany. He argued against 'giving the soft touch' to the news from Germany, lest the paper be accused of fabricating or exaggerating the situation. However, his detailed reports on the religious conflict led to his expulsion in 1937.

While reporting styles differed, the British press demonstrated a keen interest in reporting the church conflict in Germany. For the press, the struggle of the Protestant churches against attempts to control and redefine the church was a real religious struggle – it was a struggle over faith, religious doctrine and membership. Furthermore, protests by the churches against Nazi (and state) interference was seen as real and recognizable opposition to the state. For that, it deserved prominence in the British press. The press did get confused at times mistaking opposition to infringements on the freedom of the church for opposition to the Nazi regime itself. The Pastor's Emergency League and the Confessing Church were not in opposition to Hitler or the regime; for them, their opposition was religious and ideological. At no point was it the aim of the opposition pastors (or their organizations) to become leaders in political opposition to the Nazi dictatorship. Nor did they intend to organize any resistance to the tyranny taking place under the Nazis.[199] Their primary purpose was preserving the Christian faith against what they saw as heresy.[200] The church conflict has not been given as much prominence in the historical literature as other events, but the British press took as much interest in this conflict as they did in the destruction of democracy, the establishment of a Hitlerite dictatorship and the persecution of political opponents and, increasingly, the persecution and subjugation of Germany's Jewish population.

* * *

7

The Nazi persecution of the Jews

Anti-Semitism was central to Nazi Party doctrine. British correspondents, living and working in Germany, had observed and reported the rise of anti-Semitism in the country during the Weimar Republic, focusing, in particular, on the role of anti-Semitism in German politics. After Hitler came to power in January 1933, the *Manchester Guardian* discussed the possibility that the Jews would be the next to be targeted because 'Anti-Semitism has, of course, always been a cardinal point in Nazi propaganda'.[1] The *Daily Express* reported the day before the 5 March elections that the 'exodus of the Jews of Germany has begun'.[2] Many Jews had sought refuge in Czechoslovakia and Austria, and more were sure to follow: 'Faced with the menace of an anti-Semitic reign of terror in the event of a victory for the Hitlerites in to-morrow's elections, many Jews have already left Germany, and large numbers are preparing for voluntary exile.'[3] The *Daily Express* observed:

> Nothing since the mass persecution of the Jews in Czarist Russia has equalled the campaign of anti-Semitic hatred by the German Nazis. Threats of physical violence and undisguised incitements to wholesale 'pogroms' have been a feature of thousands of inflammatory speeches by the leaders and rank and file of the Nazi party.[4]

Following the election, the Nazis sought to consolidate their control over Germany. This included a brutal campaign of repression and violence against their 'enemies', including Jews. The terror and the violence against the Jews in Germany were reported internationally. A report by F. A. Voigt, special correspondent for the *Manchester Guardian*, observed: 'The anti-Semitic outrages of the last four weeks are far more horrible than could reasonably have been imagined at first. Nothing like them has been known in Germany for generations.'[5] The *Jewish Chronicle* pointed out that while the violence might not be an 'actual pogrom' 'the individual outrages – probably not all of them known – amount, in the aggregate, to something perilously approaching one'.[6] Voigt described the campaign against the Jews:

> Jewish shops have been closed and raided, Jewish homes have been searched and thrown into disorder, and hundreds of Jews have been beaten and robbed. . . . The worst excesses in Berlin occurred on March 9, most of the victims living in the Grenadierstrasse. Many Jews were beaten by Brown Shirts until the blood streamed down their heads and faces and their backs and shoulders were bruised.[7]

The violence was accompanied by a wave of dismissals as Jews were removed from their positions at universities, medical practices and law courts by SA men, local Nazi leaders and Nazi students. 'What is to become of them no one knows', Voigt reported. He commented: 'It is a most frightful comment on German civilisation that Jews should be escaping from Germany into Poland. Poland since Hitler has been Chancellor is undoubtedly a country of greater freedom than Germany.'[8] It was hoped that Hitler's call for a halt to the violence would make a difference and reduce excesses committed. But, reported the *Jewish Chronicle*, 'Even if the immediate threat of violence to person and property is lifted, the menace of the bloodless pogrom, the avowed policy of degradation and gradual pauperisation, will still remain'.[9]

The violence against the Jews was condemned by their co-religionists around the world, including the *Jewish Chronicle*. The newspaper noted that 'foreign opinion is beginning to find a voice'.[10] Hitler was conscious of foreign opinion; evidence of this could be found in his instructions calling the Storm Troops to order. But more pressure on the German government was required. The *Jewish Chronicle* called on its readers appealing for them to 'borrow from the Germans their weapon of the boycott and turn it against them'.[11] The newspaper put to readers the following declaration:

> If only half the Jewries of the world would wield it vigorously, if they would refuse to buy German goods, ignore German shipping and watering places, avoid all fresh participation in German finance . . . they would show that that force which the Prussian mentality alone understands, is not the possession of tyrants alone.[12]

Such a boycott was feared by German authorities to have 'serious economic consequences for German manufacturers and exporters', the *News Chronicle* reported.[13] Thus far, 'No central organisation has been formed yet to start any concerted action', but a number of businesses in London had already instituted a boycott of German goods.¹⁴ It was certainly not the widespread and all-encompassing action the *Jewish Chronicle* hoped for. In late March 1933, the Board of Deputies of British Jews convened for a closed meeting in London to discuss a response to the Nazi violence against their co-religionists in Germany. Many British newspapers reported the meeting, including the *Daily Mirror* which reported that the board had decided it would take 'no part in boycotts against Germany, leaving them to individual action'.¹⁵ Neville Laski, chairman of the Board, declared that 'Jews were not at war with Germany'.¹⁶ The board 'decided to resist in whatever way possible the discrimination in Germany against citizens of the Jewish faith and to hold a meeting of protest in London'.¹⁷ The lack of united action by world Jewry sent a message to the Hitler government. A key opportunity to demonstrate to Hitler and the Nazi government that action against the Jews would not be tolerated was missed.

The Nazis responded to the international condemnation of their actions against the Jews in Germany by announcing their own boycott of German Jewish businesses. In doing so, they denounced the foreign press and international Jewry. Acting Prussian Reich governor Hermann Göring reportedly declared in an address to foreign correspondents: 'The Government is shocked, indignant, and indeed speechless at the reports which have been written abroad about Jews in Germany'.¹⁸ In an interview with the *Daily Mail*'s Rothay Reynolds, Ernst Haansstaengel, a German-American businessman and 'one of Hitler's closest cooperators', argued 'reports of mishandling of Jews are barefaced lies'.¹⁹ *The Times* reported Hitler's address to his cabinet: 'International Jewry, however, must realise that a Jewish war against Germany would recoil with full force against German Jewry'.²⁰ The boycott of Jewish businesses was necessary, Hitler declared, 'as it would otherwise have burst forth spontaneously and might have taken undesirable forms'.²¹ The *Daily Express* also reported Hitler's threats; the Jews of Germany 'would be forced to recognise that a Jewish war against Germany would only hit the Jews in Germany'.²² As the *Morning Post* reported, the boycott was 'clearly intended to use the Jews and Socialists of Germany as hostages for the good behaviour of world public opinion'.²³ The boycott was to be arranged and carried out by the Nazi Party, not the German government, but as the *Morning Post* explained, 'Herr Hitler has frequently asserted that nothing happens in the Party without his knowing and desiring it'.²⁴

A wave of propaganda accompanied preparations for the boycott, which included placards displayed on the streets of Berlin declaring: 'The Jews of the whole world want to destroy Germany, German people defend yourselves; Do not buy from Jews'.²⁵ The *Daily Mail* commented: 'Not since the Jews were driven out of Germany in the Middle Ages . . . have the Jews had to face such an onslaught.'[26] Jewish shops and offices throughout Germany were to have 'a black placard with a yellow spot as was done in the Jewish ghettoes of the Middle Ages'.[27] Even before the scheduled boycott on 1 April, disturbances had broken out. Both the *Morning Post* and *The Times* reported that boycotts were already in place in some regional areas in Germany.

The boycott of Jewish businesses was held for one day, but the Nazis threatened its resumption if foreign criticism did not cease. As far as the *Manchester Guardian*'s special correspondent F. A. Voigt was concerned, foreign criticism was of little consequence because

> The world-wide protest against Hitlerites anti-Semitism is by no means the cause of the renewed drive against the Jews. That drive was intended in any case, and has long been part of the Hitlerite programme. The protest has only been exploited by the Hitlerite Dictatorship to justify that drive in the eyes of the German public – indeed, to make it commendable.[28]

Essentially, Voigt explained, 'the Jews in Germany are being made to suffer afresh not only according to plan but also with the intention of making the Jews outside Germany stop protesting. The German Government, in other words, is simply practising blackmail.'[29] *The Times* argued that since the 'racialism' of the Nazi programme was 'notorious', 'the Nazi leaders have no right to be indignant because Jews in other countries have taken their threats and their programme seriously'.[30]

Initial coverage of the boycott in British newspapers reported that it, to quote *The Times*, 'was completely effective . . . [it] completely paralysed Jewish business life'.[31] The *Daily Mail*'s Rothay Reynolds described the scenes in Berlin: 'It was the order, precision, and tranquillity of this action against a minority which made the greatest impression on detached observers.'[32] He wrote: 'Through the windows could be seen the shop assistants ready to serve customers, but nowhere did I see anybody enter . . . All the great stores in Berlin were closed except Wertheims and the Karstadt Store, which were saved by the retirement of all its Jewish directors and the dismissal of all Jewish employees.'[33] The *Daily Telegraph*'s correspondent reported his attempts to enter a Jewish shop, which was prevented by a Nazi guard.[34] Many British newspapers included photographs of the boycott; these included photographs of placards on Jewish shops and Brown Shirts patrolling the streets or standing guard outside shops.[35] One of the most widely circulated photographs was an image of a Jew being paraded through the streets of Chemnitz, in Saxony, for refusing to obey a Nazi order to clean the streets. The *News Chronicle, Jewish Chronicle, Daily Mirror* and *Manchester Guardian* all carried this photo.[36]

The response of British newspapers to the boycott was predominantly critical. For instance, a leading editorial in the *Daily Telegraph* stated it was

> certainly not a victory of Reason or Judgment. The day will come when the German people will wish the senseless story expunged from their annals, and will wonder what madness drove the leaders of the Triumphant Hitlerite Revolution to choose so shameful a way of celebrating the dawn of a new era.[37]

But there was also some misguided analysis in the *Daily Telegraph*. In contrast to the editorial featured in the newspaper, the *Daily Telegraph*'s diplomatic correspondent misguidedly ascribed the boycott as part of a 'Nazi-Jewish conflict'.[38] It was not the only newspaper to report the boycott as a part of a conflict between Nazis and Jews. However, special correspondent F. A. Voigt of the *Manchester Guardian* responded to this interpretation with some sarcasm:

> The German Jews, unarmed to the teeth and numbering one in a hundred of the population, were defeated by the armed Brown Shirts, supported by the police, the regular army, and more than half the total electorate. But their co-religionists in the five continents rallied to their relief and, bonding world opinion, especially Anglo-American opinion, to their will, launched an attack of defamatory libel against the Brown Army and the Hitler regime, spreading tales about atrocities and about a Brown Terror and other emanations of the Semitic mind so as to besmirch and smother that blameless regime amid the contempt and execrations of mankind.[39]

The *Manchester Guardian* closely followed the persecution of the Jews in 1933. The newspaper accurately captured the scope and intensity of the persecution of the Jews in early 1933. On 7 April 1933, the *Manchester Guardian* reported that the persecution of the Jews had increasingly turned to what they called the 'simple savagery of depriving them of the means by which they live'.[40] That day, in Germany, the Law for the Restoration of the Professional Civil Service (or Civil Service decree) was passed. The law prohibited the employment of any Jews in the civil service. It would have a profound impact on the lives of Jewish civil servants. The *Manchester Guardian* outlined the new law:

> Except for the few Jewish officials who were appointed before August 1, 1914, or who fought in the Great War, or whose sons or fathers fought, all Jews are to be dismissed and are in future to be debarred from the Civil Service. This law will apply to anyone of whose four grandparents one is a Jew.[41]

The new law, which would be applied not only to the Reich but also to the federal states, would:

> [P]revent Jews from being judges, professors, schoolmasters, railway officials, or from occupying any of the innumerable positions controlled by the State; combined with the persecution of the same people in business, in medicine, and all the professions, it will degrade them into a helot class with no means but the lowest of earning its living, exposed entirely to the brutality of the Nazis.[42]

For the *Manchester Guardian* the decree would take the 'degradation of Jews to second-class citizens' a step further.[43] The Jews, the *Manchester Guardian* declared, 'are scapegoats who are suffering intolerably for crimes they never committed'.[44]

The Times and *Morning Post* also reported the decree, but in passing, amid other articles on the situation in Germany. But the *Jewish Chronicle*, like the *Manchester Guardian*, understood the significance of the decree. The newspaper announced news of the decree with the headline: 'Starvation for 600,000 Jews – According to Plan; Caught Like Rats in a Trap'.[45] The persecution of the Jews essentially fell 'under two heads: (a) No Jew is to be employed in Germany (b) No Jew is to be allowed to leave Germany'.[46] For the *Jewish Chronicle*: 'It becomes increasingly difficult to consider Hitler's anti-Semitic policy as anything but Sadism.'[47] Europe had seen anti-Semitism and anti-Semitic policy before but this was a 'most refined cruelty', explained the *Manchester Guardian*.[48]

But what, asked the *Manchester Guardian*, could be done? The British government had already made it clear that it would not interfere. Sir John Simon, secretary of state for foreign affairs, declared that under the Covenant of the League of Nations, nothing could be done.[49] But, remarked the *Manchester Guardian*, the British government could 'quietly convey to the German Government the news of what this country feels about the terroristic system, and can do so in such a way that the German Government will have no difficulty in understanding what is meant'.[50] However Prime Minister Ramsey MacDonald, after being pressed by Conservative MP John Morris about whether it was possible to express 'strong feeling' against the persecution of the Jews, replied, 'it is a matter of discretion, and we are quite willing at the moment to leave it where it is'.[51] Of this the *Manchester Guardian* was incredulous:

> When in a great country freedom of thought, of speech, of life, is going down in terror, is that all that a Prime Minister of England has to say! Why was the boycott of the Jews suspended and not revived? Essentially because of international opinion.[52]

All British newspapers covered the initial outburst of anti-Semitic acts by the Hitler regime. After that, coverage was sporadic, with the exception of *The Times*, *Manchester Guardian*, and *Jewish Chronicle*. It might be expected that the *Jewish Chronicle* would regularly update its readership on the plight of its fellow Jews in Germany but *The Times* and *Manchester Guardian* also provided extensive coverage of anti-Semitic outrages.[53] Articles on the 'clean-up' of German industry, business and professions often appeared daily, and at the very least weekly.

Universities were hit especially hard, with the assault led by Nazi students. In April and May 1933 *The Times* and the *Manchester Guardian* reported pressure on Jewish professors to retire from their posts, as well as the exclusion of many Jewish students from universities, including, for instance, the exclusion of Jewish medical students from the University of Frankfurt.[54] The Nazi students' assault also extended to 'Un-German' texts and books. On 8 May 1933, Nazi students announced an act 'against the un-German spirit', in nineteen university towns throughout Germany.[55] In Berlin, for instance, students raided local libraries and stormed the Institute for Sexual Science seizing what books and manuscripts that had been left from an earlier raid. The books and printed materials were thrown into a pile in Opera Square and, in front of thousands of spectators, were set alight. Both the *Manchester Guardian* and *The Times* reported the book burnings with the latter reporting that as many as 20,000 books were destroyed.[56]

The announcement of the Civil Service decree and the drive against Jews that accompanied it influenced many clubs and associations which followed with their own restrictions on Jewish members. The process of driving Jews out of German public life was documented carefully by *The Times*. At the end of May 1933, *The Times* reported a proposal by Dr Neuendorff, the new president of the *Deutsche Turnerschaft*, to exclude Jews from the 12,852 gymnastic clubs in Germany, in line with the changes already taking place in the civil service.[57] By July 1933, *The Times* was reporting similar proposals for chess clubs. The *Manchester Guardian*, at this time, also reported the Aryanization of sporting associations, including tennis clubs in April 1933.[58] At the same time the newspaper reported how the purge of Jews had extended to engineering and the sciences.[59]

Reports in *The Times* were detailed and factual with reports appearing with a frequency that few newspapers could rival. But the *Manchester Guardian* also stood out for its reporting. The *Manchester Guardian* firmly denounced the Nazis' attack on democracy, the terrorization of the Nazis' political opponents and the subjugation and persecution of the Jews. Special correspondent Voigt was characteristically outspoken about the persecution of the Jews. In July 1933 he reported: 'the elimination of the Jews from trade, industry, and the liberal professions, as well as the general boycott (both legal and extra-legal) grows more and more systematic, more and more ruthless, so that the complete annihilation of the entire German Jewry is approaching nearer'.[60] Even though violence against Jews had lessened:

> [T]he system now exercised all over Germany, and in such a manner that there is hardly a single Jew who can escape from it, is far worse than this crude Terror, far more inhuman, far more tragic in all its consequences. An entire community of over half a million persons is being coldly and deliberately reduced to ruin, destitution, and hunger.[61]

Not all newspapers were sympathetic to the plight of the Jews. The *Daily Mail*'s proprietor, Viscount Rothermere, was highly critical of the 'influence' the Jews had on German politics and the press. He wrote in his now infamous article, 'Youth Triumphant', that the German nation 'was rapidly falling under the control of its alien elements'.[62] He alleged in the article that 'In the last days of the pre-Hitler regime there were twenty times as many Jewish Government officials in Germany as had existed before the war'. Moreover, 'Israelites of international attachments were insinuating themselves into key positions in the German administrative machine'.[63] Three ministries had direct contact with the press, wrote Rothermere, but 'in each case the official responsible for conveying new and interpreting policy to the public was a Jew'.[64] It was 'from such abuses that Hitler has freed Germany'.[65] Hitler, 'By mobilising the youth of the country in support of a vigorous national policy', had succeeded in converting 'a despondent and embittered nation into one radiant with hope and optimism'.[66] As far as Rothermere was concerned, the notion that the Nazis 'are scowling young bullies who reign by terror over a cowed and resentful population', was a 'direct inversion of the facts'; 'I am convinced by the testimony of my own eyes and ears that the sympathies of the overwhelming mass of the German population are strongly with this organisation of stalwart young patriots'.[67] The *Daily Mail* was an exceptional case; no other British newspaper in this study went as far as Viscount Rothermere in declaring support and admiration for Hitler and his movement. Rothermere was later to distance himself from Hitler's regime and Mosley's British Union of Fascists, of whom he was allied to for a while, following the groups violence at the Olympia Rally in London, and the Röhm purge in Germany in 1934.[68]

By contrast, the reporting of another popular newspaper led to the expulsion of its correspondent from Germany. The *Daily Express*' coverage of the persecution of the Jews was sporadic but highly critical of the Nazis' anti-Semitic policies. In late May 1934, Berlin correspondent Pembroke Stephens wrote of the distress of German Jews: 'Robbed of work, denied civic privileges in a country which despises them, what is the German Jew to do but follow the brutal advice of officials: "The best thing you can do is die".'[69] The article, printed following Stephens's arrest (and brief imprisonment) in Aken near Dessau, caught the attention of Nazi authorities.[70] Stephens was released after his arrest in Aken but was rearrested and then expelled from Germany. The *Daily Express* reported that his expulsion was the result of his article about the persecution of the Jews.[71] For Stephens, writing for the *Daily Express*, it was his job to:

> [T]ell the truth about Germany, even at the risk of imprisonment and expulsion . . . After my arrest a fortnight ago . . . there were two alternatives – either silence, humility, obeisance to officialdom, or the risk of continuing my work as if nothing had happened at all. I chose the second course and expulsion was the almost inevitable result.[72]

He argued: 'they [Nazis] blame me for lying when the only fault that can be laid to me is that I have been too blunt in telling the truth.'[73] Stephens followed this article with another, entitled 'Menace to Europe', in which he called Germany the 'mad dog of Europe'.[74] Stephens did not hold back, issuing a vigorous denunciation of the Nazi persecution of the Jews:

> The world revolts against the merciless war of extermination against the Jews. This war is no longer a vendetta against the guilty Jews of Germany, the cheats, the thieves, the corrupt, but a war against half a million people, including good and bad, a war against innocent women and children who have done nothing wrong but be born Jews.[75]

Following his expulsion from Germany, Pembroke Stephens would go on to work for the *Daily Telegraph and Morning Post* with whom he would cover the Spanish civil war and the Japanese invasion of China. On 11 November 1937 he was killed by machine-gun fire while observing the Japanese attack on Shanghai from a water-tower in Nantao.[76] The *Observer*, in reporting his death, wrote that 'journalism lost a gallant figure who maintained its best traditions'.[77]

* * *

The British press reported renewed campaigns against the Jews in Germany in mid-1934 (prior to the Röhm purge) and mid-1935. During this period, however, the British press regarded the struggle of the Protestant churches against attempts at Nazi coordination as more pressing. But, in 1935, it was the disgusting rhetoric of Nazi thug and notorious antisemite Julius Streicher's newspaper, *Der Stürmer*, that captured the attention of British newspapers. This latest campaign, according to the *New Statesman and Nation*, 'surpasses in blood-thirstiness and obscenity anything that even Streicher himself had ever attempted before'.[78] Some of the farcical allegations made in the Streicher's *Der Stürmer* included that the Jews sold 'wine coloured with Christian blood'; that the Talmud condoned murder and homosexuality and that 'Jewish families entice "blonde Aryan girls into their houses to minister to the sexual needs of their young boys"'.[79] Even though a 'certain section of German public opinion is quite definitely disgusted with the revolting vulgarity and sadistic brutality of Julius Streicher's anti-Semitic activity in Franconia', 'It would probably be too optimistic to claim that this section of German public opinion is entirely free from this anti-Semitism'.[80]

This newest anti-Semitic campaign was not just directed by Streicher. The *New Statesman and Nation* also reported anti-Semitic articles which had appeared in Propaganda Minister Joseph Goebbels's newspaper, *Angriff*. Furthermore, reported the *New Statesman and Nation*, 'The Streicher method of hounding personally every German who has any dealings with a Jew is being introduced into the whole of Bavaria and the entire Reich'.[81] Indeed, the boycott against Jewish businesses had been revived with a 'force not known since April, 1933'.[82] The newspaper reported: 'Jews in Germany, who for some time were left in peace, are now facing once more a new anti-Semitic drive with all the ferocity, pitilessness and brutality of the drive which shook the world two years ago.'[83]

Violence against the Jews escalated in July and August 1935. In mid-July, the *Morning Post* reported outbreaks of violence in Kurfurstendamm, one of the most famous avenues in Berlin, where 'brutal Jew baiting and window smashing' had been carried out by Storm Troops.[84] Condemned by the German public, the Nazi government issued a statement blaming 'dark elements', which were 'seeking to discredit the State and the movement'.[85] This was rather surprising, explained the *Morning Post*, because 'it is known that the Storm troopers acted not only on the encouragement of the official Nazi papers "Angriff" and "Voelkischer Beobachter", but also on the instructions from a high party official'.[86] The *Morning Post* explained that if the government wanted to end the outrages all they had to do was ban *Der Stürmer* which had been 'conducting a vigorous campaign to extend the circulation of its weekly incitements to violence and terrorism'.[87] Then in August 1934 Streicher addressed a 'monster rally of anti-Semites at the Sport Palace'.[88] With an audience of approximately 15,000, 'Germany's leading Jew-baiter' attacked the foreign press for its coverage of the violence in Kurfurstendamm in July 1934: 'A demonstration . . . is immediately described as a pogrom. What shamelessness! What provocation! If anything disagreeable to a Jew happens, a cry is raised at once. "What concern is it of yours", he asked, turning to the Press, "when we clean up our own house"?[89] Jewish leaders had issued warnings to 'all Jewish citizens to stay indoors', but a number of Jews were assaulted and beaten in the streets.[90]

In September 1935, the anti-Semitic drive that had gripped Germany culminated in new legislation which, according to the *Daily Express*, 'sent the Jews in Germany back to the Middle Ages'.[91] This legislation, commonly known as the Nuremberg laws, transformed Jews 'into a class of Untouchables in a "legal" sense', according to the *Jewish Chronicle*.[92] The new laws, reported *The Times*, included the following:

> [B]esides prohibiting mixed marriages, sexual relations between Germans and Jews, and the employment in Jewish households of German women under the age of 45, forbids Jews to fly the German flag, but permits them to fly the Jewish colours. Connected with it is the law providing for two classes of citizens. The Jew can never attain the status of a full citizen (*Reichsbürger*), which is reserved for persons of Aryan blood. He will be classed as a *Staatsangehöriger* (belonging to the State).[93]

For most British newspapers the new laws were, in the words of *The Times*, 'merely a legalization of a state of affairs already in existence'.[94] For months past, reported *The Times*, 'mixed marriages have been made impossible in many parts of the country by reason of judicial rulings supplemented by the arbitrary decrees of Nazi regional and local leaders'.[95] Similarly the *Jewish Chronicle* reported: 'The Laws, it is clear, add little, beyond the stamp of officialdom . . . The Jews are already pariahs in fact, if not in name.'[96] *The Spectator* added to this explaining the laws 'merely gives legal sanction to a prohibition which has long been enforced wither by rulings in the courts of decrees issued by Nazi leaders, to say nothing of lawless methods of forcible persuasion'.[97]

The British press overwhelmingly condemned the laws. The exception to this was the *Daily Mail*, which made no comment. The *Daily Express* declared: 'This renewed attack on Jews in Germany, not because of any individual offence, but in a blind antagonism to a race, is merely bestial.'[98] And the *Manchester Guardian* reported: 'What is happening to the German Jews, and is now being legalised, is that they are being put into a permanent quarantine. They are treated as a source of moral and physical contamination and are being at the same time segregated and slowly exterminated.'[99]

Even though most newspapers reported the announcement of the Nuremberg laws, and condemned them, they spent little time discussing the laws in depth. The *Manchester Guardian* was critical of the lack of attention the laws received, stating in October 1935, the laws had 'hardly received the attention outside of Germany that they deserved'.[100] There could be two reasons for this, the article explained – first, the press (and Europe) was occupied with the Abyssinian crisis; second, there was the belief the 'Jewish laws hardly bring any change in practice, but only legalise a status which has already been in existence for some time'.[101] But, declared the *Manchester Guardian*, the significance of the laws should not be underestimated: 'the new laws are of great fundamental importance, as they bring back a state of affairs that seemed to belong to the past, at least in Europe'.[102] And, there was another point of concern, reported the *Manchester Guardian*. The Jewish inhabitants of the Saar were included in the new law, despite the German government signing a treaty 'declaring that for one year after the return there would be no discrimination against any inhabitant of this territory for reasons of political opinion, race, or religion'.[103] The Nuremberg laws breached this treaty; the treaty was signed 'voluntarily . . . and already the Hitler Government has broken it'.[104] Other British newspapers failed to pick up on this, turning their attention instead to the Italian invasion of Abyssinia. For the *Manchester Guardian* though, it was concerning that Hitler thought so little of the 'break of faith'.[105]

* * *

Most British newspapers only returned to reporting the persecution of the Jews when Germany occupied Austria in 1938. In the meantime, coverage of the Jewish situation in Germany was intermittent. In 1936, for instance, the regime was careful to avoid any excessive violence or persecution in the lead-up to the Olympic Games which were held in Germany that year. The *Manchester Guardian* and *The Times* printed more articles than any other British newspaper, but even they were mostly preoccupied with news of the churches (which was still an evolving situation), and the increasing territorial demands of the German government. This changed with the invasion of Austria by Germany on 12 March 1938. The invasion, to enforce the *Anschluss*, was accompanied by a vigorous campaign of persecution and violence against Austria's Jews, particularly against the Jewish residents of Vienna. The *Anschluss* was reported widely by British newspapers, but it was the cruel and violent mistreatment of Austria's Jewish population that captured the attention of British correspondents.

Details about the excesses committed by Nazis against Austria's Jews were revealed by British newspapers towards the end of March 1938. The *Manchester Guardian* and the *Daily Express* reported that the looting of Jewish shops began with the influx of German troops (and Nazis) into Vienna. The correspondent for the *New Statesman and Nation* witnessed Jews being forced to scrub, 'Vote Yes for Schuschnigg' off the pavements 'while Nazis stood round jeering and cursing'.[106] For the newspaper, the 'plight of Vienna's enormous Jewish population is indescribable'.[107] The *Daily Express*' correspondent was told by many Germans that 'the Vienna terror for Jews is far worse than it ever was in Berlin'.[108] Jews were in hiding, correspondent Dennis Clarke wrote, describing how 'In a walk through Vienna I did not see a single Jewish face'.[109] The *Daily Telegraph and Morning Post*'s[110] Vienna correspondent, George Eric Rowe Gedye, reported the daily toll of suicides in the city, which included distinguished Jewish intellectuals and businessmen – few of them, remarked the correspondent, were reported in the papers.[111] He was expelled from Austria for his reporting on the persecution and violence, by order from the Gestapo. It was the second expulsion order to be issued to Gedye.[112] He went on to write *Fallen Bastions* about his time in Austria, which would include an account of the plunder of Vienna by the Nazis and the brutal treatment of the Jews.

In mid-April 1938 Professor Norman Bentwich, former League of Nations High Commissioner for Refugees,[113] wrote an article for the *Manchester Guardian* that chronicled the plight of Austrian and especially Viennese Jews. The situation was one of 'indescribable misery and hopelessness'.[114] Following the *Anschluss*, Bentwich wrote, 'there was lawlessness and brutality employed', mainly by the Austrian Nazis.[115] German police and SS leaders 'after a week introduced some measure of discipline and checked the worst abuses; but not till hundreds of shops had been looted and hundreds of people had been assaulted. There was a daily toll of suicides.'[116] The *New Statesman and Nation* correspondent reported that the 'daily roll of Jewish suicides' had 'risen as high as 130'.[117] The correspondent described the situation in Austria where Jews were

> Free game for the mob, without rights or police protection, despoiled of their property and usually deprived of all chance of earning a livelihood and even of relief from fellow-Jews, their religion outraged, [and] the frontier hermetically sealed against all chance of escape.[118]

With this in mind, the correspondent for the *News Statesman and Nation* wrote, 'mass suicide is inevitable'. He explained that 'After two days of the Nazi regime I ceased trying to dissuade any Jew who spoke of it to me from suicide'.[119]

The *Anschluss* sparked the exodus of Jews, Socialists and those who had supported the Schuschnigg government. They fled across the frontiers into neighbouring countries. This mass flight outnumbered those who had fled following Hitler's appointment as chancellor in 1933.[120] While the 'Aryanization' of German society, government, civil service and the economy had taken several years, and was still far from complete, the process of driving Jews out of the Austrian economy took just months. Looting and plundering accompanied the forcible takeover of Jewish businesses. The process of coordinating the Austrian state along National Socialist lines was extremely brutal. It garnered international attention, as did the exodus of Jews from the country. Chronicled by the British press, the appearance of refugees in Croydon (arriving by air) and many ports in Britain brought the plight of Austria's Jews to the attention of the British public.[121] The question of what to do with the refugees became an important consideration for the British government, especially the Foreign Office and the Home Office.[122]

What was to be done about the Jewish refugee crisis? The British press was certainly critical of the responses of their government. For instance, in mid-March 1938, the *Manchester Guardian* commented in a leader:

> There must be many Englishmen who, noting the treatment with which Austrian refugees from the Nazi persecution meet on reaching our shores, look back with shame for the present to the days when our reputation as a country of sanctuary stood highest in Europe.[123]

Here the article referenced the Aliens (Restriction) Act of 1919 which gave the immigration authorities the power to turn back any immigrant who did not satisfy their criteria. In effect it meant that immigration authorities could refuse entry of people of Jewish heritage. For the *Manchester Guardian* the time had come for amendments to the Act, for 'In the matter of giving asylum to the victims of brute force in Europe we have done much less than France, Holland, Switzerland, or Czechoslovakia'.[124]

On 22 March 1938, Labour MP Colonel Josiah Wedgwood, an advocate for assistance for Jewish refugees fleeing Nazism,[125] put down a motion in parliament calling for a relaxation of the Aliens Act for six months to help alleviate the situation. This would mean admitting all those who required sanctuary and refuge. It was rejected by the House, 210 to 142.[126] *The Times* called the bill a 'clumsy attempt to deal with a difficult problem'.[127] It could not be accepted, wrote *The Times*, but 'every respect must be given to the feelings which prompted it'.[128] Indiscriminate admission was impossible; every case must be treated on its merits, declared Home Secretary Sir Samuel Hoare in his critique of the bill. But the home secretary did promise that the British government would maintain the 'traditional policy of this country of offering asylum to personals who for political, racial, or religious reasons have had to leave their own countries'.[129] Of this announcement, *The Times* commented: 'It is to be hoped . . . that it will be interpreted with wide liberality, especially during the early days of the new regime in Austria, when there are certain to be many distressing cases.'[130] The *Daily Mail* went further than *The Times*, clearly displaying its anti-immigration stance. The newspaper was highly critical of the Wedgwood plan, declaring its 'misguided sentimentalism' would have had disastrous consequences 'once it was known that Britain offered sanctuary to all who cared to come, the floodgates would be opened, and we should be inundated by thousands seeking a home'.[131] For the *Daily Mail*, an 'invasion of refugees' must be avoided as the 'influx of aliens would compete seriously with our own people in the labour market'. Even limited immigration such as restricting admission to 'suitable persons' including those 'distinguished in the arts, in science and in industry' should be 'reviewed with the greatest care' as 'our own professions are already overcrowded'.[132]

The *Daily Mail*, remarkably and in spite of this article, had become more sympathetic to the plight of the Jews, covering the refugee crisis and reporting the cruelties inflicted upon the Jews. The *Daily Mail's* Berlin correspondent had witnessed the escalating persecution and, on 18 June 1938, observed how

> The feeling against the Jews in Berlin appears to be growing daily, and every night brings the threat of further violence against the poorer quarters of the city behind the Alexanderplatz. This morning I found whole streets of shops with their shutters down and with such words as 'Jewish business', 'Hang the Jews', 'Out with the Race Defilers', painted in huge white letters across them.[133]

Another article, printed in the newspaper on the same day reported that between 12,000 and 14,000 Jews were imprisoned in Austria 'not for any political crime, but merely to force their emigration'.[134] The newspaper noted that 'Hundreds have applied for permission to emigrate to Australia' and the United States.[135] However, the *Daily Mail's* compassion was limited. They concluded that Britain could only take a 'fraction' of those seeking asylum.[136] So, while the newspaper reported the increasing persecution of the Jews and was sympathetic to their plight, it did not advocate admitting large numbers into Britain.

The *Daily Mirror* also only sporadically reported the persecution of the Jews in Germany (and Austria), but in July 1938 the newspaper featured a special feature in David Walker's *Talking Shop* column on the plight of Jewish refugees. The article came several months after the *Anschluss* and on the eve of the beginning of an international conference at Évians-les-Bains in France, convened by US president Franklin D. Roosevelt, to discuss the fate of Jewish refugees. The *Daily Mirror*'s David Walker, concerned at Britain's lacklustre approach to the refugee crisis, stated that 'we are in danger here in England of behaving like a lot of half-baked hooligans towards followers of the Jewish faith'.[137] Should Britain admit more refugees? he asked. Refugees felt that Britain was more likely to treat them better than they were being treated in Germany and Austria. 'Are they justified?' asked Walker; 'The choice is implied enough, in theory. You have got to make up your mind whether to behave like a Christian or a sadist.'[138] Walker concluded his column with a request: 'If you think it would be fun to see them squirming in the gutter, write and tell me why. If you think it would be fair to violate their women, let me know the reason. That is what is happening to them abroad.'[139]

As the Évian conference commenced readers of the *Daily Mirror* responded to Walker's article. On 8 July 1938 the *Daily Mirror* printed some of the responses. Overall, Walker noted: 'Jew-baiters had outnumbered "moderates" by nearly two to one.'[140] Some of the responses were shocking in their callousness with several advocating violence against the Jews. One reader wrote: 'Our fathers built England and made it safe to live in – for these filthy swine.'[141] Another wrote: 'The Jews are entirely responsible for their own persecution because Christians are getting fed up with their methods of business.'[142] The *Daily Mirror* included some of the extreme examples of 'Jew-baiters', including: 'You ask – do you want to crucify them? Certainly not, we need the wood to build working men's houses. There is a much cheaper way to exterminate them.'[143] One reader applauded the persecution of the Jews, writing: 'Should there ever be a persecution of Jews in England, I will certainly have a hand in it and get complete satisfaction from the process.'[144] One of the most inflammatory responses came from a reader who called himself 'Jew-baiter and proud of it', who wrote: 'Instead of clearing these stinking people, we are taking Germany's scum. One day there will be an uproar against this snake, and I only hope it will be in my lifetime.'[145] Walker, with some courage, thanked his readers for responding. He specifically thanked readers who 'agree with me that persecution is filthy and unfair'. He stated that an ultimatum faced Britain:

> The fact is that either the Government, or the people (or both together, for a change) have got to make up their minds NOW on the Jewish question in England. If Evian is inconclusive, as it may well be, it will be up to us to decide for ourselves.[146]

As a whole, the British press represented a stark contrast to this particular section of the *Daily Mirror*'s readership. The *Manchester Guardian, New Statesman and Nation, The Spectator, Daily Mirror, Daily Telegraph and Morning Post, Daily Express* and *The Times* stood out in their condemnation of the dictatorship for its treatment of its Jewish citizens. The treatment of the Jews in Germany and Austria, observed *The Times*, 'is altogether unworthy of the German people, and is one of the most formidable obstacles to a better understanding with other nations'.[147] *The Times* acknowledged: 'It may be admitted that the presence of large numbers of Jews within the State presents difficult problems in certain countries, especially when they achieve an importance out of proportion to their numbers', but 'this is no sort of reason for a country with the intellectual and cultural standards of Germany to treat Jews with a callous brutality which drives even some of the most strong-minded to suicide and which for the vast majority makes life a mere hopeless misery'.[148] While Jews fleeing the regime 'will be welcome in countries where more humane standards prevail and where openings can be made for them', it must be understood and made clear that 'each country is responsible for the proper treatment of its own Jewish population'.[149]

The task before the representatives at Évian was, in the words of the *New Statesman and Nation*, 'formidable'.[150] The newspaper explained:

> [T]he problem presented by the Nazi persecution of the Jews is staggering. There were about 600,000 Jews in Germany when Hitler came to power – of whom over 100,000 have left. And now there are 200,000 more in Austria. All this pitiable host of victims is under notice to quit; they are, in effect, being coolly pushed on to the hospitality of the world – and in order to make the world's job a little harder they are first robbed of practically all their property.[151]

For the thirty-one countries represented at the conference, the primary tasks would be 'How to finance rescue work on this vast scale', and to work out 'where the refugees are to go'.[152]

Unfortunately, the conference produced few workable results. As a whole, the British press was disappointed in the lack of progress made at the conference. At its conclusion, the *New Statesman and Nation* reported: 'if it has not been a complete fiasco, it has achieved little to boast about'.[153] Even though 'All the States attending it are full of sympathy for the victims of persecution; none of them is able or willing to open its doors to a flood of refugees'.[154] The *Manchester Guardian* reported that this was 'frankly disappointing':

> The notice 'Jews Not Wanted' may commonly be seen at the entrance of cafes and swimming-pools in Nazi Germany. One would not for that reason expect to

find it displayed at an international conference on the subject of Jewish refugees, but some of the speeches made at Evian during the past fortnight suggested that it might have been found in the pockets of several delegates.[155]

The United States was prepared to take the same number as it had already admitted (approximately 27,000), while one or two of the South American states 'left the door ajar'.[156] British delegate and Conservative MP Lord Winterton suggested that Jews could be settled in East African colonies, including Kenya, but stated that it was not possible to admit any more Jews into Palestine. 'Racial antipathy' was also present, noted the *Manchester Guardian*, especially in the case of the Australian delegate. The *Daily Express* gave particular attention to the Australian delegate, Lieutenant Colonel T. W. White of the United Australia Party, who stated that Australia was only interested in British settlers. The article, with the headline 'Australia says "no hope" for refugees', quoted Colonel White.[157] 'We have no real racial problem', he said, 'We are not desirous of importing one by encouraging any scheme of large-scale foreign migration'.[158] In doing so, Colonel White 'left no doubt of his Government's attitude'.[159]

For most of the delegates, however, the impediment to the admittance of large numbers of Jews was financial. It was hoped that this was something that could be overcome. The *Daily Express* reported on 11 July 1938 that Britain, the United States and France had made the decision to approach Hitler 'at the "first favourable opportunity"', with the request to allow Jewish and other persecuted minorities in Germany and Austria '"a fair percentage", of their money and possessions if they wish to emigrate'.[160] The *New Statesman and Nation* was hopeful of the proposed 'establishment of an inter-governmental committee', based in London, to assist the emigration of Jewish refugees, which 'may help in particular to ease the financial strain by persuading the Nazi robbers to allow their victims to escape with a little more of their capital'.[161] *The Spectator* adopted a more charitable attitude:

> [I]t is an outrage, to the Christian conscience especially, that the modern world with all its immense wealth and resources cannot give these exiles a home, and food and drink, and a secure status, and there is no rational case for believing that the nationals of any country would suffer by such an act of charity.[162]

* * *

Both *The Times* and the *Manchester Guardian* remained committed to covering the persecution of the Jews following the Évian conference. Voigt of the *Manchester Guardian* uncovered the brutal treatment of Jews in the concentration camp at Buchenwald in August 1938, while *The Times* reported the continued plight of refugees. *The Times* also reported further discriminatory measures, which included a decree which forced Jews to adopt the 'Jewish' names of Israel and Sarah within their own names so that Jews in Germany could be clearly identified by those names.[163] Then, in late October 1938, both newspapers reported the forcible expulsion of Polish Jews from Germany.

In March 1938 the Polish government announced a new State Citizenship law allowed for the rescindment of citizenship for Polish nationals who had been living abroad for a long period of time. For the German government this could mean that the approximately 70,000 Polish Jews living in Germany could be left stateless and, thereby, dependent upon Germany.[164] Later in that year the Polish government introduced legislation that required Polish passports to include a special endorsement (or visa stamp) from the Polish consular (and similar authorities) if the holder wanted to return to Poland.[165] In response, and before the new legislation came into force, the German government decided to expel all Polish Jews. Both the *Manchester Guardian* and *The Times* provided detailed coverage of the expulsion of the Polish Jews. *The Times* described how 'They made a distressed and destitute picture as they crowded into the Schlesischer station seeking trains to Poland'.[166] 'Most of them were kept herded in trains for several days after having been previously confined in German gaols', reported the *Manchester Guardian*, and they 'have no luggage, nor even proper clothing, and almost all of them are without any money except the ten marks allowed to them on expulsion'.[167] Approximately 50,000 would be affected, estimated *The Times*; already 10,000 to 12,000 had been deported to the frontier where they awaited admission into Poland.[168] *The Times* explained that 'Nearly all of them wish to return to their homes and belongings in Germany, many having been born there and scarcely any of them having prospects of a livelihood in Poland, where, but for their passports, they are strangers'.[169] The *Manchester Guardian* described the 'terrible' scene at Zbonszyn where

> some 7000 Jews are living in stables and on stone floors of the railway station. Hundreds have to sleep in a yard, for there is no room in the stables. . . . About 150, mostly children and women, were taken to hospital and an epidemic is feared. Several more persons have died, and two women and one man have been driven insane by their sufferings. Even crippled and blind people were expelled from Germany, and they are now in most dire need. They include an invalid woman aged about ninety and a blind man of seventy.[170]

Less than a week later, British newspapers reported the attempted assassination of German diplomat Ernst vom Rath by a young Polish Jew, Herschel Grynszpan, at the German Embassy in Paris. Vom Rath, who had been shot five times, later died of his injuries. British newspapers, including the *Manchester Guardian*, reported that Grynszpan was motivated by the treatment of Polish Jews; his parents were believed to have been among those expelled to the frontier.[171] The Nazi press seized on the story of the assassination attempt, taking the opportunity to violently denounce the Jews. Nazi newspaper *Angriff* claimed the shooting was part of a conspiracy, the 'Work of the Agitators' International', in which there existed 'a straight path from Churchill to Grynsban'.[172] But, *Angriff* argued, as the 'murder weapon went off in the hands of a Jewish rascal', retaliation would be waged against the Jewish population in Germany.[173] Of these allegations, *The Spectator* commented:

> The murder of the German diplomat, Herr vom Rath, in Paris by a 17-year-old Polish Jew is deplored by all reasonable men. Political assassination is a crime, and a futile crime; but the Nazis, with the assassinations of June, 1934, on their consciences, have no justification for finding in it proof either of an international Jewish conspiracy or of Jewish depravity . . . no one can be surprised if the hatred and indignation inspired in a son by such acts find an outlet in the assassination for them; Herr Grynsban's guilt is less than that of the German Government. Nevertheless, the consequences for his race are likely to be appalling and out of all proportion to the crime for which, in any case, other Jews are not responsible.[174]

Jews in Germany, reported *The Spectator*, were now living 'under a terrible fear, for it is almost beyond hope that Herr Hitler will refrain from avenging on an innocent and tortured people the crime of a boy maddened by the maltreatment not merely of his race but of his own parents'.[175]

The Nazis' brutal revenge began on the night of 9 November 1938 with a violent pogrom against Germany's Jews. Reports of the violent campaign, known later as *Kristallnacht* (or Night of Broken Glass), appeared in British newspapers on 11 November 1938. Leading government figures, including Propaganda Minister Joseph Goebbels, claimed that the violence was a spontaneous reaction to the assassination of vom Rath. This was dismissed by the British press early on. Already on 11 November 1938, the *Daily Mirror*'s correspondent wrote: 'I saw Jews being rounded up like rats. . . . It was all done according to plan, ruthlessly, relentlessly.'[176] The *Daily Telegraph and Morning Post* declared that the violence was an 'officially countenanced pogrom of unparalleled brutality and ferocity', which was accompanied by 'Mob law' in Berlin, where 'hordes of hooligans indulged in an orgy of destruction'.[177] The *Manchester Guardian* reported: 'the attacks on the Jews are the responsibility of a fanatical Government whose uniformed henchmen were first in this cruel outburst of destructiveness and whose police did nothing to stop it'.[178] The *Jewish Chronicle* later attacked the regime for refusing to accept responsibility for the violence:

> Very quickly the ugly truth behind the farcical story of 'a spontaneous popular attack on the German Jewry' has come to light. It is now quite clear that these disgraceful deeds were not perpetrated by unorganised hooligans, but were the deliberately executed orders of the leaders of the Nazi regime. With shameless cynicism the Nazi rulers have clearly shown that they care not a jot for the opinion of the entire civilised world. On a pretext so flimsy that it amounts to an insult to the intelligence, they have dragged thousands of Jews to the concentration camps and seized the last property that the Jews had been left after more than five years of persecution and torture.[179]

The Times reported that the violent scenes 'seldom had their equal in a civilised country since the Middle Ages'.[180] In their report, the *Daily Telegraph and Morning Post*'s correspondent observed:

> I have seen several anti-Jewish outbreaks in Germany during the last five years, but never anything as nauseating as this. Racial hatred and hysteria seemed to have taken complete hold of otherwise decent people. I saw fashionably dressed women clapping their hands and screaming with glee, while respectable middle-class mothers held up their babies to see the 'fun'.[181]

Not all newspapers followed this line. The *Daily Express* took seriously Goebbels's radio appeal for the looting to stop and focused on what it thought was the spontaneity of mob violence.[182] There was no recognition here that the so-called spontaneity had been orchestrated by the regime.[183]

In the days that followed, British newspapers uncovered more details about the horrors of *Kristallnacht*. It was not just synagogues and shops that were targeted: 'All Jewish homes and institutes for the poor and aged and ailing have been destroyed.'[184] The Jewish hospital at Nuremberg was destroyed after all patients were ordered to file into the courtyard. A children's home at Caputh, near Berlin, was also destroyed.[185] The swiftness and completeness of the attacks made it evident 'that the excesses were planned well in advance'.[186] The *Manchester Guardian* estimated between 9,000 and 10,000 Jews were arrested in Berlin alone, and 'careful estimates' put arrests in Germany at between 35,000 and 40,000.[187] Those arrested in Berlin were taken to Sachsenhausen concentration camp, reported the *Manchester Guardian* on 18 November 1938.[188] Thousands had also been sent to Buchenwald and Dachau. Some were executed immediately. This included, according to the *Manchester Guardian*, 200 in Buchenwald alone.[189]

The executions were carried out by 'firing-squads', reported the *Manchester Guardian*.[190] In some areas, all male Jews aged between eighteen and eighty were arrested; many fled into the woods in Germany, while others had been 'trying to elude arrest by spending all their time, night and day, in trains travelling from place to place'.[191]

Despite international condemnation and criticism, more restrictions on Jews were put in place in Germany and Austria following *Kristallnacht*. Both the *Daily Mail* and *Daily Express* reported Joseph Goebbels's announcement that 'The Jewish problem will be solved very shortly in accordance with the will of the German people'.[192] The *Daily Mail* reported that rationing of food and money was being considered, as the German police had alleged that Jews had been hoarding food in their homes. The expulsion of Jews was almost certainly put forward, and the possibility of establishing ghettos for Jews was also being discussed.[193] Many British newspapers, including the *Daily Mail*, also reported the fine levied against the entire Jewish population for the death of vom Rath and the violence that followed.[194] The *Daily Mail* reported that the fine was £80,000,000 which worked out to approximately £250 per person.[195] *The Spectator* reported that, in addition to the fine, the damage to Jewish shops, businesses and homes was to be repaired at the expense of Jews. Furthermore, Jews were excluded from 'all economic activity in Germany from the end of the year onwards'.[196] The newspaper reported:

> No Jew may attend any public entertainment, no Jew may attend any German university, no Jewish child may attend any German school – but no Jew apparently may emigrate, or if he does he will go without a penny to support him or start in a new life elsewhere.[197]

Of these measures, *The Spectator* observed: 'It is true that Jews in Germany have not been formally condemned to death; it has only been made impossible for them to live.'[198] 'No foreign Power can do anything for the Jews still in Germany', reported *The Spectator*, but they could do something for the Jews who had already escaped: 'something at least can be done to alleviate suffering, and the duty to do that is a solemn charge on civilisation. A totally new effort on a totally new scale is called for. The Evian Conference of last July has led to nothing.'[199]

For the *New Statesman and Nation*, it was still important to try to 'rescue the Jews of Germany from their oppressors'.[200] And, 'That means, of course, how to get them out of Germany, and where to put them. Though at present the Nazis are preventing their escape, they would presumably offer no serious objections to international schemes which would, at other people's expense, rid them of their pariahs.'[201] But, the newspaper admitted: 'The real difficulty is to find homes for so many myriads of refugees.'[202] Palestine, even it was willing to admit more Jews, 'could only absorb a fraction', and while it was 'easy again to point to "great empty spaces" in other parts of the world . . . many of them, if they were available for settlement, would obviously be unsuitable, without immense preparation, for an almost entirely urban people from Northern Europe'.[203] The task fell to the United States and the British Empire (colonies and dominions included) to admit Jews and offer them asylum. 'We hope they [the Jews] will not look in vain, or for long. In the present temper of the Nazis, delay may mean an even more horrible fate for their victims', the *New Statesman and Nation* commented.[204]

There were extreme Nazi elements that were prepared to take the next step, as the *Manchester Guardian* reported in November 1938. The Nazi *Schutzstaffel*, SS (Protection Squad), newspaper *Schwarze Korps* (Black Corps) printed the following statement that left little doubt as to their intentions:

> Germany would be confronted by the hard necessity of exterminating the Jewish underworld exactly as it does away with criminals in the orderly state, 'with fire and sword'. This would definitely be the end of Jewry and its annihilation.[205]

The SS newspaper warned against the 'foreign quarters' trying to delay with '"further monotonous howling," by threats and blackmail, this logical and inevitable development'.[206] After all, the *Manchester Guardian* noted, the '"solution" to the Jewish problem by brutal means was favoured by "German quarters" as far back as 1933'.[207] The *Schwarze Korps* made further threats against the Jews at the end of November 1938, and again, the *Manchester Guardian* reported the German papers' inflammatory comments. This time, the SS newspaper warned against any other attempts by Jews to fight back: 'On the day a Jew or anybody with a weapon bought from a Jew dares to attack one of the leading men in Germany there will be no more Jews in Germany. We hope we have expressed ourselves with sufficient clearness.'[208]

Then, in early December 1938, the *Manchester Guardian* printed an article about a proposed location in Berlin for a ghetto (in the north and centre of Berlin), as well as a proposal (learnt by the correspondent from 'trustworthy quarters') for a decree 'compelling Jews of both sexes when outdoors to wear a badge. This is likely to be yellow in colour and to depict the Star of David.'[209] Legislation to restrict Jews on trains (to a separate carriage) and bar the owning of radios and telephones were also discussed.

With the onslaught against the Jews showing no abatement, the safety (and asylum) of Jews in Europe remained a topic of discussion in the British press. Towards the end of November 1938, the House of Commons announced plans to allow 500 Jewish children's admittance to Britain. For the *Daily Telegraph and Morning Post* this represented rapid action; 'committees were formed in the morning. By the afternoon they were already at work.'[210] The *Daily Telegraph and Morning Post* discussed the conditions attached to the admittance of the children. The children were to be provided with schooling until the age of sixteen, after which they would be resettled in the dominions or in other countries which, it is notable, were not specified.[211]

The Times also reported that there were fundraising efforts in Britain to aid Jewish refugees. Lord Stanley Baldwin's appeal for donations for victims of religious and racial persecution had reached £43,619.[212] So far, reported *The Times* (whose London office was accepting donations for the fund), over 3,000 people had donated.[213] The fund was intended to help existing agencies and organizations dedicated to helping Jewish refugees. But, as many newspapers noted, the problem was still in finding places for the refugees to go. This was illustrated in mid-1939 in the case of the liner *St Louis* which had been sailing the seas looking for a place to dock that would accept the 900 refugees on board.[214] The *Daily Express* reported the saga:

> They had sailed for Cuba. Cuba had rejected them after nearly a week's suspense during which there were several suicide attempts, and the St Louis was making her way back to Hamburg, from which she had originally set out, and to which the Jews said they dared not return. Panic-stricken, the radioed appeals to the Governments of various countries as they wandered over the seas.[215]

With front-page coverage the *Daily Express* noted that one of the pleas for asylum went to British prime minister Neville Chamberlain. The Dutch government had given permission for 200 of the 900 to land in Holland till they find somewhere else to go. The following day, the *Daily Express* reported that the British government had granted a 'proportion' of the German Jewish refugees' asylum in England. The '"exceptional circumstances" influenced the Government's decision', the *Daily Express* reported, quoting, in part, the announcement in the House of Commons. But Mr Osbert Peake, under-secretary to the Home Office, declared that this measure should not be taken as any sort of precedent.[216] It was reported that Belgium had taken 250 of the remaining Jews, while France would probably take the rest. Criticism levelled at Home Secretary Sir Samuel Hoare by Colonel Josiah Wedgwood, British MP and Zionist, that it was 'almost impossible for "Hitler's slaves" to find shelter in this country', was met with a frosty response.[217]

* * *

Throughout the 1930s, the process by which the Nazi authorities excluded Jews from society was carefully documented by the British press. Prominent focus was given in many newspapers to the exclusion of Jews from business and the economy. The effects of this – unemployment, destitution and starvation – were regularly discussed by British newspapers like the *Daily Express*, *The Spectator*, *The Times*, *Morning Post*, *Daily Telegraph (and Morning Post)* and the *Manchester Guardian*. *The Times* and the *Manchester Guardian* were particularly thorough in their coverage of the Aryanization of the German state, economy, culture and society. In 1934 and 1935 reporting by most British newspapers was sporadic. While British newspapers did report the introduction of the Nuremberg laws in 1935, their coverage of the laws was rather underwhelming. For many British newspapers, the laws merely put a legal stamp on conditions that were already a reality. For the *Manchester Guardian* this was not good enough – the newspaper criticized the lack of coverage the laws received.

But the press was, for the most part, united in condemning the violence and atrocities that accompanied the persecution of the Jews in Germany (and Austria). The exodus of German and Austrian Jews (and others targeted by the Nazis) was a pressing concern for British newspapers, particularly after the German invasion of Austria. The brutal treatment of Jews in Vienna sparked outrage in the press and dominated headlines, prompting many correspondents to call for more aid and assistance for those trying to escape the brutal dictatorship. Some newspapers urged caution in accepting large number of Jewish refugees (the *Daily Mail*); others urged the British government to implement a larger scheme of assistance (*The Spectator* and *Manchester Guardian*). And while the Évian conference was convened with the best hopes and intentions the results fell flat for many newspapers, particularly *The Spectator*. The violence of *Kristallnacht* brought the outrage felt by the press over the treatment of Jews to a new level. The press was united in their condemnation of the regime and its actions and called for greater understanding and help for refugees although they themselves could offer few workable solutions to the refugee crisis.

For a reader of a British newspaper in the 1930s it would have been hard to ignore news of the persecution of the Jews. Whether a reader picked up *Daily Mail*, *Daily Express*, *Morning Post*, *Manchester Guardian*, *The Times* or a weekly like *The Spectator* or *New Statesman and Nation*, they could expect to find something about life under the Nazi dictatorship. If they read newspapers regularly, it would have been almost impossible to ignore the fact that German (and Austrian) Jews were being violently persecuted by the Nazi regime. Even if a reader only read the sports section of a popular newspaper like the *Daily Express*, they would have been hard-pressed to avoid news of *Kristallnacht* on the front page in November 1938. This is because, throughout the 1930s, the British press, both popular and quality, daily and weekly, demonstrated a keen commitment to reporting what was happening in Germany, particularly the brutal persecution of Germany's Jews.

* * *

Conclusion

In late October 1939, just weeks after the outbreak of the Second World War on 3 September, the British Foreign Office issued a White Paper entitled 'Papers Concerning the Treatment of German Nationals in Germany'. The official White Paper chronicled the brutal mistreatment inflicted upon prisoners in concentration camps in Germany in 1938 and 1939. It uncovered instances of beatings, torture and flogging of prisoners. The bulk of the report was composed of letters and testimony received by the British government from representatives in Germany. Many British newspapers reported the release of the White Paper. Their coverage paid special attention to its findings and evidence. For *The Spectator*, the report was important as it showed 'what sort of an enemy we have to deal with' in the war.[1] Even though the details were 'incredible', explained *The Spectator*, 'the Foreign Office White Paper leaves no room for doubt' about the validity of the testimony and evidence.[2] Reactions like this were frustrating for correspondents and staff from the *New Statesman and Nation* and the *Manchester Guardian* who had worked tirelessly to uncover and report the horrors of the concentration camps since the opening of the first camp in the small town of Dachau in March 1933. It was even more frustrating that it had taken so long for the British government to publicly acknowledge these atrocities had taken place in 'peacetime'.[3] The *New Statesman and Nation* told readers that they wished

> the British authorities had not tried to hush up these things at an earlier stage when some of us really wanted to do something about them while there was still time. We were told then that we were trying to interfere in the internal affairs of a friendly nation.[4]

Both the *New Statesman and Nation* and the *Manchester Guardian* made it clear in their editorial comments that none of the details in the report were 'new news' to correspondents who had been living and working in Germany and had witnessed the rise of Nazism and the establishment of the dictatorship. For instance, the *Manchester Guardian* asserted:

The White Paper has been greeted in some quarters as though it contained 'revelations' of something new. But that is not so. The truth has been precisely indicated, though with much restraint, in the columns of this and one or two other papers – truth that was, perhaps, too little regarded by the public because to the ordinary decent man or woman it seemed incredible. But, indeed, there was nothing incredible about it.[5]

This book has chronicled the commitment of the British press in covering the Nazi regime prior to the outbreak of war in 1939. Initially it was assumed that the British press would have provided limited coverage of the situation in Germany, preferring to instead focus on themes and events that directly concerned and impacted Britain, namely Hitler's foreign policy aims, Germany's rearmament and increasing territorial aggression and expansion. Studies that examined British press responses to Hitler's foreign policy already existed. These studies drew attention to how the press considered and covered Germany's territorial aggression in light of the British government's policy of appeasement. But few had sought to examine press responses to the internal situation in Germany in any depth. Did the absence of studies focusing on this topic mean that the British press had not reported or even ignored what was happening inside Germany under Hitler's dictatorship? This gave rise to several questions that underpinned this book. First, was the press aware of what was happening in Germany under the Nazi regime in the 1930s? Second, if they were aware of what was happening, did they report the destruction of democracy, the consolidation of power and the establishment of the Nazi dictatorship? Did they cover the process of *Gleichschaltung* and the persecution of political opponents and other religious groups?

What this study has demonstrated is that the press *was* covering, and reporting in detail, the National Socialist dictatorship in Germany in the 1930s. This book establishes that the British reading public could have known about the terroristic and brutal nature of the dictatorship, if they chose to, by reading British newspapers. From the appointment of Adolf Hitler as chancellor in January 1933, the British press demonstrated a keen commitment to reporting many aspects of the Nazi dictatorship. This naturally included foreign policy (and concerns about the stability of Europe), but it also included the rise and establishment of the Nazi dictatorship, the destruction of democracy, the persecution of political and religious groups, and the economic and social policies of Hitler's government. Newspapers like *The Times, Daily Telegraph* and *Manchester Guardian* had been investigating and reporting the activities of the Nazi movement since the 1920s, paying special attention to the party's election successes in the early 1930s.[6]

Conclusion

The British press, as a whole, reported the appointment of Adolf Hitler as chancellor of Germany on 30 January 1933 as a major news story. For the press, there was initial confusion as to what Hitler's appointment might mean for German politics and the future of democracy. Hitler's aims seemed unclear, and British newspapers such as the *Daily Express*, *The Observer* and the *Daily Telegraph* seemed to believe that he was a prisoner of more powerful forces in his cabinet. Other newspapers posited that perhaps Hitler had finally given up his aims of total and undisputed power and had instead decided to work with the political parties he had previously vowed to destroy. Both *The Times* and *The Spectator*, for instance, reported that the Nazis' inclusion in government was Hitler's chance to show his ability as a statesman. In other words, in early February 1933, most British newspapers were prepared to give Hitler and his party the benefit of the doubt. However, the Nazis' brutal election campaign, as well as the wave of arrests that followed the Reichstag Fire and the brutal treatment of political opponents that followed, dispelled any confusion about both the Nazis role in the new government, and their aims. *The Times*, *News Chronicle*, *Manchester Guardian* and even the *Daily Mail* recognized that the Reichstag Fire Decree spelled the end of democracy in Germany and ushered in a dictatorship. The Nazis election victory in March 1933 meant Germany was, according to the *Manchester Guardian*, 'faced with a long period of Hitlerism'.[7] By this point, after closely following events in Germany, the British press was in a better position to report what would come next.

In the months that followed the British press captured, with some accuracy, the Nazis' destruction of democracy in each of its phases. The seizure of the German federal states, which began after the March elections, was reported primarily by the *Daily Telegraph*, *Manchester Guardian*, *The Times* and the *Daily Mail*. These newspapers understood that this was a vital step in the Nazis' pursuit of total power over Germany. The seizure of the states, which culminated in the takeover of Bavaria, was closely followed by the opening of the Reichstag at Potsdam, after the German parliament had become the target of arson in February 1933. The opening was a lavish affair, but this did not divert correspondents from reporting the passing of the Enabling Act. The *Morning Post*, *Manchester Guardian*, *The Times* and the *Daily Mail* conveyed to readers that the act was a vital step in the destruction of democracy. It paved the way for the establishment of a Nazi dictatorship. For the press it was clear that Hitler was increasing his own power at the expense of President Hindenburg.

The next step, closely followed and reported by many British newspapers, was the violent assault on the political left. Most newspapers, regardless of their political ideology, reported the destruction of the trade unions at the beginning of May 1933. This meant that the right-wing *Daily Telegraph* covered the destruction of the German trade union movement in as much detail as the left-leaning liberal *Manchester Guardian*. Further infringements on democratic values and institutions came with the (often forcible) dissolution of German political parties. British newspapers reported this process, which began with the proscription of the Socialist Party in June 1933 for Marxist corruption – a charge dismissed by *The Times* as a sham. But this time, it was not just the political left that were targeted. The Nazis undermined, intimidated and bullied every other political party in Germany including their own cabinet ally, the Nationalists, until the Nazi Party was the only party that remained. For special correspondent F. A. Voigt of the *Manchester Guardian*, it was shocking that a democratic system could be completely destroyed in just six months. In early to mid-1933, the press had followed, with interest, how the dismantling of Weimar democracy had been carried out. The frequency of reports certainly varied, but the press, as a whole, understood what was happening in Germany. It had been clear after the March elections that Hitler and the Nazis had been intent on destroying democracy.

While the press, for the most part, closely followed the destruction of democracy in Germany, the same cannot be said of the campaign of terror which accompanied it. Most newspapers reported the initial wave of arrests of Communists and Socialists following the Reichstag Fire, but they remained silent on the brutal methods of suppression and violence that followed it. This was true of the *Daily Telegraph* and *Daily Mirror* that reported initial arrests but remained largely silent on the terror campaign. A few newspapers did try to report the terror. Both the *New Statesman and Nation* and the *Jewish Chronicle* drew readers' attention to the terror and the cruelty of the concentration camps. But their reports were sporadic. *The Spectator* tried to inform readers about the atmosphere of fear and repression in Germany but was heavily criticized by their readership, and remained silent after that. *The Times* kept readers up-to-date with news of arrests and the opening of new concentrating camps but refrained from editorializing. In addition, *The Times* editor Geoffrey Dawson made excuses to refrain from printing an article that uncovered the inhuman and violent treatment of prisoners in the Dachau concentration camp. There were also newspapers that downplayed the terror and brutality of the regime. The *Morning Post*, *Observer* and the *News Chronicle* reported the existence of concentration camps but were seemingly convinced by the forced unity on display. In the few articles that were published by the *Daily Express*, the newspaper toned down the violence, citing it as a by-product of the Communists' war against Nazism. The *Daily Mail* was the most extreme case in this category. Not only did they downplay the violence but they denied the existence of a campaign of terror and criticized foreign newspapers that had sought to expose it.

What this meant was that there was a serious gap in the coverage of the Nazis' campaign of repression and violence. Luckily for readers the *Manchester Guardian* sought to fill that void, through the work of special correspondent F. A. Voigt. He clearly conveyed to readers that the violence – the campaign of terror – was an integral part of the regime. Reports by Voigt demonstrated that the violence went beyond revolutionary excesses; it continued after the Nazis had secured power, dismantled democracy, destroyed their opposition and announced themselves sole rulers of Germany. Voigt revealed that the terror had evolved with the regime from a brutal and violent campaign, led by the SA, to an organized and systematic terror run predominantly by the Gestapo and SS. The concentration camp remained integral to this system, and to the Nazi regime as a whole.

If the terror campaign had not demonstrated to all newspapers the ruthlessness and brutality of the new regime, the Röhm purge in mid-1934 certainly did. Initially the purge was seen by many British newspapers, including *The Times* and *Daily Mail*, as a victory of the moderates against extreme elements in the party. However, as details about the purge emerged, the British press questioned the validity of the action and the way it was carried out. While the press struggled with whether or not Röhm and his inner circle had been planning a putsch, newspapers, such as the *News Chronicle*, found the suggestion that Schleicher and his wife, along with the many others, had supposedly been involved as ridiculous. The brutality of the action was condemned by newspapers such as *The Spectator*, *News Chronicle*, *Daily Telegraph* and *The Times*. Increasingly, the action was seen as state-sanctioned murder against fellow Nazis and colleagues. The fact that Hitler, as head of state, had been involved in the purge was also criticized by *The Times*. The purge sparked strong criticism from the British press, and was a rare occasion in which the press, with the exception of a few popular dailies, denounced the regime. The declaration of Hitler as Führer of the German people, following President Hindenburg's death at the beginning of August 1934, was meant to demonstrate to the world the unity and strength of National Socialist Germany. However, the plebiscite, in which over 4 million voted against Hitler's appointment, only managed to convey to British newspapers, especially the *New Statesman and Nation*, that opposition to the regime still existed.

For British newspapers, the clearest form of opposition in Germany during the 1930s was the one found in Christian churches. From 1933 until the outbreak of war in 1939 the British press keenly followed the struggle of the Catholic and the Protestant churches in Germany against Nazi interference and coordination. The British press defined this struggle as a 'form of opposition' – a term contemporary historians may find problematic in this context as most of those concerned, including pastors, bishops and priests, did not oppose Hitler nor did they want to overthrow the Nazi dictatorship. At times, the press mistook protests by church groups over state interference as opposition to the Nazi regime – which it was not. But, for the most part, British newspapers recognized that the opposition that defined the church struggle was a struggle for the freedom of the faith. They protested and opposed efforts to align and coordinate the Nazi state and ideology. For the regime it was opposition nonetheless and it was brutally suppressed with its leaders thrown in gaol or concentration camps. *The Times*, *Manchester Guardian*, and the *Daily Telegraph* provided sustained coverage of the church situation. But the *Observer*, *Morning Post*, *News Chronicle* and to a lesser degree the *New Statesman and Nation* also reported the government's efforts to suppress the opposition, particularly in the late 1930s. These newspapers demonstrated that they were vitally interested in the struggle for the churches, following it throughout the 1930s.

At times, articles on the church struggle appeared more frequently than those on the persecution of the Jews. This was not because the British press cared more about the church struggle than they did about the persecution of the Jews but because the church conflict was complex, chaotic and constantly evolving. New personalities, decrees and developments demanded attention and were reported by many newspapers. The situation for the Jews was more straightforward in some ways – it was clear from 1933 that the Nazis were intent on eliminating Jews from German society. Legislation and action taken against the Jews in the 1930s furthered this. But even though, at times, the press reported the church situation in more depth, they still covered the increasingly cruel and sadistic persecution of the Jews consistently and in detail. There were certainly newspapers that, in the beginning, downplayed or denied the violent persecution. The *Daily Mail*'s proprietor Viscount Rothermere felt that the Jews had too strong an influence on German politics and business and believed any measures against them justified. However even his newspaper, the *Daily Mail*, reported the April boycott and *Kristallnacht*, as well as some of the discriminatory legislation against the Jews that was passed in the 1930s. Overall, and in spite of the Rothermere's early anti-Semitic statements, the persecution of the Jews was denounced by British newspapers. There were gaps in coverage, for instance, the Nuremberg laws did not receive the attention and analysis they deserved, even in *The Times*. But British newspapers, particularly the *Manchester Guardian* and *The Spectator*, were outspoken about the aid that the Jews needed, particularly for those wanting to flee the regime. The events of *Kristallnacht* offered further proof of the desperate situation for the Jews. The violent action by the Nazis was categorically denounced by the press for its inhuman cruelty, with the *Daily Telegraph and Morning Post* calling the violence 'nauseating'.[8] For British newspapers, the international response to the plight of the Jews and their desperate attempts to flee the regime before and, particularly, after the events of *Kristallnacht* was sorely lacking. This was especially the case for the *Manchester Guardian* and the *New Statesman and Nation* which expressed disappointment at the lack of meaningful progress on behalf of Jews suffering under Nazism. The persecution of the Jews was of vital interest for British correspondents and deserved attention and sustained coverage in the pages of British newspapers.

The British press reported many facts about the Nazi dictatorship prior to the outbreak of war in 1939 in an attempt to uncover the true nature of the regime. But various factors affected the frequency and tone of reports. The type of newspaper – whether it was a quality or popular newspaper – had bearing on the coverage given to German affairs. Political ideology or affiliation was another consideration. The quality press reported what was happening in Germany far more than the popular newspapers. Both *The Times* and the *Manchester Guardian* stood out for their coverage of German affairs in the 1930s. Articles about Germany appeared in *The Times* on an almost daily basis in 1933. In a single day there were often several lengthy articles covering various aspects of the situation in Germany. Reports by the newspaper's Berlin correspondent, Norman Ebbutt, were highly detailed and, as a result, few facts about the Nazi dictatorship were left unstated. This is an important point because *The Times* has been excoriated for its reporting on Germany in the 1930s, particularly for its endorsement of the British government's policy of appeasement. While this should not be overlooked, it should be recognized that the newspaper had covered the internal situation in Germany in the 1930s with some thoroughness. *The Times* reported the destruction of democracy in more depth than any British newspaper, even more than the *Manchester Guardian* which did not have a resident correspondent in Germany for much of 1933. It would have been difficult for a committed reader of *The Times* to have read the newspaper and not have an idea of what was happening in Germany.

The *Manchester Guardian*'s coverage of the situation in Germany quickly established the newspaper as an outspoken critic of the Nazi regime. The *Manchester Guardian*'s articles had far more editorializing than *The Times*.

The *Manchester Guardian* vigorously denounced the violence and brutality of the Nazi dictatorship. For editor W. P. Crozier, it was the paper's moral duty to uncover and report what was happening inside Germany. Special correspondent F. A. Voigt's articles did this. His investigative reports were based on months of research and were supplemented by testimony from sources in Germany, many of whom had been victims of the regime. Even though the newspaper did not have a correspondent in Germany for much of 1933, the *Manchester Guardian*'s uncompromising attitude in denouncing and exposing the regime would have also left readers with little doubt as to the nature of the regime.

Other quality newspapers also stood out for their coverage of the situation in Germany. The conservative *Daily Telegraph* and the *Morning Post* both covered the Nazi coordination and takeover of Germany as well as the church struggle and persecution of the Jews. Weekly quality newspapers, including the *New Statesman and Nation* and *The Spectator*, also sought to uncover details about what was happening in Germany, albeit less frequently. As weekly newspapers, they could not compete with the dailies in the level of detail in reporting developments in Germany, but they could, and did, keep readers informed about major events. But it can be assumed that readers would have been reading daily newspapers and so many articles contained more editorializing than some of the daily newspapers, as they surveyed the week's events and commented on them. Reports were often the result of investigations carried out over a week or several weeks. *The Spectator* and the *New Statesman and Nation* used these opportunities to issue scathing assessments of the methods of the regime. Guest writers also frequently contributed detailed articles on specific topics of themes. The *Jewish Chronicle* restricted its reports on the German situation primarily to news of the persecution of the Jews. These reports were detailed and often accompanied by photographs of the mistreatment of Jews and damage to Jewish property, especially after the April boycott in 1933. While the weekly newspapers could not match the quality daily newspapers in their coverage of events in Germany, they often still demonstrated a commitment to reporting the destruction of democracy, the establishment of the Nazi dictatorship and the persecution of political and religious groups.

Popular and pictorial newspapers did not cover events in Germany in as much detail as the quality press. But it should not be inferred from this that the popular newspapers did not report or were not interested in what was happening in Germany. Popular newspapers such as the conservative *Daily Express*, left-leaning *Daily Mirror*, liberal left-leaning *News Chronicle* and even the conservative right-wing *Daily Mail* reported many developments in Germany.

The conservative *Daily Express*, for instance, uncovered early instances of ill-treatment and violence committed by the SA and other Nazis against the Jews and were outspokenly critical of such behaviour. The articles, written by Berlin correspondent Pembroke Stephens, saw him expelled in 1934. The *Daily Mirror*, a popular left-leaning pictorial, kept news of Germany to a minimum, except for the big events. This was most probably due to the belief that its largely female readership would not be interested in reading about German affairs. But David Walker's columns on the persecution of the Jews in 1938 stood out for their unwavering criticism of both the treatment of Jews in Germany and the anti-Semitism of sections of the *Daily Mirror*'s readership. The left-leaning *News Chronicle*, out of all the popular newspapers, covered German affairs in the most depth. It did sensationalize some of the more dramatic events but still reported them in detail. The *News Chronicle* paid special attention to the destruction of democracy, the struggle for the churches and the persecution of the Jews. Photographs that accompanied articles, especially front-page features, captured important events for readers.

Of all the popular newspapers in this study, the conservative right-wing *Daily Mail* surely deserves mention on its own. The newspaper has been vilified by contemporary commentators over its reporting on Germany in the 1930s. Certainly, the newspaper had a brief flirtation with Nazism and fascism, with proprietor Viscount Rothermere and special correspondent George Ward Price using the pages of the *Daily Mail* to publicly express admiration for Hitler's dictatorship. It even offered support for Oswald Mosley's British Union of Fascists (BUF or Blackshirts) and allowed Mosley to contribute to the newspaper on several occasions in 1933 and 1934.[9] However this admiration was short-lived. The Röhm purge in Germany and the violence of the BUF at the Olympia Rally in 1934 saw Rothermere take a clear and public step away from fascism and Nazism.[10] Here it is important to consider Rothermere's admiration for both right-wing movements in their context. Rothermere's infamous 'Youth Triumphant' article, printed in July 1933, attacked detractors of the new regime, denied the terror, downplayed the persecution of the Jews and praised the strength of the new regime which had managed to attract the support of the country's youth. The article demonstrated Rothermere's ignorance and unwillingness to see the new government for what it was – a brutal regime. But his admiration for the regime focused on the strength that he considered Hitler's government had displayed and he contrasted this with what he saw as the weakness of the British government which he viewed as weak and ineffectual. The brutality of the dictatorship as it turned on its own gave Rothermere pause and he distanced himself from the regime after that. Special correspondent George Ward Price, on the other hand, continued to use the pages of the *Daily Mail* to express admiration for the regime (particularly in articles about the strength of youth and the success of the Nuremberg rallies), long after Rothermere had turned to writing about the need for Britain to rearm and prepare for a future war.

A further important point must be made here. Rothermere's (brief) admiration for fascism did not, for the most part, get in the way of the newspaper reporting what was happening in Germany, particularly in 1933. Certainly, the newspaper did not report the political terror campaign beyond the wave of arrests that followed the Reichstag Fire, but it did report the destruction of democracy in all its stages. It also reported the April boycott and efforts to 'cleanse' the civil service of Jewish employees. It seems that, for the most part, Berlin correspondent Rothay Reynolds was left to report what he had witnessed, and the *Daily Mail* printed his reports. Reports by special correspondent George Ward Price as well as any editorializing were kept separate from Reynold's reports. The dismissal of Jews from the theatre, universities, the civil service and the medical profession was all reported by Reynolds, who noted that these Jews faced 'ruin' because of the Nazi action. Reynolds also reported some developments in the church struggle, and the major excesses against the Jews in later years, including *Kristallnacht* and the plight of refugees in 1938.

Political ideology or affiliation could also affect how a newspaper covered German affairs. Whether a newspaper was right-wing or left-wing, conservative or liberal, could affect editorial decisions, and had an impact on how newspapers reported what was happening in Germany. The conservatism of the *Daily Mail*, and the influence of proprietor Rothermere, limited what the newspaper covered, particularly in terms of the ruthless suppression of the political left. The *Manchester Guardian*, on the other hand, took its liberal pedigree seriously, identifying with a moral duty to expose the brutality and cruelty of the regime. But, there were also multiple instances where newspapers overlooked political ideology reporting, for instance, the destruction of democracy in 1933. *The Times* reported each step in the destruction of democracy in detail. *The Times*, *Daily Telegraph* and *Morning Post* were all conservative newspapers but reported the suppression of the trade union movement. And *The Spectator*, a conservative newspaper, was one of the first to denounce the political terror, earning condemnation from its readers. The *Daily Mail* and *Daily Express* still gave readers an understanding (albeit an often sensational one) of what was happening in Germany, despite their conservative and right-leaning ideologies. British newspapers, regardless of their political leaning, still, for the most part, got the story across to readers, especially in 1933.

They still reported important and significant developments in the Nazis' quest for total power in Germany.

This study has demonstrated that the British press, as a whole, was vitally interested in what was happening in National Socialist Germany in the 1930s. In doing so, it has shown the efforts that many foreign correspondents, working for British newspapers, have gone to in exposing the truth and reality of life under the Nazi dictatorship. In their commitment to covering the situation in Germany, they faced obstacles and risks. The most significant was that in reporting from Germany, correspondents were at the mercy of the Nazi government and risked arrest, expulsion or worse. Editors and staff risked their newspapers being prohibited in Germany. But the correspondents risked being arrested and questioned about their activities and risked expulsion. It is no exaggeration to say that correspondents risked their livelihoods and, at times, their lives in writing about the Nazi regime.

It has been shown that foreign correspondents were under constant surveillance and scrutiny by the Gestapo and the police in Germany. Wickham Steed, journalist and former editor of *The Times*, wrote of the difficulties in working in a dictatorship in his 1938 study of the press in Britain:

> Foreign newspaper correspondents in those countries are heavily handicapped. They live under constant supervision; they may be expelled at any moment; and quite apart from censorship which controls their work; it is dangerous for them to write or suggest the truth lest they be arrested and charged with hostility to the State.[11]

Norman Ebbutt, *The Times* Berlin correspondent, wrote that it was common knowledge that foreign correspondents' phone calls were not private; phones were tapped and a 'shadowy third' would listen in to conversations.[12] Furthermore, letters were also often intercepted. To ensure his dispatches got through to *The Times* headquarters in London, Ebbutt devised a system: 'It is true that I always, merely as a precaution, duplicated or triplicated all articles which might be stopped, posting them in different letter-boxes at varying times and in different envelopes.'[13] Concerns for the safety of correspondents were also very real. Norman Ebbutt's flat in Berlin was raided in early 1933 by the police while he was out. The *Manchester Guardian*'s special correspondent F. A. Voigt also had his flat in Paris raided by Nazis. He feared that it had been part of an assassination plot to silence him.[14] The *Manchester Guardian*'s Robert Dell had to flee Germany after his reporting on the Reichstag Fire trial in late 1933 aggravated the Nazi authorities. He was warned to leave by friends and quickly did so. Pembroke Stephens of the *Daily Express* and George Eric Rowe Gedye of the *Daily Telegraph* also wrote of the dangers they faced in reporting German affairs truthfully and accurately.

While intimidation and violence were second nature to the Nazi dictatorship, often the easiest recourse available to the regime in silencing correspondents was expelling them from Germany. In the 1930s, correspondents Noel Panter, Pembroke Stephens and Norman Ebbutt were expelled from Germany while working for British newspapers. For correspondents there was a fine line in telling the truth about Germany without risking expulsion. American correspondent William L. Shirer described this in *The Nightmare Years*, a recollection of his time serving as a correspondent in Nazi Germany:

> All through my years in Berlin I was conscious of walking a real, if ill-defined line. If you strayed too far off it you risked expulsion. One soon got the feeling of how far one could go. I made up my own mind from the very beginning that as long as I could tell the essential story of Hitler's Germany, fully, truthfully and accurately, I would stay, if I were allowed to. Once that became impossible I would go.[15]

Ebbut recalled that it was necessary to moderate what he wrote for *The Times*: 'naturally it could not give voice to what I was saying in private, nor in the same uncompromising words. Otherwise I would have been outside Germany before the end of 1933.'[16] G. E. R. Gedye echoed similar sentiments in account of his time as Vienna correspondent for the *Daily Telegraph*. He wrote of the dilemma he faced following the Nazi invasion of Austria:

> I personally had a choice between two courses. Either I suppressed all the worst features of the Nazi terror in the hope of finding sufficient favour with the new masters of Austria to be able to stay on indefinitely, or I gave up the full truth without the least modification, in which case my days in Vienna would be very few.[17]

Unsurprisingly, Gedye chose the second option and, as a result, lasted a week after the Nazis took control of Austria before he was expelled.[18] For those that remained in Germany, and Austria, were faced with the unhappy reality of working in an increasingly hostile country.

At times, it was revealed, correspondents also faced obstacles in reporting on German affairs from their own newspaper staff. This made living and working in a dictatorship even harder. Tension and disagreements between correspondents and editors (and other newspaper staff) were not uncommon when it came to covering Nazi Germany, especially in the late 1930s when

Britain was in the throes of appeasement. *The Times* editor, Geoffrey Dawson, was careful about what was printed in his newspaper. In 1937, Dawson wrote to one of his correspondents H. G. Daniels: 'I do my utmost, night after night, to keep out of the paper anything that might hurt their [Nazi German] susceptibilities. . . . I can really think of nothing that has been printed now for many months past to which they could possibly take exception as unfair comment.'[19] This was certainly something that correspondent Ebbutt struggled with at times. However, *The Times* continued to print articles keeping readers up-to-date with developments in Germany, particularly the church struggle and the persecution of Jews.

F. A. Voigt, a correspondent perhaps most in line with his newspaper the *Manchester Guardian*'s policy, clashed with editor W. P. Crozier at times. It was his criticism of the newspaper's initial coverage on the terror that helped the *Manchester Guardian* become the most outspoken critic of the Nazi regime and its brutal methods. But, in another instance of criticism from Voigt, Crozier wrote back: 'it does not seem to have occurred to you for one moment that I have had, or have, to face any difficulties in your mode of presentation of the stuff you deal with', which he described as 'dogmatic and uncompromising in the highest degree'.[20] As Franklin Reid Gannon wrote in his book, Crozier faced 'the practical necessity of softening the cries, with which he was in basic agreement, of a respected colleague who yelled "Wolf!" for half a dozen years before the wolf suddenly revealed itself to the whole world in March 1939'.[21]

While it is difficult to say whether correspondents' reports were censored by editorial staff and editors, what was published was vivid enough to give a good picture of what was going on in Germany. If, from time to time, articles were toned down, the overall impression of the brutal nature of the Nazi dictatorship remained. There was nothing in reports, apart from some clear examples in the *Daily Mail*, that pointed to editors and newspaper staff trying to give a different impression. While Gannon, for instance, unearthed instances where articles on foreign policy were smoothed out or toned down, it is hard to detect the same apparatus in play when it came to reporting Germany's domestic policy. For instance, even though readers of the *Manchester Guardian* and, to a lesser degree, *The Spectator* were annoyed or outraged by reports on the terror, both newspapers continued to print the truth about Nazi barbarity. Furthermore, even in 1938 when the British government was in the throes of appeasement British newspapers continued to print articles about the brutal treatment of Jews in Germany and Austria. It is possible that British newspapers were wary or cautious about the possibility of embarrassing the British government by denouncing its foreign policy although some newspapers were critical of the official response to the refugee crisis. But for news about Germany's domestic situation, it was a different story. This was a case of a civilized state essentially going berserk. And for newspapers and correspondents it was a story that deserved to be told and the truth exposed.

The conclusions of this study have important implications for several important historiographical debates. First, the book has significant bearing on the debate surrounding appeasement in the 1930s. As the argument goes, British Prime Minister Neville Chamberlain and his government pursued a policy of appeasement in the hope of averting war on the European continent. Appeasement then arose from Chamberlain's belief that it was possible to negotiate with Hitler to avoid or, at the very least, delay war. Within this is the belief that Chamberlain could not have known who and what he was dealing with. With the benefit of hindsight, it is now clear Hitler was intent on pursuing his goals of territorial expansion, regardless of the outcome of negotiations with Britain or any other European country. How can one possibly carry out legal negotiations (in good faith) with a tyrant such as Hitler – head of an uncivilized and violent state? Did this mean then that Chamberlain and the British government were in the dark about Hitler and his intentions? In light of what this study has concluded, if the British government did not know who and what they were dealing with, namely a tyrant at the head of a brutal dictatorship, then they were surely guilty of gross negligence. It can be safely assumed that the British government had sources of information other than just newspapers but even if they only had the British press to rely on for information, they would have a fair understanding of the nature of the Nazi dictatorship. They would have known that the Nazi dictatorship had made a mockery of liberal democratic values and had ruthlessly suppressed free speech and annihilated civil liberties. The only conclusion that can reasonably be taken from this is that Chamberlain was so fearful of war, he tried to do anything and everything to prevent another breaking out. But, as scholars, we should stop trying to explain appeasement by arguing that Chamberlain and the British government simply did not know what they were dealing with.

The second debate to which this study contributes is that of knowledge about the persecution of the Jews in Germany. This concerns whether those outside of Germany knew what was happening to the Jews in Germany, and whether this knowledge could have translated into action, or at the very least, pressure on the Nazi government. There is a major debate in the historiography centring on what was known and what could have been done to help Germany's (and, later, Europe's) Jews. The question over what was known can, to some degree, be answered with the findings of this book. This study has uncovered reporting trends on the persecution of the Jews in Germany and has demonstrated that the most newspapers did report fully, and in detail, what was happening to the Jews in Germany (and later Austria). But more than that, many correspondents (and their newspapers) understood that the Jews in Germany were not just being persecuted – they were being systematically and brutally alienated and excluded from German society. The methodical way in which the Jews were targeted was juxtaposed, in British press reports, with the violent brutality in which they were often treated. The tales of beatings and torture, especially after the *Anschluss* with Austria and the events of *Kristallnacht*, was just one part in the treatment of the Jews.

The fact that this was picked up by British correspondents and their newspapers is significant to the debate surrounding knowledge of the persecution of the Jews. That the press was reporting the laws and decrees, along with the violence, as part of a campaign to rid Germany of its Jewish population bears important implications in our understanding of what was known and what could have been done. Of course, it was not clear that the persecution of the Jews would end with the Nazis' extermination programme that sought to physically annihilate the Jews in Europe, but it certainly was clear that the Jews were no longer welcome in Germany (and later Austria and Czechoslovakia). British correspondents had urged action, calling for something be done for the Jews of Germany and Austria, especially in 1938. They recognized how dire the situation was, and they recognized the failures of the international community in helping Jews flee. A reader of British newspapers could have understood that the situation was desperate. And so, the implications for the historiography are clear. What was happening to the Jews in Germany and Austria was no secret. In this line of thinking, more should have been done to help the Jews in their desperate plight before the outbreak of war in 1939.

In the 1930s British newspapers reported what was happening in Germany, as the Nazi Party exerted its control over the state. The press reported developments, with some urgency, charting the transition from Weimar democracy to ruthless dictatorship. The contrast between Britain's democratic way of life and Germany's descent into an uncivilized and oppressive state was clearly demonstrated in reports written by British correspondents. These correspondents reported the suppression of the press, free speech and religion, as well as the innumerable cases of violence, all carried out by, and for, the Nazi regime. In the years leading up to war, press commentary and criticism of Nazi Germany's aggressive foreign policy may have been toned down, but British newspapers continued to voice their disgust of Nazi methods, particularly when it came to the suppression of the churches and the persecution of the Jews.

Overall, British press reports left little doubt about the nature of the dictatorship, its intentions, methods and practice. Most correspondents did not shy away from reporting the truth. Given the level of reporting, people in Britain could have known a great deal about the Nazi dictatorship by regularly reading British newspapers. A reader of one of the quality British newspapers could, in all likelihood, have known more about the Nazi dictatorship than a reader of a popular newspaper, but even a reader of a popular newspaper would, from articles printed in the 1930s, have known that the Nazi dictatorship was a brutal and oppressive regime that had stomped out the freedoms and rights enjoyed in a democracy like Britain. The fact that these articles existed is testament to the brave commitment of the correspondents, editors and newspaper staff that made up the British press in the 1930s, in telling the truth about the Nazi regime.

Appendix
British newspaper details

Daily Express

1900–*present*
Political leaning: Centre
Proprietor: Lord Beaverbrook (William Maxwell 'Max' Aitkin)
Editor: Arthur Christiansen
Notable correspondents: Sefton Delmer; Pembroke Stephens; Alan Moorehead.
Berlin correspondents: Selkirk Panton; Noel Monks
Circulation: 2,329,000 (1938, Largest circulation of any daily in Britain)

Daily Mail

1896–*present*
Political leaning: Conservative right
Proprietor: Viscount Rothermere (Harold Sidney Harmsworth)
Editor: W. L. Warden (1931–5); A. L. Cranfield (1936–8); Robert Frew (1939–44)
Special correspondent: George Ward Price
Berlin correspondents: Rothay Reynolds; Ralph Izzard; Paul Bretherton.
Circulation: 1,580,000 (1937)

Daily Mirror

1903–*present*
Political leaning: Left (from mid-1930s)

Proprietor: Viscount Rothermere (sold by Rothermere in mid-1930s. The precise details are somewhat mysterious). Guy Bartholomew served as editorial director during the 1930s and helped revolutionize the newspaper by transforming it into a left-leaning newspaper, targeted more towards the working class. He also turned the *Daily Mirror* into a tabloid, emulating the American tabloid newspapers.
Editor: L. D. Brownlee (1931–4), Cecil Thomas (1934–48).
Circulation: Over 2,000,000 (1937)

Daily Telegraph (*Daily Telegraph and Morning Post*)

1855–1937–*present*

The *Daily Telegraph* merged with the *Morning Post* in 1937 and was known as the *Daily Telegraph and Morning Post,* before returning to the title of *Daily Telegraph.*
Political leaning: Conservative/centre right (Imperialist)
Proprietors: Berry Brothers–Lord Camrose (William Berry; later Viscount Camrose) and Lord Kemsley (Gomer Berry, later Viscount Kemsley)
Editor: Arthur E. Watson (administrative); Robert Skelton (news editor)
Notable correspondents: G. E. R. Gedye (Vienna correspondent, until left the newspaper in April 1939 over disagreements about his book *Fallen Bastions*); Victor Gordon-Lennox (diplomatic correspondent); Noel Panter (Munich correspondent until his expulsion in 1933).
Berlin correspondents: Eustace B. Wareing (until 1938); Hugh Carleton Greene (took over from Wareing in 1938 until his expulsion from Germany in May 1939. He had been Wareing's assistant in Berlin prior to being appointed lead correspondent); Anthony Mann.
Notable contributors: Austin Chamberlain; Winston Churchill.
Circulation: 637,000 (1937)

Jewish Chronicle (weekly)

1841–*present*
The *Jewish Chronicle* is the oldest continuing Jewish newspaper in the world.
Managing director: Mortimer Epstein (1931–6)

The Jewish Chronicle was governed by a board, with Neville Laski at its head as president (from 1933).
Editor: Jack M. Rich (1932–6); Ivan Greenberg (1936–46; had been assistant editor prior to that).
Notable (special) correspondent: Simon Gilbert (leading articles and important editorials such as 'In the Communal Armchair).
Circulation: 22,000 (1946)

Manchester Guardian

1821–*present*

From 1959 the name changed to *The Guardian*. Since 1961 *The Guardian* has been published in London.
Political leaning: Liberal left
Manager: John Russell Scott
Editor: William Percival Crozier (1932–44)
Notable (special/diplomatic) correspondent: Frederick Augustus Voigt
Berlin correspondents: Alexander Werth (1933); C. A. Lambert (from November 1933).
Other notable correspondents: Robert Dell (Geneva); F. A. Fodor (Central Europe and Vienna); Malcolm Muggeridge (Moscow, 1933).
Circulation: Between 25,000 and 50,000.

Morning Post

1772–1937

The *Morning Post* merged with the *Daily Telegraph* after being bought by the Berry Brothers. Prior to this the newspaper had been the oldest still running London paper.
Political leaning: Conservative right
Owner: Sold to a group headed by Duke of Northumberland (Alan Percy) in 1924.
Editor: Howell Arthur Gwynne (1910–37).
Foreign Editor: Alastair Shannon.
Chief leader writer: J. C. Johnstone
Berlin correspondents: Darsie Gillie; Karl Robson

New Statesman and Nation (weekly)

1913–*present*

The paper formed as the *New Statesman* but adopted the name *New Statesman and Nation* in 1931 after it merged with *The Nation and Athenaeum*. In 1934 the *Week-End Review* was also amalgamated into the *New Statesman and Nation*. It later returned to the name *New Statesman*.

Political leaning: Left
Manager: John Roberts (1920–57)
Editor: Basil Kingsley Martin (1931–60)
Contributors: Alexander Werth; H. N. Brailsford; C. E. M. Joad
Editorial comment: Mostyn Lloyd (on Germany)
Circulation: 18,000 approx. (1934)

News Chronicle

1930–60

The *News Chronicle* came about following the merger of the *Daily Chronicle* and *Daily News* (which had previously absorbed the *Morning Leader* and *Westminster Gazette*). The newspaper was absorbed by the *Daily Mail*, ceasing publication in 1960.

Political leaning: Left
Owner: Cadbury Family Trust with Lawrence Cadbury as Chairman.
Editor: Gerald Aylmer Vallance (1933–6); Gerald Barry (1936–47)
Political editor: A. J. Cummings
Notable (diplomatic) correspondent: Vernon Bartlett
Berlin correspondents: John Segrue (1933–6); P. B. Wadsworth (succeeded Segrue; previously assistant in Berlin); H. D. Harrison (when Harrison was expelled from Yugoslavia in 1937, he was moved to Berlin where the German government ordered his removal in March 1939); Ian Colvin (moved between Berlin and London).
Circulation: 1,324,000 (1937)

Observer (weekly)

1791–*present*
Political leaning: Liberal
Owner: Viscount Astor (Waldorf Astor)
Editor: James Louis (J. L.) Garvin (1908–1942)
Berlin Correspondent: P. B. Wadsworth (also contributed to the *News Chronicle*).
Circulation: 214,000 (1936)

The Spectator (weekly)

1828–*present*
Political leaning: Conservative
Owner: Spectator Ltd.; 61 per cent owned by Sir John Evelyn Wench (who acted as proprietor) and Sir J. Angus Watson.
Editor: Sir John Evelyn Wrench (1925–32, also major proprietor during the 1930s); Henry Wilson Harris (1932–53).
Leader writers: R. A. Scott-James (1933–5, also political editor); Goronwy Rees (1936–9).
Berlin correspondent: Harrison Brown.

The Times

1788–*present*
The newspaper was formed under the title *The Daily Universal Register* in 1785.
Political leaning: Conservative
Owner: Viscount Astor (John Jacob Astor), in conjunction with a Trust (and shareholders)
Editor: Geoffrey Dawson (1912–19, then again from 1923–41)
Assistant/deputy editor: Robert Barrington-Ward (later editor, 1941–8).

Berlin correspondents: Norman Ebbutt (Berlin correspondent until his expulsion in August 1937); Douglas Reed (Ebbutt's assistant in Berlin until 1935, then Vienna correspondent until 1938); James Holburn (Ebbutt's assistant and successor).

Other contributors/correspondents: H. G. Daniels (Geneva); A. L. Kennedy.

Circulation: 192,000 (1937)

Source of information

Cesarani, David. *The Jewish Chronicle and Anglo-Jewry, 1841-1991*. Cambridge: Cambridge University Press, 1994.

Gannon, Franklin Reid. *The British Press and Germany, 1936-1939*. Oxford: Clarendon Press, 1971.

Griffiths, Dennis ed. *The Encyclopaedia of the British Press, 1422-1922*. NY: St Martin's Press, 1992.

Hindle, Wilfrid. *The Morning Post, 1772-1937: Portrait of a Newspaper*. London: George Routledge & Sons Ltd. 1937.

Hyams, Edward. *The New Statesman: The History of the First Fifty Years, 1913-1963*. London: The Statesman & Nation Publishing Company, 1963.

Political and Economic Planning. 'Report on the British Press'. London: Political and Economic Planning, April 1938.

Notes

Introduction

1 W. H. Auden, *Another Time* (London: Faber, 1940), 112.
2 Franklin Reid Gannon, *The British Press and Germany, 1936-1939* (London: Oxford University Press, 1971), 1.
3 According to the 1939 *BBC Handbook*, the number of licences in the UK was recorded at 8,908,900 at 31 December 1939. This had risen from the 31 December 1937 figure of 8,470,600.
 The British Broadcasting Corporation, *BBC Handbook 1939* (London: Jarrold & Sons, 1939), 10.
4 James Curran and Jean Seaton, *Power without Responsibility: The Press and Broadcasting in Britain,* 5th edn (London and New York: Routledge, 1997), 44. Curran and Seaton point out that circulation figures for the interwar period are 'not entirely reliable' (see notes, page 58). While there may be some differentiation in the figures cited in sources, they do still demonstrate that more people were buying more papers and, significantly, more national papers (than regional), and 'proprietors commanded very large audiences' with their newspaper empires.
5 Viscount Rothermere (Harold Harmsworth); Lord Beaverbrook (Max Aitken); Viscount Camrose (William Berry, later became Viscount in 1941); Lord Kelmsley (James Gomer Berry, became Viscount in 1945).
6 Curran and Seaton, *Power Without Responsibility,* 44.
7 Ibid.
8 Ibid.
9 Malcolm Muggeridge, *The Thirties: 1930-1940 in Great Britain* (London: Fontana, 1972), 20.
 At one point in the 1930s, Muggeridge worked for the *Manchester Guardian* covering the Soviet Union. He later wrote for the *Daily Telegraph* and *Evening Standard* and was employed as editor of *Punch* magazine in the 1950s. He wrote several books including *The Thirties*.
10 See Appendix for biographical details of each newspaper including political leaning.
11 For instance, while the *Daily Herald* is an important newspaper it was ideologically driven. It arrived at conclusions about developments and events in Nazi Germany along already conceived ideological lines. The *Daily Herald*, therefore, offers few new perspectives for this study.

12 Other studies have included more titles but, in the end, provided only a cursory examination of the individual newspapers. This study wished to avoid that pitfall and provide a more detailed study of the press and the included newspapers.
13 Richard Cockett also looks at the press but does so by examining how Chamberlain's government sought to direct and influence the press as appeasement took hold in the late 1930s.
Richard Cockett, *Twilight of Truth: Chamberlain, Appeasement and the Manipulation of the Press* (London: Weidenfeld and Nicolson, 1989).
14 Deborah Lipstadt, *Beyond Belief: The American Press and the Coming of the Holocaust, 1933-1939* (New York: The Free Press, 1986); Laurel Leff, *Buried by the Times: The Holocaust and America's Most Important Newspaper* (Cambridge: Cambridge University Press, 2005); Robert Moses Shapiro, ed. *Why Didn't the Press Shout? American and International Journalism during the Holocaust* (Hoboken, NJ: Yeshiva University Press, 2003).
15 Dan Stone, *Responses to Nazism in Britain, 1933-1939: Before War and Holocaust* (Hampshire: Palgrave Macmillan, 2003); Russell Wallis, *Britain, Germany and the Road to the Holocaust: British Attitudes to Nazi Atrocities* (London: I.B. Taurus & Co. Ltd., 2014).
16 Colin McCullough and Nathan Wilson, eds. *Violence, Memory, and History: Western Perceptions of Kristallnacht* (New York and London: Routledge, 2015).
17 Michaela Hoenicke Moore, *Know Your Enemy: The American Debate on Nazism, 1933-1945* (Cambridge: Cambridge University Press, 2009).
18 Heidi J. S. Tworek, *News from Germany: The Competition to Control World Communications, 1900-1945* (Cambridge: Harvard University Press, 2019).
19 The Times, *History of The Times: The 150th Anniversary and Beyond, 1912-1948*, Vol. 2. (London: The Times, 1952); David Ayerst, *Guardian: Biography of a Newspaper* (London: William Collins & Sons Co. Ltd., 1971).
20 Stephen Koss, *The Rise and Fall of the Political Press in Britain: The Twentieth Century*, Vol. 2 (London: Hamish Hamilton Ltd, 1984).
21 Ian Kershaw, *Making Friends with Hitler* (London: Allen Lane, 2004).
22 John Simpson, *Unreliable Sources: How the 20th Century Was Reported* (London: Macmillan, 2010).
23 Will Wainwright, *Reporting on Hitler: Rothay Reynolds and the British Press in Nazi Germany* (London: Biteback Publishing, 2017).
24 Adrian Bingham, 'The Digitization of Newspaper Archives: Opportunities and Challenges for Historians', *Twentieth Century British History* 21, no. 2 (2010): 229–30.
25 Ibid., 230.
26 Ibid.
27 These include the John Rylands Library at the University of Manchester, the News International Archive and Record Office in London and the Bodleian Library at the University of Oxford.

Chapter 1

1. Political and Economic Planning (PEP), *Report on the British Press* (London: Political and Economic Planning, April 1938), 3.
2. Ibid.
3. Ibid.
4. Example taken from *Daily Mirror*, 20 January 1933.
5. PEP, *Report on the British Press*, 170.
6. Ibid., 160.
7. Ibid.
8. Julius Reuter founded the news agency, which quickly got the name Reuters, in 1851. The *Manchester Guardian* first used Reuter telegrams in the newspaper in 1858. Donald Read, 'Truth in News: Reuters and the *Manchester Guardian*, 1858-1964', *Northern History* 31, no. 1 (1995): 282.
9. Ibid.
10. Read, 'Truth in News', 297.
11. Donald Read, 'Reuters: News Agency of the British Empire', *Contemporary Record* 8, no. 2 (1994): 197.
12. Ibid.
13. Read, 'Truth in News', 297.
14. For a more detailed breakdown of the processing of news please refer to PEP, *Report on the British Press*, Chapter VI, 'How News Is Produced'.
15. It is possible to gain a better understanding of the editorial policy of a newspaper by examining correspondence, internal memos, proofs, diaries and so on, of newspaper personalities kept in archives, such as *The Times* at the News International Archive and Record Office in London, or *Manchester Guardian* at the John Rylands Library at the University of Manchester in Manchester, but even with this approach there are inevitably gaps.
16. PEP, *Report on the British Press*, 188.
17. Viscount Rothermere authored *My Fight to Rearm Britain* (London: Eyre & Spottiswoode Ltd., 1939).
18. Viscount Camrose, *British Newspapers and Their Controllers* (London: Cassell and Company Limited, 1947), 38.
19. Dawson was editor of *The Times* from 1912-1919 and then from 1923-1941. The Times, ed. *History of The Times: The 150th Anniversary and Beyond, 1912-1948* (London: The Times, 1952), II: 793.
20. PEP, *Report on the British Press*, 179.
21. David Ayerst, *Guardian: Biography of a Newspaper* (London: William Collins Sons & Co. Ltd., 1971), 495.
22. Franklin Reid Gannon, *The British Press and Germany, 1936-1939* (Oxford: Clarendon Press, 1971), 70.

23 Dawson's diaries are currently held in the Bodleian Library at the University of Oxford. See bibliography for collection details.
24 Gannon wrote that after the post of Foreign Editor became vacant in 1929 Dawson decided not to appoint anyone else. He wrote to friend, Lord Brand, in 1936 'A really good Foreign Editor would be a great support', but that he had not been able to find anyone that was good enough. In the end Robin Barrington-Ward served as Deputy Editor, fulfilling the function of Foreign Editor, especially in terms of Anglo-German news stories.
As quoted in Gannon, *The British Press and Germany*, 61.
25 William L. Shirer, *The Nightmare Years, 1930-1940* (Boston: Little, Brown and Company, 1984), 206.
26 Ibid.
27 Ibid.
28 See Gannon, *The British Press and Germany*, 123.
29 TNL Archive, Ebbutt Papers, Memorandum, 1 April 1933, NE/4/4/2.
30 Ibid.
31 Ebbutt to Deakin, 11 November 1934 quoted in Frank McDonough, *Neville Chamberlain, Appeasement and the British Road to War* (Manchester: Manchester University Press, 1998), 117.
32 Ibid.
33 Ibid.
34 Despite Ebbutt's complaints of interference *The Times* still printed frequent articles on the church situation. See Chapter 6.
35 Shirer, *The Nightmare Years*, 206.
36 TNL Archive, Ebbutt to Dawson, 18 December 1934, Geoffrey Dawson Internal Correspondence, TT/ED/GGD/1/.
37 Ibid.
38 Ibid.
39 TNL Archive, Dawson to Ebbutt, 20 December 1934, Geoffrey Dawson Internal Correspondence, TT/ED/GGD/1/.
40 Gannon, *The British Press and Germany*, 47.
41 Ibid., 46.
42 Ibid.
43 G. E. R. Gedye, 'Impressions of Hitler's Germany', *Contemporary Review* 143 (January/June 1933): 670.
44 Ibid., 676.
45 Gannon, *The British Press and Germany*, 47.
46 Ibid.
47 Ibid.
48 It is unclear if Voigt's criticisms stemmed from a power struggle between the two correspondents. There is nothing to suggest this in the correspondence files held at

the John Rylands Library. This author has, therefore, refrained from speculating and focused on the correspondence exchanged regarding Voigt's concerns.
49 *Manchester Guardian*, 13 March, 1933 'Growing Reports of a Nazi Terror', Berlin Corr., 9. Herafter *MG*.
50 JRL, Voigt to Crozier, 15 March 1933, Foreign Correspondence File 145e, Folder 207.
51 Ibid.
52 JRL, Werth to Crozier, 17 March, 1933, Foreign Correspondence File 153a, Folder 207.
53 Ibid.
54 JRL, Crozier to Werth, 20 March 1933, Foreign Correspondence File 160a, Folder 207.
55 JRL, Crozier, Letter to Werth, 20 March 1933, Foreign Correspondence File 160b, Folder 207.
56 JRL, Werth to Crozier, 23 March 1933, Foreign Correspondence File 172a, Folder 207, JRL.
57 Charles Lambert took over in Berlin in late November 1933. He went via Paris to meet with Voigt and discuss the German situation before traveling to Berlin, as indicated in a letter written to Crozier dated 27 November 1933.
58 Ayerst, *Guardian*, 514.
59 Ibid.
60 JRL, Voigt to Crozier, 30 April 1933, Foreign Correspondence File 186a, Folder 207.
61 Arthur Christiansen, *Headlines All My Life* (London: Heinemann, 1961), 144.
62 Sefton Delmer describes his experiences in Germany in the 1930s in the first volume of his autobiography, *Trail Sinister*. During the war Delmer was in charge of a black propaganda campaign waged by radio from Britain against Hitler and the Nazi state.
63 TNL Archive, Ebbutt to Dawson, 18 December 1934, Geoffrey Dawson Internal Correspondence, TT/ED/GGD/1/.
64 Ibid.
65 TNL Archive, Norman Ebbutt Papers, Articles and Memoirs 1939-1945, Manuscript of 'My Twelve Years in Germany and After', Notes for Chapter X, NE/2/1/1.
66 TNL Archive, Norman Ebbutt Papers, Articles and Memoirs 1939-1945, Manuscript of 'My Twelve Years in Germany and After', Introduction, NE/2/1/2.
67 *MG*, 6 March 1933 'Expulsion of Foreign Correspondents', Berlin Corr., 9.
68 *MG*, 9 March 1933 'German Communist Press Banned', Berlin Corr., 4.
69 Panter brought libel action against the British Union of Fascists newspaper *Blackshirt* over an article in the paper on 4-10 November 1933. The article called Panter a 'literary sneak' and a 'ferreting spy' who had taken 'advantage of the hospitality of a friendly country', and who would have 'already been shot in a really nice war'. *The Times* reported that after initially denying defamation, the BUF

'wished now to withdraw all those defences'. The matter was settled with an apology of 'extreme regret' and a lump sum paid to Panter 'by way of earnest of their sincerity in the matter'.
The Times, 15 November 1934, 'High Court of Justice: A Libel in the 'Blackshirt: Journalist's Suit Settled', 4.
70 *The Times*, 27 October 1933, 'Mr. Panter's Arrest', Munich Corr., 12.
71 *Daily Telegraph*, 7 November 1933, 'My Fellow Prisoners in Munich', Noel Panter, 12. *Daily Telegraph*, 8 November 1933, 'Nazis' Political Prisoners', Noel Panter, 12.
72 *Daily Express*, 17 May 1934, 'Nazis arrest "*Daily Express*" Berlin correspondent; Pembroke Stephens in Custody', 1. Stephens described his arrest in a follow-up article published on 18 May 1934 entitled My arrest by the Nazis; Freed but charges may follow; '*Daily Express*' man returns to Berlin' (p1-2).
73 *Daily Express*, 1 June 1934 'Pembroke Stephens Arrested Again', Reginald Steed, Daily Express Corr., 1. Hereafter *DE*.
74 *DE*, 2 June 1934, 'My Expulsion by the Nazis', By Pembroke Stephens, 1.
75 Ibid.
76 TNL Archive, Norman Ebbutt Papers, Articles and Memoirs 1939-1945, Manuscript of 'My Twelve Years in Germany and After', Chapter IX, NE/2/1/12.
77 Ibid.
78 Voigt often used the term 'Gestappa' interchangeably with 'Gestapo' in his correspondence and articles.
JRL, Voigt to Crozier, 1 December 1933, Foreign Correspondence File 172a, Folder 210.
79 Ibid.
80 Ibid.
81 JRL, Voigt to Crozier, 18 December 1933, Foreign Correspondence File 256b, Folder 210. Emphasis in text.
82 Ibid.
83 JRL, Voigt to Crozier, 26 December 1933, Foreign Correspondence File 270, Folder 210.
84 Ibid.
85 JRL, Voigt to Crozier, 29 December 1933, Foreign Correspondence File 276, Folder 210. Emphasis in text.

Chapter 2

1 *Daily Telegraph*, 31 January 1933, 'Hitler's Triumph and Test', Leader, 10. Hereafter *DT*.
2 Ibid.

3 *The Times*, 31 January 1933, 'Herr Hitler in Office', Leader, 11. Hereafter *TT*.
4 *The Spectator*, 3 February 1933, 'Hitlerism on Trial', 140. Hereafter *TS*.
5 Ibid.
6 *News Chronicle*, 31 January 1933, 'Herr Hitler's Triumph', Leader, 6. Hereafter *NC*.
7 *Daily Express*, 31 January 1933, 'Hitler Smashes Military Plot', 1. Hereafter *DE*.
8 Ibid.
9 *DT*, 1 February 1933, 'Hitler Shorn of Real Power', 11.
10 Ibid.
11 Ibid.
12 *NC*, 31 January 1933, 'Hitler's Message to the World', 1.
13 *DE*, 22 February 1933, 'Germany's 21-Day Chancellor', 'D. Sefton Delmer', 10.
14 *Daily Mirror*, 31 January 1933, 'Hitler May Rule as Dictator', 1. Hereafter *DMirror*.
15 *Manchester Guardian*, 31 January 1933, 'Hitler Forms His First Cabinet', Berlin Corr., 9. Hereafter *MG*.
16 Ibid.
17 Ibid.
18 *DMirror*, 31 January 1933, 'Hitler May Rule as Dictator', 1.
19 *The New Statesman and Nation*, 4 February 1933, 117. Hereafter *NS&N*.
20 *DT*, 31 January 1933, 'Hitler's Triumph and Test', Leader, 110.
21 *MP*, 31 January 1933, 'Hitler Chancellor of Germany', Berlin Corr., 11.
22 Ibid.
23 Ibid.
24 *Jewish Chronicle*, 3 February 1933, 'Hitler's Victory', 7. Hereafter *JC*.
25 *NC*, 31 January 1933, 'Hitler's Plans', Berlin Corr., 2.
26 *TS*, 3 February 1933, 'Hitlerism on Trial', 140.
27 *TT*, 31 January 1933, 'Herr Hitler in Office', Leader, 11.
28 *MG*, 1 February 1933, 'Hitler's First Days in Power', Berlin Corr., 9.
29 Ibid.
30 Ian Kershaw, *Hitler, 1889-1936* (London: Penguin Books, 1998), 439.
31 *MG*, 6 February 1933, 'Political Murders in Germany', Berlin Corr., 12.
32 *MP*, 7 February 1933, 'Confusion in Germany', Berlin Corr., 13.
33 Ibid.
34 *TT*, 6 February 1933, 'Election Moves in Germany', Berlin Corr., 12.
35 *MG*, 4 February 1933, 'Effort to Dissolve the Prussian Diet', Berlin Corr., 15.
36 *DE*, 22 February 1933, 'Germany's 21-Day Chancellor', 'By Telephone from D. Sefton Delmer', 10.
37 *DT*, 16 February 1933, 'Herr Hitler Prepares to Suppress Opponents', Berlin Corr., 13.
38 *DT*, 20 February 1933, 'Hitler Defies German Constitution', Berlin Corr., 13.
39 *TT*, 13 February 1933, 'Hitlerism', Berlin Corr., 11.

40 *TS*, 17 February 1933, 'Hitler's Campaign', 201.
41 *TT*, 16 February 1933, 'A Hitlerist State', Berlin Corr., 12.
42 *TT*, 17 February 1933, 'Dangers in Germany', Berlin Corr., 13.
43 *MG*, 16 February 1933, 'A Change of Regime in Germany', Berlin Corr., 9.
44 Ibid.
45 *DT*, 20 February 1933, 'Hitler Defies German Constitution', Berlin Corr., 13.
46 Ibid.
47 *Obs.*, 26 February 1933, 'South Germany and Hitler', Corr., 10.
48 *MG*, 18 February 1933, 'Hitler's Widening Control', Berlin Corr., 15.
49 Ibid.
50 *MG*, 27 February 1933, 'The Election in Germany', Berlin Corr., 12.
51 *DE*, 25 February 1933, 'Whirlwind Election Tour by Airplane', By D. Sefton Delmer, 3.
52 Ibid.
53 Ibid.
54 *DE*, 25 February 1933, 'Nothing Shall Stop Us Now', By D. Sefton Delmer, 1.
55 Ibid.
56 Ibid.
57 Ibid.
58 *DE*, 'Nothing Shall Stop Us Now', 'By D. Sefton Delmer', continued on 11.
59 *DMail*, 28 February 1933, 'German House of Deputies Destroyed by Fire', Berlin Corr., 1.
60 *TT*, 28 February 1933, 'Reichstag on Fire', Berlin Corr., 14.
61 There is a general consensus of the 'single culprit' thesis, originally put forth by Fritz Tobias, that Marinus van der Lubbe was responsible for the fire. A few historians, including Benjamin Carter Hett, have recently come out and argued against this thesis, citing new evidence. See Benjamin Carter Hett, *Burning the Reichstag: An Investigation into the Third Reich's Enduring Mystery* (New York: Oxford University Press, 2014). This has been vigorously refuted by others, most notably Richard J Evans, in the *London Review of Books* in 2014. See Richard J. Evans, 'The Conspiracists', Review of *Burning the Reichstag: An Investigation into the Third Reich's Enduring Mystery*, by Benjamin Carter Hett, *London Review of Books* 36 no. 9 (2014): 3–9, http://www.lrb.co.uk/v36/n09/richard-j-evans/the-conspiracists.
62 *MP*, 1 March 1933, "German Constitution Suspended', Berlin Corr., 11.
63 *DMail*, 1 March 1933, 'Berlin Reds Raided', Berlin Corr., 12.
64 Richard J Evans, *The Coming of the Third Reich* (New York: The Penguin Press, 2004), 332–3.
65 *MG*, 'German Dictatorship', 9.
66 *DMail*, 'Sensational German Decree to Smash Communism', 11.

67 Hans Mommsen, *The Rise and Fall of Weimar Democracy*, translated by Elborg Forster and Larry Eugence Jones (Chapel Hill: The University of North Carolina Press, 1996), 542; Evans, *The Coming of the Third Reich*, 332.
68 *TT*, 1 March 1933, 'The German Crisis', Berlin Corr., 14.
69 *News Chronicle*, 1 March 1933, 'Hitler's Death Decree, 'From John Segrue', 1.
70 Ibid.
71 *NC*, 1 March 1933, 'Hitler's Death Decree', From John Segrue Berlin Corr., 1.
72 Ibid.
73 *MP*, 1 March 1933, 'German Constitution Suspended', Berlin Corr., 11.
74 *MG*, 'German Dictatorship', 9 and, *DM*, 'Sensational German Decree to Smash Communism', 11.
75 *TT*, 1 March 1933, 'Tension in Berlin', Leader, 15.
76 *DT*, 1 March 1933, 'Martial Law Proclaimed in Germany', Berlin Corr., 13.
77 *MP*, 'German Constitution Suspended', 11.
78 *NC*, 2 March 1933, 'Germany under the Iron Hand', Berlin Corr., 1.
79 *MG*, 2 March 1933, 'Berlin a City of Rumours', Reuter, 13.
80 Ibid.
81 *NS&N*, 4 March 1933, 241.
82 *NS&N*, 11 February 1933, 'The Nazi Heaven', Berlin Corr., 153.
83 Ibid.
84 Ibid.
85 Ibid.
86 *TS*, 3 March 1933, 'Terror in Germany', By Harrison Brown, 279.
87 Ibid.
88 Ibid.
89 Ibid., 273.
90 Ibid.
91 Ibid.
92 Ibid.
93 *Obs.*, 5 March 1933, 'The German Revolution', 16.
94 *TT*, 4 March 1933, 'Germany Polls To-Morrow', Leader, 13.
95 *DT*, 4 March 1933, 'Will Hitler Get His Majority?', Berlin Corr., 11.
96 *DMail*, 4 March 1933, 'Germany's Third Election in Eight Months', Berlin Corr., 13.
97 *MG*, 4 March 1933, 'Germany's Choice', Leader, 10.
98 *MG*, 4 March 1933, 'Eve of the Elections in Germany', Berlin Corr., 11.
99 Ibid.
100 Ibid.
101 *TT*, 4 March 1933, 'Eve of Poll in Germany', Berlin Corr., 12.
102 *TT*, 6 March 1933, 'Elections in Germany', Berlin Corr., 12.
103 *TT*, 7 March 1933, 'Herr Hitler's Election', Leader, 15.

104 *TS*, 10 March 1933, 'The German Elections', 321.
105 *DMail*, 6 March 1933, 'Nazis Seize Hamburg', 11; *DE*, 6 March 1933, 'Sweeping Victory for Hitler in German Elections', By D. Sefton Delmer, Daily Express' Corr., 1.
106 *TT*, 7 March 1933, 'Triumph for the Nazis', Berlin Corr., 15; *Morning Post*, 6 March 1933, 'Hitler Sweeps Germany', 11.
107 *TT*, 6 March 1933, 'Elections in Germany', Berlin Corr., 12.
108 Ibid.
109 *TT*, 7 March 1933, 'Triumph of the Nazis', Berlin Corr., 15.
110 *DMail*, 6 March 1933, 'Nazi Coup at Hamburg', Berlin Corr., 12.
111 *NS&N*, 11 March 1933, 'Hitler's Victory', 241.
112 *NC*, 6 March 1933, 'Hitler's Day', From John Segrue 'News-Chronicle' Corr., 9.
113 Figures taken from *TT*, 'Triumph of the Nazis', Berlin Corr., 15.
114 *MG*, 6 March 1933, 'Nazis Win the General Election', 9.
115 *NC*, 'Hitler's Day', 9.
116 *DMail*, 6 March 1933, 'Record Poll', Berlin Corr., 12.
117 *DT*, 6 March 1933, 'A Triumph for Hitler', 11.
118 *MG*, 7 March 1933, 'Fruits of Efficient Propaganda', Berlin Corr., 9.
119 Ibid.
120 *MG*, 6 March 1933, 'Nazis Win the General Election', 9.
121 *TS*, 10 March 1933, 'The German Elections', 321.
122 Ibid.
123 Ibid.
124 *MG*, 'Nazis Win the General Election', 9.
125 Ibid.
126 *TT*, 'Triumph of the Nazis', 15.

Chapter 3

1 *Daily Mail*, 6 March 1933, 'Nazis Seize Hamburg', Berlin Corr., 11. Hereafter *DMail*.
2 Ibid.
3 Ibid.
4 *The Times*, 7 March 1933, 'Triumph of the Nazis', Berlin Corr., 15. Hereafter *TT*.
5 *News Chronicle*, 8 March 1933, 'Nazis Besiege Building in Defiant City', John Segrue, 9. Hereafter *NC*.
6 *Manchester Guardian*, 8 March 1933, 'Nazi Coup in Hessen', Berlin Corr., 12. Hereafter *MG*.
7 *DMail*, 9 March 1933, 'Nazis Take Control of the Police in Four More States', 'From Our Own Correspondent, Berlin', 12.

8 *News Chronicle*, 9 March 1933, 'Nazis Raid on the Reichsbank', 'From Our Own Correspondent, Berlin', 1.
9 *Daily Telegraph*, 9 March 1933, 'Bavarian Cabinet: Reconstruction Urged by Nazis', Munich Corr., 11. Hereafter *DT*.
   The 'high officials' mentioned were Ernst Röhm and Gaulitier Adolf Wagner who, with orders from Hitler, travelled to Munich to demand the resignation of the Bavarian Prime Minister Heinrich Held and the appointment of Ritter von Epp in his place as Reich Commissioner.
10 Ibid.
11 *DT*, 10 March 1933, 'Hitlerites Seize Control in Bavaria', Munich Spec. Corr., 13.
12 Ibid.
13 Ibid.
14 Ibid.
15 Ibid.
16 *DT*, 11 March 1933, 'Hitler Urges His Men to Keep Order', Berlin Corr., 11.
17 Ibid.
18 Ibid.
19 *NC*, 10 March 1933, 'Nazi Troops Besiege Bavarian Cabinet', John Segrue, 1 and *Daily Express*, 10 March 1933, 'Hitlerites Capture Bavaria', Spec. Corr., 1. Hereafter *DE*.
20 *MP*, 10 March 1933, 'Nazis Seize Bavaria', Berlin Corr., 11.
21 *TT*, 10 March 1933, 'Nazi Coup in States', Berlin Corr., 14.
22 *MG*, 11 March 1933, 'Ease of Nazi Revolution', Berlin Corr., 15.
23 Ibid.
24 *TT*, 10 March 1933, 'Nazi Coup in States', Berlin Corr., 14.
25 *The Observer*, 12 March 1933, 'Bavaria Bows to the Storm', Berlin Corr., 12. Hereafter *Obs*.
26 *TT*, 11 March 1933, 'Nazi Rule in Germany', Berlin Corr., 10.
27 Ibid.
28 *MG*, 11 March 1933, 'Ease of Nazi Revolution', 'From Our Own Correspondent, Berlin', 15.
29 *Daily Telegraph*, 13 March 1933, 'Secrets of Nazi Plots Revealed', 'From Our Own Correspondent, Berlin', 11.
30 Ibid.
31 Ibid., 11, and continued 'Reign of Terror in Germany', 9.
32 *Daily Telegraph*, 14 March 1933, 'Great Exodus of Jews from Germany', 'From Our Own Correspondent, Berlin', 11.
33 *MG*, 14 March 1933, 'Nazi Successes in Council Elections', Berlin Corr., 13.
34 *TT*, 15 March 1933, 'The Hitler Revolution', Leader, 15.
35 Ibid.

36 *MG*, 11 March 1933, '"No Communists in Reichstag"', Berlin Corr., 15.
37 *MG*, 11 March 1933, 'Ease of Nazi Revolution', Berlin Corr., 15.
38 Ibid.
39 *MG*, 11 March 1933, '"No Communists in Reichstag"', Berlin Corr., 15.
40 *TT*, 13 March 1933, 'Reichstag Session', Berlin Corr., 13.
    Most British newspapers referred to the Enabling Act or Law to Remedy the Distress of People and Reich, as an Enabling Bill.
41 *TT*, 18 March 1933, 'Nazis and the Reichstag', Berlin Corr., 11.
42 *The Times* also used the term 'blank cheque' to refer to the bill in its article published on 21 March 1933, 'Nazi Powers in the Reich', From Our Own Correspondent, Berlin, 14.
    DE, 21 March 1933, 'Hitler to Rule as Dictator', Berlin Corr., 1.
43 *DMail*, 16 March 1933, 'Reichstag to Shut?', Berlin Corr., 12.
44 *MP*, 21 March 1933, 'Hitler as Absolute Dictator', Berlin Corr., 13.
45 Ibid.
46 Ibid.
47 *MG*, 21 March 1933, 'Absolute Power for Hitler', Berlin Corr., 9.
48 *TT*, 22 March 1933, 'The Spirit of Potsdam', Leader, 15. And *MG*, 21 March 1933, 'Reichstag Opens Today', Berlin Corr., 13.
49 *MG*, 22 March 1933, 'Hitlerism', Leader, 10.
50 *TT*, 22 March 1933, 'The Spirit of Potsdam', Leader, 15.
51 *NC*, 22 March 1933, 'The Potsdam Spirit', Berlin Corr., 2, cont. from 1.
52 Ibid.
53 *TT*, 23 March 1933, 'Nazis and the Reichstag', Berlin Corr., 14.
54 *MG*, 23 March 1933, 'German Declaration for Unity with Austria', Reuter, 13.
55 Ibid.
56 *NC*, 25 March 1933, 'German Trade Unions to Go', Spec. Corr. John Segrue, 1.
57 *MG*, 24 March 1933, 'Dictatorship Bill Passed in Germany', Reuter, 11.
58 *DMail*, 24 March 1933, 'Hitler's New Powers', Berlin Corr., 14.
59 *MG*, 24 March 1933, 'Dictatorship Bill Passed in Germany', 11. And *TT*, 24 March 1933, 'Power for the Nazis', Berlin Corr., 14.
60 *DE*, 21 March 1933, 'Hitler to Rule as Dictator', Berlin Corr., 1.
61 *NC*, 25 March 1933, 'German Trade Unions to Go', Spec. Corr., John Segrue, Berlin, 1.
62 Ibid.
63 Ibid.
64 Ibid.
65 Ibid.
66 Ibid.
67 Ibid.

68 Ibid.
69 *TT*, 1 May 1933, 'Nazi May Day', Berlin Corr., 14.
70 Ibid.
71 *MG*, 2 May 1933, 'May Day', Leader, 8.
72 Ibid.
73 Ibid.
74 *Daily Mirror*, 3 May 1933, 'Hitler's Surprise Blow at Socialism', 5. Hereafter *DMirror*.
75 Ibid.
76 *NS&N*, 6 May 1933, 'Adolf Hitler Will Give You – ?', 561.
77 *TT*, 3 May 1933, 'Another Nazi Coup', Berlin Corr., 14.
78 Ibid.
79 *MG*, 3 May 1933, 'Nazis Take Over German Trade Unions', Reuter, 9.
80 Ibid.
81 *DT*, 3 May 1933, 'Hitler's Blow at Trade Unions', Berlin Corr., 11.
82 Ibid.
83 Ibid.
84 *TT*, 3 May 1933, 'Another Nazi Coup', Berlin Corr., 14.
85 *DMail*, 3 May 1933, 'Hitler Takes Over Trade Unions', Berlin Corr., 11.
86 Ibid.
87 Ibid.
88 As quoted in *TT*, 3 May 1933, 'Another Nazi Coup', 14.
89 *DMirror*, 3 May 1933, 'Hitler's Surprise Blow at Socialism', 5.
90 *MP*, 3 May 1933, 'Hitler's New Coup', Berlin Corr., 13.
91 *TT*, 3 May 1933, 'Another Nazi Coup', Berlin Corr., 14.
92 Ibid.
93 Ibid.
   In fact, on 5 May all other trade unions dissolved and submitted to the authority of Hitler, including the Christian trade unions.
94 *Obs.*, 7 May 1933, 'Whither Germany?' By J. L. Garvin, 18.
95 *NS&N*, 6 May 1933, 'Adolf Hitler Will Give You – ?', 561.
96 *TT*, 11 May 1933, 'New Blow by Nazis', Berlin Corr., 14.
97 Ibid.
98 Ibid.
99 *The Times*, 11 May 1933, 'New Blow by Nazis', 'From Our Own Correspondent, Berlin', 14.
100 *TT*, 11 May 1933, 'New Blow By Nazis', 14.
101 *MP*, 11 May 1933, 'Hitler the Ruthless', Berlin Corr., 12.
102 *Daily Mirror*, 11 May 1933, 'Hitler Crushes Socialism in Germany'', 3.
103 *MG*, 11 May 1933, 'Nazis Strike at the Socialists', Reuter, 9.
104 Ian Kershaw, *Hitler, 1889-1936* (London: Penguin Books, 1998), 477.

105 *MG*, 7 June 1933, 'Opposition to Hitler; Socialists Organise', Geneva Corr., 12.
106 *TT*, 23 June 1933, 'Nazi Blow at Socialists', Berlin Corr., 14.
107 Ibid.
108 Ibid.
109 Ibid.
110 *DE*, 23 June 1933, 'Hitler Wipes Out 7,000,000 Voters in One Night', 1.
111 The Stahlhelm had aligned itself with the Nationalist Party but was not part of the party. The Nationalist Party instead had the Nationalist Fighting League, also known as the Green Shirts, as its paramilitary wing.
112 *TT*, 29 March 1933, 'Nazis and the Stahlhelm', Berlin Corr., 13.
113 *TS*, 31 March 1933, 'News of the Week', 447.
114 *DT*, 29 March 1933, 'Nazi-Nationalist Rivalry', Leader, 12.
115 *TT*, 29 March 1933, 'Nazis and Stahlhelm', Berlin Corr., 13.
116 *TT*, 17 April 1933, 'Nazi-Stahlhelm Conflicts', Berlin Corr., 9.
117 *MG*, 28 April 1933, 'Gain to Nazis', Reuter, 9.
118 *TT*, 28 April 1933, 'Stahlhelm and Nazis', Berlin Corr., 13.
119 *TT*, 6 May 1933, 'Nationalists and Nazis', Berlin Corr., 11.
120 *DMail*, 22 June 1933, 'Nazis Swoop on German Nationalists', Corr., 11.
121 *MP*, 22 June 1933, 'Hitler Suppresses His Rivals', Berlin Corr., 11.
122 *DMail*, 28 June 1933, 'Hugenberg Resigns', Berlin Corr., 12.
123 *NC*, 28 June 1933, 'Hugenberg Bows to Storm', Berlin Corr., 1.
124 Ibid.
125 *NC*, 29 June 1933, 'Hindenburg and Hitler', Berlin Corr., 1.
126 *TT*, 28 June 1933, 'Nazi Hold on Power', Berlin Corr., 14.
127 *MP*, 28 June 1933, 'Dr. Hugenberg Resigns', Berlin Corr., 13.
128 Ibid.
129 *MG*, 26 June 1933, 'Resignation of Hugenberg', Reuter, 12.
130 *MG*, 27 June 1933, 'Hugenberg Meeting Banned', Reuter, 14.
131 *MP*, 29 June 1933, 'Hugenberg's Fate', Berlin Corr., 15.
132 *DT*, 28 June 1933, 'Hitlerites Absorb Nationalists', Berlin Corr., 11.
133 *TT*, 30 June 1933, 'Nationalists in Germany', Berlin Corr., 14.
134 *NS&N*, 1 July 1933, 'The Nazis' Progress, 1.
135 *MG*, 29 June 1933, 'Hindenburg and Hitler', Reuter, 9.
136 *NC*, 27 June 1933, 'Hitler Strikes Again', Berlin Corr., 1.
137 *TT*, 22 June 1933, 'New Coup in Germany', Berlin Corr., 14.
138 *TT*, 30 June 1933, 'Nationalists in Germany', Berlin Corr., 14.
139 The negotiations and the aftermath of the negotiations will be discussed further in Chapter 6.
140 *DMail*, 1 July 1933, 'Catholic Heads Join Nazis; End of a Great Party', Berlin Corr., 10.
141 *MG*, 1 July 1933, 'A One-Party Germany', Reuter, 13.

142 *MG*, 7 July 1933, 'Catholicism in Germany', Reuter, 6.
143 Ibid.
144 *TT*, 7 July 1933, 'German Centre Party', Berlin Corr., 14.
145 *DE*, 12 July 1933, 'Hitler Puts the Brake On; 'Ruthless Measures', Berlin Corr., 1.
146 Ibid.
147 *The Times*, 12 July 1933, 'Check to Nazi Extremism', Berlin Corr., 13.
148 *Obs*, 16 July 1933, 'The New Nazi Decrees', Spec. Corr. Berlin, 17.
149 *NS&N*, 5 August 1933, 'The Revolutionary Movement in Nazi Germany', Ernst Henri, 153.
150 *MG*, 30 June 1933, 'The Nazi Dictatorship; Why German Labour Collapsed', Spec. Corr., 5.
151 Ibid.
152 Ibid.
153 *MG*, 28 June 1933, 'The Nazi Dictatorship; I. Its Real Nature', Spec. Corr., 11.
154 *MG*, 3 July 1933, 'The Nazi Dictatorship; III. Terror', Spec Corr., 9.
155 Ibid.

Chapter 4

1 *The Spectator*, 3 March 1933, 'The Terror in Germany', 279. Hereafter *TS*.
2 Ibid.
3 Ibid.
4 *TS*, 10 March 1933, Letters to the Editor, 'Terror in Germany?' 337.
5 Ibid.
6 Ibid.
7 Ibid.
8 Ibid.
9 *The Spectator*, 7 April 1933, Letter to the Editor 'The Terror in Germany' (A. Munthe), 501.
10 Ibid.
11 Ibid.
12 Sir John Evelyn Wrench would take a much more critical stance on Germany under Nazism in his 1940 book *I Loved Germany*. In this book he would recall that it was the violence towards the Jews in 1933 that removed any sympathy he held for the Germans following the war.
Sir Evelyn Wrench, *I Loved Germany* (London: Michael Joseph, 1940).
13 *The Times*, 26 October 1933, 'Nazi Germany', Letter to the Editor, Harrison Brown, 10. Hereafter *TT*.
14 Ibid.
15 Ibid.

16　Ibid.
17　*TT*, 26 August 1933, 'Nazi Camp for Unbelievers', Corr., 7.
18　*The Times,* 19 September 1933, 'Life in a Nazi Camp', German Corr., 13.
19　JRL, Voigt to Crozier, 2 February 1933, Foreign Correspondence File 46, Folder 207.
20　TNL Archive, Simpson to Deakin, 20 December 1933, Ralph Deakin Correspondence, TT/FN/1/RD/1.
21　Ibid.
22　TNL Archive, Barrington-Ward to Deakin, 5 January 1934, Ralph Deakin Correspondence, TT/FN/1/RD/1/.
23　Ibid.
24　TNL Archive, Ebbutt to Deakin, 12 January 1934, Ralph Deakin Correspondence, TT/FN/1/RD/1/.
25　Ibid.
26　TNL Archive, Barrington-Ward to Deakin, 15 February 1934, Ralph Deakin Correspondence TT/FN/1/RD/1/.
27　Lee Kersten, 'The Times and the Concentration Camp at Dachau, December 1933–February 1934: An Unpublished Report', *Shofar: An Interdisciplinary Journal of Jewish Studies* 18, Issue 2 (Winter 2000): 101.
28　*NS&N*, 26 January 1934, 'The Terror Continues', 77.
29　Ibid.
30　*News Chronicle*, 17 June 1933, 'Nazis' 20,000 Prisoners', Robert Bernays, 1. Hereafter *NC*.
　　Robert Bernays was a British Liberal MP (serving 1931–45) who worked as a correspondent and journalist till late 1933. He subsequently published a book about his experiences *Special Correspondent* (London: Victor Gollancz, 1934).
31　Ibid.
32　Ibid.
33　Margot Asquith, or Lady Oxford and Asquith, was the widow of Herbert Henry Asquith, 1st Earl of Oxford and Asquith, former British prime minister (1908–16).
34　*NC*, 9 May 1933, 'Lady Oxford Meets the Mystery Man', 1 and 2.
35　*NC*, 11 May 1933, 'News-Chronicle Sold Out', Berlin Corr., 1.
36　*Morning Post*, 20 September 1933, 'Behind Bars in Germany', Spec. Corr., 13.
37　Ibid.
38　*DMail*, 10 July 1933, 'Youth Triumphant', By Viscount Rothermere, 10.
39　Ibid.
40　Ibid.
41　JRL, Werth to Crozier, 2 February 1933, Foreign Correspondence, File 46, Folder 207.
42　JRL, Crozier to Werth, 6 February 1933, Foreign Correspondence, File 54, Folder 207.

43 *Manchester Guardian*, 13 March 1933, 'Growing Reports of a Nazi Terror', Berlin Corr., 9.
   Subeditors heading referred to in unsent message, JRL, Crozier to Voigt, 16 March 1933, Foreign Correspondence File 144, Folder 207.
44 JRL, Voigt to Crozier, 15 March 1933, Foreign Correspondence File 145a/b/c, Folder 207.
45 Ibid.
46 Ibid.
47 JRL, Crozier to Dell, 15 March 1933, Foreign Correspondence Fie 141a/b, Folder 207.
48 There was suggestion that Werth might return to Germany after Voigt's articles had appeared.
49 *MG*, 25 March 1933, 'Nazi Terror Reports Not Exaggerated', Spec. Corr., 13.
50 Ibid.
51 Ibid.
52 *MG*, 28 February 1933, 'The Terror in Germany', Spec. Corr., 9.
53 Ibid.
54 *MG*, 24 March 1933, 'Letters to the Editor', 20.
55 Ibid (Joan Gray).
56 Ibid.
57 *MG*, 1 April 1933, 'Letters to the Editor: Germany Under the Nazis' (Englishman in Germany), 8.
58 Ibid (K. H. Abshagen et al.).
59 *MG*, 24 March 1933, 'Letters to the Editor: The Revolution in Germany' (Hilda Smith), 20.
60 *MG*, 28 March 1933, 'Letters to the Editor: The Persecution' (I. W. Slotki), 18.
61 *MG*, 29 March 1933, 'Letters to the Editor: Germany Under the Nazis' (A. L. Rowse), 18.
62 *MG*, 30 March 1933, 'Letters to the Editor: Germany Under the Nazis' (Harold Picton), 18.
63 Ibid.
64 JRL, Voigt to Crozier, 30 March 1933, Foreign Correspondence File 186a, Folder 207.
65 Ibid.
66 JRL, Voigt to Crozier, 1 April 1933, Foreign Correspondence File 198a, Folder 207.
67 *MG*, 8 April 1933, 'More Facts About the Nazi Terror', 15.
68 *MG*, 8 April 1933, 'Forbidden in Germany', Leader, 14.
69 JRL, Werth to Crozier, 4 April 1933, Foreign Correspondence File 209a, Folder 207.
70 JRL, Werth to Crozier, 30 March 1933, Foreign Correspondence File 196a, Folder 207.

71 JRL, Voigt to Crozier, 11 April 1933, Foreign Correspondence File 223a/b, Folder 207.
72 JRL, Crozier to Voigt, 18 April 1933, Foreign Correspondence File 243a, Folder 207.
73 JRL, Crozier to Voigt, 2 May 1933, Foreign Correspondence File 4, Folder 208.
74 JRL, Voigt to Crozier, 4 November 1933, Foreign Correspondence File 104a, Folder 210.
75 JRL, Dell to Crozier, 4 November 1933, Foreign Correspondence File 105, Folder 210.
76 *MG*, 8 April 1933, 'Examples of Nazi Terror', Spec. Corr., 15.
77 Ibid.
78 *MG*, 12 April 1933, 'Investigation of the Nazi Terror', Spec. Corr., 12.
79 Ibid.
80 Ibid.
81 Ibid.
82 Ibid.
83 Ibid.
84 *MG*, 20 April 1933, 'Nazi Cabinet's Responsibility for Terrorism', Spec. Corr., 3.
85 Ibid.
86 *MG*, 13 April 1933, 'Nazi Torture Chambers in Berlin', Spec. Corr., 6.
87 Ibid.
88 *MG*, 8 June 1933, 'In a Brown House; A Doctor's Story', 9.
89 Ibid.
90 *MG*, 23 June 1933, 'The Terror in Germany', Spec. Corr., 11.
91 Ibid.
92 Ibid.
93 Ibid.
94 Ibid.
95 Ibid.
96 *MG*, 13 July 1933, 'The Triumph of the Nazis', Spec. Corr., 5.
97 Ibid.
98 Ibid.
99 Ibid.
100 *MG*, 4 October 1933, 'The New Nazi Secret Police', Corr., 15.
101 *MG*, 11 October 1933, 'Germany's New Detention Barracks', Corr., 12.
102 Ibid.
103 JRL, Voigt to Crozier, (7–12) November 1933, Foreign Correspondence File 118b, Folder 210.
104 Ibid.

105 JRL, Voigt to Crozier, 15 December 1933, Foreign Correspondence File 251a–e, Folder 210.
106 Franklin Reid Gannon, *The British Press and Germany, 1936–1939* (Oxford: Clarendon Press, 1971), 77.

Chapter 5

1. *The Times*, 1 January 1934, 'A "Happy and Free" Germany', Berlin Corr., 12. Hereafter *TT*.
2. Ibid.
3. Ibid.
4. *Manchester Guardian*, 16 January 1934, 'The Terror in Germany', From Our Special Correspondent, 12. Hereafter MG.
5. *MG*, 8 December 1933, 'Storm Troops More Than Two Million Strong', Berlin Corr., 14.
6. Ibid.
7. *Daily Mail*, 17 February 1934, 'Hitler's Momentous Talk to the "Daily Mail"', 'From G. Ward Price', 11, 12. Hereafter *DMail*.
8. *The Spectator*, 2 February 1934, 'Germany To-Day: I – Hitler's Supremacy', By H. Powys Greenwood, 151. Hereafter *TS*.
9. Ibid.
10. Ibid. Italics present in original text.
11. *Observer*, 4 February 1934, 'Hitler Faces His Second Year', Spec. Corr., 15. Hereafter *Obs*.
12. *New Statesman and Nation*, 28 April 1934, 'The Second Spring', Corr., 631. Hereafter *NS&N*.
13. Ibid.
14. Ibid.
15. *NS&N*, 16 June 1934, 'The Nazis' Domestic Troubles', 902.
16. Ibid.
17. *MG*, 26 June 1934, 'Von Papen's Banned Speech', 6.
18. *MG*, 26 June 1934, 'Dr. Goebbels and Herr von Papen', Leader, 10.
19. *TT*, 27 June 1934, 'Nazi Dissension', Berlin Corr., 15.
20. Ibid.
21. Ibid.
22. *News Chronicle*, 20 June 1934, 'Upheaval in Nazi Cabinet', 1. Hereafter *NC*. MG, 27 June 1934, 'Germany and the Nazis', Spec. Corr., 9.
23. *MG*, 27 June 1934, 'Germany and the Nazis', Spec. Corr., 9.

24 Ibid.
25 Ibid.
26 Ibid.
27 *NC*, 27 June 1934, 'Germany To-Day and To-Morrow', By Vernon Bartlett, 10.
28 Ibid.
29 *NC*, 2 July 1934, 'Hitler Week-End of Ruthless Slaughter', 1.
30 Ibid.
31 Ibid.
32 Ibid.
33 *TT*, 2 July 1934, 'Herr Hitler's Coup', 16.
34 Ibid.
35 *TT*, 2 July 1934, 'Story of the Crisis', Berlin Corr., 16.
36 Ibid.
37 Ibid.
38 Ibid.
39 Ibid.
40 Ibid.
41 Ibid.
42 Ibid.
43 Ibid.
44 Ibid.
45 Norbert Frei, *National Socialist Rule in Germany: The Führer State, 1933-1945*, translated by Simon B Steyne (Oxford: Blackwell, 1993), 18–23; Richard J. Evans, *The Third Reich in Power* (London: Penguin Books, 2006), 31–41; Volker Ullrich, *Hitler: A Biography, Volume I Ascent*, translated by Jefferson Chase (London: The Bodley Head, 2016), 458–76.
46 *TT*, 2 July 1934, 'Story of the Crisis', Berlin Corr., 16.
47 Ibid.
48 Ibid.
49 Ibid.
50 Ibid.
51 Ibid.
52 Ibid.
53 Ibid.
54 *DMail*, 2 July 1934, 'Why Hitler Swooped: Midnight Disclosures', 11.
55 Ibid.
56 *DMail*, 2 July 1934, 'The Rebel Plot Disclosed', Spec. Corr., Sunday, Midnight, 11.
57 *Daily Express*, 2 July 1934, 'Captain Roehm Executed', 1. Hereafter *DE*.
58 *DE*, 2 July 1934, 'Storm Troop Leader Cries "Heil Hitler" to Firing Squad', 2.
59 *Obs.*, 1 July 1934, 'Plotters' Plans Discovered', Spec. Corr., Saturday night, 17.

60 Ibid.
61 *MG*, 2 July 1934, 'Storm Troops' Future', 6.
62 Ibid.
63 Ibid.
64 Ibid.
65 *NC*, 2 July 1934, 'A Very Remarkable "Plot"', John Segrue, Berlin, 1, continued on 2 under 'Was There a Plot?'
66 ,Ibid.
67 *NC*, 2 July 1934, 'Was There a Plot?', 2.
68 *Daily Telegraph*, 3 July 1934, 'Germany Under the New Terror', Leader, 14. Hereafter *DT*.
69 *MG*, 5 July 1934, 'Von Papen to Stay in Office as Vice-Chancellor', Berlin Corr., 9.
70 Ibid.
71 *TS*, 6 July 1934, 'The Terror in Germany', 4.
72 *NC*, 3 July 1934, 'The Price of Tyranny', Leader, 8.
73 *TT*, 3 July 1934, 'Medieval Methods', Leader, 15.
74 Ibid.
75 Ibid.
76 Ibid.
77 Ibid.
78 Ibid.
79 *NS&N*, 7 July 1934, 1.
80 *TT*, 5 July 1934, 'The Hitler Coup', Berlin Corr., 14.
81 *DT*, 11 July 1934, 'Dr. Goebbels Attacks the World's Press', From Our Own Correspondent, Berlin, 13.
82 Ibid.
83 *MP*, 11 July 1934, 'Dr. Goebbels Angry', Berlin Corr., 13.
84 *NC*, 11 July 1934, 'A Tottering Idol?', Leader, 10.
85 *NS&N*, 14 July 1934, 33.
86 *DT*, 11 July 1934, 'More Papers Banned', B.U.P. and Reuter, 13.
87 *DE*, 11 July 1934, 'Germany and the "Daily Express"', 1.
88 *MP*, 11 July 1934, 'Dr. Goebbels Angry', Berlin Corr., 13.
The article in the *Morning Post* criticized by Goebbels seems to be from 5 July in which the paper reported that Papen was to remain in office: 'It may be taken as probable that Herr von Papen has adopted the course he has in deference to the wishes of President von Hindenburg.' 5 July 1933, 'Germany Grows Restive', Berlin Corr., 11.
89 *MP*, 11 July 1934, 'Dr. Goebbels Angry', Berlin Corr., 13.
90 *MP*, 12 July 1934, 'Germany Shrugs Her Shoulders', Berlin Corr., 11.
91 *TT*, 11 July 1934, 'The Reichstag Summoned', Berlin Corr., 14.

92 *MG*, 16 July 1934, 'Herr Hitler's Speech', Leader, 8.
93 *NC*, 11 July 1934, 'A Tottering Idol?', Leader, 10.
94 *DE*, 14 July 1934, 'Hitler Answers for 77 Deaths', 1.
95 *DE*, 14 July 1934, 'How the Speech Sounded', By a 'Daily Express Representative Who Listened In', 1.
96 *MG*, 14 July 1934, 'Story of Mutiny', Reuter, 13.
97 Ibid.
98 Ibid.
99 *MP*, 14 July 1934, 'Hitler's Own Story of the Plot to Kill Him', 11.
100 *DT*, 16 July 1934, 'Germany Not Convinced', Berlin Corr., 11.
101 Ibid.
102 *TS*, 20 July 1934, 'Hitler's Next Move', 76.
103 Ibid.
104 Ibid.
105 Ibid.
106 Ibid.
107 Professor Guglielmo Ferrero was an Italian historian, journalist, and novelist, who wrote *The Greatness and Decline of Rome* (5 volumes). He fled fascism in Italy and took up a post at the University of Geneva.
108 *TS*, 20 July 1934, 'Byzantine Germany', By Professor Guglielmo Ferrero, 79.
109 *TT*, 16 July 1934, 'Herr Hitler's Apologia', Berlin Corr., 12.
110 *TT*, 2 August 1934, 'Hindenburg Sinking', Berlin Corr. 10.
111 *DT*, 1 August 1934, 'Hitler Ready to Fly to Hindenburg', Berlin Corr., 11.
112 *MG*, 1 August 1934, 'The Question All Germany Is Asking: Possible Candidates', Reuter, 9.
113 *DMail*, 2 August 1934, 'Hindenburg in War and Peace', By the Rt. Hon. Winston S. Churchill, P.C. M.P., 8 and *DE*, 2 August 1934, 'My Old Enemy', By the Rt. Hon. David Lloyd George, 10.
114 *DMail*, 3 August 1934, 'Hitler the World's Most Powerful Ruler', 11.
115 *NC*, 3 August 1934, 'Hitler Out-Kaisers the Kaiser', Berlin Corr., 1.
116 Ibid.
117 Ibid.
118 *MG*, 3 August 1934, 'How the News Was Announced', Berlin Corr., 9.
119 Ibid.
120 *MG*, 3 August 1934, 'Constitution Swept Aside', Press Association Foreign Special, 9.
121 *DT*, 18 August 1934, 'A Plebiscite Which Can Tell Nothing', Leader, 10.
122 Ibid.
123 Ibid.
124 *NS&N*, 25 August 1934, 'Opposition to Hitler', 226.

125 *TS*, 24 August 1934, 'After the Plebiscite', By H. Powys Greenwood, Munich, 247.
126 Ibid.
127 *TS*, 24 August 1934, 'After the Plebiscite', By H. Powys Greenwood, Munich, 248.
128 *MP*, 5 September 1934, 'Hitler Hailed Like a King', 11.

Chapter 6

1 *The Spectator*, 28 September 1934, 'The Cross and the Swastika', 424. Hereafter *TS*.
2 Ibid.
3 Ibid.
4 Ibid.
5 Ibid.
6 Ibid.
7 Ibid.
8 Volker Ullrich, *Hitler: A Biography, Volume I Ascent*, translated by Jefferson Chase (London: The Bodley Head, 2016), 639.
9 *Manchester Guardian*, 8 May 1933, 'The Centre Party in Germany', 12. Hereafter *MG*.
10 *Daily Mail*, 1 July 1933, 'Catholic Heads Join Nazis', Berlin Corr., 10. Hereafter *DMail*.
11 *MG*, 10 July 1933, 'Motives of Both Sides', Spec. Corr., 12.
12 *DMail*, 1 July 1933, 'Catholic Heads Join Nazis', 10.
13 *MG*, 10 July 1933, 'Motives of Both Sides', 12.
14 Ibid.
15 According to the article the Journeymen's Societies were 'associated with the Catholic Bavarian People's Party'.
The Times, 12 June 1933, 'Disorders in Munich', 'From Our Own Correspondent, Berlin', 14. Hereafter *TT*.
16 Ibid.
17 *MG*, 10 July 1933, 'Motives of Both Sides', 12.
18 *MG*, 10 July 1933, 'Nazi Agreement with the Vatican', 12.
19 Ibid.
20 *MG*, 10 July 1933, 'Motives of Both Sides', 12.
21 *Morning Post*, 10 July 1933, 'Priests Released', Berlin Corr., 13. Hereafter *MP*.
22 The speech was given by Bishop for Tyrol and for Vorarlberg at a meeting of Catholic teachers at Dornbirn in Vorarlberg, Austria, according to the article in the *Morning Post*.
MP, 15 November 1933, 'The Pope Indicts Germany', Vienna Corr., 13.
23 Ibid.

24 *MG*, 1 December 1933, 'Atrocity Tales' in Germany', Berlin Corr., 13.
25 *MG*, 25 January 1934, 'Church and State in Germany', Leader, 8.
26 Ibid.
27 Ibid.
28 Ibid.
29 Ibid.
30 *TT*, 4 April 1934, 'Germany and the Vatican', Leader, 13.
31 Ibid.
32 *Observer*, 8 April 1934, 'First Shots in the Conflict', 'From Our Special Correspondent, Berlin', 19. Hereafter *Obs*.
33 The judgement was concerning the distribution of newspapers and possible discriminations for Roman Catholic households who abstained from subscribing to the National Socialist *NationalZeitung*. The Roman Catholic newspaper *Neuer Tag* had requested that this particular canvasser be refrained from 'threatening possibly subscribers with disadvantages'. The request was refused by the Duisburg Provincial Court.
TT, 4 April 1934, 'German Press Rivalry', Berlin Corr., 12.
34 *TT*, 4 April 1934, 'Germany and the Vatican', 13.
35 Ibid.
36 It also succeeded in getting Catholic patients excluded from the measure. For a further discussion of this policy see Chapter 7.
Daily Express, 31 January 1934, 'Vatican Beats Nazis', 1. Hereafter *DE*.
37 *Obs.*, 8 April 1934, 'Hitler Sends Emissary to the Pope', Central News, 19.
38 *TS*, 5 February 1937, 'The 'Kultur Kampf'', 206.
39 Ibid.
40 *DMail*, 22 March 1937, 'The Pope and Germany', Berlin Corr., 14.
41 Ibid.
42 Ibid.
43 *TT*, 3 May 1933, 'Protestantism in Germany', 'By a German Churchman', 13.
44 Ibid.
45 *TT*, 29 May 1933, 'German Church Politics', Berlin Corr., 13.
46 *TT*, 26 May 1933, 'Nazis and Church Reform', Berlin Corr., 13.
Ludwig Müller was appointed to this role on 25 April 1933.
47 Edward Snyder, 'Friedrich von Bodelschwingh and the Protestant Appeasement of the Nazi Regime, 1933-34', in *From Weimar to Hitler: Studies in the Dissolution of the Weimar Republic and the Establishment of the Third Reich, 1932-1934*, edited by Hermann Beck and Larry Eugene Jones (New York: Berghahn Books, 2019), 313.
48 Ibid., 310.
49 *TT*, 6 June 1933, 'German Protestant Primate', Berlin Corr. 10.

50 Klaus Scholder, *The Churches and the Third Reich, Volume One: Preliminary History and the Time of Illusions, 1918-1934*, translated by John Bowden (London: SCM Press Ltd., 1987), 351.
51 Victoria Barnett, *For the Soul of the People: Protestant Protest Against Hitler* (Oxford: Oxford University Press, 1992), 34.
52 J. S. Conway, *The Nazi Persecution of the Churches, 1933-45* (London: Weidenfeld and Nicolson, 1968), 37.
53 *TT*, 26 June 1933, 'New Church Politics', Berlin Corr., 13.
54 *TT*, 27 June 1933, 'New Nazi Action', Berlin Corr., 14.
55 Ibid.
56 *The Times*, 30 June 1933, 'German Church Crisis', Berlin Corr., 13.
57 *TT*, 30 June 1933, 'German Church Crisis', Berlin Corr., 13.
58 Ibid.
59 *TT*, 1 July 1933, 'Nazi Church Politics', Berlin Corr., 12.
60 *News Chronicle*, 1 July 1933, 'Hindenburg's Clash with Hitler', Berlin Corr., 1. Hereafter *NC*.
61 Ibid.
62 Ibid.
63 *MP*, 22 July 1933, 'German Church Elections', Berlin Corr., 13.
64 Ibid.
65 Ibid.
66 *TT*, 24 July 1933, 'German Church Elections', Berlin Corr., 11.
67 *TT*, 25 July 1933, 'Extremist Majority in Church Elections', Berlin Corr., 13.
68 *TT*, 28 July 1933, 'German Church Changes', Berlin Corr., 14.
69 Ibid.
70 Doris L. Bergen, *Twisted Cross: The German Christian Movement in the Third Reich* (Chapel Hill: University of North Carolina Press, 1996), 88.
71 *MG*, 24 November 1933, 'The German Church', Leader, 8.
72 *The Times*, 15 November 1933, 'Nazis and the Church', Berlin Corr., 13.
73 Ibid.
74 For a detailed description and assessment of the Sport Palace Rally, see Klaus Scholder, *The Churches and the Third Reich, Volume One*, Chapter 13.
75 *The Times*, 15 November 1933, 'Nazis and the Church', Berlin Corr., 13.
76 Barnett, *For the Soul of the People*, 35.
77 Ibid.
78 Ibid.
79 Klaus Scholder, *The Churches and the Third Reich, Volume Two: The Year of Disillusionment: 1934 Barmen and Rome*, translated by John Bowden (London: SCM Press Ltd, 1988), 20.
80 *TT*, 6 January 1934, 'German Church Conflict', Berlin Corr., 9.

81 *MP*, 8 January 1934, 'Nazi Primate Defied', Berlin Corr., 13.
82 Ibid.
83 *NC*, 8 January 1934, 'Pastors Defy German Primate', Berlin Corr., 1.
84 Ibid.
85 Ibid.
86 Ibid.
87 Ibid.
88 *NC*, 10 January 1934, 'Will Hindenburg Act? Church Conflict Spreads', Berlin Corr., 2.
89 Ibid.
90 *NC*, 26 January 1934, 'Storm Over Germany: Goering and Hitler in Conflict', 1.
91 *NC*, 16 January 1934, 'Storm Troops to Expel Pastors', Berlin Corr., 9.
92 *NC*, 26 January 1934, 'Storm Over Germany: Goering and Hitler in Conflict', 1.
93 *TT*, 26 January 1934, 'Herr Hitler and the Church', Berlin Corr', 12.
94 *TT*, 27 January 1934, 'German Church Conference', Berlin Corr., 10.
95 For more details on the meeting, see Ullrich, *Hitler*, 645; Scholder, *The Churches and the Third Reich, Volume Two*, 40–3; Conway, *The Nazi Persecution of the Churches*, 73–5.
96 Historian Klaus Scholder alleges that the colleague Niemöller had the conversation with was Walter Künneth, a theologian and member of the Confessing Church. Klaus Scholder, *The Churches and the Third Reich, Volume Two*, 40.
97 *TT*, 27 January 1934, 'German Church Conference', Berlin Corr., 10.
98 Ibid.
99 Ibid.
100 Ibid.
101 *TT*, 29 January 1934, 'German Church Conflict', Berlin Corr., 11.
102 *MG*, 26 February 1934, 'Nazi Primate's Opponents', Berlin Corr., 13.
103 Ibid.
104 *MG*, 13 August 1934, 'The German Evangelical Church', Leader, 8.
105 Ibid.
106 *MG*, 13 August 1934, 'Pastors Fight in Germany', Berlin Corr., 9.
107 ,Ibid.
108 Ibid.
109 Ibid.
110 Ibid.
111 *TT*, 13 September 1934, 'German Church Friction', Berlin Corr., 9.
112 *TT*, 17 September 1934, 'German Church Dispute', Berlin Corr., 11.
113 Ibid.
114 *New Statesman and Nation*, 22 September 1934, 'The Religious War in Germany', 346. Hereafter *NS&N*.

115 Ibid.
116 Ibid.
117 Ibid.
118 *TT*, 20 September 1934, 'The Churches in Germany', Berlin Corr., 9.
119 Ibid.
120 Ibid.
121 *NC*, 20 September 1934, 'The Nazi Church Militant', Leader, 8.
122 Ibid.
123 *DMail*, 15 October 1934, 'German Church Quarrel', Berlin Corr., 16.
124 *TT*, 13 October 1934, 'Church Crisis in Bavaria', Berlin Corr., 11.
125 Ibid.
126 Ibid.
127 Ibid.
128 Ibid.
129 Ibid.
130 Ibid.
131 *MG*, 20 October 1934, 'A New German Church', 13.
132 Ibid.
133 Ibid.
134 Ibid.
135 *NC*, 16 October 1934, 'German Pastors Winning', Berlin Corr., 11.
136 Ibid.
137 *TT*, 19 October 1934, 'German Church Conflict', Berlin Corr., 13.
138 Ibid.
139 *DT*, 20 October 1934, 'Hitler's Alarm over Church Conflict', Munich Corr., 13.
140 *NC*, 27 October 1934, 'Hitler Removes Church Goering', Berlin Corr., 1.
141 *TT*, 29 October 1934, 'South German Church', Berlin Corr., 14.
142 Ibid.
143 Ibid.
144 *NC*, 31 October 1934, 'German Protestant Church Regains Its Freedom', Berlin Corr., 11.
145 Ibid.
146 Ibid.
147 Ibid.
148 *MG*, 26 November 1934, 'Dr. Mueller's New Move', Berlin Corr., 12.
149 *Obs.*, 4 November 1934, 'Bishop Müller's Future', Berlin Corr., 21.
150 *MP*, 26 November 1934, 'Nazi Primate in Trouble', Berlin Corr., 13.
151 *MG*, 14 November 1934, 'Rules for German Editors', Spec. Corr., 12.
152 Ibid.
153 *MP*, 26 November 1934, 'Nazi Primate in Trouble', Berlin Corr., 13.

154 *TT*, 8 December 1934, 'German Church Conflict', Berlin Corr., 11.
155 Conway, *The Nazi Persecution of the Churches, 1933-1945*, 135; *TT*, 30 September 1935, 'A German Church 'Dictator'', Berlin Corr., 13.
156 Ibid.
157 *Obs.*, 8 December 1935, 'The Church in Germany', Berlin Corr., 12.
158 Ibid.
159 Ibid.
160 Ibid.
161 *NC*, 13 January 1936, 'Churches Defy Nazis', Berlin Corr., 2.
162 Ibid.
163 Ibid.
164 *TT*, 21 January 1936, 'Nazi Secret Police and the Church', Berlin Corr., 11.
165 *MG*, 11 February 1936, 'Niemoeller's Attack on Nazi Church Policy', Spec. Corr., 6.
166 Ibid.
167 *DE*, 17 July 1936, 'Pastors Challenge "Deified" Hitler', Reuter, 2.
168 *TT*, 2 July 1937, 'New Nazi Blow at Churches', Berlin Corr., 16.
169 *NC*, 2 July 1937, 'Nazis Arrest Niemoeller, Famous Protestant Leader', NC Corr., British United Press and Reuter, 1.
170 *MG*, 2 July 1937, 'Famous Pastor Arrested', Berlin Corr., 11.
171 *NC*, 2 July 1937, 'Nazis Arrest Niemoeller, Famous Protestant Leader', 1.
172 Ibid.
173 Ibid.
174 *MG*, 2 July 1937, 'Third Realm and Religion', Leader, 12.
175 *TT*, 13 July 1937, 'Nazi Police and the Church', Berlin Corr., 13.
176 Ibid.
177 *TT*, 10 August 1937, 'German Protestants' Defiance', Berlin Corr., 9.
178 *TT*, 3 August 1937, 'Nazi Police and the Church', Berlin Corr., 9.
179 *TT*, 11 August 1937, 'Germany and "The Times"', Berlin Corr., 12.
180 *TT*, 12 August 1937, 'Nazi Press and "The Times"', Berlin Corr., 10.
181 Ibid.
182 *TT*, 11 August 1937, 'Nazis and "The Times"; Foreign Comment', Berlin Corr., 14.
183 *MG*, 21 August 1937, 'The Foreign Journalist in Germany', Berlin Corr., 15.
184 Ibid.
185 *NS&N*, 12 March 1938, 'Pastor Niemöller', 395.
186 *MG*, 3 March 1938, 'Dr. Niemöller', Leader, 8.
187 Ibid.
188 *NS&N*, 12 March 1938, 'Pastor Niemöller', 395.
189 Ibid.
190 *NC*, 4 March 1938, 'Justice Undone', Leader, 10.
191 In 1941 he was transferred to Dachau concentration camp.

192 *MG*, 4 March 1938, 'Fate of Dr. Niemöller', Berlin Corr., 6.
193 *MG*, 8 March 1938, 'Gestapo and Dr. Niemöller', Spec. Corr., 6.
194 *NS&N*, 12 March 1938, 'Pastor Niemöller', 395.
195 *Daily Telegraph and Morning Post*, 19 January 1938, 'Church Leader to be Tried in Germany', 'From Our Own Correspondent, Berlin', 11.
196 Conway, *The Nazi Persecution of the Churches, 1933-1945*, 220.
197 *Manchester Guardian*, 1 July 1938, 'Pastor Niemöller', Leader, 10.
198 Ibid.
199 Conway, *The Nazi Persecution of the Churches*, 84.
200 Ibid.

Chapter 7

1 *Manchester Guardian*, 3 March 1933, '2,000 Arrests in Two Prussian Provinces Alone', Berlin Corr., 9. Hereafter *MG*.
2 *Daily Express*, 4 March 1933, 'Jews Flee from Vengeance of the Hitlerites', 9. Hereafter *DE*.
3 Ibid.
4 Ibid.
5 *MG*, 27 March 1933, 'Facts about the Nazi Terror', Spec. Corr., 9.
6 *Jewish Chronicle*, 17 March 1933, 'Germany: An Appeal for Sanity', 9. Hereafter *JC*.
7 *MG*, 27 March 1933, 'Facts about the Nazi Terror', Spec. Corr., 9.
8 Ibid.
9 *JC*, 17 March 1933, 'Germany: An Appeal for Sanity', 9.
10 *JC*, 17 March 1933, 'Anti-Jewish Terror in Germany', 22.
11 *JC*, 24 March 1933, 'A Jewish Retort to the Nazis', 9.
12 Ibid.
13 *News Chronicle*, 25 March 1933, 'German Fears; Rewards for Evidence', Berlin Corr., 13. Hereafter *NC*.
14 *NC*, 25 March 1933, 'Jewish Storm Against Hitler', 13.
15 *Daily Mirror*, 27 March 1933, 'Jews Not to Wage War Against Germany', 3. Hereafter *DMirror*.
16 Ibid.
17 Ibid.
18 *Daily Mail*, 27 March 1933, 'Hitler and the Jews', Rothay Reynolds, Berlin Corr., 16. Hereafter *DMail*.
19 Ibid.
20 Hitler in this instance referred to anti-German placards on motor cars in London. *TT*, 30 March 1933, 'Nazi Boycott of Jews', Berlin Corr., 13.

21 Ibid.
22 *DE*, 30 March 1933, 'First Steps in Nazi Boycott Against Jews', Berlin Corr., 11.
23 *Morning Post*, 30 March 1933, 'Hitler on the Boycott', Berlin Corr., 13. Hereafter *MP*.
24 *MP*, 30 March 1933, 'Hitler on the Boycott', Berlin Corr., 13.
25 *DMail*, 1 April 1933, 'Germany's Boycott Surprise', Rothay Reynolds Berlin Corr., 13.
26 Ibid.
27 Ibid.
28 *MG*, 30 March 1933, 'Hitler's New Drive Against the Jews', Spec. Corr., 9.
29 Ibid.
30 *TT*, 3 April 1933, 'According to Plan', Leader, 15.
31 *TT*, 3 April 1933, 'Boycott of the Jews', Berlin Corr., 14.
32 *DMail*, 3 April 1933, 'Germany's Jewish Boycott', Rothay Reynolds Berlin Corr., 13.
33 Ibid.
34 *Daily Telegraph*, 3 April 1933, 'Heavy Cost of Germany's One-Day Boycott', Berlin Corr., 11. Hereafter *DT*.
35 For instance, *MG*, 4 April 1933, 12; *NC*, 3 April 1933, 'Jew-Baiting in Germany', 9; *DE*, 3 April 1933, 11 and 14.
36 *NC*, 3 April 1933, 'Jew-Baiting in Germany', 9; *JC*, 7 April 1933, 25; *DMirror*, 3 April 1933, 3; *MG*, 4 April 1933, 12.
37 *DT*, 3 April 1933, 'Germany's One Day Boycott', Leader, 10.
38 *DT*, 3 April 1933, 'Efforts Behind the Scenes', Dip. Corr., 12.
39 *MG*, 5 April 1933, 'The Great Nazi Victory on the Shop Front', Corr., 12.
40 *MG*, 7 April 1933, 'The German Persecution', Leader, 10.
41 Ibid.
42 Ibid.
43 Ibid.
44 Ibid.
45 *JC*, 14 April 1933, 'The Tragedy of German Jewry', 16.
46 Ibid.
47 Ibid.
48 *MG*, 7 April 1933, 'The German Persecution', Leader, 10.
49 Ibid.
50 Ibid.
51 *MG*, 7 April 1933, 'The German Persecution', 10.
52 Ibid.
53 For most of 1933, the *Manchester Guardian* did not have a resident correspondent in Berlin. It relied on news agencies such as Reuter, as well as news from the newspaper's other European correspondents, and features by special correspondent

Voigt, until December 1933 when C. A. Lambert took over. In May 1933, for instance, there were approximately ten articles about the persecution of the Jews provided by Reuter, compared with four articles provided by correspondents or special correspondent Voigt.

54 *MG*, 5 May 1933, 'Nazi Pressure on Jews', 15. *TT*, 4 May 1933, 'Nazi Racial Ideas', 'From Our Own Correspondent, Berlin', 11. *TT*, 4 May 1933, 'Limitation of Jewish Students', Frankfurt Corr., 11.
55 Richard J. Evans, *The Coming of the Third Reich* (London: Penguin Books, 2004), 430.
56 *TT*, 11 May 1933, '"Un-German" Books Destroyed', Berlin Corr., 13.
57 *TT*, 20 May 1933, 'The Ostracism of German Jews', Berlin Corr., 11.
58 *MG*, 24 April 1933, 'Nazi "Purge" Extends', Reuter, 9. And *MG*, 25 April 1933, 'Nazi "Purge" of Sport', Press Association Foreign Special, 11.
 To his credit, Walter von Cramm, ranked number 2 in the world, refused to be co-opted by the Nazis for their purposes. He was persecuted for his homosexuality and sentenced to a year's imprisonment in 1938.
59 *MG*, 24 April 1933, 'Nazi "Purge" Extends', Reuter, 9.
60 *MG*, 17 July 1933, 'Confiscatory Legislation in Germany', Spec. Corr., 12.
61 Ibid.
62 *DMail*, 10 July 1933, 'Youth Triumphant', By Viscount Rothermere, 10.
63 Ibid.
64 Ibid.
65 Ibid.
66 Ibid.
67 Ibid.
68 On 19 July 1934, the *Daily Mail* printed an exchange of letters between Mosley and Rothermere which clearly demonstrated their 'divergence of ideas'. Rothermere wrote:

> As you know, I have never thought that a movement calling itself 'Fascist' could be successful in this country, and I have also made it quite clear in my conversations with you that I never could support any movement with an anti-Semitic bias, any movement which had dictatorship as one of its objectives, or any movement which will substitute a 'Corporate State' for the Parliamentary institutions of this country.
>
> *Daily Mail*, 19 July 1934, 'Lord Rothermere and Sir Oswald Mosley', 11 and 12.

Mosley claimed that Rothermere had been pressured by Jewish advertisers, but it seems that the publicity from the Olympia rally made Rothermere think twice about (publicly) supporting the BUF. Furthermore, the Röhm purge had demonstrated, beyond a doubt, the stark reality of the brutality of the dictatorship. Rothermere's admiration for the Nazi dictatorship seemed to come more from an admiration of a strong government than of a fascist state model (something Britain was lacking at the time).

69 *DE*, 25 May 1934, 'German Jews Are Facing Their Darkest Days', By Pembroke Stephens, 2.
Philip Pembroke Stephens took over the post as Berlin correspondent from Sefton Delmer at the end of 1933. He had previously worked in Paris and Vienna for the *Daily Express*.

70 Aken is situated near Dessau, approximately two hours drive south-west of Berlin.

71 *DE*, 2 June 1934, 'My Expulsion by the Nazis', By Pembroke Stephens, 1.
In reporting his death in 1937 the *Observer* and *New York Times* attributed his expulsion to his reports on the secret rearming of Germany. This was in reference to his article following his first arrest in Aken where he had observed what he thought was the building of factories, possibly for armaments.

72 Ibid.

73 Ibid.

74 A statement, according to the article, attributed to the French Military Governor of Metz. *Daily Express*, 9 June 1934, 'Menace to Europe', 'By Pembroke Stephens, 10.

75 *DE*, 9 June 1934, 'Menace to Europe', By Pembroke Stephens, 10.

76 *MG*, 11 November 1937, 'British War Correspondent Killed in Shanghai', 11.
There seems to be some confusion about the date of Pembroke Stephens's death in Shanghai. Some have accurately put his death as occurring on 11 November 1937 while others such as John Simpson have mistakenly identified his death as occurring on 18 November 1937. The precise date of his death is not difficult to determine if one does some research of newspaper archives. This author was able to determine the date, nature and details of Stephens's death with a quick search of newspaper coverage in November 1937. John Simpson is also wrong in his supposition that the *Daily Express* was the only British newspaper to accurately report the devastating effect the Nazi regime had on people's lives, particularly Jewish lives.

77 *The Observer*, 14 November 1937, 'The World: Week by Week', 18. Hereafter *Obs*.

78 *New Statesman and Nation*, 20 April 1934, 'Frustrated Jewish Hopes in Germany', Corr., 545. Hereafter *NS&N*.

79 Ibid.

80 Ibid.

81 Ibid.

82 Ibid.

83 Ibid.

84 *MP*, 17 July 1935, 'German Disgust at Jew Baiting', Berlin Corr., 13.

85 Ibid.
86 Ibid.
87 Ibid.
88 *MP*, 16 August 1935, 'Berlin's Day of Jew-Hate', 11.
89 Ibid.
90 Ibid.
91 *DE*, 16 September 1935, 'Nazis Proclaim Anti-Jew Laws', '"Daily Express" Special Correspondent, Nuremberg', 1.
92 *JC*, 20 September 1935, 'Germany: Disgraceful "Jew-Laws"', 16.
93 *TT*, 18 September 1935, 'Isolation of Jews in Germany', Berlin Corr., 9.
94 *TT*, 17 September 1935, 'New German Laws', Berlin Corr., 13.
95 Ibid.
96 *JC*, 20 September 1935, 'Germany: Disgraceful "Jew-Laws"', 16.
97 *The Spectator*, 20 September 1935, 'Anti-Jewish Laws in Germany', 414. Hereafter *TS*.
98 *DE*, 17 September 1935, 'Jews', Opinion, 10.
99 *MG*, 17 September 1935, 'Hitler Marks Time', Leader, 8.
100 *MG*, 5 October 1935, 'The Nuremberg Decrees', Corr., 13.
101 Ibid.
102 Ibid.
103 Ibid.
104 Ibid.
105 Ibid.
106 *NS&N*, 26 March 1938, 'The Rape of Vienna', Corr., 511.
107 Ibid.
108 *DE*, 19 March 1938, 'Vienna Silent as Hitler Speaks', Dennis Clarke, Vienna Staff Reporter, 2.
109 Ibid.
110 The *Daily Telegraph* and *Morning Post* merged in late 1937 and was retitled (briefly) the *Daily Telegraph and Morning Post* before later becoming the *Daily Telegraph*.
111 *Daily Telegraph and Morning Post*, 21 March 1938, 'Daily Toll of Suicide Among Vienna Jews', Vienna Corr., 4. Hereafter *DT&MP*.
112 According to the *Daily Telegraph and Morning Post* (29 March 1938, 15), the first expulsion order had been withdrawn.
113 Norman Bentwich was a barrister and academic who served as League of Nations director of High Commission for Refugees from Germany between 1933 and 1935. He was also a Professor of International Relations at Jerusalem University from 1932 to 1951, and a keen Zionist.
114 *MG*, 13 April 1938, 'The Jews in Austria', By Professor Norman Bentwich, 9.
115 Ibid.

116 Ibid.
117 *NS&N*, 23 April 1938, 'Farewell to Austria', Corr., 680.
118 Ibid.
119 Ibid.
120 A. J. Sherman, *Island Refuge: Britain and Refugees from the Third Reich, 1933-1939* (London: Paul Elek, 1973), 85.
121 Ibid., 86.
122 For the pressures and considerations that faced the British Home Office and Foreign Office, see Sherman, *Island Refuge*, Chapter Four.
123 *MG*, 19 March 1938, 'The Refugees', Leader, 12.
124 Ibid.
125 Colonel Josiah Wedgwood was a British Labour politician (previously a member of the Liberal party), who was a critic of appeasement and a proponent of increased Jewish immigration to Britain and Palestine. He worked vigorously to assist Jewish refugees.
126 The proposal put to parliament was 'That leave be given to bring in a Bill to amend the Aliens Acts and Naturalisation Acts so as to give the Secretary of State for the Home Department powers with regard to the immigration into Great Britain and Northern Ireland of refugees from Austria for a period of six months from the date of the passing of this Act, and the granting of British nationality to such immigrants'.
Hansard, Commons Sitting, HC Deb 22 March 1938 vol 333, cc1003-12, 'Austrian Refugees Immigration and Naturalisation', Colonel Wedgwood.
127 *TT*, 23 March 1938, 'Austrian Refugees', Leader, 15.
128 Ibid.
129 Ibid.
130 Ibid.
131 *DMail*, 23 March 1938, 'Refugees', 10.
132 Ibid.
133 *DMail*, 18 June 1938, 'Nazis Arrest 1,487 Jews', Berlin Corr., 12.
134 *DMail*, 18 June 1938, 'Jews and Germany', 12.
135 Ibid.
136 Ibid.
137 *DMirror*, 5 July 1938, 'David Walker's Talking Shop', 9.
138 Ibid.
139 Ibid.
140 *DMirror*, 8 July 1938, 'David Walker's Talking Shop', 10.
141 Ibid.
142 Ibid.
143 Ibid.

144 Ibid.
145 Ibid.
146 Ibid.
147 *TT*, 6 July 1938, 'The Refugees', Leader, 17.
148 Ibid.
149 Ibid.
150 *NS&N*, 9 July 1938, 'The Refugee Problem', 61.
151 Ibid.
152 Ibid.
153 *NS&N*, 16 July 1938, 'Evian and the Refugees', 102.
154 Ibid.
155 *MG*, 16 July 1938, 'After Evian', Leader, 12.
156 Ibid.
157 *DE*, 8 July 1938, 'Australia Says "No Hope" for Refugees', Reporter at Evian, 2.
158 Ibid.
159 Ibid.
160 *DE*, 11 July 1938, 'Britain, U.S. to Approach Hitler on Refugees', Reporter at Evian, 2.
161 *NS&N*, 16 July 1938, 'Evian and the Refugees', 102.
162 *TS*, 29 July 1938, 'The Refugees', 189.
163 *The Times*, 20 August 1938, 'Jewish Names for German Jews', Berlin Corr., 10.
164 Peter Longerich, *Holocaust: The Persecution and Murder of the Jews*, translated by Jeremy Noakes (Oxford: Oxford University Press), 109.
165 *MG*, 29 October 1938, 'Wholesale Arrest of Polish Jews in Germany', Berlin Corr., 13.
166 *TT*, 29 October 1938, 'Polish Jews Expelled', Berlin Corr., 11.
167 *MG*, 31 October 1938, 'Berlin and Warsaw to Negotiate on Expelled Jews', Warsaw Corr., 12.
168 *TT*, 2 November 1938, 'Polish Jews Plight', Warsaw Corr., 13.
169 Ibid.
170 *MG*, 1 November 1938, 'Expelled Jews' Dark Outlook', Warsaw Corr., 6.
171 *MG*, 8 November 1938, 'Diplomat Shot', Paris Corr., 11.
172 *MG*, 9 November 1938, 'Germany Begins Reprisals against the Jews', Berlin Corr., 11.
173 Ibid.
174 *TS*, 11 November 1938, 'The Paris Assassination', 793.
175 Ibid.
176 *DMirror*, 11 November 1938, 'Nazi Hate Day', Spec. Corr., 36.
177 *DT&MP*, 11 November 1938, 'German Mobs' Vengeance on Jews', 17.
178 *MG*, 11 November 1938, 'The Disorders in Germany', Leader, 10.

179 *JC*, 18 November 1938, 'The Nazi Pogroms', By Bernhard Reichenbach, 30.
180 *The Times*, 11 November 1938, 'Nazi Tactics on Jews', Berlin Corr., 14,
181 *DT&MP*, 11 November 1938, 'German Mobs' Vengeance on Jews', 17.
182 *DE*, 11 November 1938, 'Looting Mobs Defy Goebbels', 1, 2.
183 Ibid.
184 Ibid.
185 Ibid.
186 Ibid.
187 *MG*, 18 November 1938, 'Extent of German Pogrom', Dip. Corr., 11.
188 Ibid.
189 Ibid.
190 Ibid.
191 Ibid.
192 *DE*, 14 November 1938, 'Goebbels Renews Onslaught on the Jews, "Now We Must Make Them Suffer"', 1.
193 *DMail*, 12 November 1938, 'Nazis Threaten to Ration Jews' Food', By Paul Bretherton, Berlin, 11.
194 *MG*, 18 November 1938, 'Extent of German Pogrom', 11.
195 Ibid.
196 *TS*, 18 November 1938, 'The New Barbarism', 836.
197 Ibid.
198 Ibid.
199 Ibid., 836–7.
200 *NS&N*, 19 November 1938, 'Nazis and Jews', 816.
201 Ibid.
202 Ibid.
203 Ibid., 816–17.
204 *NS&N*, 19 November 1938, 'Nazis and Jews', 817.
205 The pretext for this was the *Schwarze Korps* allegation that after the Jews had their assets seized ('the jugular veins of the parasites have been cut') 'their capital will soon be exhausted. The rich Jews will be forced to support the poor, with the definite result that all of them become destitute and then necessarily criminals- according to their intrinsic nature', and the 'result would be an underworld conspiracy' to take revenge.
MG, 23 November 1938, 'Still Darker Threats Against the Jews', Berlin Corr., 11.
206 Ibid.
207 Ibid.
208 *MG*, 30 November 1938, 'A Black Guard Threat to Massacre All Jews', 6.
209 This measure was not implemented until 1941, when Reinhard Heydrich issued a decree in the protectorates of Moravia and Bohemia. It was later, gradually, implemented throughout the Reich.

  MG, 5 December 1938, 'Berlin Ghetto Site Chosen: A Crowded Quarter', Berlin Corr., 6.
210 *DT&MP*, 23 November 1938, 'Plans for 500 Child Refugees in Britain', Spec. Corr., 16.
211 Ibid.
212 *TT*, 13 December 1938, 'The Refugees Fund', 16.
213 Ibid.
214 In 1976 a film was made about this incident called *Voyage of the Damned*.
215 *DE*, 13 June 1939, '900 Wandering Jews SOS to Premier', 1.
216 Ibid.
217 Ibid.

Conclusion

1 *The Spectator*, 3 November 1939, 'A Reversion to Barbarism', 609. Hereafter *TS*.
2 Ibid.
3 *New Statesman and Nation*, 4 November 1939, 'A London Diary', 638. Hereafter *NS&N*.
4 Ibid.
5 *Manchester Guardian*, 1 November 1939, 'The Camps and the System', Leader, 6. Hereafter *MG*.
6 See Brigitte Granzow, *A Mirror of Nazism: British Opinion and the Emergence of Hitler, 1929-1933* (London: Victor Gollancz Ltd., 1964).
7 *MG*, 6 March 1933, 'Nazis Win the General Election', 9.
8 *Daily Telegraph and Morning Post*, 11 November 1938, 'German Mobs' Vengeance on Jews', 17.
9 This included, for instance, an article written by Mosley entitled 'A World Re-born under Fascism', on 1 May 1933 (page 12).
10 The *Daily Mail* printed an exchange of letters between Mosley and Rothermere in which the proprietor distanced himself from the BUF and support of their ideology. *Daily Mail*, 19 July 1934, 'Lord Rothermere and Sir Oswald Mosley', 11.
11 Wickham Steed, *The Press* (London: Penguin, 1938), 165.
  Steed was a foreign correspondent for *The Times* based, at various times, in Berlin, Vienna, and Rome. He became Editor of *The Times* in 1919, serving until 1922.
12 TNL Archive, Norman Ebbutt Papers, Articles and Memoirs 1939-1945, Manuscript of 'My Twelve Years in Germany and After', Chapter IX, NE/2/1/12, News International Archive and Record Office.
13 Ibid.
14 Voigt referred to them as 'Nazis'; whether they were working under official orders or on their own initiative was unclear.

15 Shirer, *The Nightmare Years*, 138.
16 TNL Archive, Norman Ebbutt Papers, Articles and Memoirs 1939-1945, Manuscript of 'My Twelve Years in Germany and After', Chapter XII, NE/2/1/19.
17 G. E. R. Gedye, *Fallen Bastions* (London: Victor Gollancz, 1939), 327.
18 Ibid.
19 H. G. Daniels was a correspondent for *The Times*, based Geneva and Paris. Dawson to Daniels, 23 May 1937, in John Evelyn Wrench, *Geoffrey Dawson and Our Time* (London: Hutchison & Co., 1955), 361.
20 JRL, Crozier to Voigt, 16 June 1936, Foreign Correspondence File 344c, Folder 215.
21 Franklin Reid Gannon, *The British Press and Germany, 1936-1939* (Oxford: Clarendon Press, 1971), 85.

Bibliography

Primary sources

Newspapers and periodicals

Daily Express
Daily Mail
Daily Mirror
Daily Telegraph (1933–1937)
Daily Telegraph & Morning Post (1937–1939)
Jewish Chronicle
Manchester Guardian
Morning Post (1933–1937)
New Statesman and Nation
News Chronicle
Observer
The Spectator
The Times

Archival sources

Bodleian Library, University of Oxford, UK
MSS DAWSON
Personal Papers, 37–43 Diaries, 1933–1939
Special Correspondence, 56, 60, Letters and Correspondence
General Correspondence and Papers 78–81, 1933–1941
Correspondence and Papers of Cecilia Dawson, 93
News International Archive and Record Office, London, UK
TT/ED/GGD/1/ *George Geoffrey Dawson Correspondence*
TT/ED/GGD/2/ *George Geoffrey Dawson Correspondence*
TT/ED/GGD/3/ *George Geoffrey Dawson Correspondence*
TT/ED/RMBW/1/ *Robert Barrington-Ward Correspondence*
TT/FN/1/RD/1/ *Ralph Deakin Correspondence*
NE/1/1/ *Norman Ebbutt Correspondence*
NE/2 *Norman Ebbutt Articles and Memoirs, 1939–1945*
NE/2/2 *Articles and Talks By Norman Ebbutt*

NE/3/1 *Published references to Norman Ebbutt*
NE/3/2 *Personal Items relating to Norman Ebbutt's life*
NE/4 *Ebbutt papers held by The Times*
John Rylands Library, The University of Manchester, UK
95–6 General Cuttings books: W. P. Crozier with MS. Indices
97–8 Cuttings books: W. P. Crozier
97 2 January 1933–19 September 1937
145/14/1-52 *Miscellaneous documents etc, mainly relating to; the editorship of W.P. Crozier, 1932–47*
207–221 *Foreign Correspondence 1933–39*
223/47/1-39 *Nazi Germany 1933-44 – miscellaneous correspondence, cuttings etc.*
283/7 *Foreign Distribution agents, 1932–67*
317/2-3 *Photographs, W.P. Crozier*
387/3. *MG Distribution and Sales Stats, 1931–47*
B/V51A.1-181 *F. Voigt Correspondence, 1920–57*

Published sources, commentary (1930s)

Anon. *Why Nazi? Not to Accuse, Nor to Defend, but to Explain*. London: Faber and Faber Ltd, 1933.
Anon. 'Englands World Opinion of Germany After the Purge. *World Affairs* 97, no. 3 (September, 1934): 141–3.
Barnes, J. S. *Fascism*. London: Thornton Butterworth Ltd, 1934.
Bartlett, Vernon. *Nazi Germany Explained*. London: V. Gollancz, 1933.
Bernays, Robert. *Special Correspondent*. London: V. Gollancz, 1934.
Brady, Robert A. *The Spirit and Structure of German Fascism*. London: V. Gollancz, 1937.
Chamberlain, Neville. *The Struggle for Peace*. London: Hutchison, 1939.
Churchill, Winston. *Step by Step, 1936–1939*. London: T. Butterworth Ltd., 1939.
Delmer, Sefton. *Trail Sinister: Top Newsman Remembers Europe*. London: Secker & Warburg, 1961.
Fyfe, Hamilton. *My Seven Selves*. London: George Allen & Unwin Ltd., 1935.
Gedye, G. E. R. 'Impressions of Hitler's Germany'. *Contemporary Review*, 143 (January/June 1933): 669–76.
Gedye, G. E. R. *Fallen Bastions*. London: Victor Gollancz Ltd, 1939.
Gibbs, Philip. *Across the Frontiers*. London: The Right Book Club, May 1939.
Golding, Louis. *The Jewish Problem*. Harmondsworth: Penguin, 1938.
Henderson, Nevile. *Failure of a Mission: Berlin 1937–1939*. London: Hodder and Stoughton Ltd. 1940.
Henri, Ernst. *Hitler Over Europe*. London: Dent, 1934.
Henri, Ernst. *Hitler Over Russia: The Coming Fight between the Fascist and Socialist Armies*. London: J. M. Dent & Sons Ltd., 1936.

Hillson, Norman. *I Speak of Germany: A Plea for Anglo-German Friendship*. London: George Routledge & Sons, Ltd., 1937.
Jameson, Storm. *Civil Journey*. London: Cassell, 1939.
Kennedy, A. L. *Britain Faces Germany*. London: Cape, 1937.
L. H. 'Germany's Second Revolution'. *Bulletin of International News* 11, no. 1 (5 July 1934): 3–11.
Lorimer, E. O. *What Hitler Wants*. Harmondsworth: Penguin Books, 1939.
Madge, Charles and Tom Harrison. *Britain by Mass-Observation*. Harmondsworth: Penguin Books, 1939.
Martin, Kinglsey. *Fascism, Democracy and the Press*. New Statesman Pamphlet. London: The New Statesman and Nation, 1938.
Middleton, Edgar C. *Beaverbrook: Statesman and Man*. London: Stanley Paul, 1934.
Mosley, Leonard O. *Report From Germany*. Left Book Club Edition. London: Victor Gollancz, 1945.
Neumann, Franz. *Behemoth: The Structure and Practice of National Socialism*. Left Book Club Edition. London: Victor Gollancz, 1942.
Nicolson, Harold. *Diplomacy*. London: Thornton Butterworth Ltd., 1939.
Olden, Rudolf. *Hitler the Pawn*. London: Victor Gollancz, 1936.
Pieck, Wilhelm. *Germany: The Workers Fight Against the Hitler Terror*. Sydney: Modern Publishers, 1934.
Political and Economic Planning. 'Report on the British Press'. London: Political and Economic Planning, April 1938.
Pope, Ernst R. *Munich Playground*. Sydney and London: Angus and Robertson, 1942.
Price, George Ward. *I Know These Dictators*. London: George G. Harrap, 1937.
Price, George Ward. *Extra-Special Correspondent*. London: George G. Harrap, 1957.
Reed, Douglas. *Insanity Fair*. London: Jonathan Cape, 1939.
Reed, Douglas. *A Prophet At Home*. London: Jonathan Cape, 1941.
Roberts, Stephen H. *The House that Hitler Built*. 3rd edn London: Methuen, 1937.
Rothermere, Viscount. *My Fight to Rearm Britain*. London: Eyre and Spottiswoode, 1939.
Rothermere, Viscount. *Warnings and Predictions*. London: Eyre and Spottiswoode, 1939.
Schuman, Frederick L. *The Nazi Dictatorship: A Study in Social Pathology and the Politics of Fascism*. 2nd edn New York: Knopf, 1936.
Seton-Watson, R. W. *Britain and the Dictators*. London: Cambridge University Press, 1938.
Spivak, John L. *Europe Under the Terror*. London: Victor Gollanczz Ltd., 1936.
Steed, Wickham. *The Meaning of Hitlerism*. London: Nisbet, 1934.
Steed, Wickham. *The Press*. Harmondsworth: Penguin Books, 1938.
Voigt, Frederick Augustus. *Unto Caesar*. London: Constable & Co. Ltd, 1938.
Ward Price, George. *I Know These Dictators*. London: George G. Harrap & Co., 1937.
Wise, James Waterman. *Swastika, the Nazi Terror*. New York: H. Smith and R. Haas, 1933.

World Committee of Victims of Fascism. *The Brown Book of the Hitler Terror and the Burning of the Reichstag*. London: Victor Gollancz, 1933.
Wrench, Evelyn. *I Loved Germany*. London: Michael Joseph, 1940.
Zilliacus, K. 'Vigilantes'. *Between Two Wars? The Lessons of the Last World War in Relation to the Preparations for the Next*. Harmondsworth: Penguin Books Limited, 1939.

Published sources

Books, chapters and journal articles

Abel, T. *Why Hitler Came to Power*. New York: AMS Press, 1981.
Alexandroff, Alan and Richard Rosecrance. 'Deterrence in 1939'. *World Politics* 29, no. 3 (April 1977): 404-24. doi: 10.2307/2010003.
Allen, Robert and John Frost. *Daily Mirror*. Cambridge: Patrick Stephens, 1981.
Allen, Robert and John Frost. *Voice of Britain: The Inside Story of the Daily Express*. Cambridge: Patrick Stephens, 1983.
Allen, William Sheridan. *The Nazi Seizure of Power: The Experience of a Single Town*. Chicago: Quadrangle Books, 1965.
Anderson, Gerald D. *Fascists, Communists, and the National Government: Civil Liberties in Great Britain, 1931-1937*. Columbia: University of Missouri, 1983.
Ascher, Abraham. *Was Hitler a Riddle: Western Democracies and National Socialism*. Stanford: Stanford University Press, 2012.
Ayerst, David. *Guardian: Biography of a Newspaper*. London: William Collins & Sons Co. Ltd., 1971.
Ayerst, David. *The Guardian Omnibus, 1821-1971: An Anthology of 150 Years of Guardian Writing*. London: Collins, 1973.
Bajohr, Frank. *Aryanisation in Hamburg: The Economic Exclusion of the Jews and the Confiscation of their Property in Nazi Germany*. New York: Berghahn Books, 2002.
Balfour, Michael. *Withstanding Hitler in Germany, 1933 - 45*. London: Routledge, 1988.
Bankier, David. *The Germans and the Final Solution: Public Opinion under Nazism*. London: Oxford University Press, 1992.
Bankier, David, ed. *Probing the Depths of German Antisemitism: German Society and the Persecution of the Jews*. New York: Berghahn Books, 2000.
Baranowski, Shelley. *The Confessing Church, Conservative Elites, and the Nazi State*. Text and Studies in Religion, Vol. 28. New York: E. Mellen Press, 1986.
Barkai, Avraham. *From Boycott to Annihilation: The Economic Struggle of German Jews, 1933 — 1943*. Translated by William Templer. USA: University Press of New England, 1989.
Barnes, James J. and Patience P. Barnes. *Hitler's Mein Kampf in Britain and America: A Publishing History, 1930-39*. Cambridge: Cambridge University Press, 1980.

Barnes, James J. and Patience P. Barnes. *Nazis in Pre-War London, 1930–1939: The Fate and Role of German Party Members and British Sympathizers*. Portland: Sussex Academic Press, 2005.

Barnett, Victoria. *For the Soul of the People: Protestant Protest Under Hitler*. Oxford: Oxford University Press, 1992.

Barth, Karl. *The German Church Conflict*. London: Lutterworth Press, 1965.

Beck, Hermann. *The Fateful Alliance: German Conservatives and Nazis in 1933: The Machtergreifung in a New Light*. New York: Berghahn Books, 2008.

Benewick, Robert. *The Fascist Movement in Britain*. London: Allen Lane, 1972.

Bentwich, Norman. *My 77 Years: An Account of My Life and Times, 1883–1960*. London: Routledge & Kegan Paul Limited, 1962.

Berenbaum, Michael. *A Mosaic of Victims: Non-Jews Persecuted and Murdered by the Nazis*. New York: New York University Press, 1990.

Bergen, Doris L. *Twisted Cross: The German Christian Movement in the Third Reich*. Chapel Hill: University of North Carolina Press, 1996.

Berghahn, Marion. *Continental Britons: German-Jewish Refugees from Nazi Germany*. New York: Berghahn Books, 2007.

Berman, Sheri. *The Social Democratic Moment: Ideas and Politics in the Making of Interwar Europe*. Cambridge: Harvard University Press, 1998.

Besier, Gerhard. *The Holy See and Hitler's Germany*. Translated by W. R. Ward. New York: Palgrave Macmillan, 2007.

Bessel, Richard. *Political Violence and the Rise of Nazism: The Storm Troops in Eastern Germany, 1925–1934*. New Haven: Yale University Press, 1984.

Bessel, Richard, ed. *Life in the Third Reich*. Oxford: Oxford University Press, 1987.

Bingham, Adrian. 'The Digitization of Newspaper Archives: Opportunities and Challenges for Historians'. *Twentieth Century British History* 21, no. 2 (2010): 225–31. doi: 10.1093/tcbh/hwq007.

Blinkhorn, Martin, ed. *Fascists and Conservatives: The Radical Right and the Establishment in Twentieth-Century Europe*. London: Unwin Hyman, 1990.

Bloxham, David and Tony Kushner. *The Holocaust: Critical Historical Approaches*. Manchester: Manchester University Press, 2005.

Boas, Jacob. 'Germany or Diaspora? German Jewry's Shifting Perceptions in the Nazi Era, 1933–1938'. *Leo Baeck Institute Yearbook* 27, no. 1 (1982): 109–26. doi: 10.1093/leobaeck/27.1.109.

Boas, Jacob. 'Countering Nazi Defamation: German Jews and the Jewish Tradition, 1933–1938'. *Leo Baeck Institute Yearbook* 34, no. 1 (1989): 205–26. doi: 10.1093/leobaeck/34.1.205.

Bolchover, Richard. *British Jewry and the Holocaust*. Cambridge: Cambridge University Press, 1994.

Bösch, Frank. *Mass Media and Historical Change: Germany in International Perspective, 1400 to the Present*. Translated by Freya Buechter. New York: Berghahn Books, 2015. Accessed 22 July 2016. eBook Collection (EBSCOhost), EBSCOhost.

Bourne, Richard. *Lords of Fleet Street: The Harmsworth Dynasty*. London: Unwin Hyman, 1990.

Bouverie, Tim. *Appeasing Hitler: Chamberlain, Churchill and the Road to War*. London: The Bodley Head, 2019.

Boyce, George, James Curran and Pauline Wingate, eds *Newspaper History: From the Seventeenth Century to the Present Day*. London: Constable, 1978.

Bracher, Karl Dietrich. *The German Dictatorship*. Translated by Jean Steinberg. New York: Praeger Publishers, 1972.

Bramsted, Ernest Kohn. *Goebbels and National Socialist Propaganda*. London: Cresset Press, 1965.

Branson, Noreen and Margot Heinemann. *Britain in the Nineteen Thirties*. London: Weidenfeld and Nicolson, 1971.

Breitman, Richard. *Official Secrets: What the Nazis Planned, What the British and Americans Knew*. New York: Hill and Wang, 1999.

Brendon, Piers. *The Dark Valley: A Panorama of the 1930s*. London: Jonathan Cape, 2000.

Briggs, Asa. *The Golden Age of Wireless*. London: Oxford University Press, 1965.

British Broadcasting Corporation. *The BBC Year Book, 1933*. London: British Broadcasting Corporation, 1933.

British Broadcasting Corporation. *The BBC Year Book, 1935*. London: British Broadcasting Corporation, 1935.

British Broadcasting Corporation. *The BBC Year Book, 1939*. London: British Broadcasting Corporation, 1939.

Broszat, Martin. *The Hitler State: The Foundation and Development of the Internal Structure of the Third Reich*. Translated by John W. Hiden. London: Longman, 1981.

Browder, George C. *Foundations of the Nazi Police State: The Formation of Sipo and SD*. Kentucky: University Press of Kentucky, 1990.

Brown, Timothy S. *Weimar Radicals: Nazis and Communists between Authenticity and Performance*. New York: Berghahn Books, 2009.

Bullock, Alan. *Hitler: A Study in Tyranny*. England: Pelican Books, 1962.

Bullock, Alan. *Hitler and Stalin: Parallel Lives*. London: Fontana Press, 1993.

Burleigh, Michael. *The Third Reich: A New History*. London: Macmillan, 2000.

Burleigh, Michael and Wolfgang Wippermann. *The Racial State: Germany, 1933 – 1945*. Cambridge: Cambridge University Press, 1991.

Burnham, Lord. *Peterborough Court: The Story of the Daily Telegraph*. London: Cassell & Company, 1955.

Burrin, Philippe. *Hitler and the Jews: The Genesis of the Holocaust*. Translated by Patsy Southgate. London: Edward Arnold, 1994.

Burrin, Philippe. *Nazi Anti-Semitism: From Prejudice to the Holocaust*. Translated by Janet Lloyd. New York: The New Press, 2005.

Campbell, Bruce B. 'The SA After the Rohm Purge'. *Journal of Contemporary History* 28, no. 4 (October 1993): 659–74.

Camrose, William Ewert Berry, Viscount. *British Newspapers and Their Controllers*. London: Cassell and Company Ltd, 1947.

Caplan, Jane, ed. *Nazi Germany*. Oxford Short History of Germany Series. Oxford: Oxford University Press, 2008.

Caquet, P. E. *The Bell of Treason: The 1938 Munich Agreement in Czechoslovakia*. London: Profile Books, 2018.

Carr, E. H. *International Relations between the Two World Wars, 1919–1939*. London: Macmillans & Co. Ltd, 1950.

Carr, William. *A History of Germany, 1815 – 1985*. 3rd edn London: Edward Arnold, 1988.

Carsten, F. L. *The Rise of Fascism*. London: B. T. Batsford Ltd., 1967.

Catterall, Peter, Colin Seymour-Ure and Adrian Smith, eds *Northcliffe's Legacy: Aspects of the British Popular Press*, 1896 – 1996. Basingstoke: Macmillan Press, 2000.

Cesarani, David. *The Jewish Chronicle and Anglo-Jewry, 1841 – 1991*. Cambridge: Cambridge University Press, 1994.

Cesarani, David. *The Final Solution: Origins and Implementation*. London: Routledge, 1994.

Cesarani, David, and Paul A. Levine. *Bystanders to the Holocaust: A Re-Evaluation*. London: Frank Cass, 2002.

Chalaby, Jean K. 'Twenty Years of Contrast: The French and British Press During the Inter-War Period'. *European Journal of Sociology* 37, no. 1 (May 1996): 143–59. doi: 10.1017/S0003975600008006.

Chandler, Andrew. 'Munich and Morality: The Bishops of the Church of England and Appeasement'. *Twentieth Century British History* 5, no. 1 (1994): 77–99. doi: 10.1093/tcbh/5.1.77.

Chapoutot, Johann. *The Law of Blood: Thinking and Acting as a Nazi*. Translated by Melinda Richmond Mouillot. Cambridge: The Belknap Press of Harvard University Press, 2018.

Chrisholm, Anne and Michael Davie. *Beaverbrook: A Life*. London: Hutchison, 1992.

Christiansen, Arthur. *Headlines All My Life*. London: Heinemann, 1961.

Churchill, Winston S. *The Second World War: Volume I, The Gathering Storm*. London: Cassell & Co. Ltd, 1949.

Clarke, Tom. *Northcliffe in History: An Intimate Study of Press Power*. London: Hutchison and Co., 1950.

Cochrane, Arthur C. *The Church's Confession under Hitler*. 2nd edn Pittsburgh: The Pickwick Press, 1976.

Cockett, Richard. *Twilight of Truth: Chamberlain, Appeasement and the Manipulation of the Press*. London: Weidenfeld and Nicolson, 1989.

Cohen, Michael Joseph. *Churchill and the Jews*. London: Frank Cass, 1985.

Confino, Alon. *A World Without Jews: The Nazi Imagination from Persecution to Genocide*. New Haven: Yale University Press, 2014.

Conway, J. S. *The Nazi Persecution of the Churches, 1933 – 45*. London: Weidenfeld and Nicolson, 1968.

Copsey, Nigel. *Anti-Fascism in Britain*. New York: Palgrave, 2000.

Copsey, Nigel and Andrzej Olechnowicz, eds *Varieties of Anti-Fascism: Britain in the Inter-War Period*. Basingstoke: Palgrave Macmillan, 2010.

Cornwell, John. *Hitler's Pope: The Secret History of Pope Pius XII*. London: Viking, 1999.
Cowling, Maurice. *The Impact of Hitler: British Politics and British Policy, 1933–1940*. Chicago: The Univerity of Chicago Press, 1975.
Craig, Gordon A. *Germany, 1866 – 1945*. Oxford: Clarendon Press, 1978.
Crankshaw, D. F. *Gestapo: Instrument of Tyranny*. London: Putnam, 1956.
Crew, David F. *Nazism and German Society, 1933 – 1945*. New York: Routledge, 1994.
Cross, Colin. *The Fascists in Britain*. London: Barrie and Rockliff, 1961.
Crozier, William Percival and A. J. P. Taylor, ed. *Off the Record: Political Interviews, 1933–1943*. London: Hutchison, 1973.
Cudlipp, Hugh. *Publish and Be Damned! The Astonishing Story of the Daily Mirror*. London: Andrew Dakers Limited, 1953.
Curran, James and Jean Seaton. *Power Without Responsibility: The Press and Broadcasting in Britain*. 5th edn London and New York: Routledge, 1997.
Curran, James, Anthony Smith and Pauline Wingate. *Impacts and Influences: Essays on Media Power in the Twentieth Century*. London: Methuen, 1987.
Dawidowicz, Lucy S. *The War Against the Jews, 1933 – 45*. London: Penguin Books, 1990.
Deli, Peter. 'The Quality Press and the Soviet Union: A Case Study of the Reactions of the Manchester Guardian, The New Statesman and The Times to Stalin's Great Purges, 1936–38'. *Media History* 5, no. 2 (1999): 159–80. doi: 10.1080/13688809909357958.
Desmond, Robert W. *Crisis and Conflict: World News Reporting between the Two World Wars, 1920 – 1940*. Iowa City: University of Iowa Press, 1982.
Dorpalen, Andreas. *Hindenburg and the Weimar Republic*. Princeton: Princeton University Press, 1964.
Driberg, Tom. *Beaverbrook: A Study in Power and Frustration*. London: Weidenfeld and Nicolson, 1956.
Dutton, David. 'Sir Austen Chamberlain and British Foreign Policy, 1931–37'. *Diplomacy and Statecraft* 16, no. 2 (2005): 281–95. doi: 10.1080/09592290590948342.
Eatwell, Roger. *Fascism: A History*. London: Chatto & Windus, 1995.
Edelman, Maurice. *The Mirror: A Political History*. London: Hamish Hamilton, 1966.
Engel, Matthew. *Tickle the Public: One Hundred Years of the Popular Press*. London: Victor Gollancz, 1996.
Engelmann, Bernt. *In Hitler's Germany: Everyday Life in the Third Reich*. Translated by Krishna Winston. London: Methuen Mandarin, 1986.
Evans, Erin Lovell. *The German Centre Party, 1870 – 1933: A Study in Political Catholicism*. Carbondale: Southern Illinois University Press, 1981.
Evans, Richard J. *Rituals of Retribution: Capital Punishment in Germany, 1600 – 1987*. Oxford: Oxford University Press, 1996.
Evans, Richard J. *The Coming of the Third Reich*. London: Penguin Books, 2004.
Evans, Richard J. *The Third Reich in Power*. London: Penguin Books, 2006.
Evans, Richard J. 'The Conspiracists'. Review of *Burning the Reichstag: An Investigation into the Third Reich's Enduring Mystery*, by Benjamin Carter Hett. *London Review of*

Books 36 no. 9 (2014): 3–9, http://www.lrb.co.uk/v36/n09/richard-j-evans/the-conspiracists.
Evans, Richard J. *The Third Reich in History and Memory*. London: Little, Brown, 2015.
Eyck, Erich. *A History of the Weimar Republic: From the Locarno Conference to Hitler's Seizure of Power*. Translated by Harlan P. Hanson and Robert G. L. Waite. Vol. II. New York: Atheneum, 1970.
Ferris, Paul. *The House of Northcliffe: The Harmsworth's of Fleet Street*. London: Weidenfeld and Nicolson, 1971.
Fest, Joachim. *The Face of the Third Reich*. Translated by Michael Bullock. London: Penguin Books, 1970.
Fest, Joachim. *Hitler*. Translated by Richard and Clara Winston. New York: Harcourt, 1974.
Fischer, Conan. *Stormtroopers: A Social, Economic and Ideological Analysis, 1929 – 35*. London: George Allen & Unwin, 1983.
Fischer, Conan. *The Rise of the Nazis*. Manchester: Manchester University Press, 1995.
Foster, Alan. 'The Times and Appeasement: The Second Phase'. *Journal of Contemporary History* 16, no. 3, The Second World War: Part 2 (July 1981): 441–65. doi:10.1177/002200948101600303.
Foster, Alan. 'The Beaverbrook Press and Appeasement: The Second Phase'. *European History Quarterly* 21, no. 1 (1991): 5–38. doi: 10.1177/026569149102100101.
Fowler, Roger. *Language in the News: Discourse and Ideology in the Press*. London: Routledge, 1991.
Franklin, Bob, ed. *Pulling Newspapers Apart: Analysing Print Journalism*. Abingdon, Oxon: Routledge, 2008.
Frei, Norbert. *National Socialist Rule in Germany: The Führer State 1933 – 1945*. Translated by Simon B. Steyne. Oxford: Blackwell, 1983.
Friedlander, Henry. *The Origins of Nazi Genocide: From Euthanasia to the Final Solution*. Chapel Hill and London: The University of North Carolina Press, 1995.
Friedlander, Saul. *Pius XII and the Third Reich: A Documentation*. Translated by Charles Fullman. London: Chatto & Windus, 1966.
Friedlander, Saul. *The Years of Persecution: Nazi Germany and the Jews, 1933–39*. London: Phoenix, 2007.
Frischer, Willi. *The Rise and Fall of Hermann Goering*. London: Four Square Books, 1960.
Fuchser, Larry William. *Neville Chamberlain and Appeasement: A Study in Politics*. New York: Norton, 1982.
Fulda, Bernhard. *Press and Politics in Weimar Germany*. Oxford: Oxford University Press, 2009.
Gallo, Max. *The Night of the Long Knives: Hitler's Purge of Roehm and the S.A. Brown Shirts*. Translated by Lily Emmet. Great Britain: Harper & Row, 1972.
Gannon, Franklin Reid. *The British Press and Germany, 1936–1939*. Oxford: Clarendon Press, 1971.
Gardner, Juliet. *The Thirties: An Intimate History*. London: Harper Press, 2011.
Gay, Peter. *Weimar Culture*. Harmondsworth, Middlesex: Penguin Books, 1974.

Geary, Dick. *Hitler and Nazism*. London: Routledge, 2000.
Gellately, Robert. *The Gestapo and German Society: Enforcing Racial Policy 1933 – 1945*. Oxford: Clarendon Press, 1991.
Gellately, Robert. 'Denunciations in Twentieth-Century German: Aspects of Self-Policing in the Third Reich and the German Democratic Republic'. *Journal of Modern History* 68 (1996): 931–67. http://www.jstor.org/stable/2946725.
Gellately, Robert. 'The Prerogatives of Confinement in Germany, 1933 – 1945'. In *Institutions of Confinement: Hospitals, Asylums, and Prisons in Western Europe and North America, 1500–1950*, edited by N. Finzsch and R. Jütte, 191–212. New York: Cambridge University Press, 1996.
Gellately, Robert. *Backing Hitler: Consent and Coercion in Nazi Germany*. Oxford: Oxford University Press, 2001.
Gellately, Robert and Nathan Stoltzfus, eds *Social Outsiders in Nazi Germany*. Princeton: Princeton University Press, 2001.
Gerwarth, Robert. *Hitler's Hangman: The Life of Heydrich*. New Haven: Yale University Press, 2011.
Gilbert, Martin. *The European Powers, 1900 – 45*. London: Weidenfeld and Nicolson, 1965.
Gilbert, Martin. *The Holocaust: The Jewish Tragedy*. London: Fontana Press, 1987.
Gilbert, Martin. *Churchill and the Jews*. London: Simon & Schuster, 2000.
Godman, Peter. *Hitler and the Vatican: Inside the Secret Archives that Reveal the New Story of the Nazis and the Church*. New York: Free Press, 2004.
Goldhagen, Daniel Jonah. *Hitler's Willing Executioners: Ordinary Germans and the Holocaust*. London: Abacus, 2006.
Gollancz, Victor. *'Let My People Go': Some Practical Proposals for Dealing with Hitler's Massacre of the Jews and an Appeal to the British Public*. London: Victor Gollancz, 1943.
Gollancz, Victor. *Our Threatened Values*. Left Book Club ed. London: Victor Gollancz Ltd, 1946.
Goltz, Anna von der. *Hindenburg: Power, Myth and the Rise of the Nazis*. Oxford: Oxford University Press, 2011.
Gorodetsky, Gabriel, ed. *The Maisky Diaries: Red Ambassador to the Court of St James, 1932 – 1943*. Translated by Tatiana Sorokina and Oliver Ready. New Haven: Yale University Press, 2015.
Görtemaker, Manfred, ed. *Britain and Germany in the 20th Century*. German Historical Perspectives XVIII. Oxford: Berg, 2006.
Gourlay, Logan. *The Beaverbrook I Knew*. London: Quartet Books, 1984.
Grant, Thomas D. *Stormtroopers and Crisis in the Nazi Movement: Activism, Ideology and Dissolution*. New York: Routledge, 2004.
Granzow, Brigitte. *A Mirror of Nazism: British Opinion and the Emergence of Hitler, 1929 — 1933*. London: Victor Gollancz, 1964.
Grebling, Helga. *The History of the German Labour Movement*. Translated by Edith Körner. Abridged by Mary Saran. Leamington Spa, Dover: Berg Publishers, 1985.

Gregor, Neil. *How to Read Hitler*. London: Granta Books, 2014.
Griffiths, Dennis, ed. *The Encyclopaedia of the British Press, 1422 – 1922*. New York: St Martin's Press, 1992.
Griffiths, Richard. *Fellow Travellers of the Right: British Enthusiasts for Nazi Germany, 1933-39*. London: Constable, 1980.
Grunberger, Richard. *A Social History of the Third Reich*. Harmondsworth: Penguin Books, 1974.
Hale, Oron J. *The Captive Press in the Third Reich*. Princeton: Princeton University Press, 1964.
Halperin, S. William. *Germany Tried Democracy*. New York: W.W. Norton and Company, 1946.
Hambro, Carl Joachim. *Newspaper Lords in British Politics*. London: Macdonald, 1958.
Hamerow, Theodore S. *Why We Watched: Europe, America and the Holocaust*. New York: W.W. Norton & Co., 2008.
Hampton, Mark. *Visions of the Press in Britain, 1850 – 1950*. Urbana: University of Illinois Press, 2004.
Hancock, Eleanor. *Ernst Röhm: Hitler's SA Chief of Staff*. Basingstoke, Hampshire: Palgrave Macmillan, 2011.
Hancock, Eleanor. 'The Purge of the S.A. Reconsidered: An Old Putschist Trick?'. *Central European History* 44, no. 4 (December 2011): 669-83.
Hardy, Alexander G. *Hitler's Secret Weapon: The 'Managed' Press and Propaganda Machine of Nazi Germany*. New York: Vantage Press, 1968.
Hart-Davis, Duff. *Hitler's Games: The 1936 Olympics*. London: Century, 1986.
Hart-Davis, Duff. *The House the Berry's Built*. Toronto: Stoddart, 1990.
Hattersley, Roy. *Borrowed Time: The Story of Britain Between the Wars*. London: Little Brown, 2007.
Havighurst, Alfred F. *Twentieth Century Britain*. New York: Row, Peterson and Company, 1962.
Haworth, Bryan. 'The British Broadcasting Corporation, Nazi Germany and the Foreign Office, 1933–1936'. *Historical Journal of Film, Radio and Television* 1, no. 1 (1981): 47–55. doi: 10/1080/01439688100260041.
Heberle, Rudolf. *From Democracy to Nazism: A Regional Case Study on Political Parties in Germany*. New York: Howard Fertig, 1970.
Heiden, Konrad. *A History of National Socialism*. London: Methuen, 1971.
Helmreich, Ernst Christian. *The German Churches under Hitler: Background, Struggle and Epilogue*. Detroit: Wayne State University Press, 1979.
Herd, Harold. *The March of Journalism: The Story of the British Press from 1622 to the Present Day*. London: George Allen & Unwin Ltd, 1952.
Herzberg, Arno. 'The Jewish Press under the Nazi Regime – Its Mission, Suppression and Defiance – A Memoir'. *Leo Baeck Institute Yearbook* 36, no. 1 (1991): 367-88. doi: 10.1093/leobaeck/36.1.367.
Heschel, Susannah. *The Aryan Jesus: Christian Theologians and the Bible in Nazi Germany*. Princeton and New York: Princeton University Press, 2008.

Hett, Benjamin Carter. *Burning the Reichstag: An Investigation into the Third Reich's Enduring Mystery*. New York: Oxford University Press, 2014.

Hett, Benjamin Carter. 'This Story Is About Something Fundamental': Nazi Criminals, History, Memory, and the Reichstag Fire'. *Central European History* 48 (2015): 199–224. doi:10.1017/S0008938915000345

Hett, Benjamin Carter. *The Death of Democracy: Hitler's Rise to Power and the Downfall of the Weimar Republic*. New York: Henry Holt and Company, 2018.

Hilberg, Raul. *The Destruction of the European Jews*. Vol. I. New York: Holmes & Meier, 1985.

Hilberg, Raul. *Perpetrators, Victims, Bystanders: The Jewish Catastrophe, 1933–1945*. New York: HarperPerrenial, 1993.

Hilton, Christopher. *Hitler's Olympics: The 1936 Berlin Olympic Games*. Stroud: Sutton, 2006.

Hindle, Wilfrid. *The Morning Post, 1772 – 1937: Portrait of a Newspaper*. London: George Routledge & Sons Ltd. 1937.

Hitler, Adolf. *Mein Kampf*. Translated by Ralph Manheim. Boston and New York: Houghton and Mifflin Company, 1999.

Hobsbawm, Eric. *The Age of Extremes: The Short Twentieth Century, 1914 – 1991*. London: Abacus, 2013.

Hodder-Williams, Richard. *Public Opinion Polls and British Politics*. London: Routledge & K. Paul, 1970.

Hodgson, Guy. 'Sir Neville Henderson, Appeasement and the Press: Fleet Street and the Build-Up to the Second World War'. *Journalism Studies* 8, no. 2 (2007): 320–34. doi: 10.1080/14616700601148952.

Hoenicke Moore, Michaela. *Know Your Enemy: The American Debate on Nazism, 1933–1945*. Cambridge: Cambridge University Press, 2009.

Hohenberg, John. *Foreign Correspondence: Great Reporters and Their Times*. New York: Columbia University Press, 1964.

Höhne, Heinz. *The Order of the Death's Head: The Story of Hitler's S.S.* Translated by Richard Barry. London: Secker & Walburg, 1969.

Holborn, Hajo, ed. *Republic to Reich: The Making of the Nazi Revolution*. Translated by Ralph Manheim. New York: Pantheon Books, 1972.

Holman, Brett. 'The Air Panic of 1935: British Press Opinion Between Disarmament and Rearmament'. *Journal of Contemporary History* 46, no. 2 (2011): 288–307. doi: 10.1177/0022009410392407.

Holmes, Colin. *Antisemitism in British Society, 1876 – 1939*. London: Edward Arnold, 1979.

Horrie, Chris. *Tabloid Nation: The Birth of the Daily Mirror to the Death of the Tabloid*. London: André Deutsch, 2003.

Hutt, Allen. *The Changing Newspaper: Typographic Trends in Britain and America, 1622–1972*. London: Gordon Fraser, 1973.

Hyams, Edward. *The New Statesman: The History of the First Fifty Years, 1913–1963*. London: The Statesman & Nation Publishing Company, 1963.

Ingaro, Christian. *Believe and Destroy: Intellectuals in the SS War Machine*. Translated by Andrew Brown. Cambridge: Polity Press, 2013.

Jantzen, Kyle. *Faith and Fatherland: Parish Politics in Hitler's Germany*. Minneapolis: Fortress Press, 2008.

Jenkins, Roy. *Churchill: A Biography*. New York: Farrar, Straus and Giroux, 2001.

Johnson, Eric A. *Nazi Terror: The Gestapo, Jews, and Ordinary Germans*. London: John Murray, 2000.

Johnson, Eric and Karl-Heinz Reuband. *What We Knew: Terror, Mass Murder and Everyday Life in Nazi Germany*. London: John Murray, 2005.

Johnson, Gaynor, ed. *The Foreign Office and British Diplomacy in the Twentieth Century*. London: Routledge, 2005.

Jones, Nigel. *The Birth of the Nazis: How the Freikorps Blazed a Trail for Hitler*. London: Constable and Robinson, 2004.

Kaplan, Marion A. *Between Dignity and Despair: Jewish Life in Nazi Germany*. New York: Oxford University Press, 1998.

Kater, Michael, H. *Culture in Nazi Germany*. New Haven and London: Yale University Press, 2019.

Kennedy, P. M. 'Idealists and Realists: British Views of Germany, 1864–1939'. *Transactions of the Royal Historical Society* 24 (December 1975): 137–56. doi: 10.2307/3679090.

Kershaw, Ian, ed. *Weimar: Why Did German Democracy Fail?* New York: St. Martin's Press, 1990.

Kershaw, Ian. '"Working Towards the Führer": Reflections on the Nature of the Hitler Dictatorship'. *Contemporary European History* 2 (1993): 103–18.

Kershaw, Ian. *Hitler: 1889–1936: Hubris*. London: Penguin Books, 1998.

Kershaw, Ian. *Hitler: 1936–1945: Nemesis*. London: Penguin Books, 2001.

Kershaw, Ian. *Making Friends with Hitler: Lord Londonderry and Britain's Road to War*. London: Allen Lane, 2004.

Kershaw, Ian. *To Hell and Back: Europe 1914–1949*. London: Allen Lane, 2015.

Kersten, Lee. 'The Times and the Concentration Camp at Dachau, December 1933 – February 1934: An Unpublished Report'. *Shofar: An Interdisciplinary Journal of Jewish Studies* 18, no. 2 (Winter 2000): 101–9.

Kirsch, Jonathan. *The Short, Strange Life of Herschel Grynszpan: A Boy Avenger, A Nazi Diplomat, and a Murder in Paris*. New York: Liveright, 2014.

Kitchen, Martin. *Europe Between the Wars: A Political History*. London: Longman, 1994.

Klemperer, Victor. *I Shall Bear Witness: The Diaries of Victor Klemperer, 1933 – 41*. Translated and Abridged by Martin Chalmers. London: Weidenfeld & Nicolson, 1998.

Klemperer, Victor. *The Language of the Third Reich*. Translated by Martin Brady. London: Continuum, 2008.

Koch, H. W., ed. *Aspects of the Third Reich*. Hampshire and London: Macmillan Education Ltd., 1988.

Kohn, Ralph. 'Nazi Persecution: Britain's Rescue of Academic Refugees'. *European Review* 19, no. 2 (May 2011): 255–83. doi: 10.1017/S1062798710000542.

Kolb, Eberhard. *The Weimar Republic*. Translated by P. S. Falla. London and NY: Routledge, 1988.

Koss, Stephen. *The Rise and Fall of the Political Press in Britain: Volume 2: The Twentieth Century*. London: Hamish Hamilton, 1984.

Krausnick, Helmut and Martin Broszat. *Anatomy of the SS State*. Translated by Dorothy Long and Marian Jackson. St Albans: Paladin, 1973.

Krüger, Arnd and William Murray, eds *The Nazi Olympics: Sport, Politics and Appeasement in the 1930s*. Urbana: University of Illinois Press, 2003.

Kulka, Otto Dov, and Eberhard Jäckel, ed. *The Jews in the Secret Nazi Reports on Popular Opinion in Germany, 1933 – 1945*. Translated by William Templer. New Haven: Yale University Press, 2010.

Kurlander, Eric. *Living with Hitler: Liberal Democrats in the Third Reich*. New Haven and London: Yale University Press, 2009.

Kushner, Tony. *The Holocaust and the Liberal Imagination: A Social and Cultural History*. Oxford: Blackwell, 1994.

Kushner, Tony and Katharine Knox. *Refugees in an Age of Genocide: Global, National and Local Perspectives During the Twentieth Century*. London: Frank Cass, 1999.

Lacquer, Walter. *The Terrible Secret: An Investigation into the Suppression of Information about Hitler's 'Final Solution'*. London: Weidenfeld and Nicolson, 1980.

Lake, Brian. *British Newspapers: A History and Guide for Collectors*. London: Sheppard Press, 1984.

Langer, Walter, C. *The Mind of Adolf Hitler*. London: Pan Books, 1972.

Large, David Clay, ed. *Contending with Hitler: Varieties of German Resistance in the Third Reich*. Cambridge: Cambridge University Press, 1991.

Large, David Clay. *Where Ghosts Walked: Munich's Road to the Third Reich*. New York: W.W. Norton and Company, 1997.

Large, David Clay. *Nazi Games: The Olympics of 1936*. New York: W.W. Norton, 2007.

Larson, Erik. *In the Garden of Beasts: Love, Terror and an American Family in Hitler's Berlin*. Melbourne: Scribe Publications, 2011.

Laver, James. *Between the Wars*. London: Vista Books, 1961.

Lee, Stephen L. *The European Dictatorships, 1918 – 1945*. London: Routledge, 1995.

Lees-Milne, James. *Harold Nicolson: A Biography, 1930 – 1968*. London: Chatto & Windus, 1981.

Leff, Laurel. *Buried by the Times: The Holocaust and America's Most Important Newspaper*. Cambridge: Cambridge University Press, 2005.

LeMahieu, D. L. *A Culture for Democracy: Mass Communication and the Cultivated Mind Between the Wars*. Oxford: Clarendon Press, 1988.

Levitsky, Steven and Daniel Ziblatt. *How Democracies Die: What History Reveals about Our Future*. Great Britain: Viking, 2018.

Lewis, Jeremy. *Shades of Greene: One Generation of an English Family*. London: Jonathan Cape, 2010.

Lewy, Guenter. *The Catholic Church and Nazi Germany*. London: Weidenfeld and Nicolson, 1968.

Linehan, Thomas P. *British Fascism, 1918-39: Parties, Ideology and Culture*. Manchester: Manchester University Press, 2000.

Lipstadt, Deborah. *Beyond Belief: The American Press and the Coming of the Holocaust, 1933-1939*. New York: The Free Press, 1986.

Longerich, Peter. *Holocaust: The Nazi Persecution and Murder of the Jews*. Oxford: Oxford University Press, 2010.

Longerich, Peter. *Heinrich Himmler*. Translated by Jeremy Noakes and Lesley Sharpe. Oxford: Oxford University Press, 2012.

Longerich, Peter. *Goebbels: A Biography*. Translated by Alan Blance, Jeremy Noakes and Lesley Sharpe. London: The Bodley Head, 2015.

Longerich, Peter. *Hitler: A Life*. Translated by Jeremy Noakes and Lesley Sharpe. Oxford: Oxford University Press, 2019.

Love, Gary. 'The Periodical Press and the Intellectual Culture of Conservatism in Interwar Britain'. *The Historical Journal* 57, no. 4 (December 2014). doi: 10.1017/S00018246X14000429.

Low, David. *Years of Wrath: A Cartoon History, 1932-1945*. London: Gollancz, 1949.

Lubrich, Oliver, ed. *Travels in the Reich, 1933 - 1945: Foreign Authors Report from Germany*. Chicago: The University of Chicago Press, 2010.

Lukacs, John. *The Hitler of History*. New York: Vintage Books, 1998.

Lunn, Kenneth and Richard C. Thurlow, eds *British Fascism: Essays on the Radical Right in Interwar Britain*. London: Croom Helm, 1980.

Lutzer, Erwin W. *Hitler's Cross*. Chicago: Moody Press, 1995.

McCallum, J. A. *Hitler and the Trade Unions*. 'Through Australian Eyes Pamphlets on World Affairs, No. 6'. Sydney: Angus and Robertson, 1940.

McConagha, W. A. *Development of the Labor Movement in Great Britain, France and Germany*. Chapel Hill: The University of North Carolina Press, 1942.

McCullough, Colin and Nathan Wilson, eds *Violence, Memory, and History: Western Perceptions of Kristallnacht*. New York and London: Routledge, 2015.

MacDonogh, Giles. 1938: *Hitler's Gamble*. London: Constable, 2010.

McDonough, Frank. 'The Times, Norman Ebbut and the Nazis, 1927 - 1937'. *Journal of Contemporary History* 27, no. 3 (July 1992): 407-24. doi: 10.1177/002200949202700302.

McDonough, Frank. *Neville Chamberlain, Appeasement and the British Road to War*. Manchester: Manchester University Press, 1998.

McDonough, Frank. *Hitler and the Rise of the Nazi Party*. New York: Pearson/Longman, 2003.

McDonough, Frank. *Hitler, Chamberlain, and Appeasement*. Cambridge: Cambridge University Press, 2003.

McLachlan, Donald. *In the Chair: Barrington-Ward of The Times, 1927 – 1948*. London: Weidenfeld and Nicolson, 1971.

Manvell, Roger and Heinrich Fraenkel. *Heinrich Himmler*. London: William Heinemann Ltd. 1965.

Maracin, Paul R. *The Night of the Long Knives: Forty-Eight Hours that Changed the History of the World*. Guilford: Lyons, 2007.

Martel, Gordon. *The Times and Appeasement: The Diaries of A.L. Kennedy, 1932 – 1939*. New York: Cambridge University Press, 2000.

Martin, Kingsley. *Critic's London Diary*. London: Martin Secker & Warburg Ltd, 1960.

Martin, Kingsley. *Kingsley Martin: Portrait and Self-Portrait*. London: Barrie & Jenkins, 1969.

Maser, Werner. *Hitler: Legend, Myth & Reality*. Translated by Peter and Betty Ross. New York: Harper Torchbooks, 1974.

Mason, Paul T., ed. *Totalitarianism: Temporary Madness or Permanent Danger?* Lexington, MA: D.C. Heath and Company, 1968.

Mason, Timothy W. *Social Policy in the Third Reich: The Working Class and the National Community*. Translated by John Broadwin. Edited by Jane Caplan. Providence: Berg, 1993.

Mason, Timothy W. *Nazism, Fascism and the Working Class*. Edited by Jane Caplan. Cambridge: Cambridge University Press, 1995.

Matheson, Peter, ed. *The Third Reich and the Christian Churches*. Grand Rapids, MI: William B. Eerdmans Publishing Company, 1981.

Mau, Hermann. "'The 'Second Revolution" – June 20, 1934'. In *Republic to Reich: The Making of the Nazi Revolution*, edited by Hajo Holborn, translated by Ralph Manheim, 223–48. New York: Pantheon Books, 1972.

Merkl, P. H. *Political Violence under the Swastika*. Princeton: Princeton University Press, 1975.

Merrill, John C. and Harold A. Fisher. *World's Great Dailies: Profiles of Fifty Newspapers*. New York: Hastings House, 1980.

Meyer, Henry Cord, ed. *The Long Generation: Germany from Empire to Ruin, 1913 – 1945*. New York: Walker and Company, 1973.

Michael, Robert. 'Theological Myth, German Antisemitism and The Holocaust: The Case of Martin Niemoeller'. *Holocaust and Genocide Studies* 2, no. 1 (1987): 105–22. doi: 10.1093/hgs/2.1.105.

Miller, Susanne and Heinrich Potthoff. *A History of German Social Democracy, From 1848 to the Present*. Translated by J. A. Underwood. Leamington Spa: Berg, 1986.

Mitchell, Otis C. *Hitler's Stormtroopers and the Attack on the German Republic, 1919 – 1933*. North Carolina: McFarland & Company, 2008.

Mommsen, Hans. 'The Free Trade Unions and Social Democracy in Imperial Germany'. In *The Development of Trade Unionism in Great Britain and Germany, 1880 – 1914*. ed Wolfgang J. Mommsen and Hans-Gerhard Husung, 371–89. The German Historical Institute. London: George Allen and Unwin, 1985.

Mommsen, Hans. *The Rise and Fall of Weimar Democracy*. Translated by Elborg Forster and Larry Eugene Jones. Chapel Hill: The University of North Carolina Press, 1996.

Mommsen, Hans. *Alternatives to Hitler: German Resistance Under the Third Reich*. Translated and Annotated by Angus McGeoch. Introduction by Jeremy Noakes. London: I.B. Tauris, 2003.

Mommsen, Wolfgang J. and Lothar Kettenacker, eds *The Fascist Challenge and the Policy of Appeasement*. London: Allen & Unwin, 1983.

Morgenthaler, Sibylle. 'Countering the Pre-1933 Nazi Boycott Against the Jews'. *Leo Baeck Institute Yearbook* 36, no. 1 (1991): 127–49. doi: 10.1093/leobaeck/36.1.127.

Morris, Benny. *The Roots of Appeasement: The British Weekly Press and Nazi Germany During the 1930s*. London: Frank Cass, 1991.

Moses, John A. *Trade Unionism in Germany from Bismarck to Hitler, 1919 – 1933*. Vol. 2. London: George Prior Publishers, 1982.

Mosley, Leonard. *The Reich Marshal: A Biography of Hermann Goering*. New York: Doubleday & Company Inc., 1974.

Mosse, George L. *Nazi Culture: Intellectual, Cultural and Social Life in the Third Reich*. Translated by Salvator Attanasio. New York: Grosset & Dunlap, 1968.

Mowat, Charles Loch. *Britain Between the Wars, 1918 – 1940*. London: Methuen & Co. Ltd, 1962.

Muggeridge, Malcolm. *The Thirties: 1930 – 1940, A Great Britain*. London: Fontana, 1972.

Muller, Ingo. *Hitler's Justice: The Courts of the Third Reich*. Translated by Deborah Lucas Schneider. Cambridege, MA: Harvard University Press, 1991.

Neville, Peter. *Appeasing Hitler: The Diplomacy of Sir Neville Henderson*. Basingstoke: Macmillan, 1999.

Neville, Peter. *Hitler and Appeasement: The British Attempt to Prevent the Second World War*. London: Hambledon Continuum, 2006.

Nicosia, Francis R. and Lawrence D. Stokes, eds *Germans Against Nazism: Nonconformity, Opposition and Resistance in the Third Reich: Essays in Honour of Peter Hoffmann*. New York: St. Martin's Press, 1990.

Nolte, Ernst. *Three Faces of Fascism*. Translated by Leila Vennewitz. New York: Holt, Reinhart & Winston, 1966.

Nyomarky, Joseph. *Charisma and Factionalism in the Nazi Party*. Minneapolis: University of Minnesota Press, 1967.

O'Brien, P. 'The Prison on the Continent: Europe, 1865 – 1965'. In *The Oxford History of the Prison*, edited by N. Morris and D. J. Rothman, 199–225. New York: Oxford University Press, 1995.

Olson, Kenneth E. *The History Makers: The Press of Europe From Its Beginnings Through 1965*. Baton Rouge: Louisiana State University Press, 1966.

Orlow, Dietrich. *The History of the Nazi Party, 1919 – 1933*. Pittsburgh: University of Pittsburgh Press, 1969.

Orlow, Dietrich. *The History of the Nazi Party, 1933 – 1945*. Pittsburgh: University of Pittsburgh Press, 1973.

Overy, Richard. *Goering*. London: Phoenix Press, 2000.

Overy, Richard. *The Dictators: Hitler's Germany, Stalin's Russia*. London: Penguin Books, 2005.

Overy, Richard. *1939: Countdown to War*. London: Allen Lane, 2009.

Overy, Richard. *The Twilight Years: The Paradox of Britain Between the Wars*. New York: Viking, 2009.

Palmier, Jean-Michel. *Weimar in Exile: The Antifascist Emigration in Europe and America*. London: Verso, 2006.

Panayi, Panikos, ed. *Weimar and Nazi Germany: Continuities and Discontinuities*. Harlow: Longman, 2001.

Parker, R. A. C. *Chamberlain and Appeasement: British Policy and the Coming of the Second World War*. Basingstoke: Macmillan Press, 1993.

Parker, R. A. C. *Churchill and Appeasement*. London: Macmillan, 2000.

Pascal, Roy. *The Growth of Modern Germany*. New York: Russell & Russell, 1969.

Patch, William L. *The Christian Trade Unions in the Weimar Republic, 1918 – 1933*. New Haven: Yale University Press, 1985.

Patch, William L. *Heinrich Brüning and the Dissolution of the Weimar Republic*. Cambridge: Cambridge University Press, 1998.

Peele, Gillian and Chris Cook, eds *The Politics of Reappraisal, 1918 – 1939*. London: Macmillan, 1975.

Pegg, Mark. *Broadcasting and Society, 1918 — 1939*. London: Croom Helm, 1983.

Peukert, Detlev. *Inside Nazi Germany: Conformity, Opposition and Racism in Everyday Life*. Translated by Richard Deveson. Harmondsworth: Penguin, 1989.

Pinder, John, ed. *Fifty Years of Political and Economic Planning: Looking Forward, 1931–1981*. London: Heinemann, 1981.

Pine, Lisa. *Hitler's 'National Community': Society and Culture in Nazi Germany*. London: Hodder Education, 2007.

Pound, Reginald and Geoffrey Harmsworth. *Northcliffe*. London: Cassell & Company Ltd., 1959.

Prittie, Terence. *Germans Against Hitler*. London: Hutchison & Co Ltd., 1964.

Pugh, Martin. *The Making of Modern British Politics, 1867 – 1939*. Oxford: Basil Blackwell, 1982.

Pugh, Martin. *'Hurrah for the Blackshirts': Fascists and Fascism in Britain Between the Wars*. London: Jonathan Cape, 2005.

Quinlan, Kevin. *The Secret War Between the Wars: MI5 in the 1920s and 1930s*. Suffolk: Boydell Press, 2014.

Read, Anthony and David Fisher. *Kristallnacht: Unleashing the Holocaust*. London: Papermac, 1991.

Read, Donald. 'Reuters: News Agency of the British Empire'. *Contemporary British History* 8, no. 2 (1994): 195–212. doi: 10.1080/1361946908581290.

Read, Donald. 'Truth in News: Reuters and the Manchester Guardian, 1858 – 1964'. *Northern History* 31, no. 1 (1995): 281–97. doi: 10.1179/007817295790175345.

Rees, Laurence. *The Dark Charisma of Adolf Hitler: Leading Millions into the Abyss.* London: Ebury Press, 2012.

Reitlinger, Gerald. *The SS: Alibi of a Nation, 1922 – 1945*. New York: Viking Press, 1968.

Reitlinger, Gerald. *The Final Solution*. London: Sphere Books, 1971.

Richardson, John E. *Analysing Newspapers: An Approach from Critical Discourse Analysis*. Basingstoke, Hampshire: Palgrave Macmillan, 2007.

Ripsman, Norrin M. and Jack S. Levy. 'Wishful Thinking or Buying Time? The Logic of British Appeasement in the 1930s'. *International Security* 33, no. 2 (Fall 2008): 148–81. http://www.jstor.org/stable/40207135.

Robbins, Alan Pitt. *Newspapers to-Day*. Oxford: Oxford University Press, 1956.

Robbins, Keith. *Present and Past: British Images of Germany in the First Half of the Twentieth Century and Their Historical Legacy*. Göttingen: Waldstein Verlag, 1999.

Roberts, J. M. *The Penguin History of the Twentieth Century: The History of the World, 1901 to the Present*. London: Penguin Books, 2000.

Rosenhaft, Eva. *Beating the Fascists? The German Communists and Political Violence, 1929 – 1933*. New York: Cambridge University Press, 1983.

Ross, Robert W. *So It Was True: The American Protestant Press and the Nazi Persecution of the Jews*. Minneapolis: University of Minnesota Press, 1980.

Roth, Cecil. *The Jewish Chronicle, 1841 – 1941: A Century of Newspaper History*. London: The Jewish Chronicle, 1949.

Roth, Joseph. *On the End of the World*. Translated by Will Stone. London: Hesperus Press Ltd., 2013.

Roth, Joseph. *The Hotel Years: Wanderings in Europe Between the Wars*. London: Granta Books, 2013.

Rothfels, Hans. *The German Opposition to Hitler: An Assessment*. Translated by Lawrence Wilson. London: Oswald Wolff Limited, 1973.

Rowse, A. L. *All Souls and Appeasement: A Contribution to Contemporary History*. London: Macmillan, 1961.

Sassoon, Donald. *The Culture of The Europeans from 1800 to the Present*. London: Harper Collins, 2006.

Schad, Martha. *Hitler's Spy Princess: The Extraordinary Life of Stephanie von Hohenlohe*. Translated by Angus McGeoch. Stroud: Sutton Publishing, 2004.

Schneider, Michael. *A Brief History of the German Trade Unions*. Translated by Barrie Selman. Bonn: J.H.W. Dietz, 1991.

Schoenbaum, David. *Hitler's Social Revolution: Class and Status in Nazi Germany, 1933 – 1939*. New York: Anchor Books, 1967.

Scholder, Klaus. *The Churches and the Third Reich: Preliminary History and the Time of Illusions, 1918–1934*. Vol. I. Translated by John Bowden. London: SCM Press Ltd, 1987.

Scholder, Klaus. *The Churches and the Third Reich: The Year of Disillusionment: 1934, Barmen and Rome*. Vol. II. Translated by John Bowden. London: SCM Press Ltd, 1988.

Schwarz, Angela. 'British Visitors to National Socialist Germany: In a Familiar or in a Foreign Country?' *Journal of Contemporary History* 28, no. 3 (July 1993): 487–509. doi: 10.1177/002200949302800305.

Schweitzer, Arthur. *Big Business in the Third Reich*. London: Eyre & Spottiswoode, 1964.

Semmens, Kristen. *Seeing Hitler's Germany: Tourism in the Third Reich*. New York: Palgrave Macmillan, 2005.

Sereny, Gitta. *Albert Speer: His Battle with Truth*. London: Macmillan, 1995.

Seul, Stephanie. '"Plain, Unvarnished News"?' *Media History* 21, no. 4 (2015): 378–96. doi: 10.1080/13688804.2015.1011108.

Seul, Stephanie. 'Journalists in the Service of British Foreign Policy: The BBC German Service and Chamberlain's Appeasement Policy, 1938 - 1939'. In *Journalists as Political Actors: Transfers and Interactions between Britain and Germany Since the Late 19th Century*, edited by Frank Bösch and Dominik Geppert, 88–109. Augsburg: Wissner, 2008.

Seul, Stephanie. '"A Menace to Jews Seen If Hitler Wins": British American Press Comment on German Antisemitism, 1918 - 1933'. *Jewish Historical Studies* 44 (2012): 75–102. http://www.jstor.org/stable/41806166.

Seul, Stephanie. '"Herr Hitler's Nazis Hear an Echo of World Opinion": British and American Press Responses to Nazi Anti-Semitism, September 1930 - April 1933'. *Politics, Religion & Ideology* 14, no. 3 (September 2013): 412–30. doi: 10.1080/21567689.2013.820453.

Shapiro, Robert Moses, ed. *Why Didn't the Press Shout? American and International Journalism during the Holocaust*. Hoboken, NJ: Yeshiva University Press, 2003.

Sharf, Andrew. 'Nazi Racialism and British Opinion'. *Race & Class* 5, no. 2 (1963): 15–24. doi:10.1177/030639686300500202.

Sharf, Andrew. *The British Press and Jews under Nazi Rule*. London: Oxford University Press, 1964.

Sharf, Andrew. *Nazi Racialism and the British Press, 1933 - 1945*. Noah Barou Memorial Lecture, 1963. London: World Jewish Congress, British Section, 1968.

Sherman, A. J. *Island Refuge: Britain and Refugees from the Third Reich, 1933 - 1939*. London: Paul Elek, 1973.

Shirer, William L. *The Rise and Fall of the Third Reich: A History of Nazi Germany*. London: Secker and Warburg, 1962.

Shirer, William L. *Berlin Diary, 1934–1941*. London: Sphere Books Limited, 1972.

Shirer, William L. *The Nightmare Years, 1930–1940*. Boston: Little, Brown and Company, 1984.

Siemens, Daniel. *Stormtroopers: A New History of Hitler's Brownshirts*. New Haven and London: Yale University Press, 2017.

Simpson, John. *Unreliable Sources: How the 20th Century Was Reported*. London: Macmillan, 2010.

Simpson, John. *We Chose to Speak of War and Strife: The World of the Foreign Correspondent*. London: Bloomsbury, 2016.

Smith, Anthony. *The Newspaper: An International History*. London: Thames and Hudson Ltd., 1979.

Snowman, Daniel. *The Hitler Emigres: The Cultural Impact on Britain of Refugees from Nazism*. London: Chatto & Windus, 2002.

Snyder, Timothy. *Bloodlands: Europe between Hitler and Stalin*. London: Vintage Books, 2011.

Sofsky, Wolfgang. *The Order of Terror: The Concentration Camp*. Princeton: Princeton University Press, 1997.

Soucy, Robert J. 'French Press Reactions to Hitler's First Two Years in Power'. *Contemporary European History* 7, no. 1 (March 1998): 21–38. doi: 10.1017/S0960777300004744.

Sparks, Colin and John Tulloch. *Tabloid News: Global Debates Over Media Standards*. Lanham, MD: Rowman & Littlefield Publishers, 2000.

Speck, W. A. *A Concise History of Britain, 1707 – 1975*. Cambridge: Cambridge University Press, 1993.

Speer, Albert. *Inside the Third Reich: Memoirs*. Translated by Richard and Clara Winston. New York: Simon & Schuster Paperbacks, 1970.

Spicer, Kevin. *Resisting the Third Reich: The Catholic Clergy in Hitler's Berlin*. De Kalb: Northern Illinois University Press, 2004.

Spicer, Kevin. *Hitler's Priests: Catholic Clergy and National Socialism*. De Kalb: Northern Illinois University Press, 2008.

Stachura, Peter D., ed. *The Shaping of the Nazi State*. London: Croom Helm, 1978.

Stannage, Tom. *Baldwin Thwarts the Opposition: The British General Election of 1935*. London: Croom Helm, 1980.

Stargardt, Nicholas. *The German War: A Nation Under Arms, 1939–45*. London: The Bodley Head, 2015.

Steigmann-Gall, Richard. *The Holy Reich: Nazi Conceptions of Christianity, 1919 – 1945*. Cambridge: Cambridge University Press, 2003.

Steinberg, Michael Stephen. *Sabers and Brown Shirts: The German Students' Path to National Socialism, 1918–1935*. Chicago: University of Chicago Press, 1977.

Steinberg, S. H. *Five Hundred Years of Printing*. Middlesex: Penguin Books, 1977

Steiner, Zara. *The Triumph of the Dark: European International History, 1933–1939*. Oxford: Oxford University, 2011.

Stern, J. P. *Hitler: The Führer and the People*. Glasgow: Fontana, 1975.

Stevenson, John. *British Society, 1914–1945*. Harmondsworth: Penguin Books, 1984.

Stolleis, Michael. *The Law Under the Swastika: Studies on Legal History in Nazi Germany*. Translated by Michael Dunlap. Chicago: University of Chicago, 1998.

Stone, Dan. *Responses to Nazism in Britain, 1933 – 1939: Before War and Holocaust.* Hampshire: Palgrave Macmillan, 2003.

Stone, Dan, eds *The Historiography of the Holocaust.* Hampshire and New York: Palgrave Macmillan, 2004.

Storer, Colin. *A Short History of the Weimar Republic.* London: I.B. Tauris, 2013.

Strobl, Gerwin. *The Germanic Isle: Nazi Perceptions of Britain.* Cambridge: Cambridge University Press, 2000.

Swift, Will. *The Kennedy's: Amidst the Gathering Storm: A Thousand Days in London, 1938 – 1940.* London: JR Books, 2008.

Symons, Julian. *The Thirties: A Dream Revolved.* London: Faber, 1975.

Tal, Uriel. *Religion, Politics and Ideology in the Third Reich: Selected Essays.* London: Routledge, 2004.

Taylor, A. J. P. *The Trouble Makers: Dissent Over Foreign Policy, 1792 – 1939.* London: Hamilton, 1957.

Taylor, A. J. P. *English History, 1914–1945.* London: Oxford University Press, 1965.

Taylor, A. J. P. *Beaverbrook.* England: Penguin Books, 1972.

Taylor, A. J. P. *The Origins of the Second World War.* London: Penguin, 1991.

Taylor, S. J. *The Great Outsiders: Northcliffe, Rothermere and the Daily Mail.* London: Weidenfeld & Nicolson, 1996.

Thalmann, Rita and Emmanuel Feinermann. *Crystal Night: 9 – 10 November 1938.* Translated by Gilles Cremonesi. London: Thames and Hudson Ltd., 1974.

The Times. *History of The Times: The 150th Anniversary and Beyond, 1912 – 1948*, Vol. 2. London: The Times, 1952.

Thompson, Neville. *The Anti-Appeasers: Conservative Opposition to Appeasement in the 1930s.* Oxford: Clarendon Press, 1971.

Thurlow, Richard C. *Fascism in Britain: A History, 1918–1985.* Oxford and New York: Blackwell, 1987.

Tobias, Fritz. *The Reichstag Fire: Legend and Truth.* Translated by Arnold J. Pomerans. London: Secker & Warburg, 1962.

Tunstall, Jeremy. *The Media in Britain.* London: Constable, 1983.

Turner Jr., Henry Ashby. *Hitler's Thirty Days to Power: January 1933.* London: Bloomsbury, 1997.

Tworek, Heidi. 'The Creation of European News: News Agency Cooperation in Interwar Europe'. *Journalism Studies* 14, no. 5 (October 2013): 730–42. doi: 10.1080/1461670X.2013.810908

Tworek, Heidi J. S. *News From Germany: The Competition to Control World Communications, 1900–1945.* Cambridge: Harvard University Press, 2019.

Ullrich Volker. *Hitler: A Biography: Volume I, Ascent.* Translated by Jefferson Chase. London: The Bodley Head, 2016.

Unger, Aryeh L. *The Totalitarian State: Party and People in Nazi Germany and Soviet Russia.* London: Cambridge University Press, 1974.

Vella, Stephen. 'Newspapers'. In *Reading Primary Sources: The Interpretation of Texts From Nineteenth and Twentieth Century History*, edited by Miriam Dobson and Benjamin Ziemann. Hoboken: Taylor and Francis, 2008. E-edition. doi:10.4324/9780203892213.

Wachsmann, Nikolaus. '"Annihilation through Labor": The Killing of State Prisoners in the Third Reich'. *Journal of Modern History* 71 (1991): 624–59.

Wachsmann, Nikolaus. 'Between Reform and Repression: Imprisonment in Weimar Germany'. *The Historical Journal* 45 (2002): 411–32.

Wachsmann, Nikolaus. *Hitler's Prisons: Legal Terror in Nazi Germany*. London: Yale University Press, 2004.

Wachsmann, Nikolaus. *KL: A History of the Nazi Concentration Camps*. London: Little, Brown, 2015.

Wainwright, Will. *Reporting on Hitler: Rothay Reynolds and the British Press in Nazi Germany*. London: Biteback Publishing, 2017.

Wallis, Russell. *Britain, Germany and the Road to the Holocaust: British Attitudes to Nazi Atrocities*. London: IB Taurus & Co. Ltd., 2014.

Waln, Nora. *The Approaching Storm: One Woman's Story of Germany, 1934 - 1938*. Cresset Women's Voices. London: Century Hutchinson, 1988.

Ward Price, G. *Extra-Special Correspondent*. London: George G. Harrap & Co., 1957.

Wark, Wesley K. *The Ultimate Enemy: British Intelligence and Nazi Germany, 1933 - 1939*. Ithaca and London: Cornell University Press, 2010.

Watkins, Alan. *A Short Walk Down Fleet Street: From Beaverbrook to Boycott*. London: Duckbacks, 2001.

Weale, Adrian. *Army of Evil: A History of the SS*. New York: NAL Caliber, 2013.

Weber, Thomas. *Becoming Hitler: The Making of a Nazi*. Oxford: Oxford University Press, 2017.

Welch, David. *Nazi Propaganda: The Power and Limitations*. London: Barnes and Noble, 1983.

Welch, David. *The Third Reich: Politics and Propaganda*. 2nd edn London: Routledge, 2002.

Wait, Eric D. *Weimar Germany: Promise and Tragedy*. Princeton: Princeton University Press, 2009.

Williams, A. T. *A Passing Fury: Searching for Justice at the End of World War II*. London: Jonathan Cape, 2016.

Williams, Francis. *Press, Parliament and People*. London: W. Heinemann, 1946.

Williams, Francis. *Dangerous Estate: The Anatomy of Newspapers*. London: Longmans, 1957.

Williams, Kevin. *Read All About It! A History of the British Newspaper*. Oxon: Routledge, 2010.

Wilson, Jim. *Nazi Princess: Hitler, Lord Rothermere and Princess Stephanie von Hohlenlohe*. Gloucestershire: The History Press, 2011.

Wiskemann, Elizabeth. *Europe of the Dictators, 1919–1945*. London: Fontana Press, 1966.
Wistrich, Robert S. *Anti-Semitism: The Longest Hatred*. London: Thames Mandarin, 1992.
Wistrich, Robert S. *Who's Who in Nazi Germany*. London and New York, 2002.
Wolfers, Arnold. *Britain and France between Two War: Conflicting Strategies of Peace from Versailles to World War II*. New York: W.W. Norton & Company, 1966.
Woolf, S. J. *The Nature of Fascism*. New York: Random House, 1968.
Woolf, S. J. *Fascism in Europe*. London: Methuen, 1981.
Wrench, John Evelyn. *Geoffrey Dawson and Our Times*. London: Hutchison & Co., 1955.
Wünschmann, Kim. *Before Auschwitz: Jewish Prisoners in the Prewar Concentration Camps*. Massachusetts: Harvard University Press, 2015.
Young, Kenneth. *Churchill and Beaverbrook: A Study in Friendship and Politics*. London: Hutchinson, 1955.
Zahn, Gordon C. *German Catholics and Hitler's Wars: A Study in Social Control*. London and New York: Sheed and Ward, 1963.
Ziegler, Philip. *Between the Wars: 1919–1939*. New York and London: MacLehose Press, 2017.

Other sources

Theses

Kehoe, Barbara Benge. 'The British Press and Nazi Germany'. PhD diss., University of Illinois, 1980.
Lai, Chun-yue, Eric. 'Reading Hitler: British Newspapers' Representation of Nazism, 1930 – 39'. PhD diss., University of Hong Kong, 2004.
Mazzarella, Mario D. 'The British Press and the Rise of Nazi Germany, 1933 – 1940'. PhD diss., The American University, 1977.

Index

Angriff 143, 158, 168
Anschluss 2, 20, 146, 160-2, 164, 189
anti-Semitism 6, 87, 125, 127, 133, 149, 152, 154, 158
appeasement 3, 5, 7, 19, 176, 181, 187, 188
Aryanization 132-3, 155, 158, 159, 162, 173
Asquith, Emma Margaret (Margot) 80
Austria 2, 122, 146, 161, 186, 187, 189
   Jews fleeing to 149
   persecution of Jews 160-5, 170, 173, 174

Baldwin, Stanley 172
Barmen Declaration 128
Barrington-Ward, Robin 16, 79
Bartlett, Vernon 100-1
Bavaria 158, 177
   Protestant church 134-8
   seizure of 50-5, 72
Bavarian People's Party (*Bayerische Volkspartei*, BVP) 59, 122, 123
   dissolution of 73
   Nazi attacks on 69
Beaverbrook, Lord (William Maxwell Aitken) 1, 15, 21, 191
Bentwich, Norman 161
Bernays, Robert
   concentration camps 80
Bodelschwingh, Friedrich von 129, 130
Bone, James 26
boycott (April 1933) 150-1, 158, 184
British government 3, 5, 16, 21, 89, 154, 162, 163, 172, 173, 175, 176, 181, 183, 187, 188
British press
   Anschluss 160
   appeasement 3
   appointment of Hitler 30-1, 177
   boycott (April 1933) 153
   church struggle 122, 126, 127, 128, 131, 132, 135-6, 138, 144, 146, 147, 150, 179-80

concentration camps 78-9
Concordat 123
coverage of German news 119, 176, 184-5, 187, 188, 190
criticism of Nazi dictatorship 118
destruction of democracy 33, 48, 49, 73-4, 177, 178
dissolution of political parties 73
election campaign (1933) 33, 35, 44
Enabling Act 56, 59
Evian conference 165
Führer 115
German press 34
Hindenburg, death of 98
Hitler 29
Kristallnacht 169, 181
makeup of 11
March 1933 election 44, 45, 46, 48, 52, 178
Nazi attack on opposition 64, 177
Nazi regime 176, 181, 184-5, 190
Nazi revolution 55, 115
Nazi seizure of states 50, 51, 53, 55, 177
Nazi seizure of trade unions 61, 62
Night of the Long Knives 97-8, 101
opposition to regime 180
Papen's 1934 speech 100
persecution of Jews 157, 159, 162, 165, 172, 173, 180, 188-9
photograph evidence 39, 45, 90, 102, 152, 182
political parties 66, 68
prohibition in Germany 110, 111
refugees 162, 165
Reichstag Fire 38-9
Reichstag Fire decree 40
Röhm purge 97, 98, 109-10, 113, 117-18, 179
terror in Germany 81-2, 94-5
trial of Martin Niemöller 144
British Union of Fascists 156, 183
Brown, Harrison 43, 78
   terror in Germany 75-6, 77

Brown Houses 90, 91, 93
Brüning, Heinrich 70, 122
Buchenwald concentration camp 167, 169

Catholic Church 123, 126, 127, 137, 146
  associations 125
  Nazi persecution of 92
  Nazi violence against 123
  Press 126
  struggle against Nazis 122, 141, 142, 180
  youth 123
Centre Party (*Deutsche Zentrumspartei*) 68, 122, 123, 146
  dissolution of 68–71, 73
  Enabling Act 56, 59
  in the Reichstag 58
Chamberlain, Neville 16, 172, 188
Christiansen, Arthur 21, 191
Churches 118, 119, *see also* Catholic Church; Protestant Churches
  arrests 141
  creation of German church 98
  elections 131
  southern churches 134–5
  struggle of 118, 121, 126, 134, 140, 141, 142, 144, 147
Churchill, Winston 116, 168, 192
Civil Service decree, *see* Law for the Restoration of the Professional Civil Service (Civil Service decree)
Clarke, Dennis 161
Communist Party of Germany (*Kommunistische Partei Deutschlands*) (KPD) 34, 44, 48, 49, 53, 54, 55, 61, 63, 65, 69–72, 76–7
  arrest of 45, 75, 76, 80, 81, 86
  election 46–7
  Nazi oppression of 56, 65, 86, 87, 118, 178, 179
  Nazi terror 89, 145
  opening of Reichstag 58
  raid of offices 50
  Reichstag Fire 38–9, 41, 42, 43
concentration camps 56, 58, 75
  coverage in British press 78–80, 90, 91, 92, 145, 167, 169, 178
  existence of 78, 81
  release of Catholic priests 125
  use by Nazis 75, 117, 145
  White Paper 175
Concordat between the Holy See and the German Reich (*Reichskonkordat*) 69, 70, 73, 123–7, 137, 146
Confessing Church 128, 133, 136, 138, 139, 141, 146, 147
correspondents 2, 6, 9, 13, 14, 16, 19, 22, 26, 33, 187, 188
  dangers 23–5, 95, 135, 144, 185, 186
  expulsion 186
  reporting on German news 5, 17, 21, 35, 39, 41, 47, 48, 49, 50, 52, 56, 72, 74, 75, 78, 82, 83, 87, 97, 99, 101, 108, 110, 112, 114–17, 123, 145, 149, 151, 160, 173, 175, 177, 181, 185, 186, 189, 190
Crozier, William Percival 9, 78, 193
  Berlin correspondent 94
  concern for correspondents 26, 27, 83, 88, 93
  editorial control 16
  editorial stance 94, 187
  letters to editor 86–7
  removal of Berlin correspondent 20–1, 58, 83
  truth about Germany 82, 83, 87, 93, 182
Czechoslovakia 22, 189
  Jews fleeing to 149, 162

Dachau concentration camp 58, 169, 175
  opening of 75
  press coverage 78, 80, 91, 125, 178
Daily Express 1, 4, 8, 11, 15, 34, 66, 71, 73, 191
  appointment of Hitler 30, 177
  boycott (April 1933) 151
  Catholic Church 126
  circulation 15
  concentration camps 141
  Concordat 123
  coverage of German news 29, 31, 37, 182–3, 184
  danger to correspondent 186
  death of Hindenburg 116
  editorial policy towards Germany 21, 22
  election (March 1933) 45, 46

Enabling Act 56, 59
expulsion of correspondent 23, 24, 25, 157
Hitler 112
Kristallnacht 169, 170, 174
lack of reporting on terror 178
Nazi arrest of Communists 80-1
Nazi arrest of Socialists 81
Nazi seizure of Bavaria 52, 55
Nazi seizure of states 55
Nuremberg laws 159
Persecution of Jews 81, 149, 151, 156-7, 161, 165, 166, 169, 170, 173, 174
prohibition of 111
refugees 165, 172
Reichstag Fire 38-9
Röhm purge 101, 106, 111, 112
St Louis 172
Daily Mail 4, 7, 8, 15, 66, 68, 111, 191
boycott (April 1933) 151-2
Centre Party 70
Church struggle 126, 137, 141
Concordat 70, 123, 127
coverage of German news 15, 182, 183-4, 187
death of Hindenburg 116
election (March 1933) 44-8
Enabling Act 57, 59, 177
Hugenberg's position 68
interview with Hitler 98-9
Kristallnacht 170
lack of reporting on terror 81, 179
March 1933 election 44, 47
Nazi raid of communist headquarters 39
Nazi seizure of states 50, 55, 177
Nazi seizure of trade unions 62, 73
Nazi takeover of Hamburg 49
Nuremberg laws 159
persecution of Jews 151, 152, 156, 159, 163, 170, 173, 174, 180
pro-German 7
refugees 163
Reichstag Fire 39
Reichstag Fire Decree 40, 41, 177
Röhm purge 101, 105, 179
Daily Mirror 4, 15, 39, 191-2
appointment of Hitler 31, 32

boycott (April 1933) 151
coverage of German news 55, 182, 183
election (March 1933) 45, 55
Evian conference 164, 165
Kristallnacht 168
lack of reporting on terror 81, 178
layout of newspaper 12
Nazi seizure of states 55
Nazi seizure of trade unions 61, 62
Nazi suppression of Socialist party 65
persecution of Jews 151, 153, 163-5, 168
refugees 163-4, 165
Röhm purge 101
Daily Telegraph 4, 19, 111, 192
appointment of Hitler 29, 31, 32, 177
arrest of Martin Niemöller 142
boycott (April 1933) 151, 153
church struggle 139, 142, 147, 180
coverage of German news 34, 82, 176, 177, 182, 184, 186
danger to correspondent 24, 186
editorial policy towards Germany 19, 20
election (March 1933) 44, 46, 47, 48
expulsion of correspondent 186
lack of reporting on terror 81, 178
March 1933 election 36
Nazi conflict with Nationalist Party 67, 69
Nazi control of Germany 36, 116
Nazi oppression of opponents 54, 117
Nazi seizure of Bavaria 51, 52, 55
Nazi seizure of states 49, 177
Nazi seizure of trade unions 62, 73, 178
Nazi suppression of German press 35
persecution of Jews 152, 153, 157, 165, 173
plebiscite (1934) 117
prohibition of newspapers 34-5, 110, 111
Reichstag Fire 38
Reichstag Fire Decree 41
Röhm purge 108, 110, 113, 179
Daily Telegraph and Morning Post 4, 192
expulsion of Pembroke Stephens 157
imprisonment of Martin Niemöller 146
Kristallnacht 168, 169

persecution of Jews   161, 165, 168, 169, 172, 173, 181
  refugees   165, 172
Daladier, Édouard   87
Daniels, H. G   187
Dawson, Geoffrey   9, 18–19, 22, 195
  editorial freedom   16
  editorial stance   7, 79–80, 178, 187
  terror in Germany   79, 178
Deakin, Ralph   18, 79
Decree for the Protection of the German People (1933)   33
  British press commentary   34
  effect of   34
Decree of the Reich President for the Protection of People and State (1933) (Reichstag Fire Decree)   40, 76
Dell, Robert   2, 83, 88, 92, 95, 185
Delmer, Sefton   191
  Hitler's election tour   37–8
  interview with Hitler   21, 29
  Nazi suppression of German press   34
  Reichstag Fire   38
  reporting style   22, 27, 37
democracy   19, 33, 35, 36, 41–4, 56, 115, 177, 190
  destruction of   2, 3, 10, 17, 32, 48, 49, 50, 55, 57, 59, 71–2, 73, 74, 117, 122, 129, 147, 155, 176, 177, 179, 181–4, 189
Der Stürmer   158
dictatorship   41, 87, 92, 101, 110, 114, 115, 117, 124, 147, 173, 174, 175, 177, 183, 185, 186, 187, 188, 190

Ebbutt, Norman   10, 17, 196
  Church struggle   147
  concentration camps   78, 79
  danger and risk   22, 25, 185
  editorial interference   18–19, 78, 87, 187
  expulsion   19, 22, 143–4, 186
  ill-health   22, 144
  information resources   37
  March 1933 election   36
  reporting style   36, 37, 128, 147, 181
  terror in Germany   78–80, 87
  trial of Martin Niemöller   146
  editor   2, 7, 9, 12, 14, 15, 16, 18–21, 26, 27, 58, 74, 79, 80, 82, 89, 178, 182, 185, 186, 187, 190, 191–5
  letters to   76–8, 85–6
election (March 5 1933)   52, 74, 83, 149, 177
Enabling Act (Bill) (Law to Remedy the Distress of the People and the Reich)   56, 57, 58, 73, 74, 177
Epp, Franz Ritter von   51
Evian conference (1938)   164, 165, 166

fascism   43, 114
foreign correspondents   19
  danger   22–3
  editorial interference   17–21
  importance of   27
  supply of news   17
Foreign Office (British)   27, 162, 175
Frick, Wilhelm   31, 56, 65, 87, 131, 140
Führer   98, 103, 104, 115, 118, 121, 135, 146, 179
Funk, Walther
  March 1933 speech   36
Gannon, Franklin Reid   5, 19, 95, 187
Gedye, George Eric Rowe   192
  danger to   186
  editorial interference   19, 186
  Fallen Bastions   9, 20, 161
Gerlack, Fritz   122
German Christians (Deutsche Christen)   127, 129, 138
  Aryan paragraph   132
  attempts to restructure churches   128, 137
  church elections   131
  Reich Bishop   129–30
  repression of opponents   134
  rhetoric of   125
German Government   18, 25, 27, 29, 30, 41, 65, 70, 79, 82, 84, 89, 90, 97, 110, 127, 137, 150, 151, 152, 154, 160, 167, 168
German National People's Party (Deutschnationale Volkspartei, DNVP)   53, 178
  forced dissolution   67, 68, 69, 73
  struggle against Nazi interference   66
Germany
  federated states   49, 177

as a news centre   1, 2, 16, 17
Gestapo   81, 92, 93, 142, 145, 146
  violence of   98, 179
ghetto   170, 171
Gillie, Darsie   14, 82
Gleichschaltung   3, 127, 176
Goebbels, Paul Joseph   21, 23, 38, 39, 59, 68, 69, 77, 79, 100, 103, 110, 111, 140, 143, 158, 168, 169, 170
  May Day   60
  press interference   23
Göring, Hermann   21, 31, 37, 38, 39, 76, 77, 84, 151
  boycott (April 1933)   151
  church struggle   134–5
  May Day   60–1
  Nazi seizure of states   49
  press interference   23
  Röhm purge   102, 104, 106, 110
Greenwood, H. Powys   99, 114, 118
Grynszpan, Herschel   167, 168

Haansstaengel, Ernst   151
Hamburg   49, 172
Hanover   135, 137
Heines, Edmund   102, 103, 104, 106
Held, Heinrich   51
Hess, Rudolf   100
Hindenburg, Paul von   31, 45, 63, 73, 76, 101, 111, 177
  appointment of Hitler   29, 30, 32
  church struggle   130–1, 134
  death of   10, 98, 115, 116, 118, 179
  Hugenberg's resignation   68, 69
  March 1933 election   45
  Reichstag Fire Decree   40
Hitler, Adolf   2, 3, 6, 7, 8, 10, 19, 23, 34, 37–8, 40, 49, 51, 54, 64, 66, 67, 68, 72, 78, 79, 124, 183, 186, 188
  appointment as Chancellor   29, 30–1, 33, 43, 48, 82, 99, 122, 146, 177
  Catholicism   124
  church struggle   125, 129, 130–1, 134, 135, 138–41, 145, 146, 147, 180
  Concordat   123, 126
  control over Germany   32, 35, 36, 44, 47, 51, 57, 59, 61, 63, 70, 71, 73, 74, 99, 100, 118, 176, 177, 179
  election (March 1933)   21, 22, 45, 46
  Enabling Act   59–60
  foreign policy   3, 80, 188
  Führer   116–17, 121
  and Hugenberg   66, 68
  interview by George Ward Price   98
  May Day   60
  Night of the Long Knives   101–6, 108, 110, 111–14, 117
  persecution of Jews   149, 150, 151, 154, 155, 156, 160, 162, 165, 166, 168, 173, 176, 186
  plebiscite (1934)   121
  Reichstag Fire   38–9
  Röhm purge   103, 105, 106, 108, 110–14, 179
  Storm Troops   92, 97, 98, 100
  suppression of Socialist party   65
  trade unions   61–2
  and violence   77, 79, 84, 86, 92, 93, 110, 115, 183
Hitler Youth (*Hitler Jugend Bund der deutschen Arbeiterjugend*)   126
Hoare, Simon James   163, 172
Home Office (British)   162
Hossenfelder, Joachim   132
House of Commons   172
Hugenberg, Alfred   31, 37, 66
  forced resignation   67, 68, 69, 73

Jäger, August   129, 130, 135–8
  dismissal of   139
Jewish Chronicle   4, 192–3
  appointment of Hitler   32
  boycott (April 1933)   151
  coverage of German news   182
  Kristallnacht   169
  Nuremberg laws   159
  persecution of Jews   149–51, 153, 154, 155, 159, 169, 170
  photograph evidence   182
  terror in Germany   80, 178
Jews
  Anschluss   160–2
  boycott (April 1933)   150, 180
  concentration camps   166, 169–70
  dismissal of   150
  execution of   169–70
  expulsion of Polish Jews   167
  extermination of   171
  Kindertransport   172
  Kristallnacht   168–70, 173, 180

Nazi terror and violence   87, 89, 90
Nuremberg laws   180
persecution of   98, 119, 146, 147, 155,
  166, 173, 180, 182, 183, 188-9
refugees   149, 150, 161, 162, 165, 166,
  171, 173, 184
restrictions of   170
safety of   87
violence against   158, 189

Kerrl, Hans   140, 141
Kindertransport   172
Krause, Reinhold   132
Kristallnacht   168-70, 173, 174, 180,
  181, 184

Lambert, Charles A.   21, 88, 94
Laski, Neville   151, 193
Law for the Restoration of the Professional
  Civil Service (Civil Service
  decree)   132, 153, 155, 184
League of Nations   161
Leipart, Theodor   60, 61
Ley, Robert   62
Lloyd George, David   116

MacDonald, James Ramsey   154
Marahrens, Bishop August Friedrich
  Karl   134
Manchester Guardian   2, 4, 9, 11, 12,
  13, 193
  Anschluss   160
  appointment of Hitler   31, 32, 37
  arrest of Martin Niemöller   141-2,
    145, 146
  arrest of Nazi opponents   48, 61
  Aryan paragraph   132
  Catholic Church   123, 124, 125, 127
  Centre Party   69, 70
  church struggle   122, 125, 128,
    133, 135, 136, 138-42, 144, 146,
    147, 180
  concentration camps   91, 145, 175
  Concordat   70, 123-4
  conflict between Stahlhelm and SA   67
  correspondent in Berlin   14, 17, 20,
    21, 45, 58, 82, 83, 88
  coverage of German news   10, 20-1,
    176, 179, 181, 182, 184, 187
  criticism of   85-6

  danger to correspondents   25-6, 88,
    95, 185
  death of Hindenburg   116
  destruction of democracy   33, 36, 48,
    71, 178
  dictatorship   41, 110, 182
  difficulty obtaining information   37
  discontent in Germany   100
  election (March 1933)   36, 44, 46, 47
  Enabling Act   57-8, 59, 177
  execution of Jews   169-70
  expulsion of Ebbutt   144
  Führer   117
  German readership   16, 85
  Kristallnacht   168, 169
  Letters to editor   85-6
  May Day   60
  Nazi attack on Communists   48, 56,
    61, 85
  Nazi attack on Socialists   56, 61
  Nazi attack on trade unions   61, 178
  Nazi revolution   42, 54, 55, 85, 94
  Nazi seizure of states   49, 52-3, 177
  Nazi suppression of Socialist party
    65, 66
  Nazi takeover of police   53
  Nuremberg laws   159-60
  opening of Reichstag   58
  Pastors Emergency League   133
  persecution of Jews   90, 149, 152-6,
    159, 160, 161, 162, 165, 166, 167,
    169, 171, 173, 181
  photograph evidence   90
  political parties in Germany   68-9, 70
  prohibition of newspapers   34
  refugees   161, 162, 165, 166, 167-8
  Reichstag Fire Decree   40-1, 177
  removal of Werth   14, 21, 88
  reporting considerations   88
  reporting style   155, 181
  and Reuters   13, 21
  Röhm purge   97-8, 106-8, 110,
    111, 112
  safety of correspondents   88, 185
  suppression of   23, 87-8
  terror in Germany   20, 75, 82, 83, 85,
    88-95, 98, 175, 179, 187
  trial of Martin Niemöller   144
Marxism (Marxist)   46, 60, 62, 63, 64,
  66, 178

Meiser, Bishop Hans   134, 136–9
monarchy   76, 106, 109, 115
Morning Post   4, 11, 192, 193
   appointment of Hitler   32
   arrest of Martin Niemöller   142
   boycott (April 1933)   151, 152
   Catholic Church   125, 127
   Church struggle   128, 131, 133, 139, 140, 142, 147, 180, 182
   Civil Service decree   154
   Communist involvement in Reichstag Fire   42
   concentration camp   178
   Concordat   123
   coverage of German news   93, 110, 182, 184
   destruction of democracy   42
   dictatorship   41
   election (March 1933)   34, 45, 46, 48
   Enabling Act   57, 59, 73, 177
   Hugenberg's resignation   68, 69
   Nazi seizure of Bavaria   52
   Nazi seizure of trade unions   62, 184
   Nazi suppression of Socialist party   64, 66, 180
   persecution of Jews   151, 154, 158, 173, 181, 182
   prohibition of newspapers   34
   raid of communist headquarters   39
   Reichstag Fire   39
   Reichstag Fire decree   41
   Röhm purge   110, 111, 113, 118
   terror in Germany   80, 82, 93, 178
Morris, John   154
Mosley, Oswald   156, 183
Muggeridge, Malcom   2
Müller, Ludwig   129–32, 134, 136–9
   decree   133
   Reich Bishop   130, 131
   sidelining of   140

Nationalist Party, *see* German National People's Party (*Deutschnationale Volkspartei*, DNVP)
National Socialist German Workers' Party (*Nationalsozialistische Deutsche Arbeiterpartei*, Nazi Party, NSDAP)   17, 18, 19, 22, 26, 29, 30, 31, 33, 37, 64, 67, 69, 80, 87, 122, 123, 130, 141, 146, 151, 189
   and anti-Semitism   149
   book burning   155
   election campaign   44, 46, 75, 177
   rally   118
   Röhm purge   97, 100, 114
   quest for total power   36, 48, 63, 177
   as sole party   68, 69, 70, 73, 74, 123, 178
   suppression of political parties   64, 98
   tension with SA   99
Nazification   3
   churches   121, 131
   police   50
   trade unions   62
   universities   155
Nazism   5, 6, 9, 15, 19, 22, 24, 81, 107, 121, 122, 127, 128, 131, 145, 162, 175, 179, 181, 183
Neurath, Constantin von   137
News Chronicle   4, 194
   appointment of Hitler   30, 31, 32
   arrest of Martin Niemöller   142, 145
   boycott (April 1933)   150, 153
   church struggle   131, 133–4, 137, 138, 139, 141, 144, 146, 147, 180
   Communist involvement in Reichstag Fire   42
   concentration camps   80, 178
   coverage of German news   182, 183
   discontent in Germany   100
   election (March 1933)   45, 46, 47
   Enabling Act   59
   Hindenburg's death   116
   Hitler's position   112, 116, 131
   Hugenberg's resignation   68
   Nazi seizure of states   50, 52
   Nazi seizure of trade unions   59–60
   Nazi suppression of opposition   180
   opening of Reichstag   58
   photograph evidence   39, 153, 183
   political Catholicism   69
   Reichstag Fire   39
   Reichstag Fire Decree   41, 177
   Röhm purge   101–2, 107, 108, 110, 111, 112, 179
   Storm Troops   50, 100
   terror in Germany   42, 80
   trade unions   59–60
newspapers
   advertisers   14–15
   collection of news   12

digitization of 8
editors 15
foreign news 13
freedom of 33
as historical sources 7–8
layout 11–12
methodological approach 8
political ideology 181
popular newspapers 181
proprietors 15
quality newspapers 181
New Statesman and Nation 4, 32, 194
appointment of Hitler 32
arrest of political opponents 69, 145–56, 178
atmosphere in Germany 99
church struggle 122, 136–7, 144, 145, 147, 180
concentration camps 79, 175, 178
coverage of German news 182
dissolution of Nationalist party 68, 69
election (March 1933) 43, 46, 69
Hugenberg's resignation
persecution of Jews 158, 161, 174
plebiscite (1934) 118, 179
Nazi control over Germany 43, 71
Nazi seizure of trade unions 61, 63
Nazi violence 80
persecution of Jews 158, 161, 165, 170, 174, 181
refugees 165, 166, 170, 171
Reichstag Fire 42, 43
Röhm purge 110, 111
Sonnenburg concentration camp 80
Storm Troops 99
terror in Germany 79, 80
trial of Martin Niemöller 144–5
White Paper (1939) 175
Niemöller, Martin 122, 128, 133–6, 141
arrest of 141
imprisonment of 145, 146
trial of 144–5
Night of the Long Knives (Röhm purge) 97, 101, 102, 122, 156, 178, 183
criticism by British press 108–10
death toll 108, 113
Hitler's address to Reichstag 111–12
initial reports 101
justification for 103, 112, 113, 114

reaction to 104–5, 109–10, 179
Schleicher's role 107
Nuremberg laws 159–60, 173

Observer 4, 37, 44, 53, 57, 71, 195
Catholic church 126, 139
church struggle 139, 140, 144, 180
dissolution of political parties 70
Hindenburg's death 157
Hitler's position 99, 177
March 1933 election 44
opposition to Nazis 63, 66, 180
prohibition of 111
Röhm purge 106
terror in Germany 80, 178
Olympic Games (1936) 160
Operation Hummingbird 97, 101
Oranienburg concentration camp 78, 90

Panter, Noel 24, 186, 192
Papen, Franz von 30, 31, 33, 36–9, 69, 99, 123, 125
1934 speech 99–100, 101
Röhm purge 104, 107–8
Pastor's Emergency League (*Pfarrenotbund*), *see also* Confessing Church
Protest against Aryan paragraph 133
Peake, Osbert 172
Phipps, Sir Eric 24
Poland 10
political parties (German), *see also* *individual party entries*
Jewish refugees 150, 167
Nazi destruction of 66, 76, 123, 178
suppression of 86
Pope, Pius XI 126, 127
popular newspaper press 2, 4, 11, 12, 13, 15, 21, 34, 45, 52, 55, 56, 57, 73, 81, 98, 101, 106, 112, 118, 133, 156, 174, 179, 181, 182, 183, 190
Price, George Ward 183
admiration of regime 184
interview with Hitler 98
Röhm purge 105
Protestant churches 132, 134, 138
arrest of members 92
coordination of 121, 128, 129, 137, 139
National synod 135

struggle of 122, 127, 134, 140–3, 147, 157, 180

quality newspaper press 4, 11, 12, 16, 34, 45, 52, 67, 98, 122, 164, 181, 182, 190

Rath, Ernst vom 167, 170
rearmament 15, 21, 119, 122, 176
Reed, Douglas 87, 196
refugees
  Aliens Restriction Act (1919) 162
  attitudes to 163–4
  in Britain 162
  Jewish 149, 150, 161, 162, 165, 166, 171, 173, 184
  Kindertransport 172
Reich Bishop 129, 130, 131
Reich (National) Church 128, 129, 131, 135, 137, 138, 139
  Aryan paragraph 132–3
  constitution 132
Reichstag 47, 48, 55–7
  Enabling Act 59
  opening of 58, 177
Reichstag Fire 38, 75, 83, 177, 178
Reichstag Fire Decree, *see* Decree of the Reich President for the Protection of People and State (1933) (Reichstag Fire Decree)
Reichstag Fire trial 88, 185
Reichswehr (German Army) 53, 57, 98–102, 107
  oath of loyalty 98
  Röhm purge 102
Reuters 10, 13, 14, 21
revolution (Nazi) 39, 42, 47, 50, 52–5, 63, 64, 66, 69–73, 76, 77, 84, 85, 92, 94, 97, 98, 118, 153
  second revolution 99, 100, 102, 103, 105, 111, 112, 113
Reynolds, Rothay 7, 151, 152, 184, 191
Röhm, Ernst 10, 22, 97, 104, 115, 117, 118, 156, 157, 179, 183
  death 102, 106
  homosexuality 102, 103
  role of SA 98, 99
  second revolution 102–5, 107, 112, 179
Roosevelt, Franklin D. 2, 164
Rosenberg, Alfred 80

Rothermere, Viscount (Harold Sydney Harmsworth) 1, 15, 183, 191
  denial of terror 81
  Jews in Germany 180
  rearmament 184
  Youth Triumphant article 81, 156, 183
Rowse, A. L. 86–7

Sachsenhausen concentration camp 145, 169
St Louis 172
Schirach, Baldur von 126
Schleicher, Kurt von
  death 106
  dismissal from office 30
  plot involving 102, 103, 104, 107, 108, 112
Schuschnigg, Kurt Alois Josef Johann 162
Schutzstaffel (SS) 78, 81, 89, 92, 93, 161, 171, 179
Scott, John R. 16
Segrue, John 194
  Enabling Act 59
  Nazi attack on trade unions 60
  opposition to Nazis 46
  Reichstag Fire Decree 41
  Röhm purge 102, 107–8
Seldte, Franz 66, 67
Shirer, William L. 6, 17, 186
Simon, Sir John 24, 154
Simpson, Stanley
  article on concentration camp 78, 79, 80
Social Democratic Party of Germany (*Sozialdemokratische Partei Deutschlands*, SPD)
  arrest of 75, 80, 178
  ban on party 65
  raid of offices 50
  in Reichstag 58
  Nazi interference with 56
  Nazi seizure of assets 64
  persecution of 66
  suppression of 64, 65
  and trade unions 60
Socialism 19, 56, 60, 61, 64, 65, 107
Spectator, The 4, 13, 195
  appointment of Hitler 30, 32, 99, 177

church struggle 121–2, 126, 127, 147
concentration camps 175
coverage of German news 48, 182, 184, 187
criticism of Nazi regime 114
destruction of democracy 35
election (March 1933) 45, 47–8
fascism in Germany 43
Kristallnacht 168, 170
letters to editor 76–7, 178, 184
Nazi revolution 99
Nazi suppression of Stahlhelm 66
Nuremberg laws 159
opposition to Nazis 63, 118
persecution of Jews 165, 170, 173, 174, 181
plebiscite (1934) 118
refugees 166
Röhm purge 108, 110, 113–14, 179
terror in Germany 75–6, 77, 85, 178, 184
White Paper (1939) 175
State Governors (*Statthalter*)
states (federated, Germany)
Nazi takeover of 49–52
southern 50
Steed, Wickham 185
Steel Helmets (*Stahlhelm*)
seizure of states 50
suppression of 66
under Nazi control 67
Stephens, Pembroke 21, 81, 191
arrest 157
danger to 186
death 157
expulsion 24–5, 157, 183, 186
Sterilization 126
Storm Troops (SA) (*Sturmabteilung*) 53, 66, 67, 68, 70, 74, 81, 139
plot 107
position in Germany 100
purge of 97, 98, 101–2, 104, 106, 109, 117
seizure of states 50, 51
suppression of opposition 50
tension with Nazi government 97, 98, 99
terror in Germany 75, 81, 83, 84, 89–93, 97, 118, 178

violence of 23, 24, 49, 66, 75, 76, 84, 92, 134, 150, 158, 179, 183
Streicher, Julius 158
terror
campaign 75, 76, 78, 81, 82–4, 87, 89–92, 94, 117, 149, 161, 178, 183
Thälmann, Ernst 145
The Times 4, 5, 7, 9, 11, 12, 13, 17, 18, 19, 195–6
Anschluss 160
appeasement 7
appointment of Hitler 29, 32, 177
arrest of Martin Niemöller 141–3
arrest of Nazi opponents 61, 143
Aryan paragraph 132
ban on Socialist party 65–6
Berlin correspondent 18, 22, 36, 37, 39, 78–80, 87, 143–4, 185, 186
book burning 155
Catholic church 126
Centre Party 69, 70
Church struggle 122, 127–31, 133–41, 143, 146, 147, 180
Concordat 123
conflict between Stahlhelm and SA 67
coverage of German news 36, 55, 82, 93, 160, 176, 178, 181, 184, 187
danger to correspondent 25
destruction of democracy 55, 184
dictatorship 55
dissolution of political parties 70
editor 16, 187
election (March 1933) 36, 44–8
Enabling Act 56, 59, 177
expulsion of Ebbutt 143–4
freedom of voting 45
Hugenberg's resignation 68, 69
Kristallnacht 169
letters to the editor 77
May Day 60
Nazi attack on opposition 49, 67, 69–70
Nazi conflict with Nationalist Party 67, 69
Nazi control over Germany 48, 53, 70, 71, 97, 100, 177
Nazi election tactics 35
Nazi Germany 97
Nazi revolution 54

Nazi seizure of states   52, 177
Nazi seizure of trade unions   60–3, 73
Nazi suppression of German press   34
Nazi suppression of Socialist party
   64, 65, 66, 178
Nazi takeover of Hamburg   49
Nuremberg laws   159
opening of Reichstag   58
Papen's 1934 speech   101
persecution of Jews   152, 154, 155,
   159, 160, 162, 163, 165, 166, 167,
   169, 173, 181
prohibition of newspapers   34
refugees   162, 165, 166, 167, 172
Reichstag Fire   39
Reichstag Fire Decree   40, 41, 177
reporting style   55, 103–4, 181
Röhm purge   102, 103–5, 109, 110,
   111, 115, 179
second revolution   100, 102, 105
terror in Germany   78–9, 80, 82, 178
trust   15–16
totalitarian   70, 71, 124, 125
trade unions
   Nazi attack on   59, 60, 63, 73, 178

van der Lubbe, Marinus   39, 42
Vatican   68, 70, 124, 137, 146
Voigt, Frederick Augustus   9, 14, 17, 20,
   21, 88, 100, 187, 193
   church conflict   128, 141, 145
   Concordat   124
   danger to   25–7, 95, 185
   destruction of democracy   71–2, 178
   exposing brutality of regime   20,
      82–3, 93–5, 182
   persecution of Jews   149–50, 152, 153,
      155, 166
   reporting on Germany   82, 88, 128, 155

Storm Troops   100
terror in Germany   23, 83, 84, 85, 87,
   89–95, 179, 187
terror in second stage   91–3
Völkischer Beobachter   158
   March 1933 election   35
   undermines Socialist party   56
Vorwärts
   suppression of   34

Wagner, Adolf   69
Walker, David
   Talking Shop article   163–4, 183
Wedgewood, Colonel Josiah   162, 172
   Wedgewood plan   163
Weekly press   1, 4, 5, 11, 13, 43, 44, 106,
   122, 155, 164, 182, 192, 194, 195
Weimar Republic   17, 32, 36, 40, 56, 73,
   117, 149, 178, 189
Wels, Otto   65
Werth, Alexander   14, 78, 87, 193
   danger to   58
   editorial interference   20–1
   Jewish background   88
   March 1933 election   45
   proposed return to Germany   88
   removal from Germany   20, 58, 83
   reporting on Germany   82, 85
White, Thomas Walter   166
White Paper   175
Winterton, Lord (Edward Turnour)   166
Wrench, Sir Evelyn   77
Wurm, Bishop Theophil   134, 136,
   137, 139
Württemberg
   Protestant church   135, 136–7
   seizure of   50

Young Reformers League   128